Leon Spivak

Bricks and Shadows

BOSTON · 2025

ISBN 978-1-960533-91-3 (hardcover)
Library of Congress Control Number: 2025947872

Published by M·GRAPHICS | BOSTON, MA
　　　www.mgraphics-books.com
　　　mgraphics.books@gmail.com

Book Design by M·GRAPHICS © 2025
Photography by L. Spivak © 2025

Printed in the USA

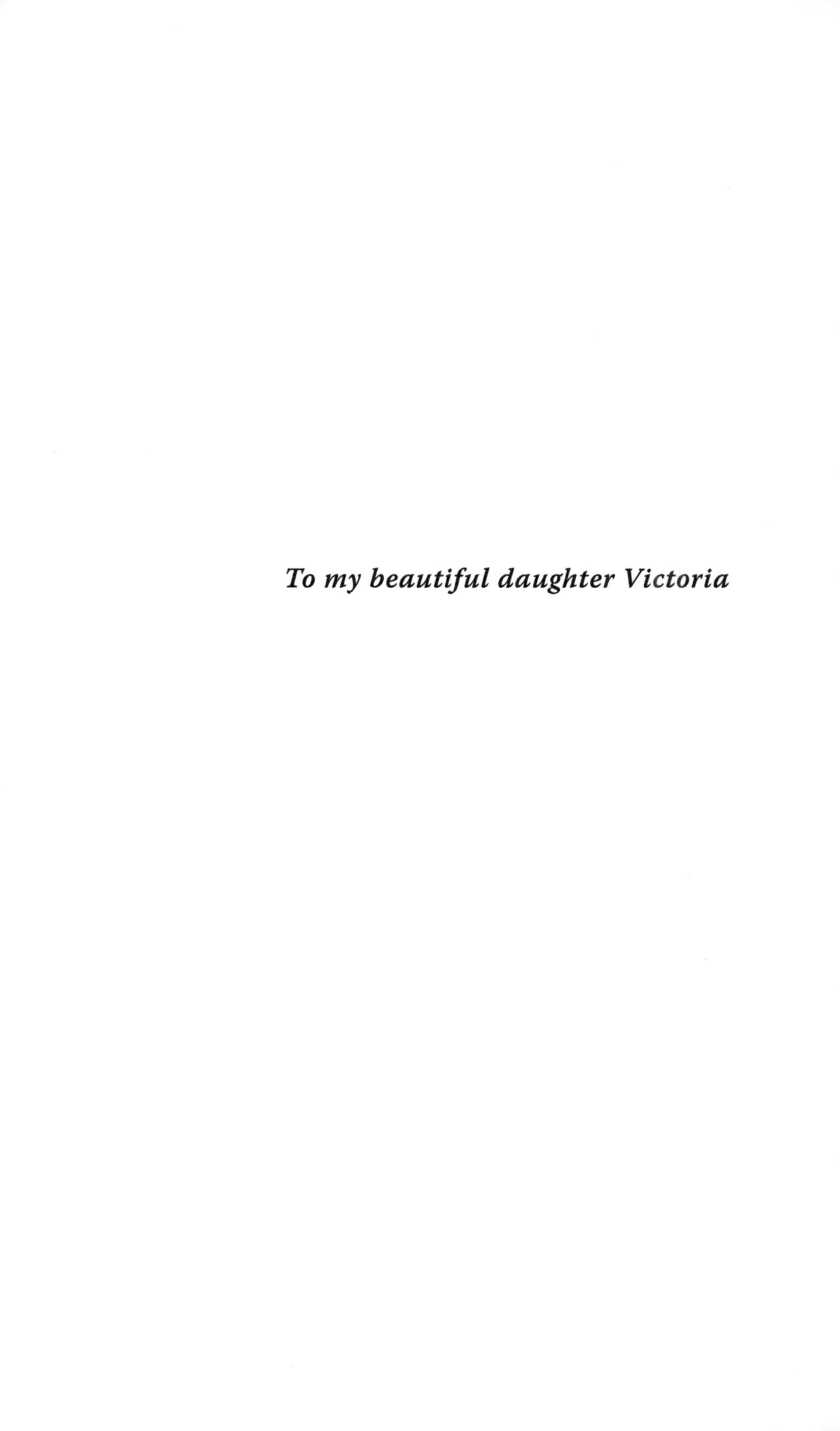

To my beautiful daughter Victoria

Acknowledgments

*The author would like to thank all his friends
who supported him in the creation of this book.*

*Special thanks to Michael Minayev, Alexander Litvak,
Michael Efroimsky, Dmitriy Dribinskiy,
Ivan and Ludmila Kurilla, Lana Arefyeva,
Margarita Mozgovaya, and Svetlana Yarmolinskaya
for their valuable corrections
and critical comments*

Three cities have shaped my life. I was born in Chernivtsi, in Western Ukraine. This old city has miraculously preserved the legacy of the Austro-Hungarian Empire. It was barely touched by the two world wars. My early childhood unfolded in the Soviet Union, behind the Iron Curtain but the colorful backdrop for all the city's residents was the atmosphere of the Old World — narrow cobblestone streets, urban legends, and European architecture: Italianate, Beaux Arts, and Art Nouveau.

I lived in St. Petersburg, Russia for twenty-five years. It is a city of palaces and canals, imperial splendor and opulence beneath the northern sky, where the enduring spirit of the Golden Age of Russian culture is still alive.

Boston is my third city, where a new chapter of my life began in 1993.

Massachusetts is a heaven for history lovers. Not every European province can boast such a lineage: Pilgrims and Puritans, preachers and merchants, pirates and witches, rebels, philosophers, and authors. As Oscar Wilde quipped back in the 19th century, Americans have been joking about their youth for two hundred years.

Boston is a city of subtle details, free from pretension of being a dominant capital. This is why wandering the narrow streets of neighborhoods like the North End, Beacon Hill, and Back Bay feels so inviting.

Boston is a graphic city. Black-and-white photography captures so well the mood and texture of its old red brick and gray granite from local quarries, its authentic cast-iron lanterns and wrought-iron balcony railings. Boston is often described by visitors as the most European city in the United States.

I have lived in Boston for over thirty years. This small photo album is my tribute to my new home.

Leon Spivak
August 2025

Boston Sketches

I'm gonna tell you a big fat story, baby;
Aw, it's all about my town;

Yeah, down by the river;
Down by the banks of the river Charles;
Aw, that's what's happenin' baby;
That's where you'll find me;
Along with lovers, muggers, and thieves;
Aw, but they're cool people;

Well I love that dirty water;
Oh, Boston, you're my home;
Oh, you're the number one place.

Edward Cornelius Cobb (1938 – 1999)
musician and songwriter

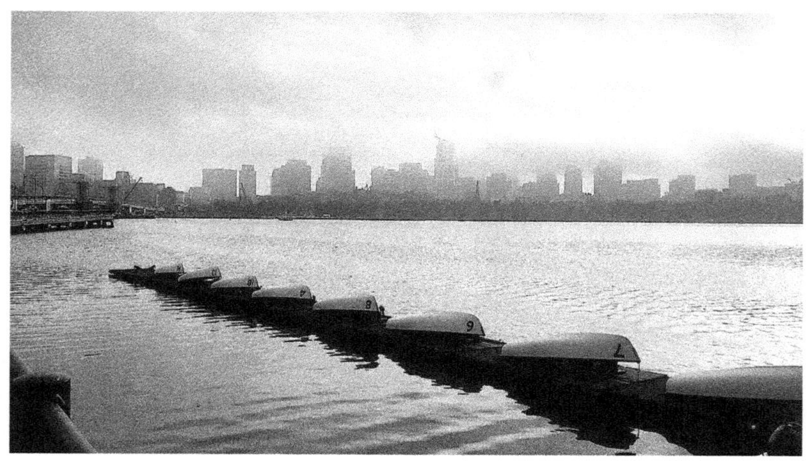

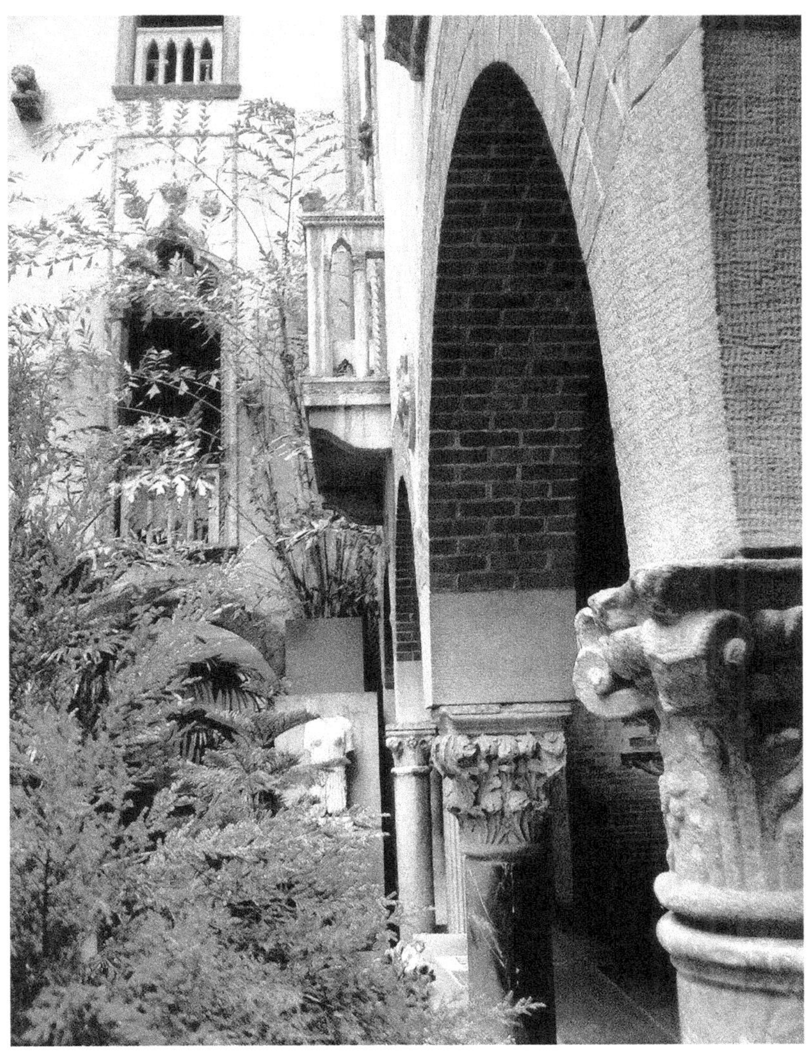

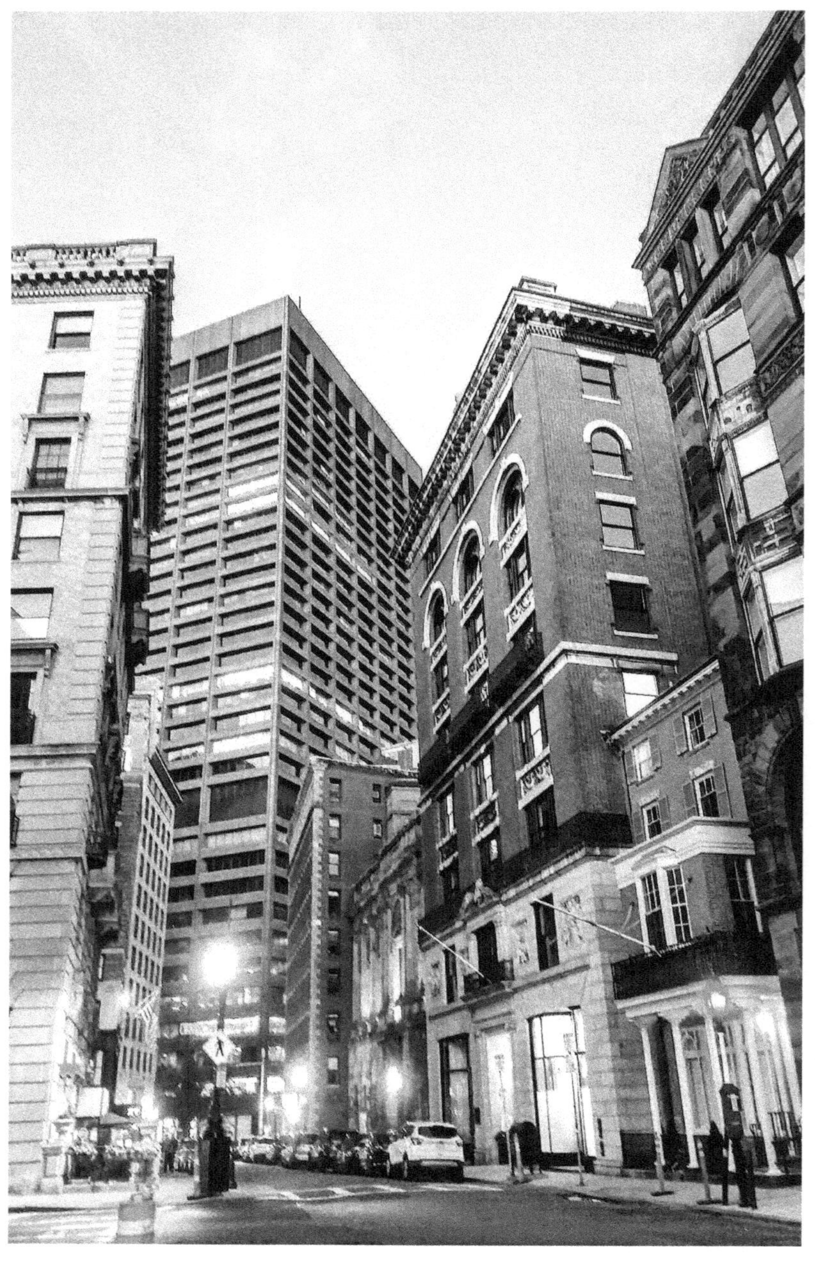

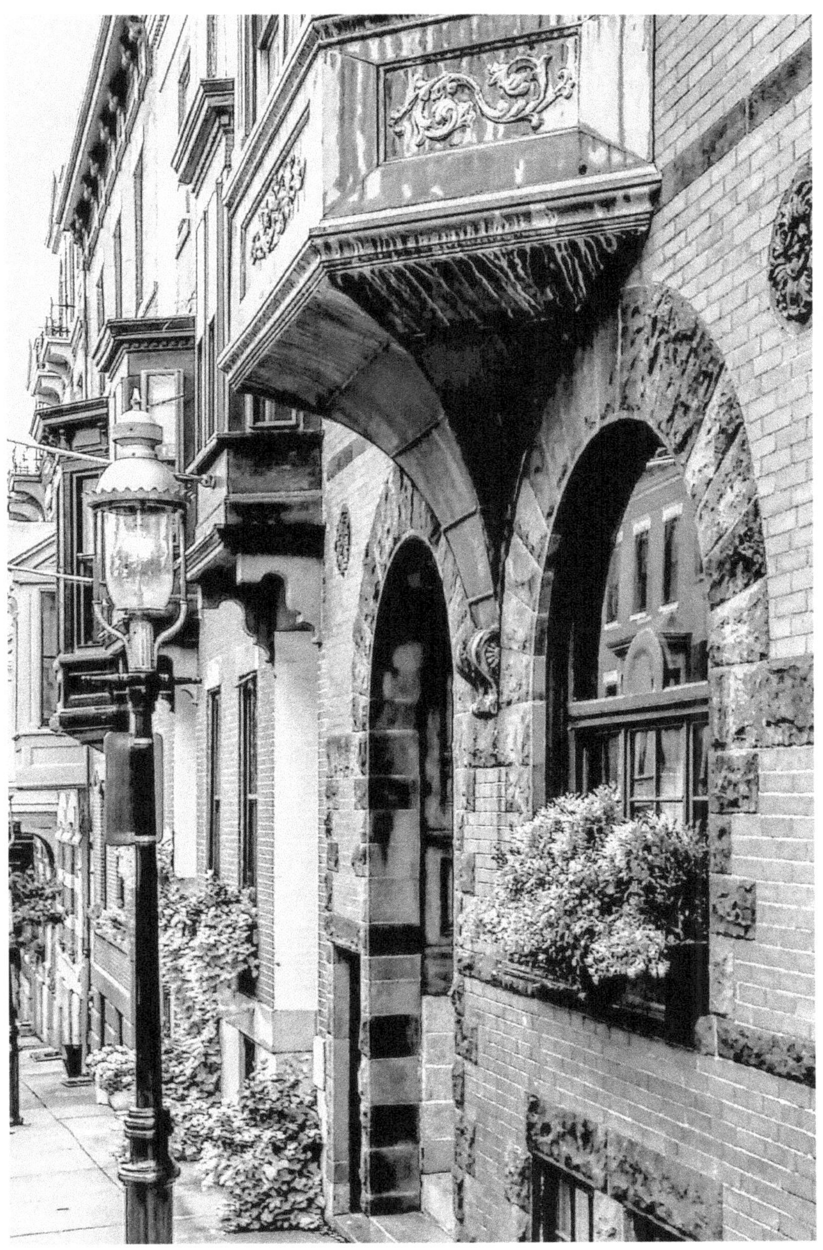

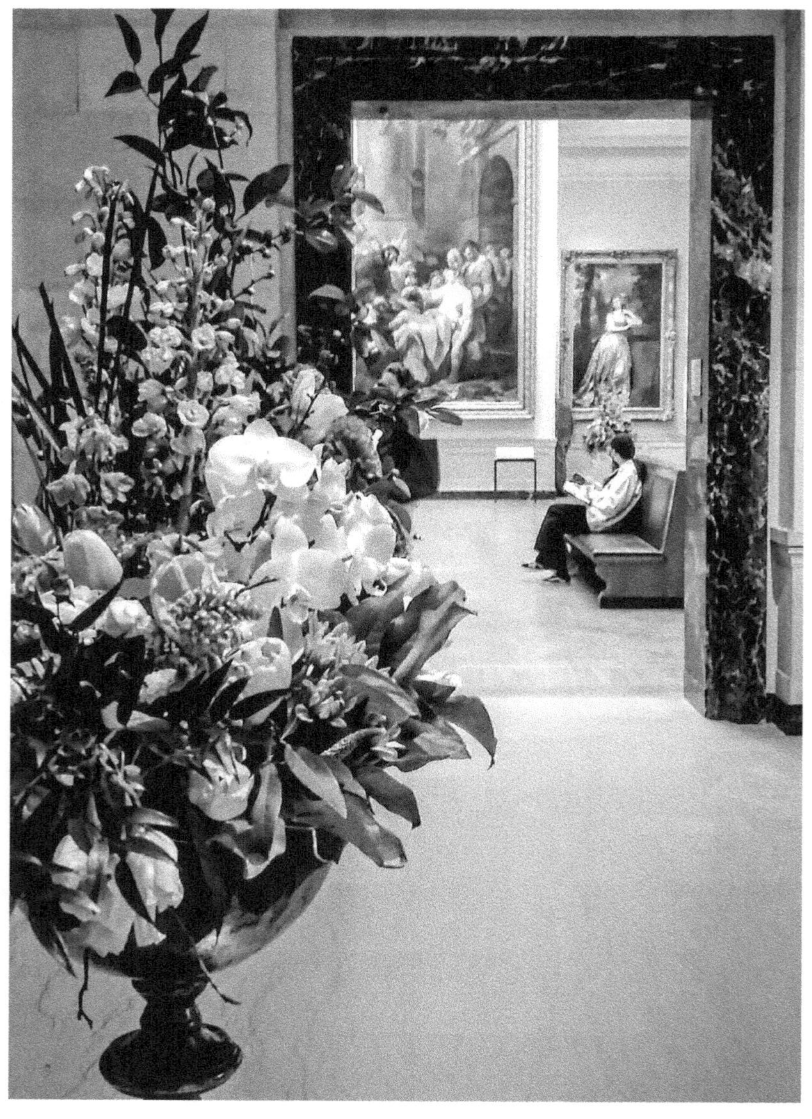

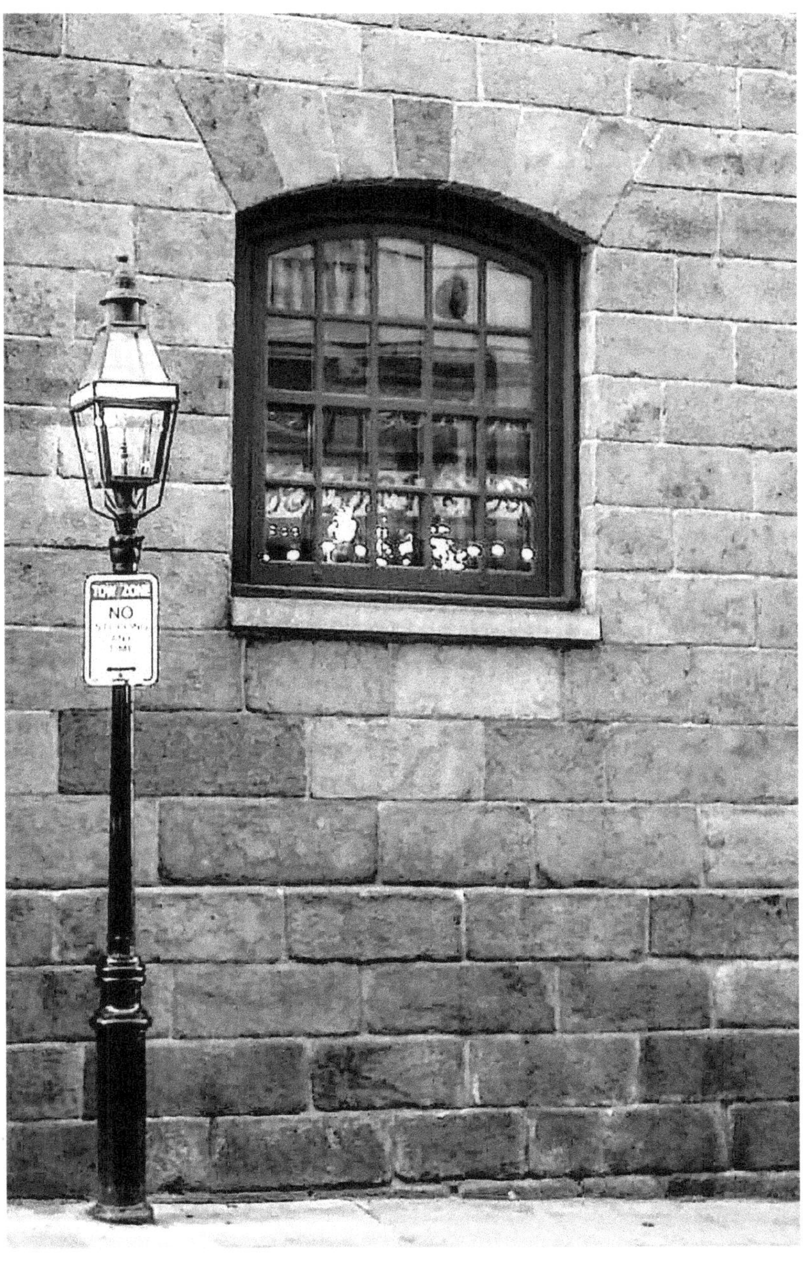
TOW ZONE
NO

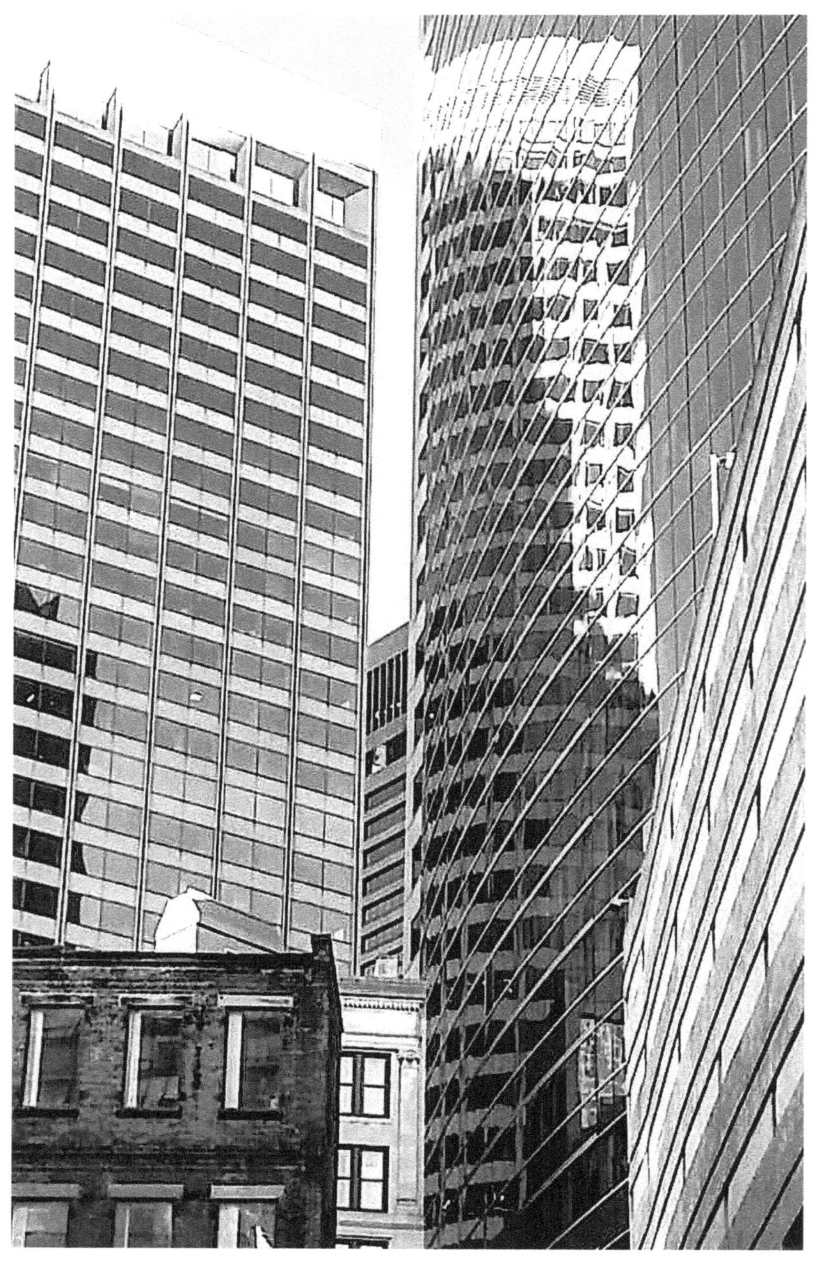

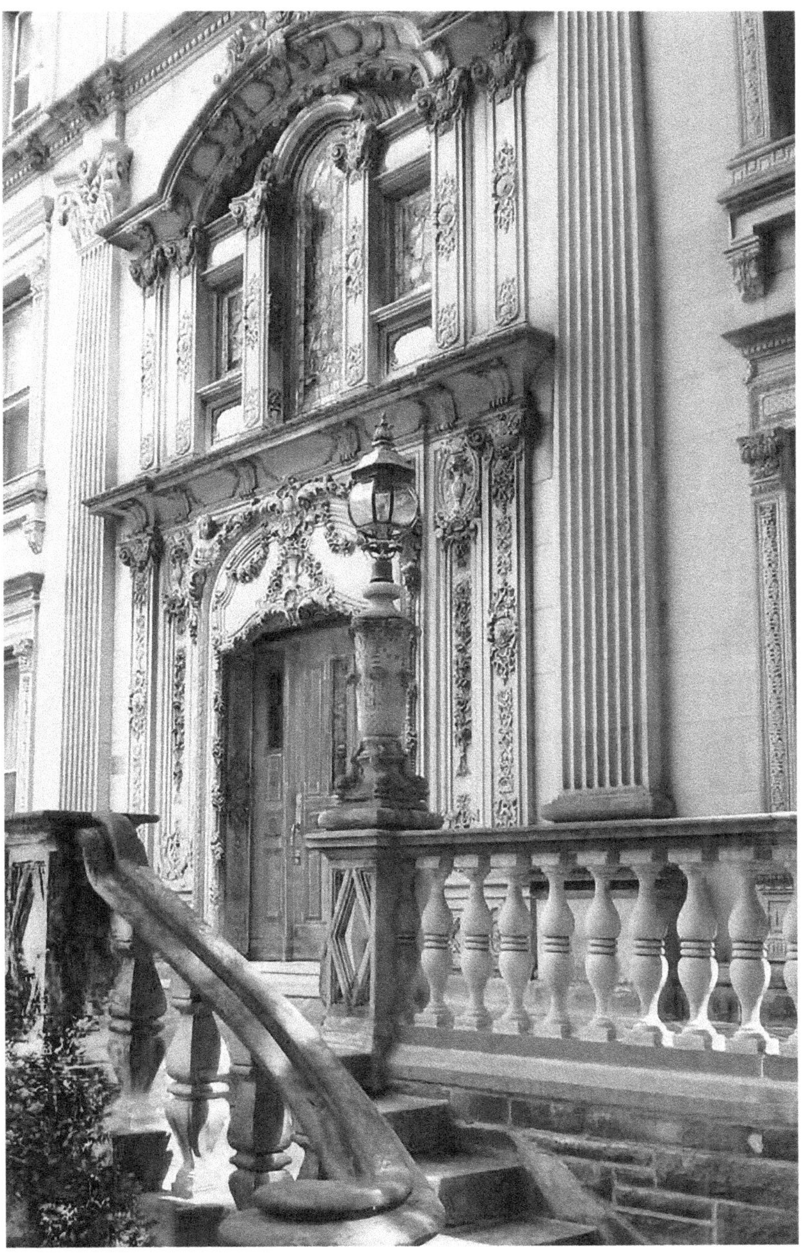

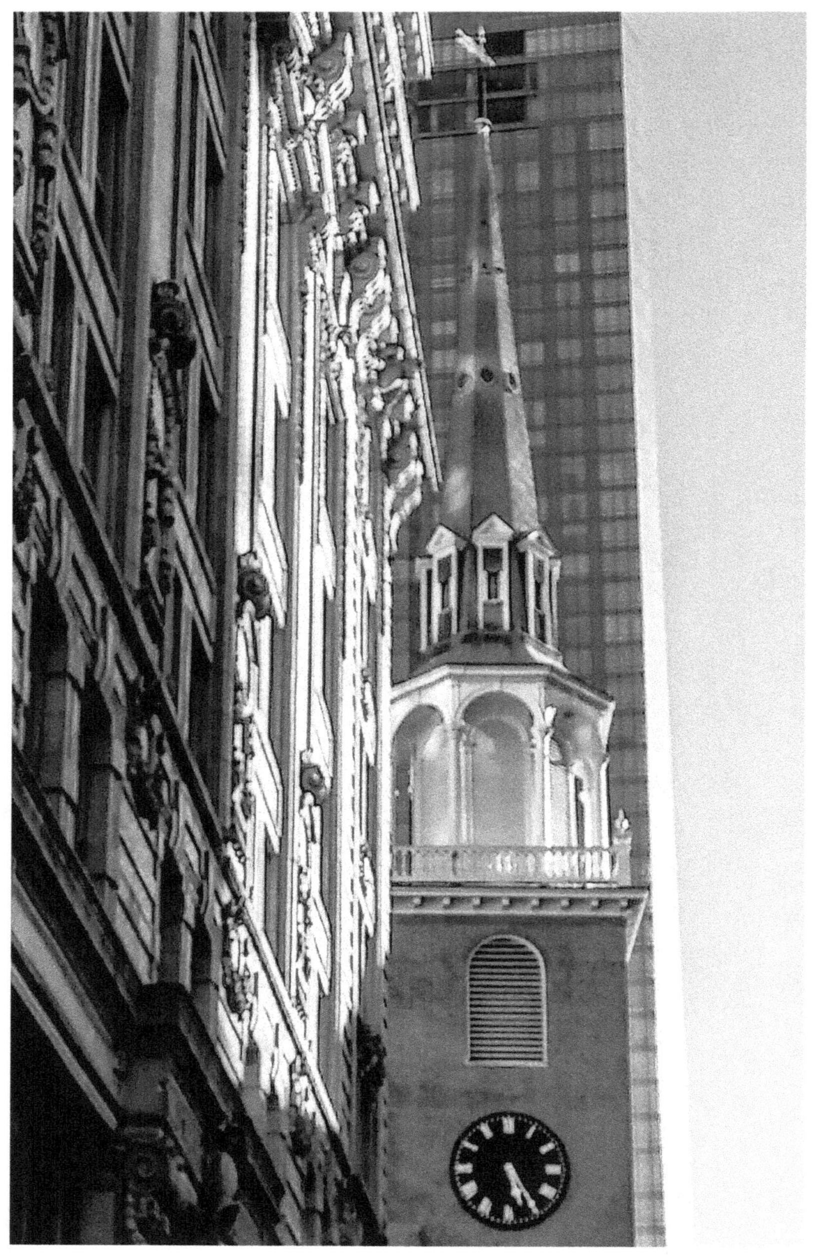

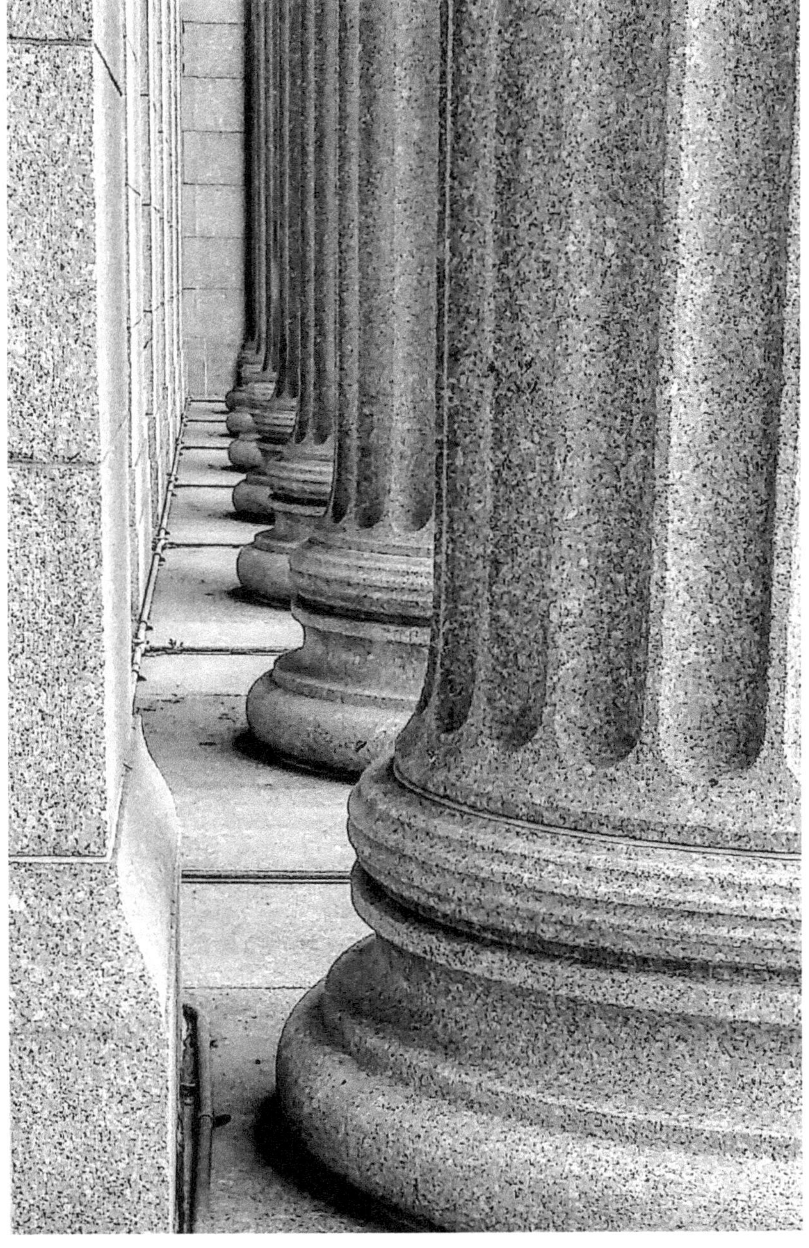

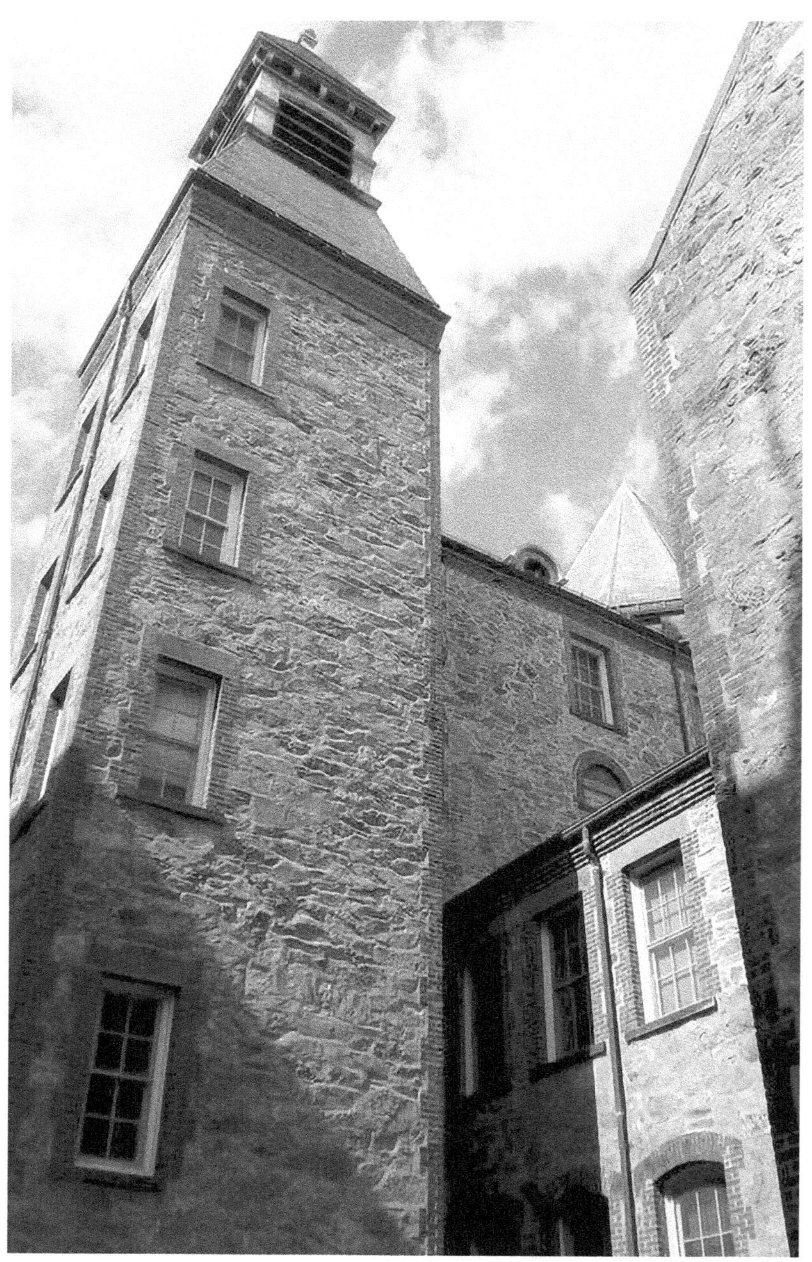

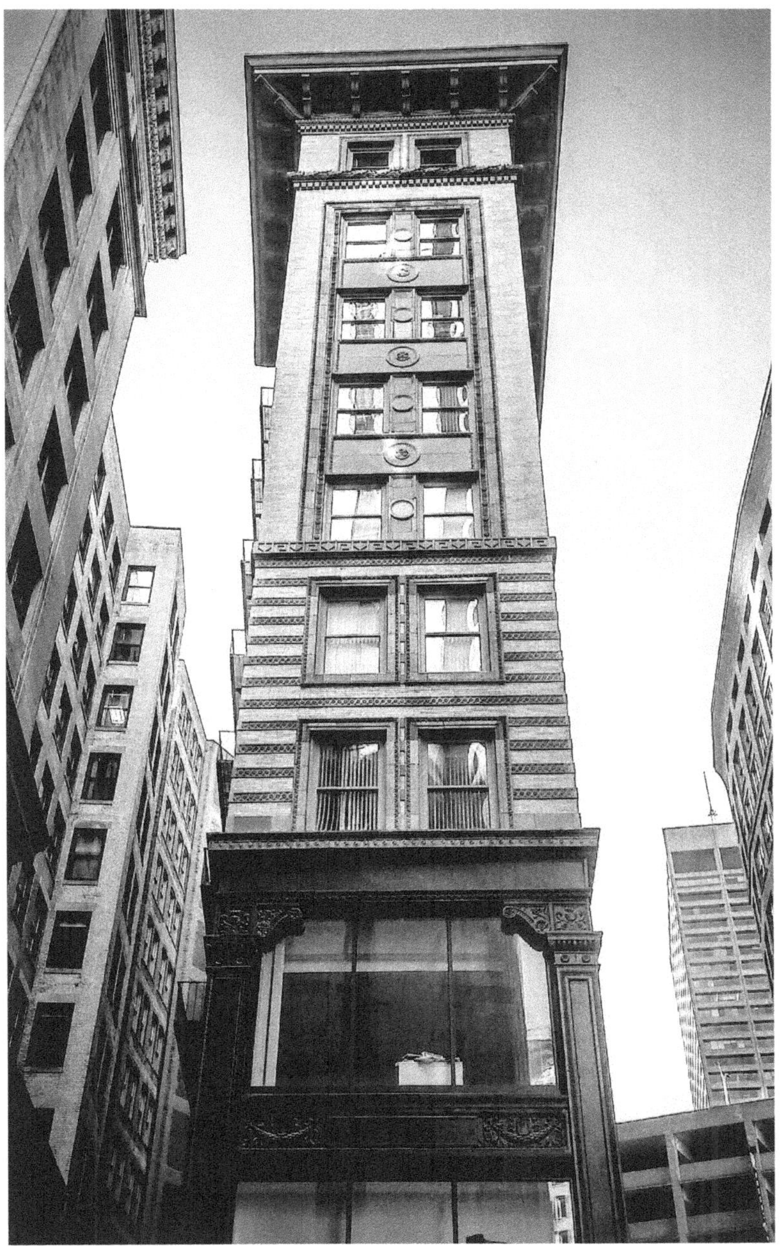

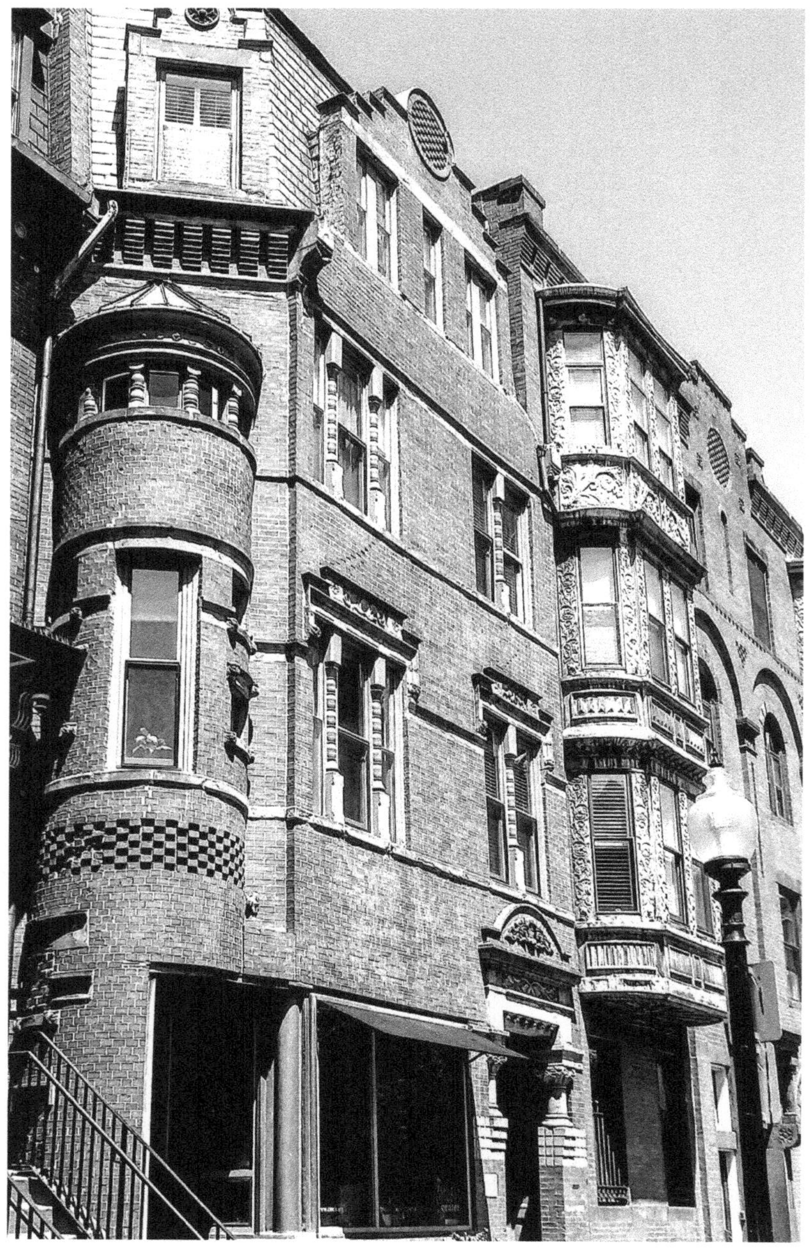

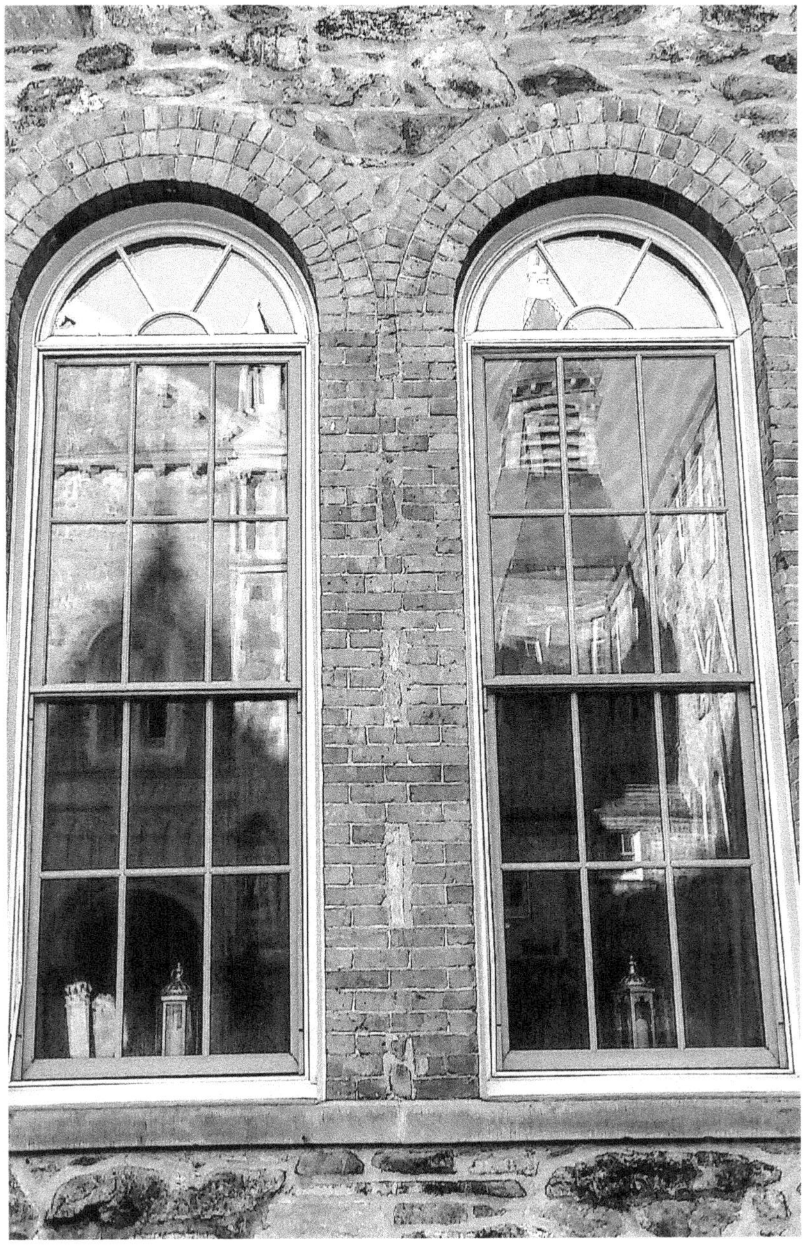

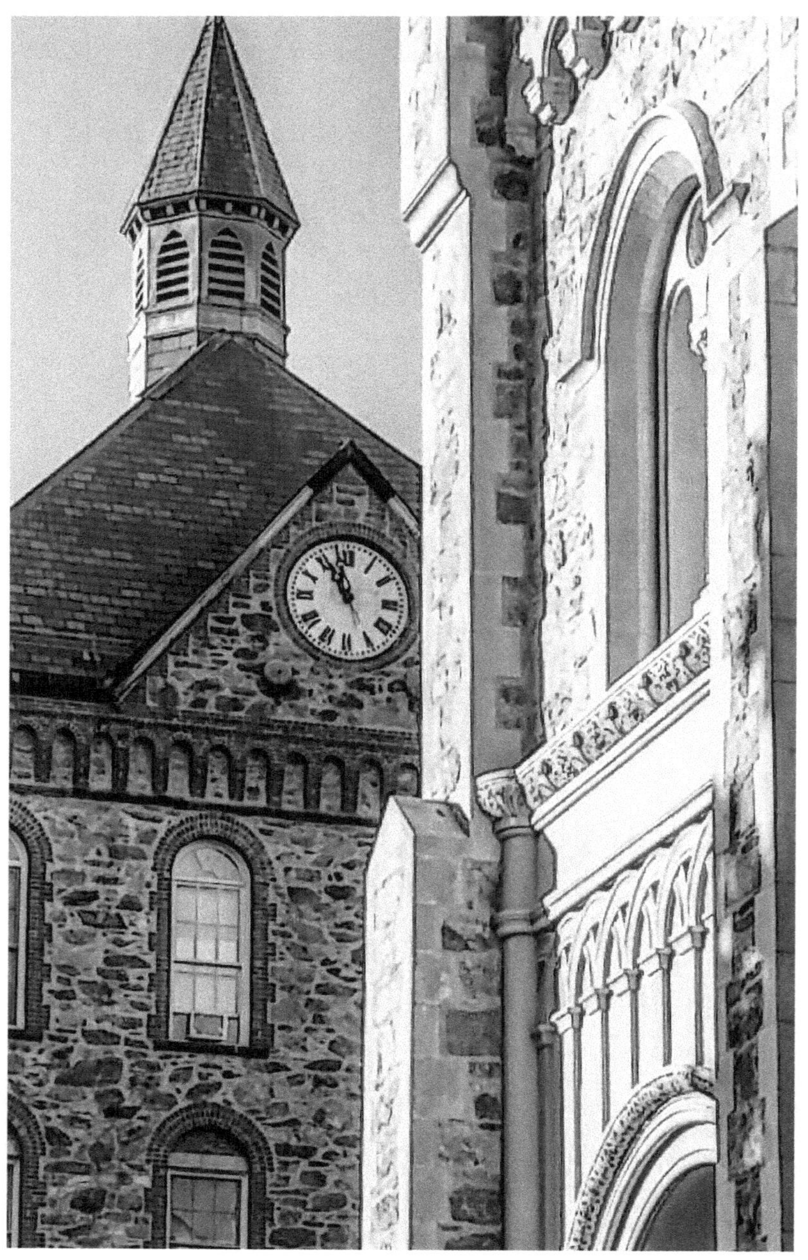

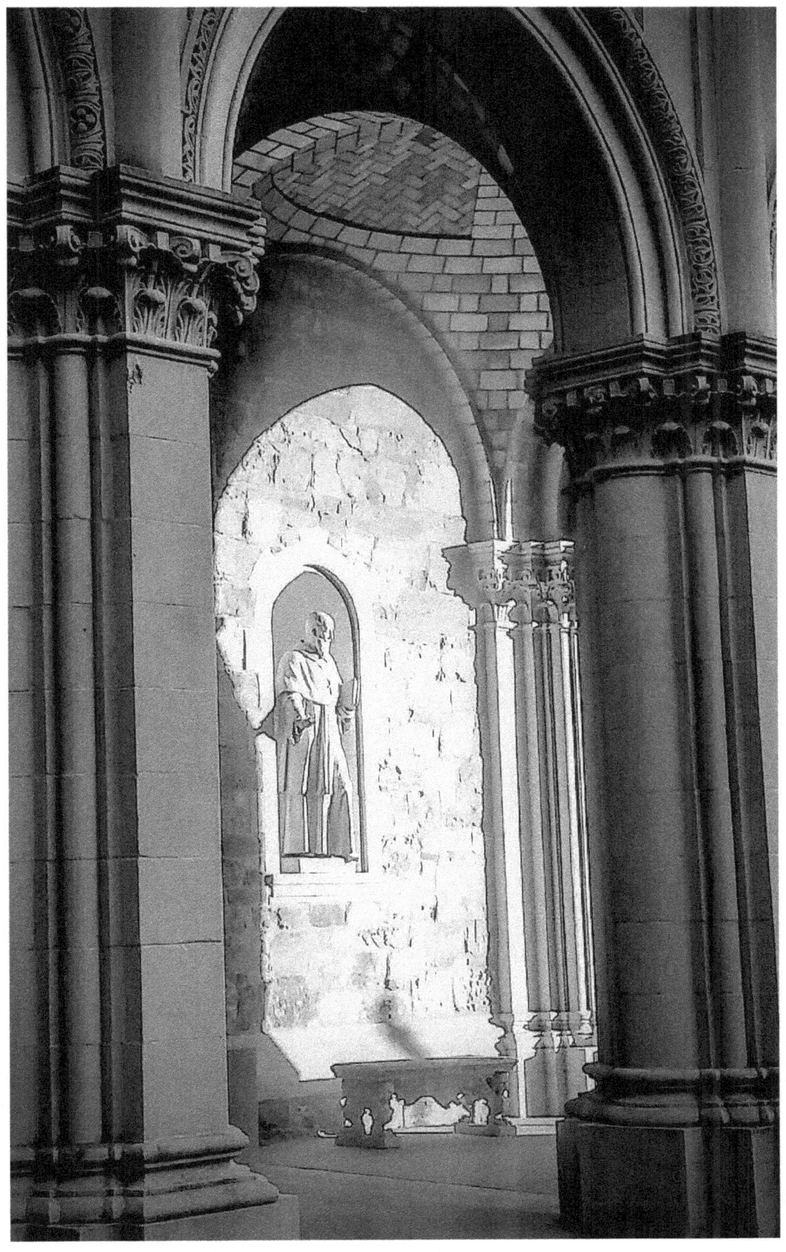

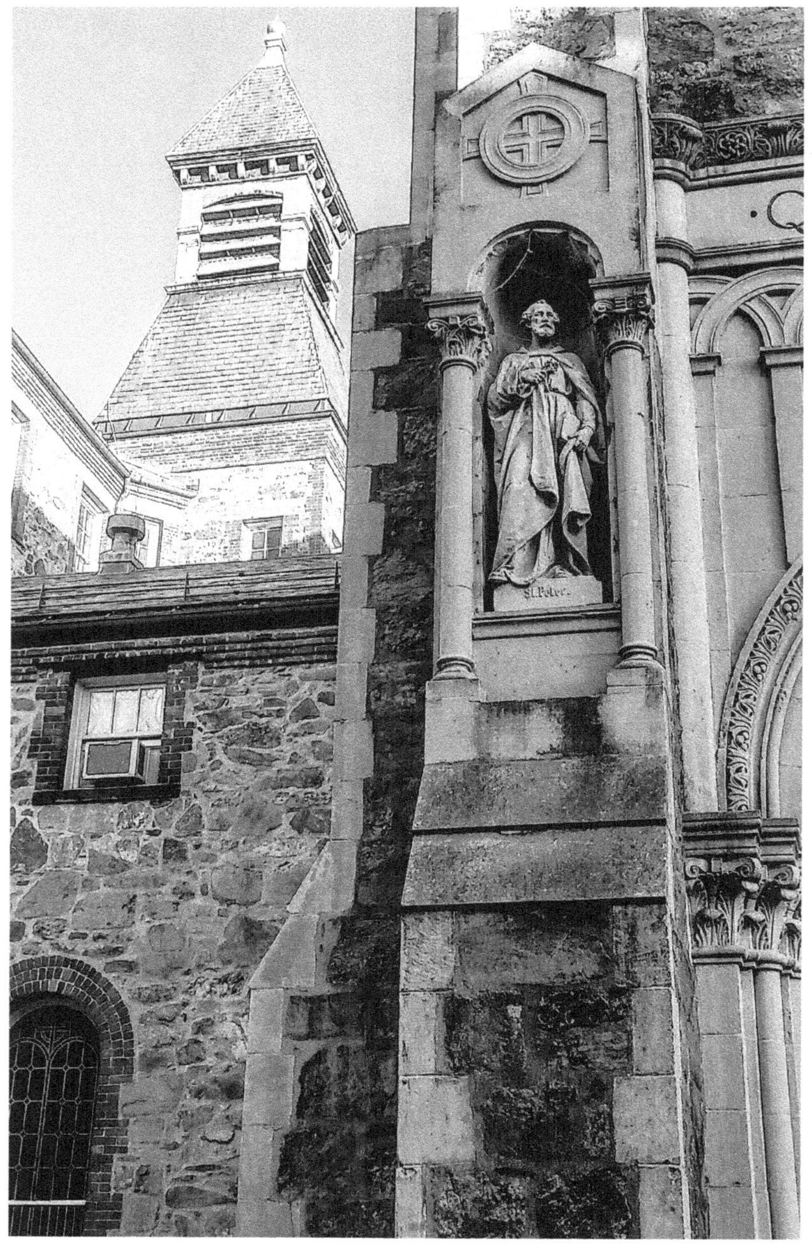

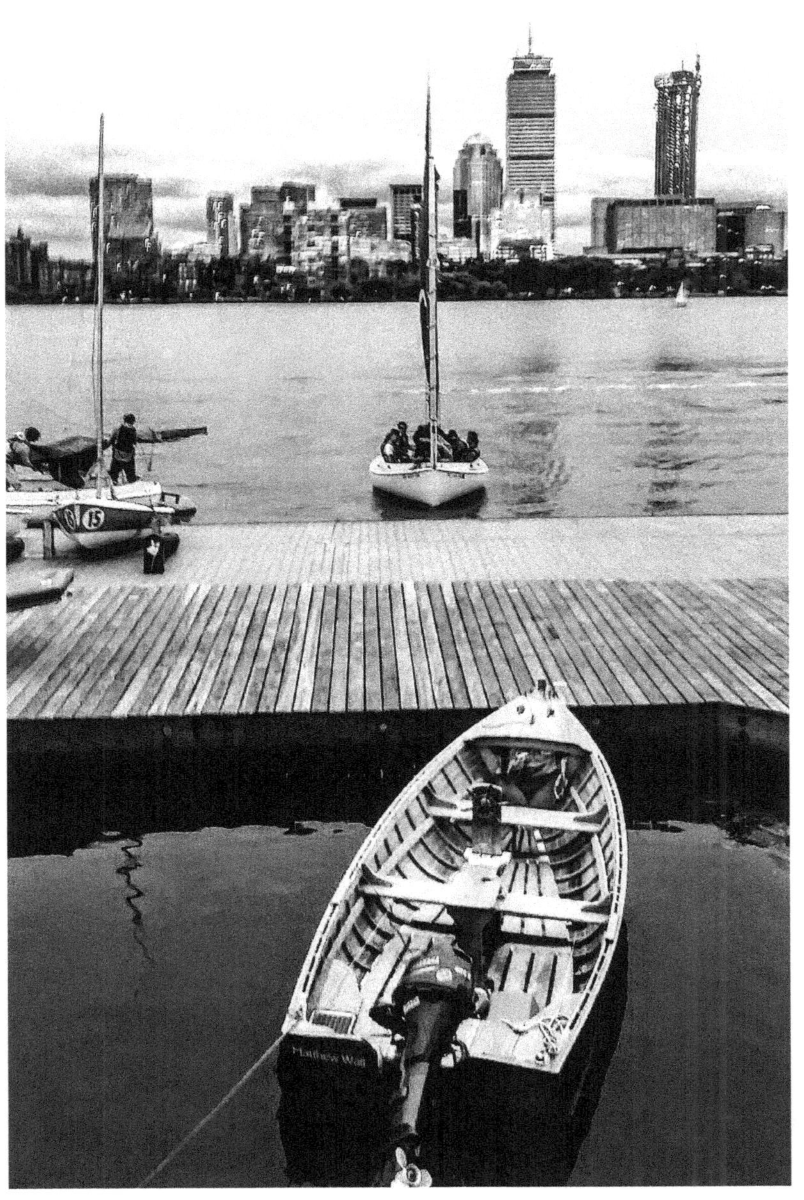

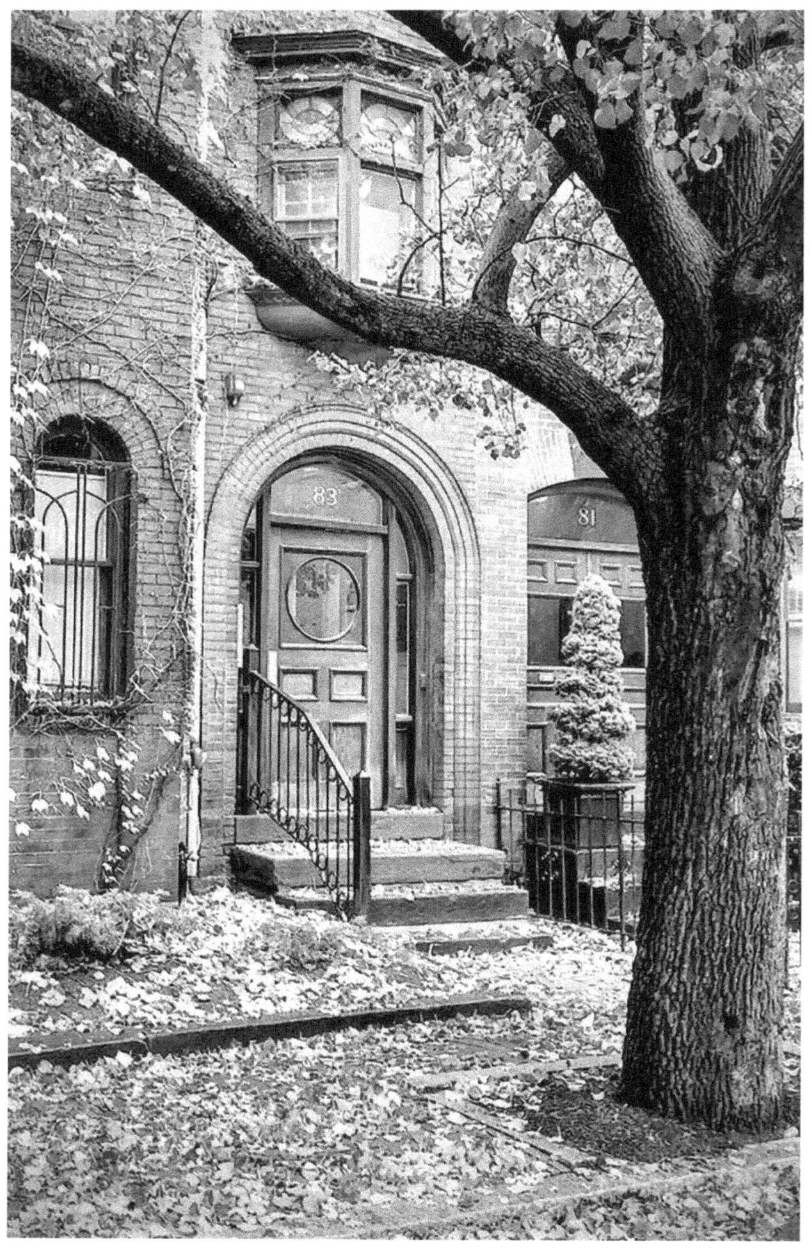

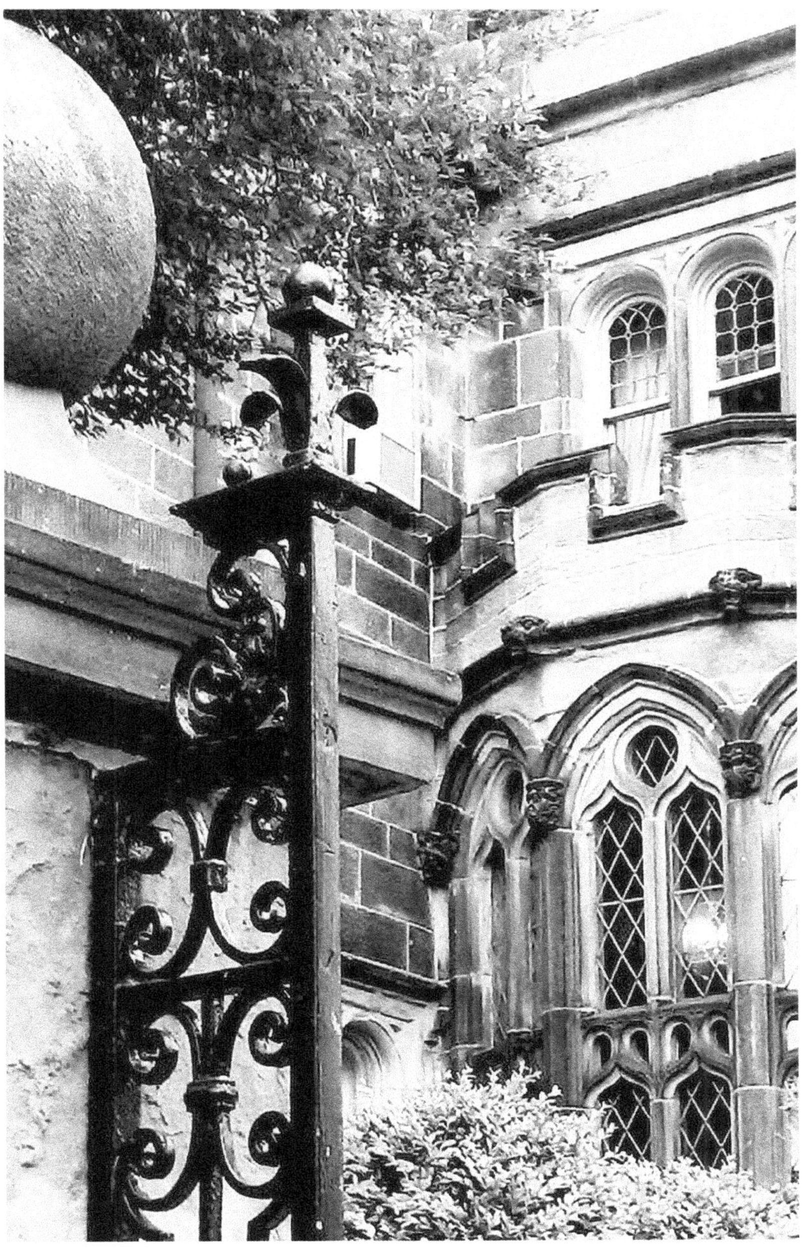

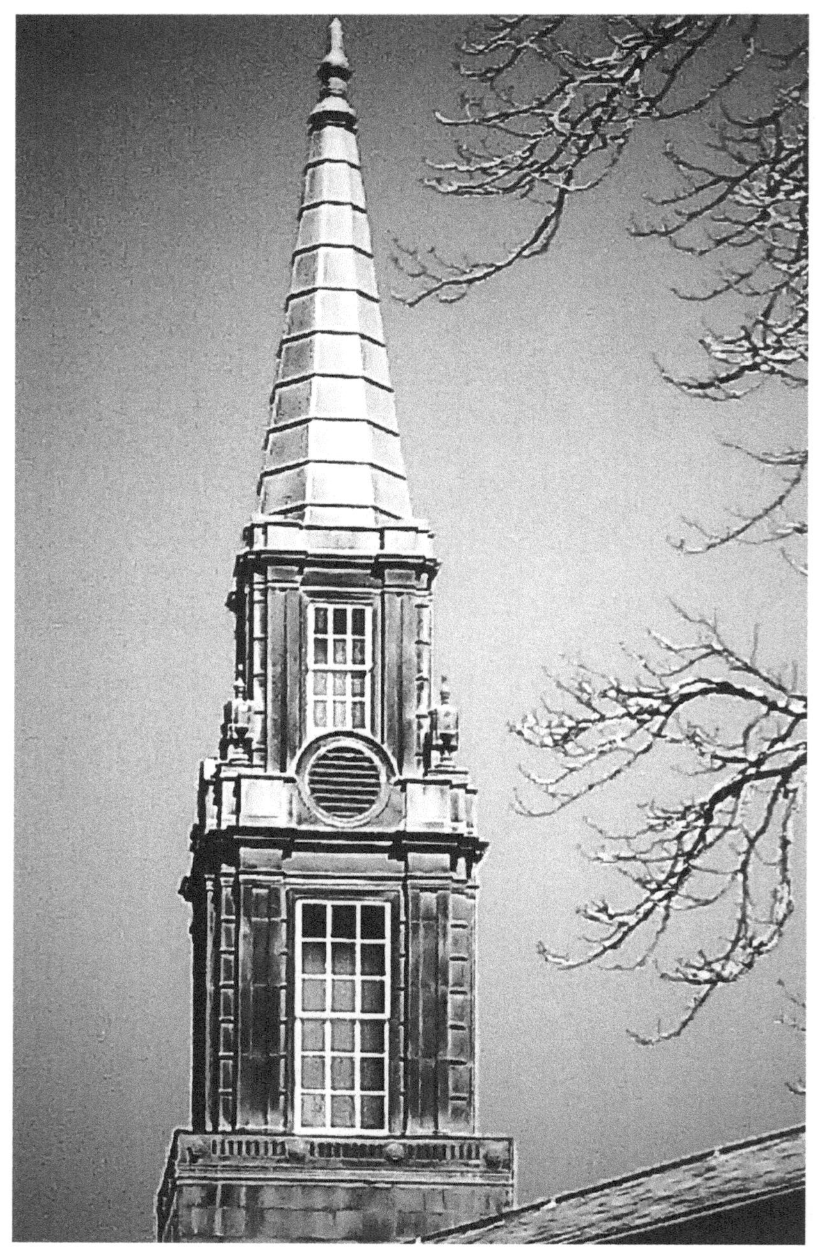

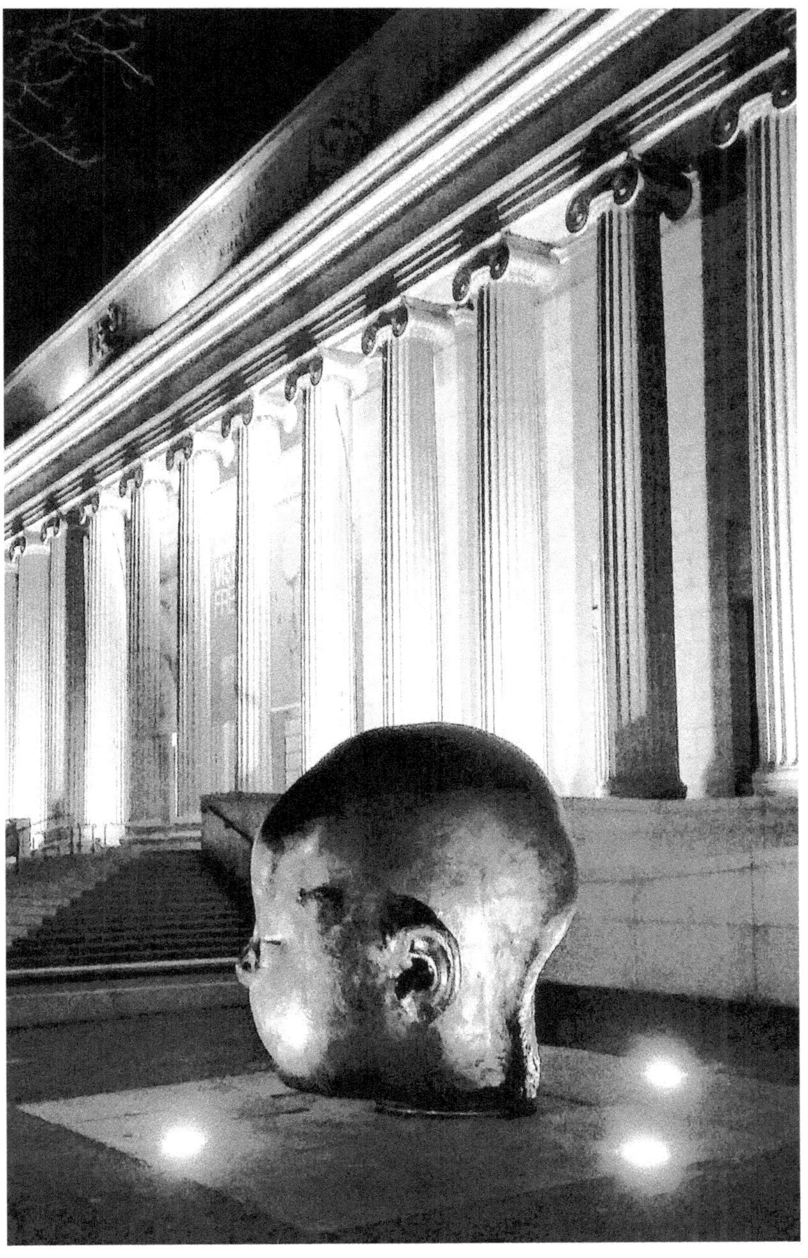

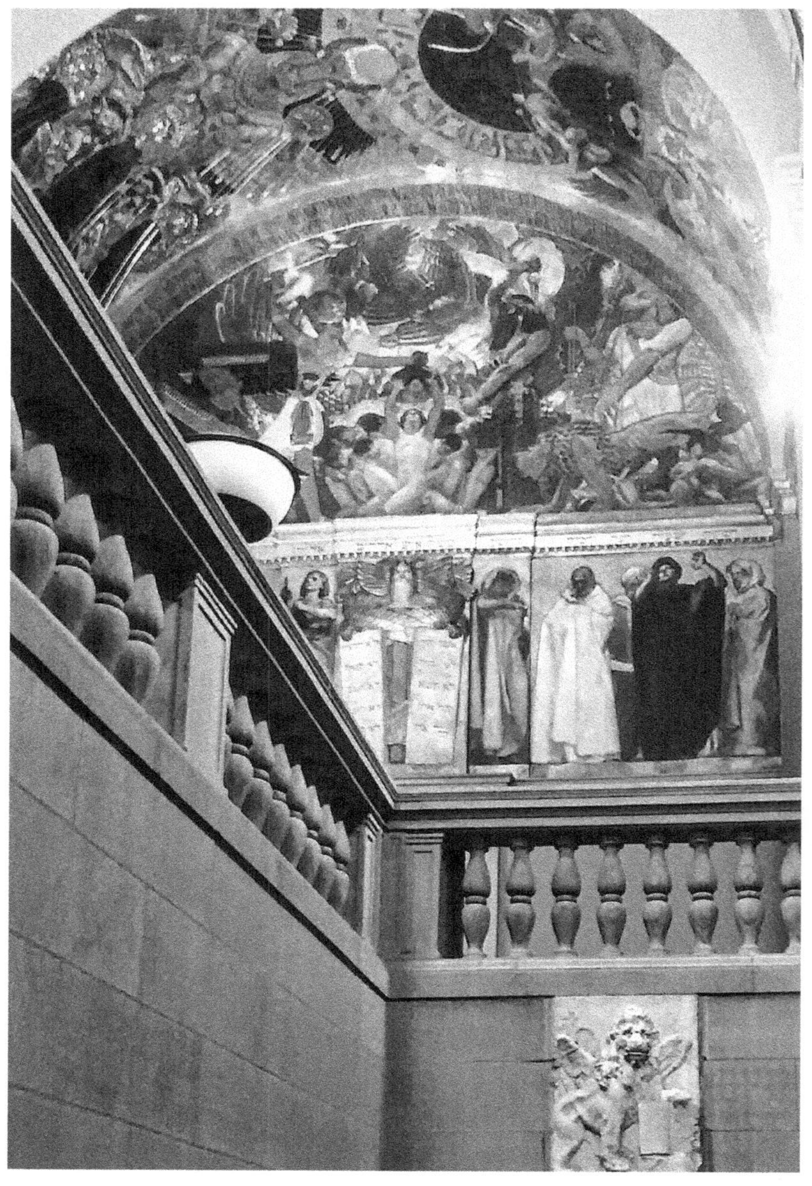

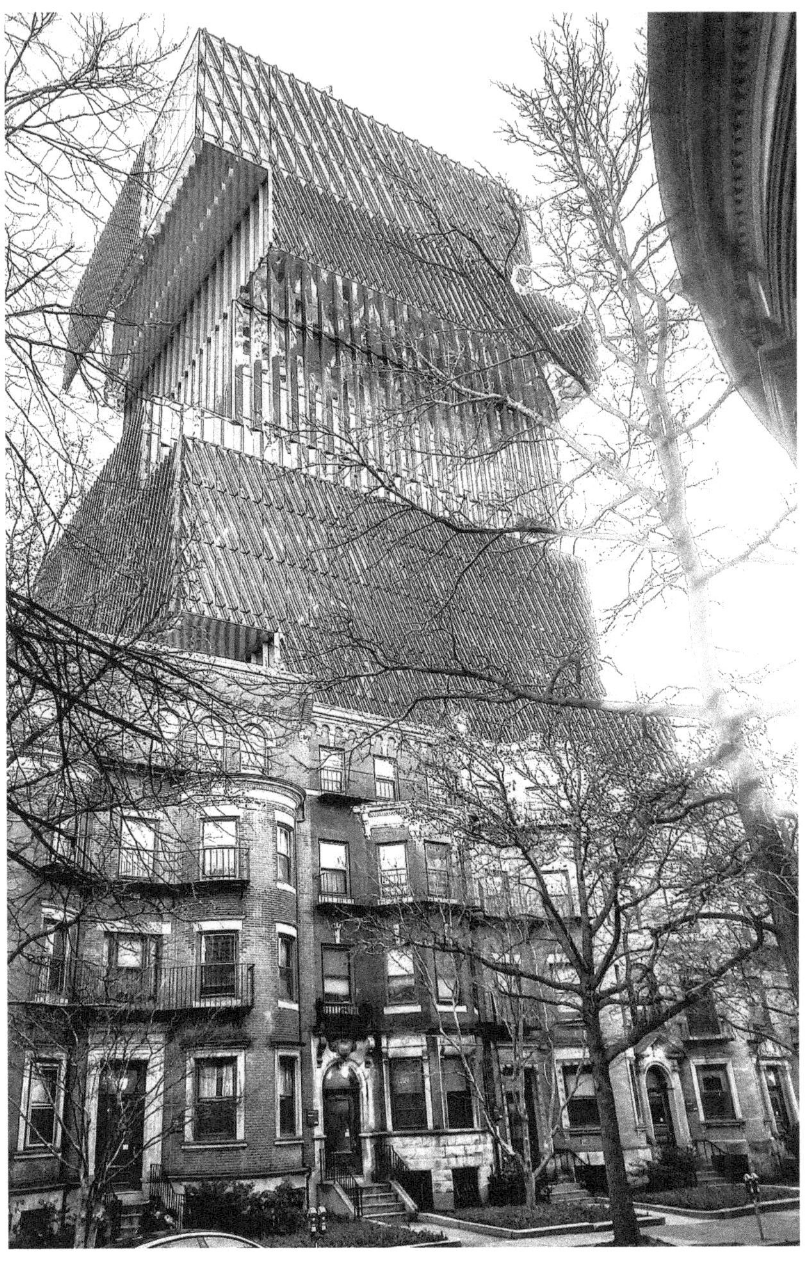

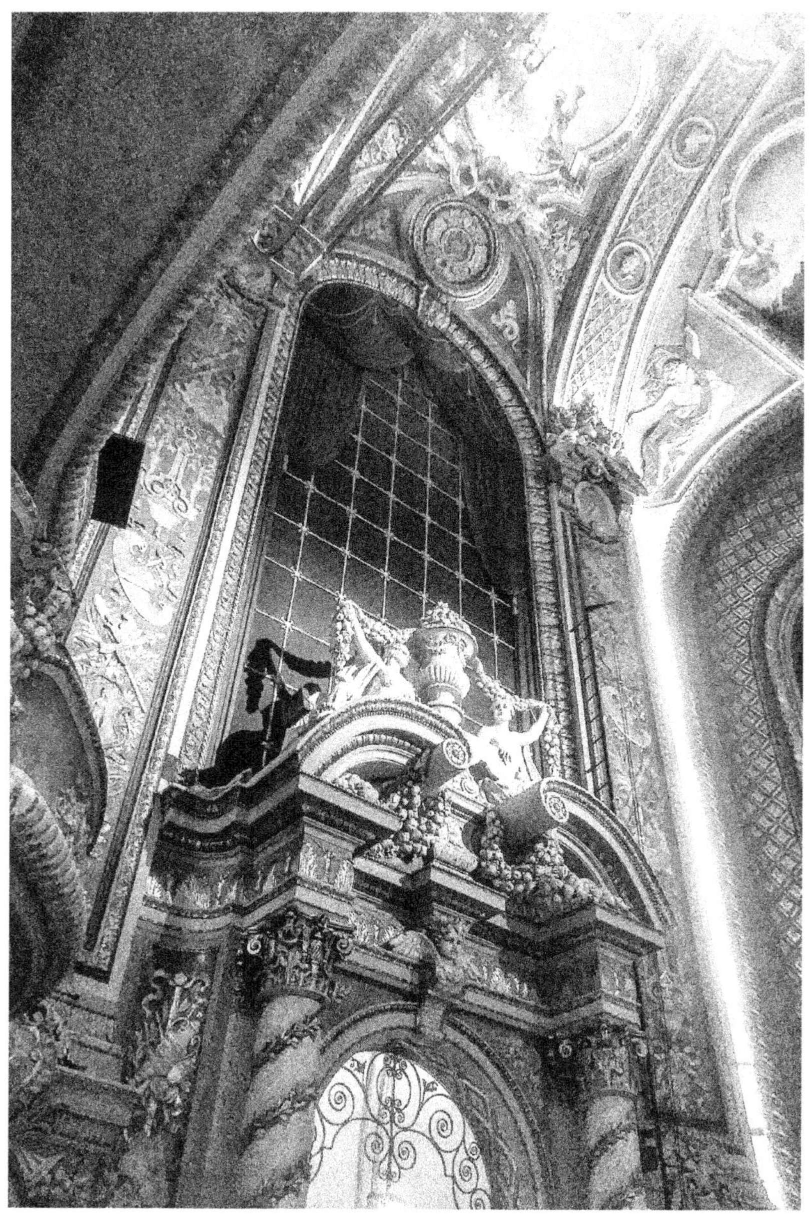

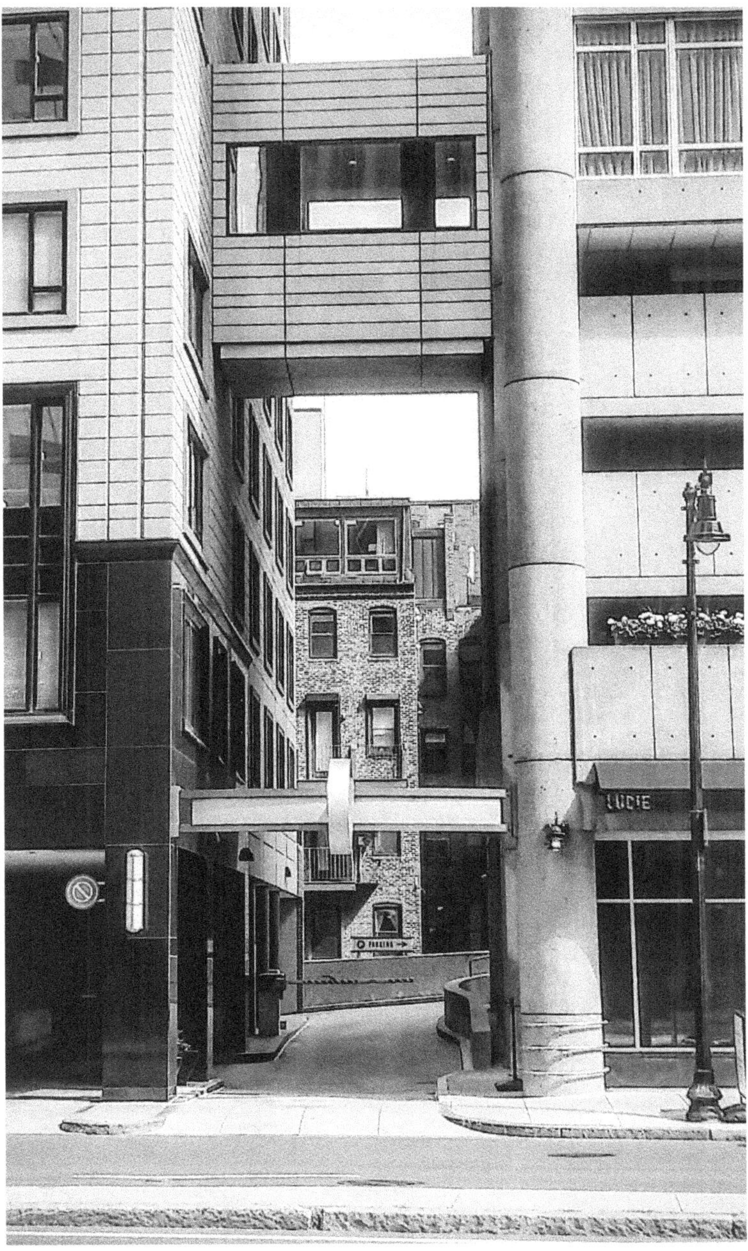
LUCIE
PARKING →

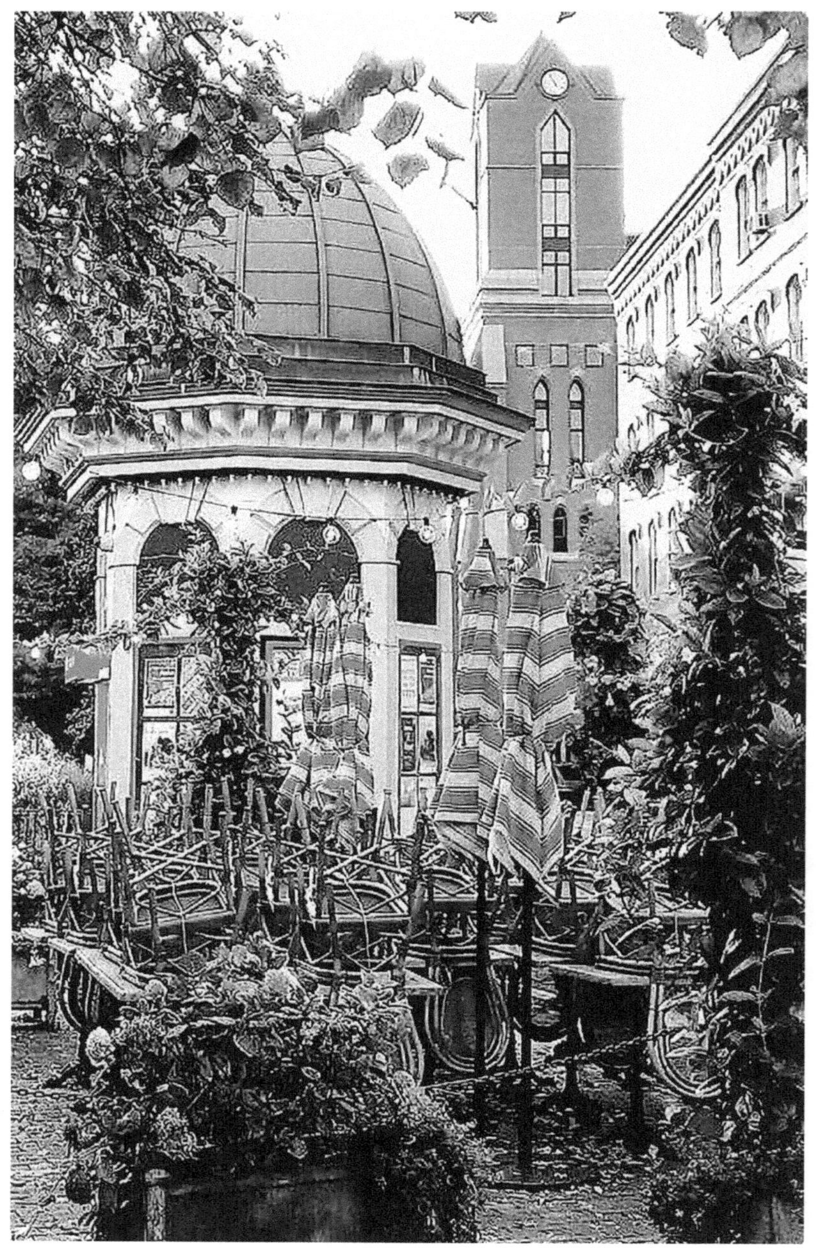

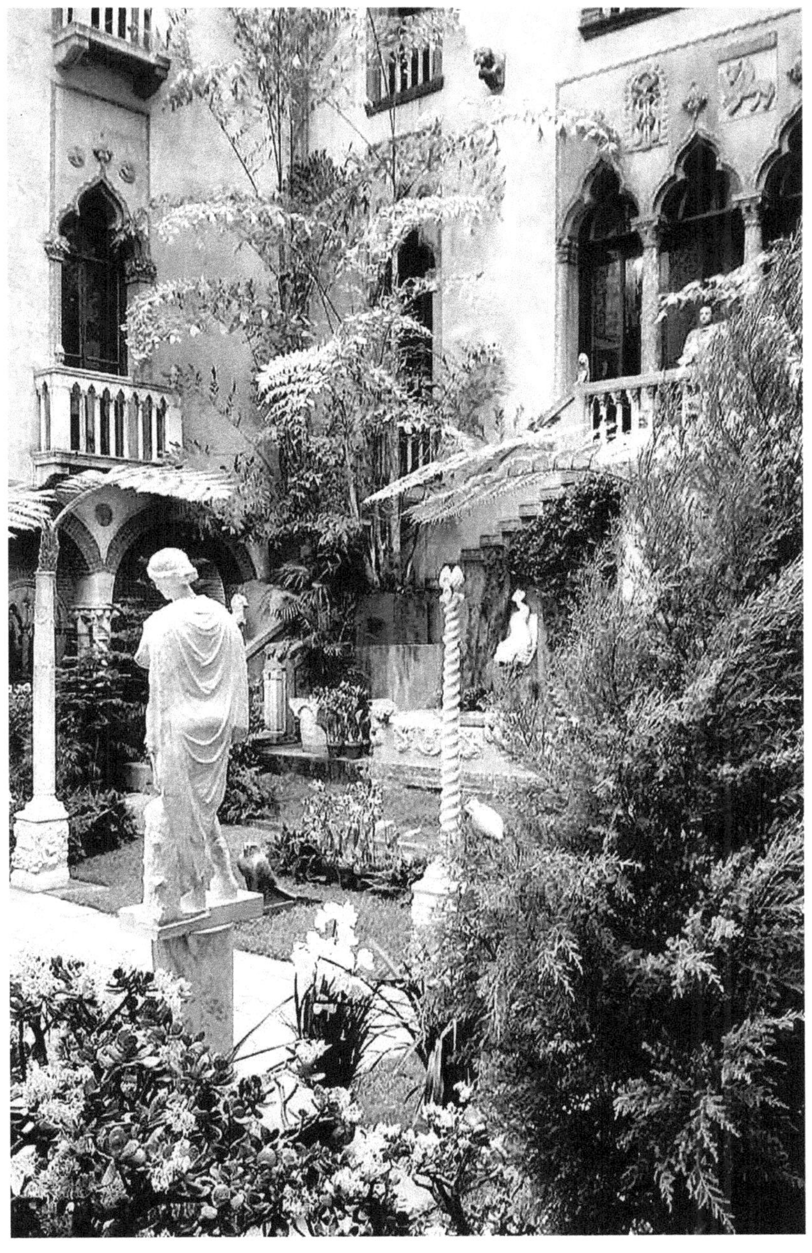

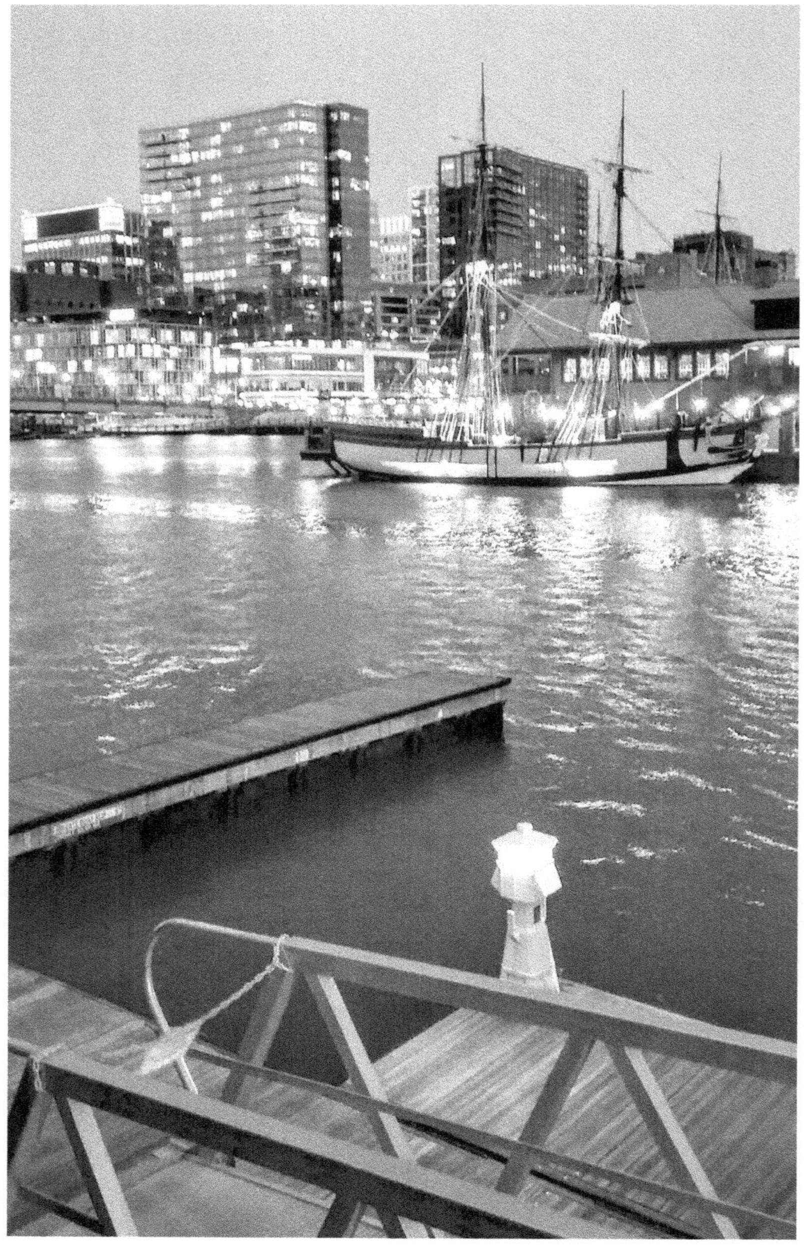

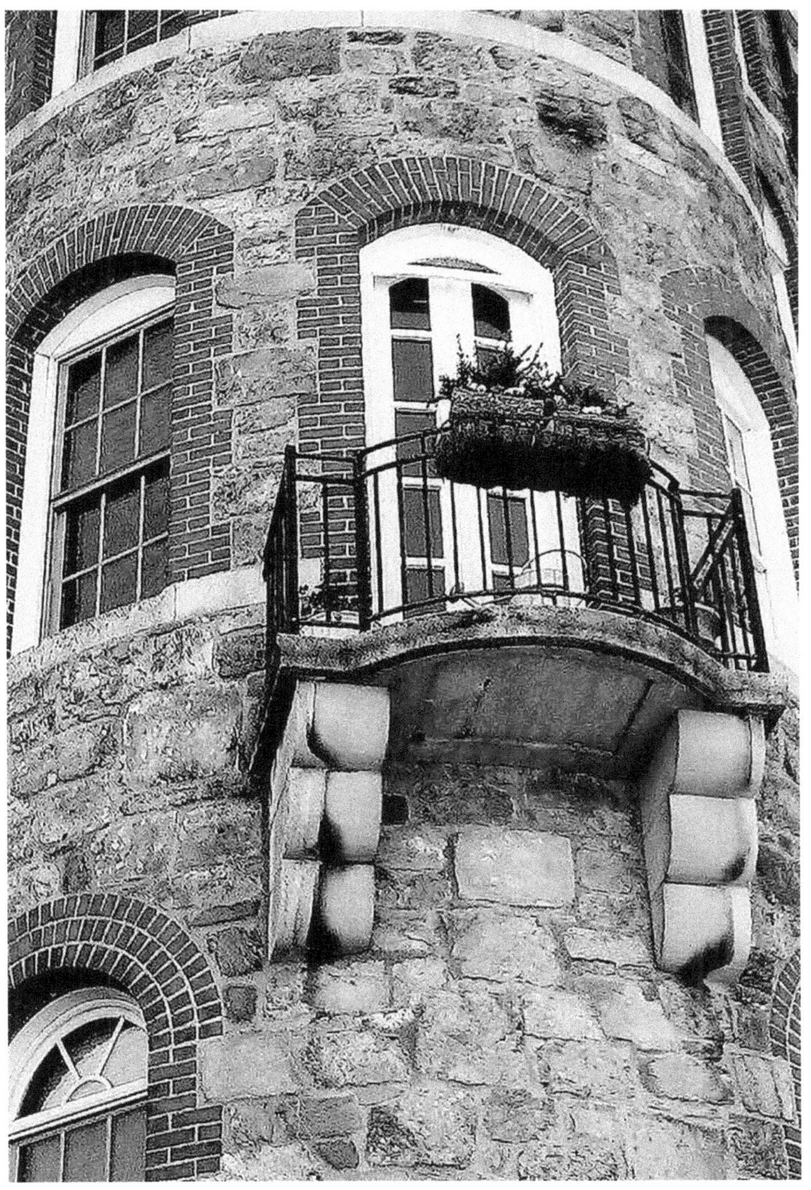

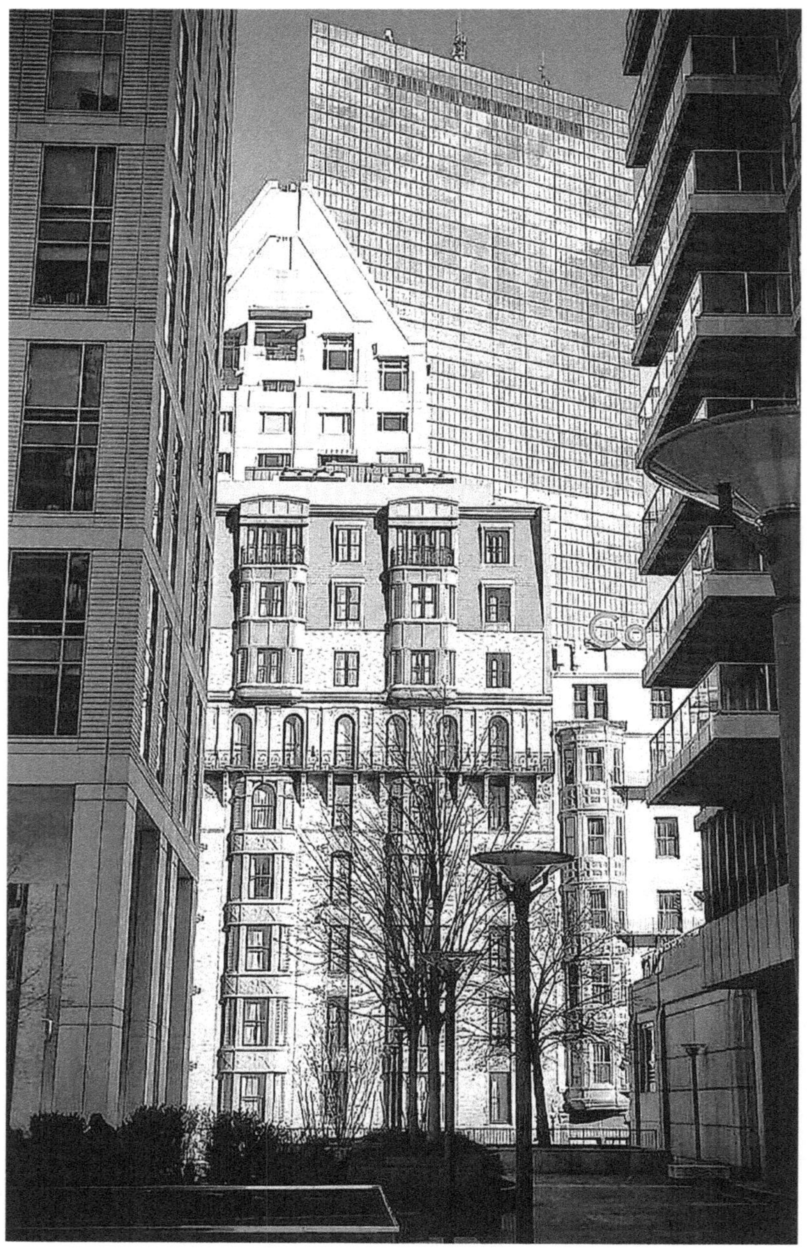

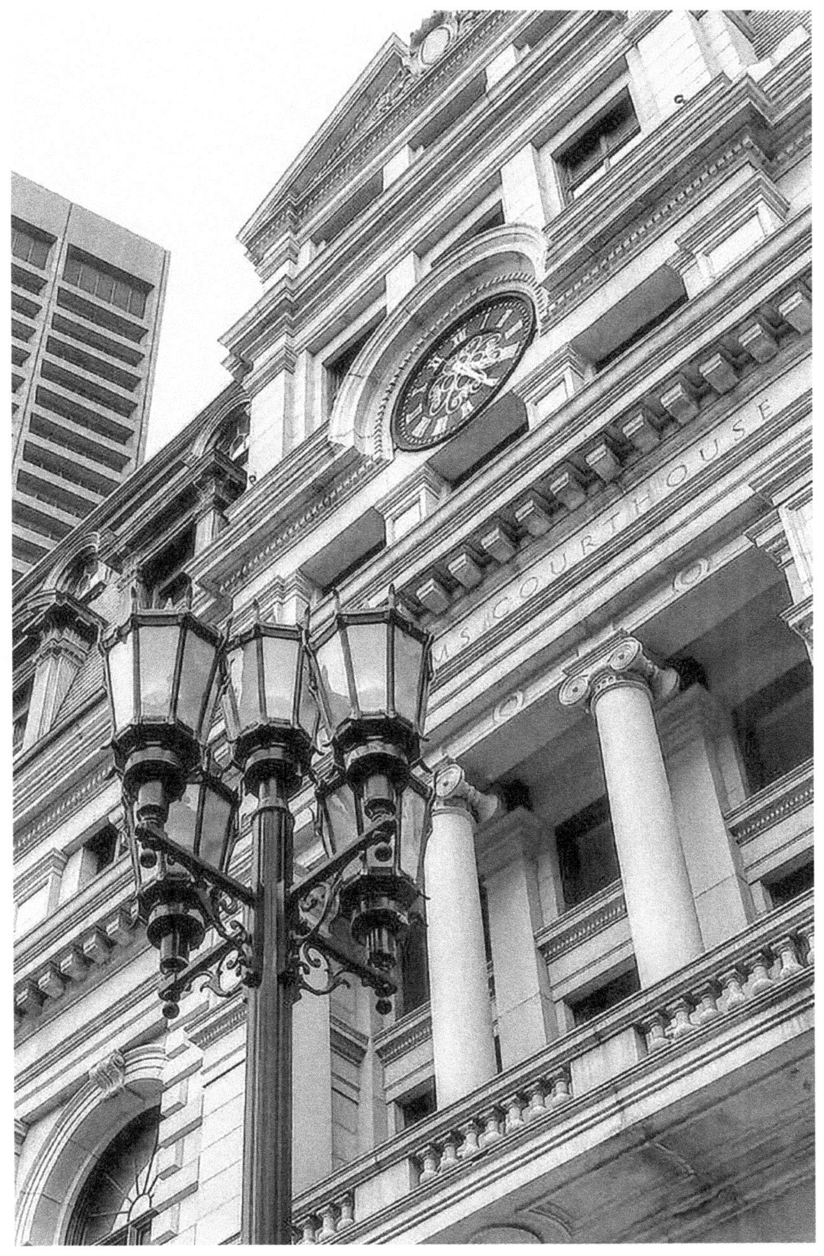

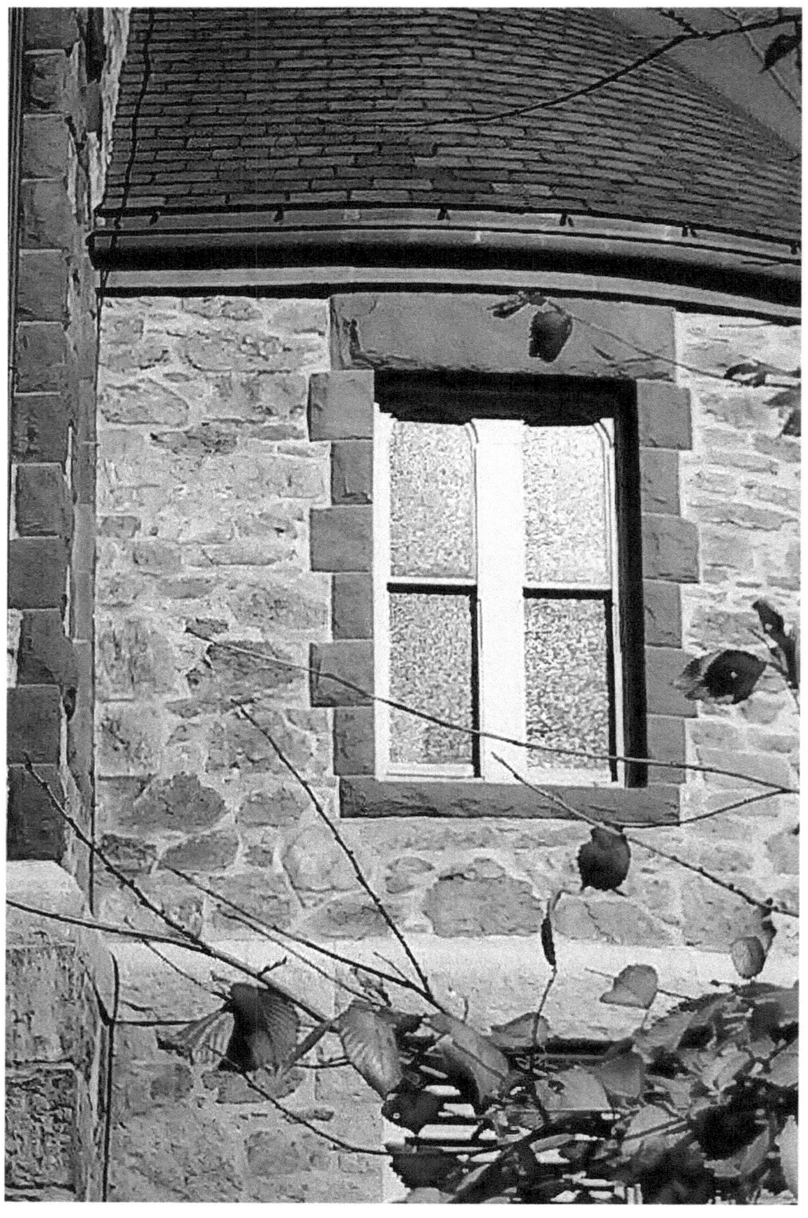

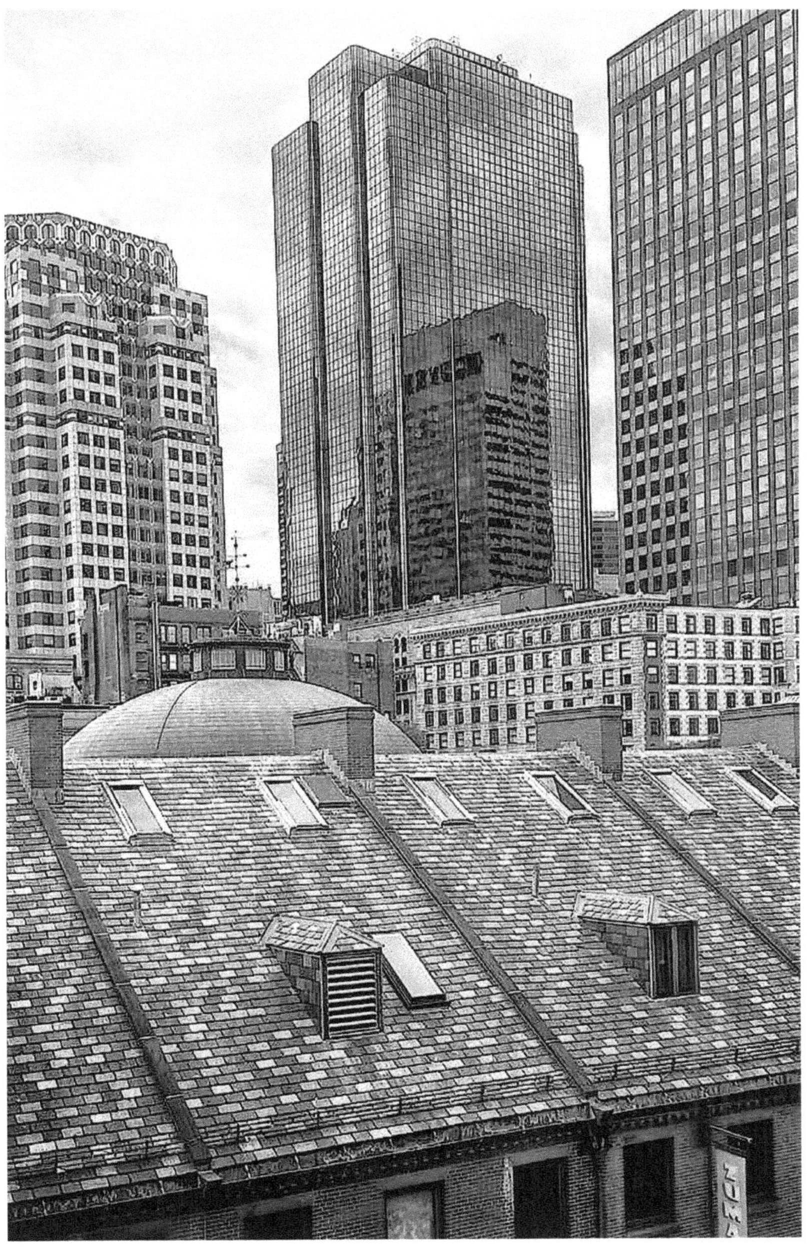

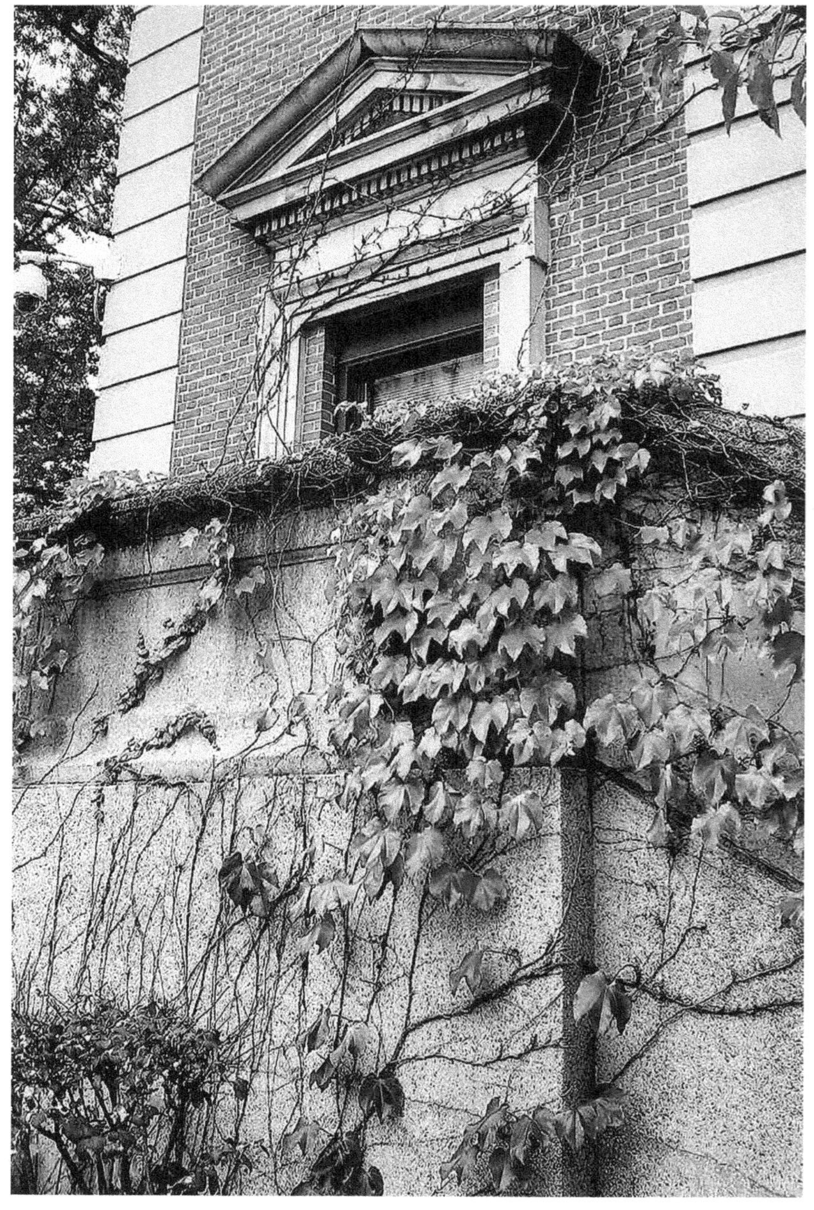

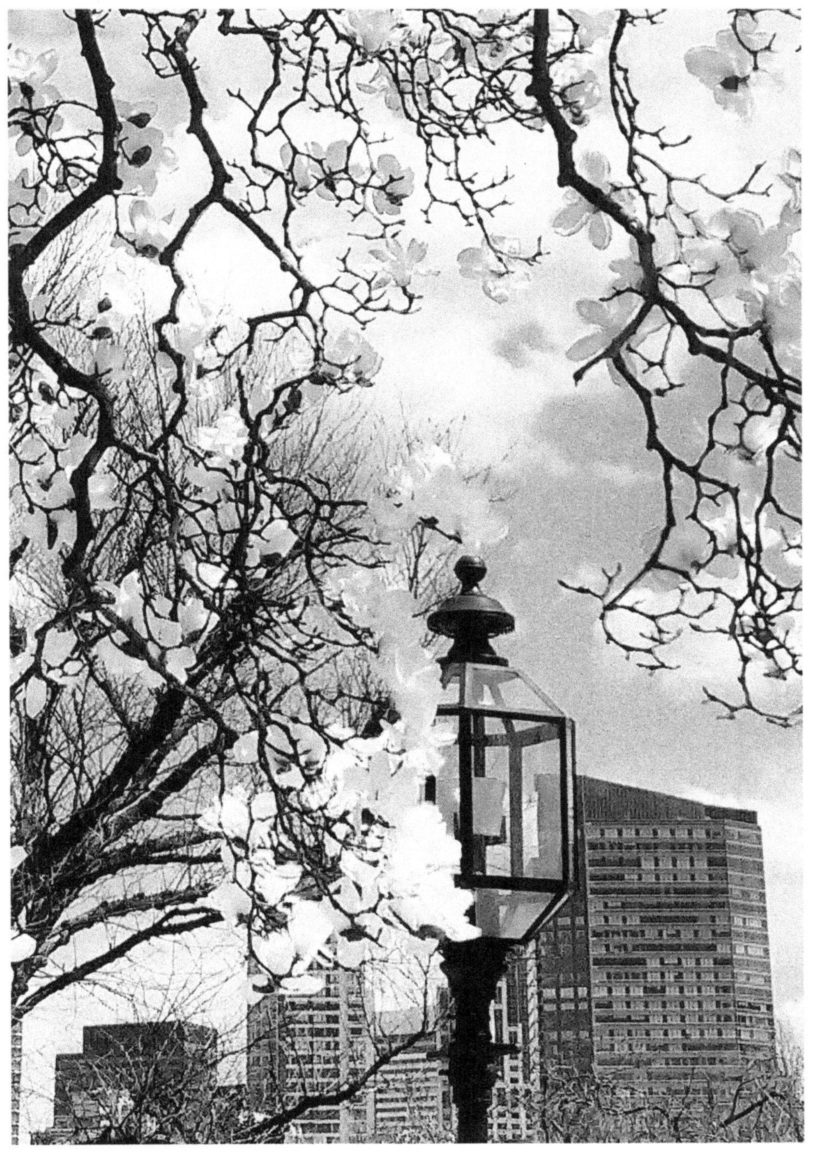

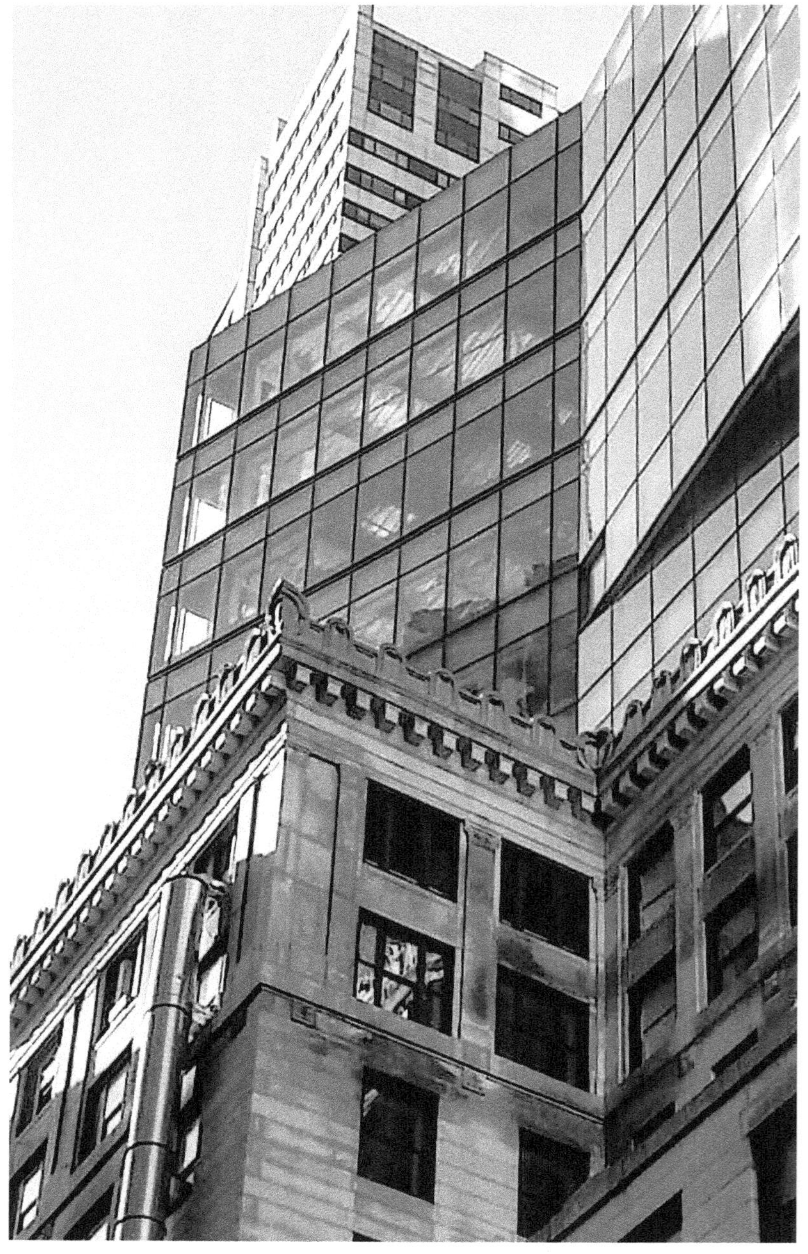

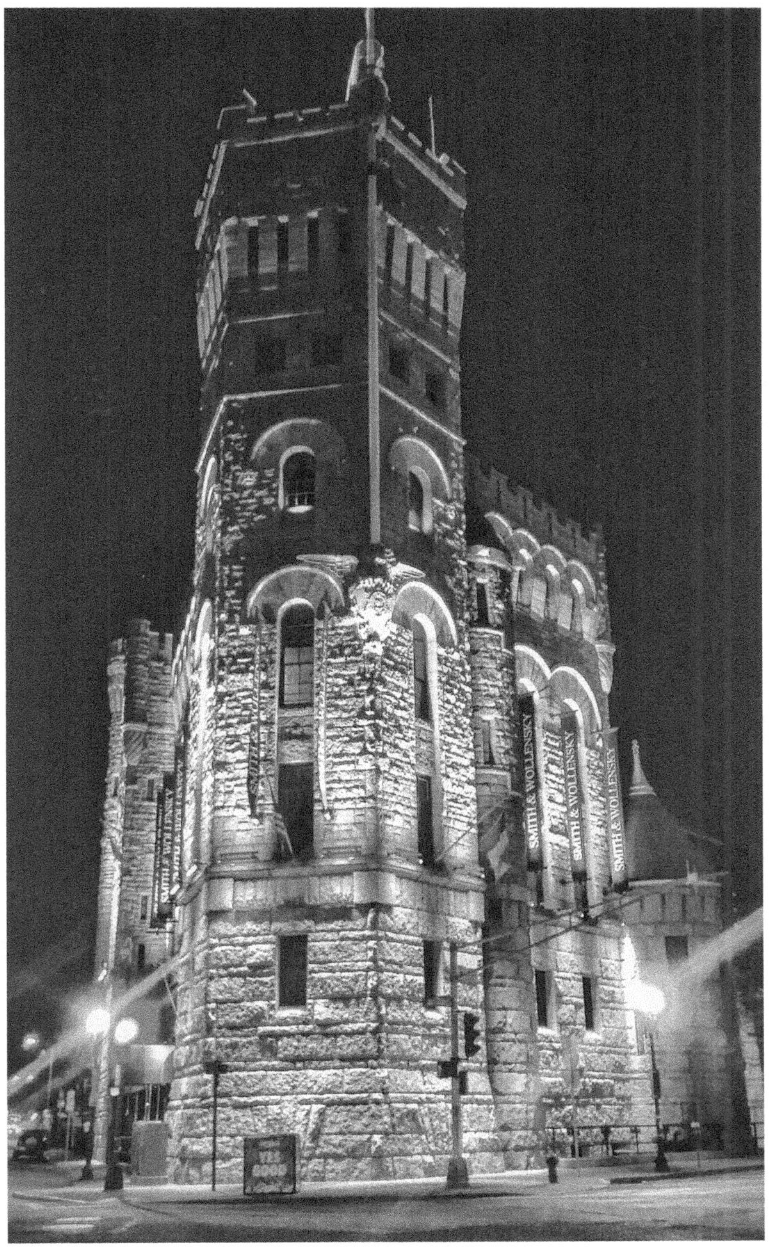

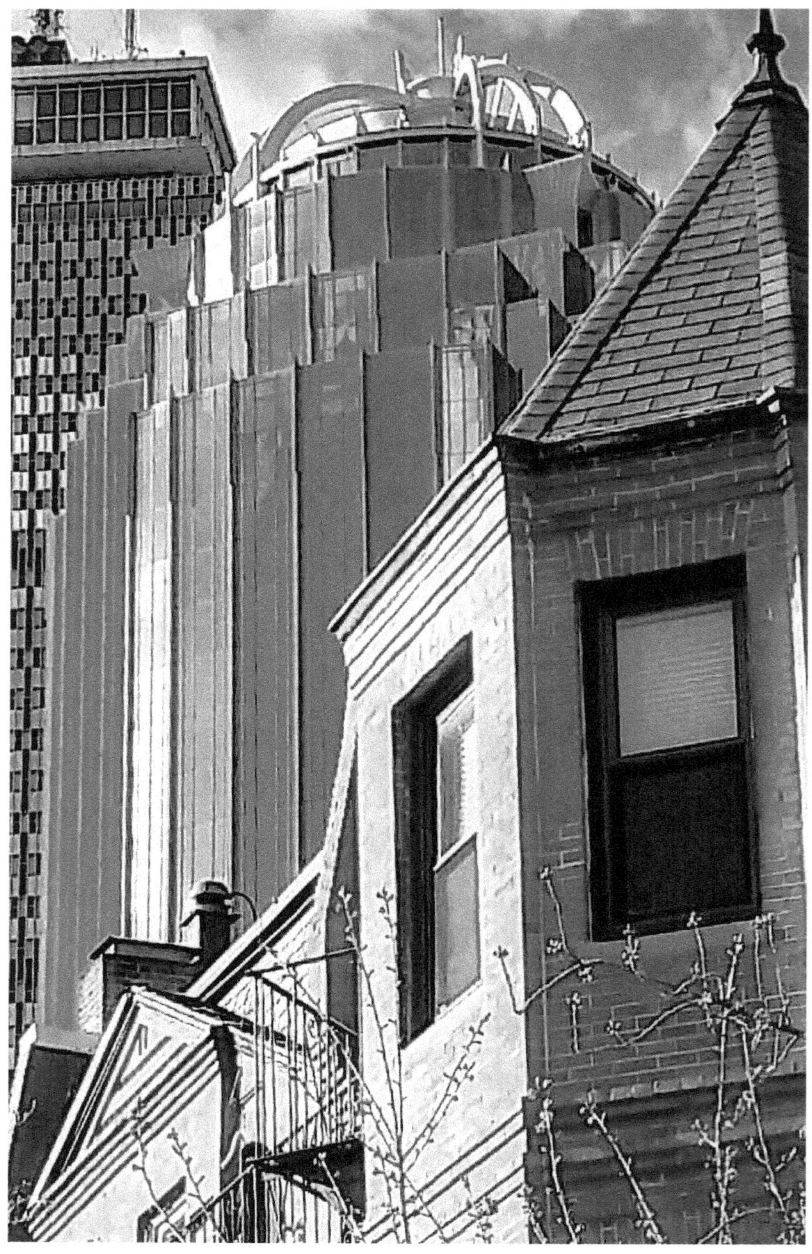

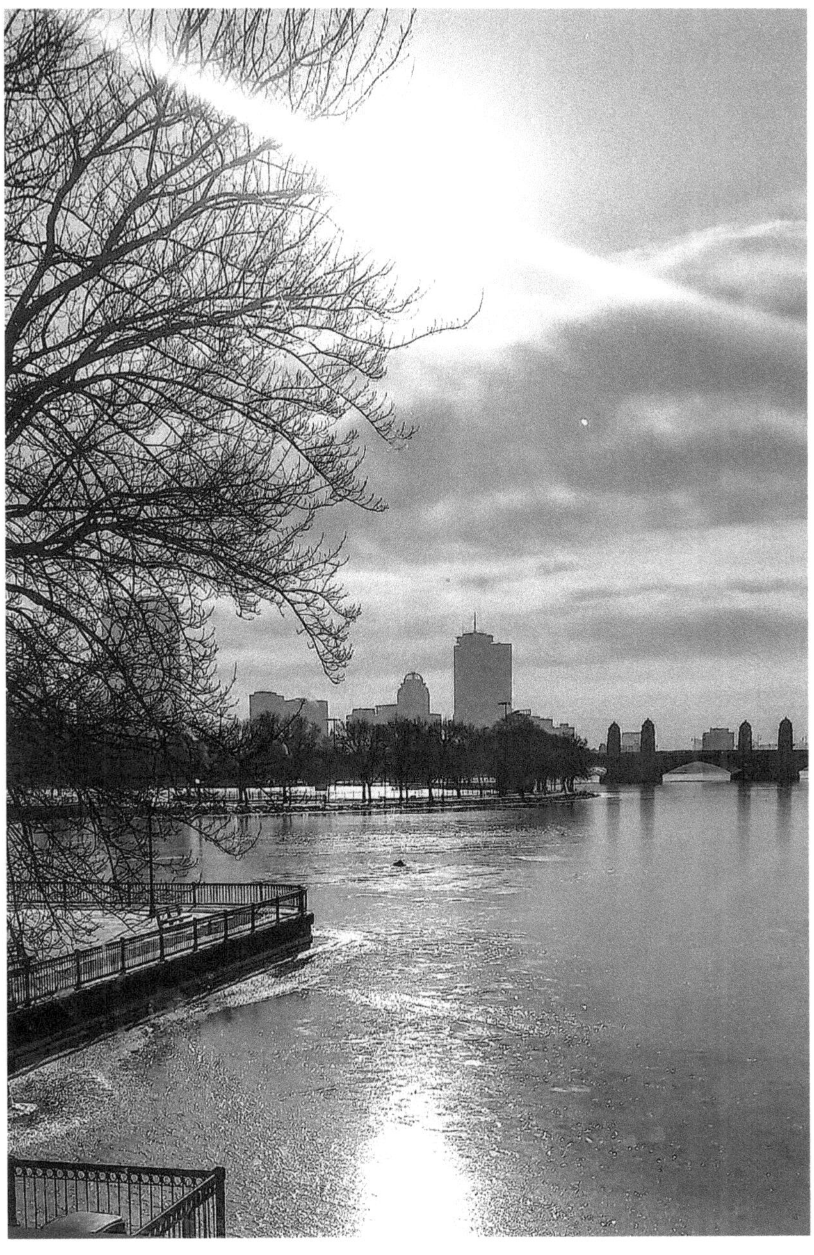

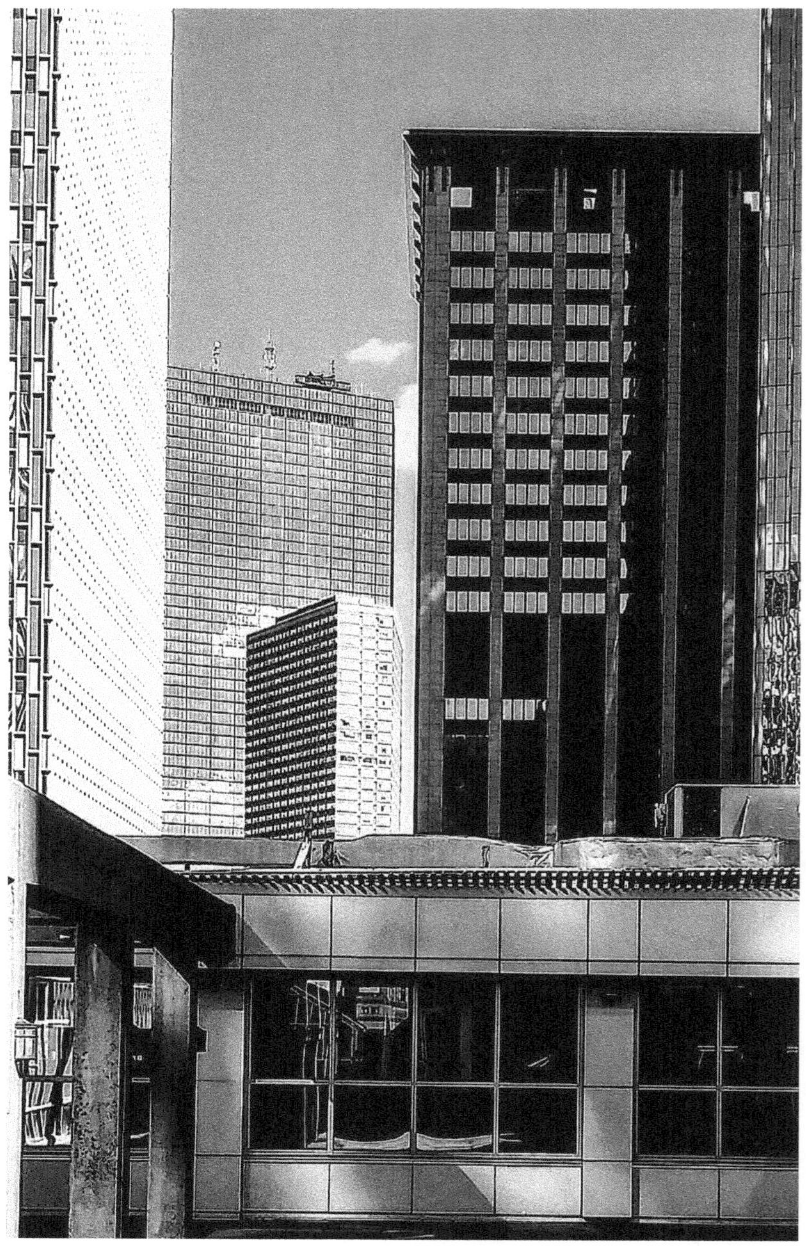

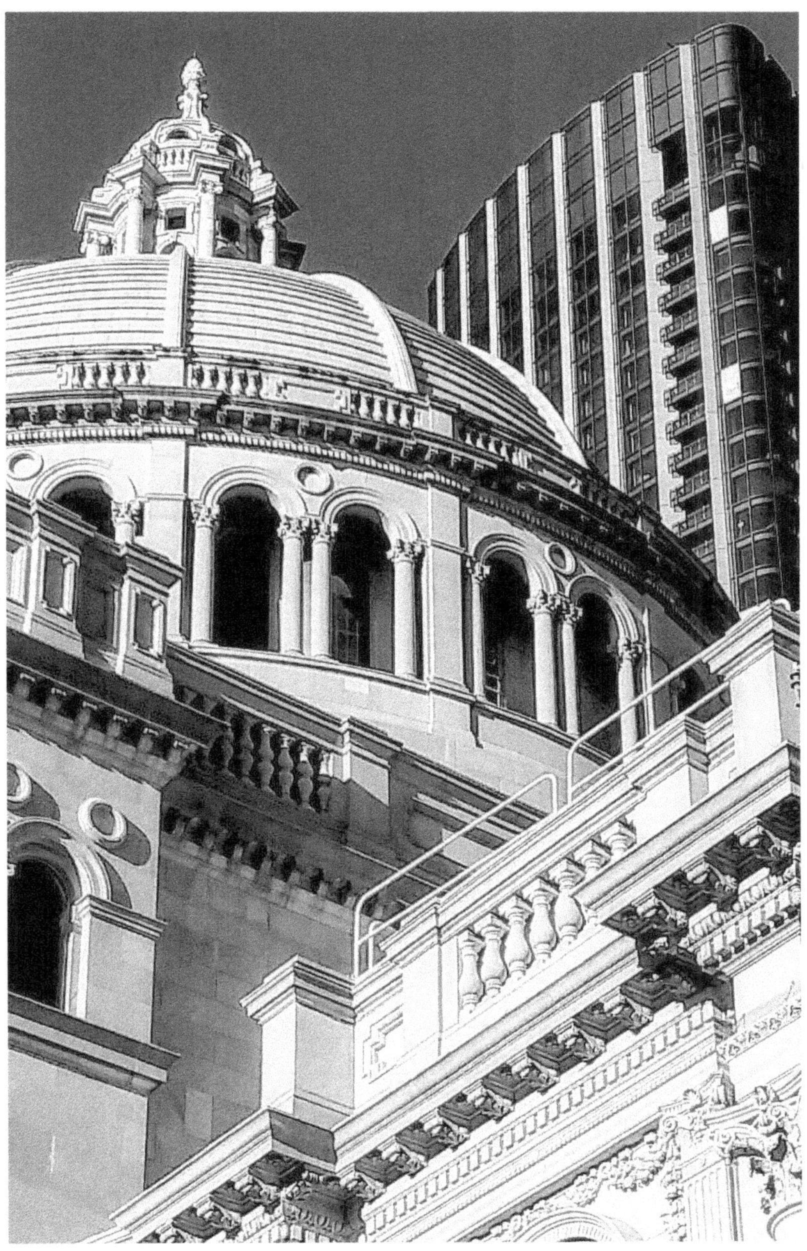

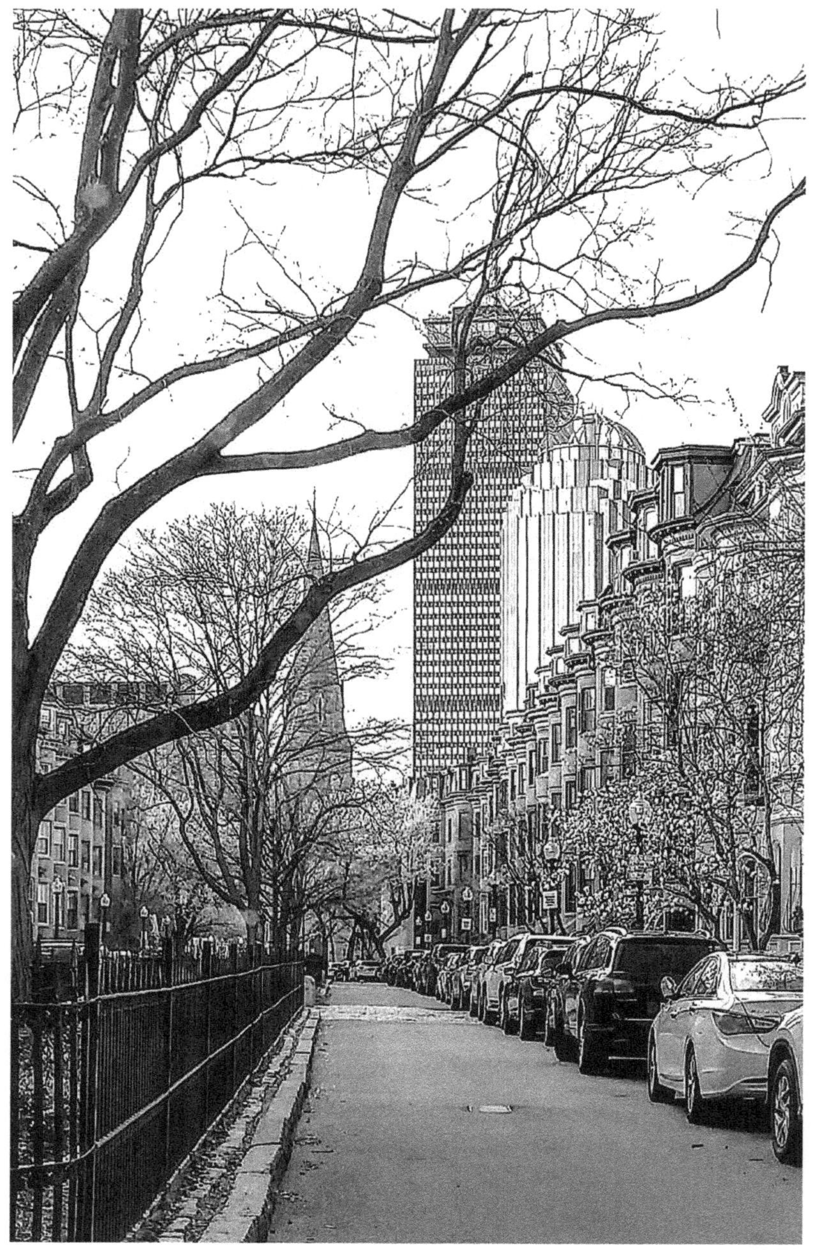

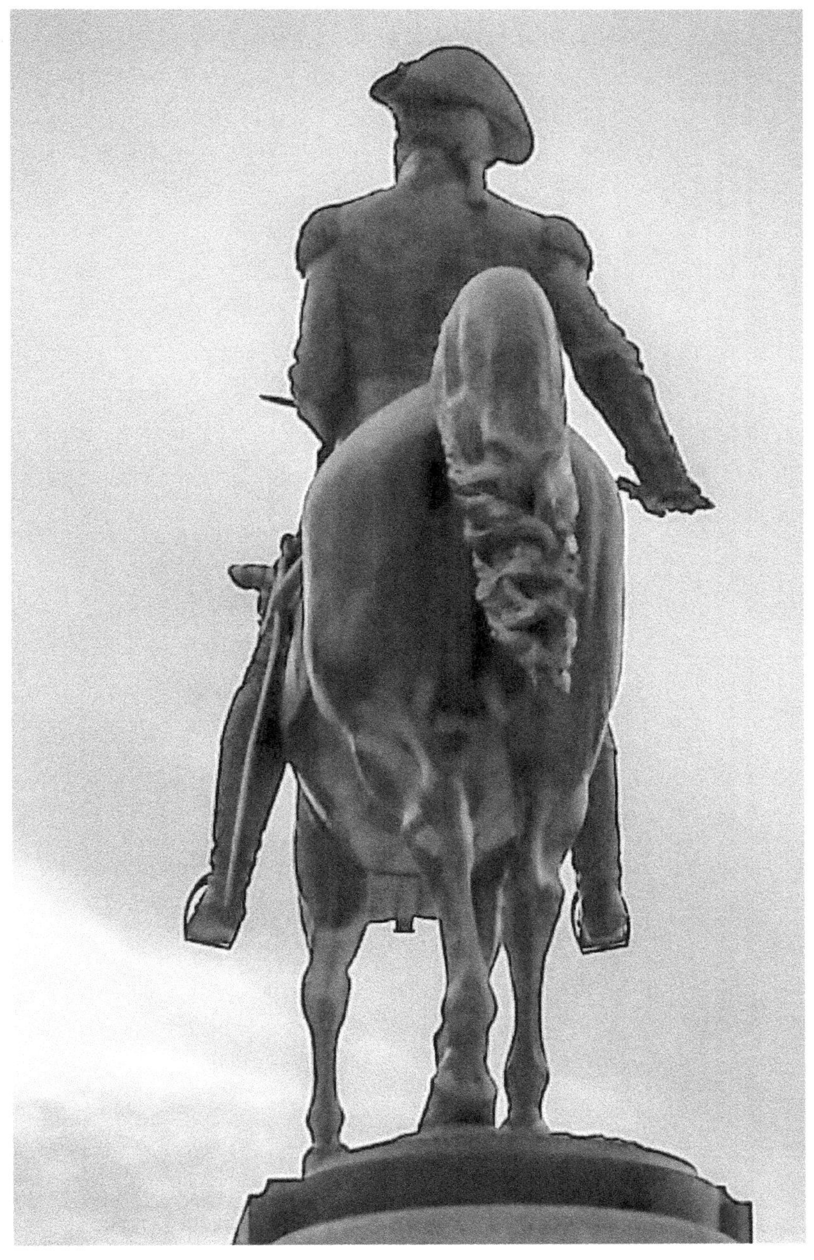

North End

A Boston man is the east wind made flesh.

Thomas Gold Appleton (1812 – 1884)
writer and artist

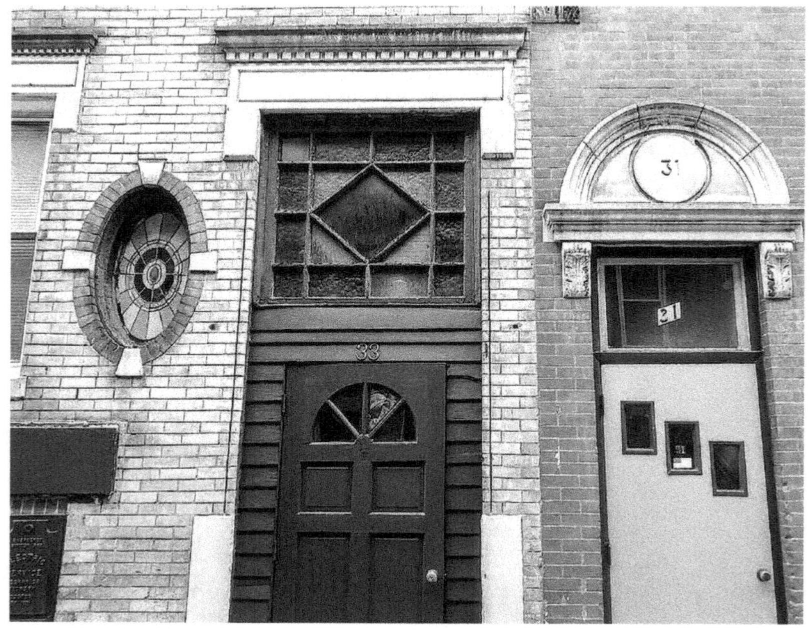

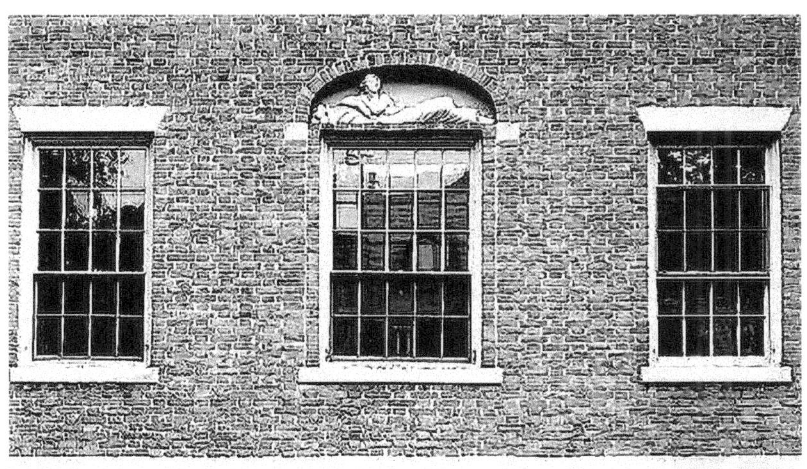

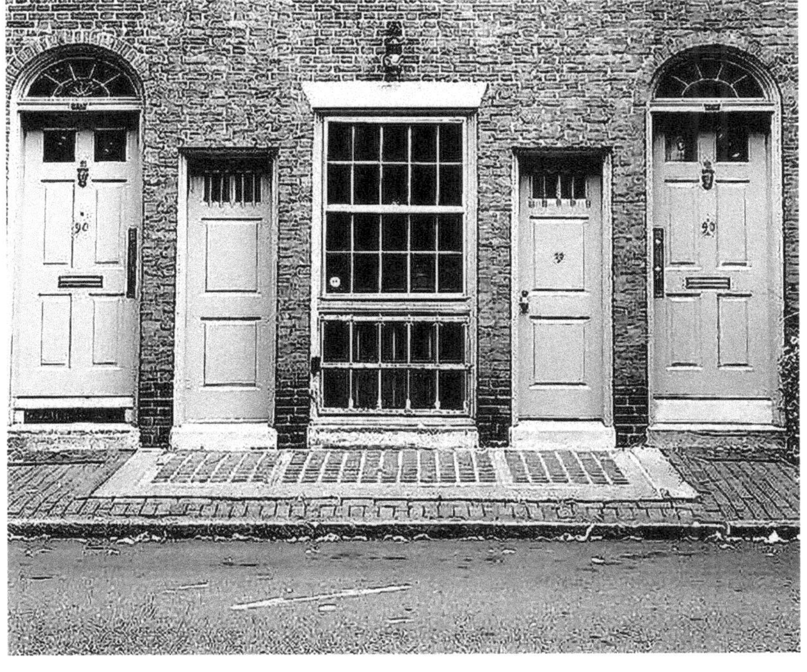

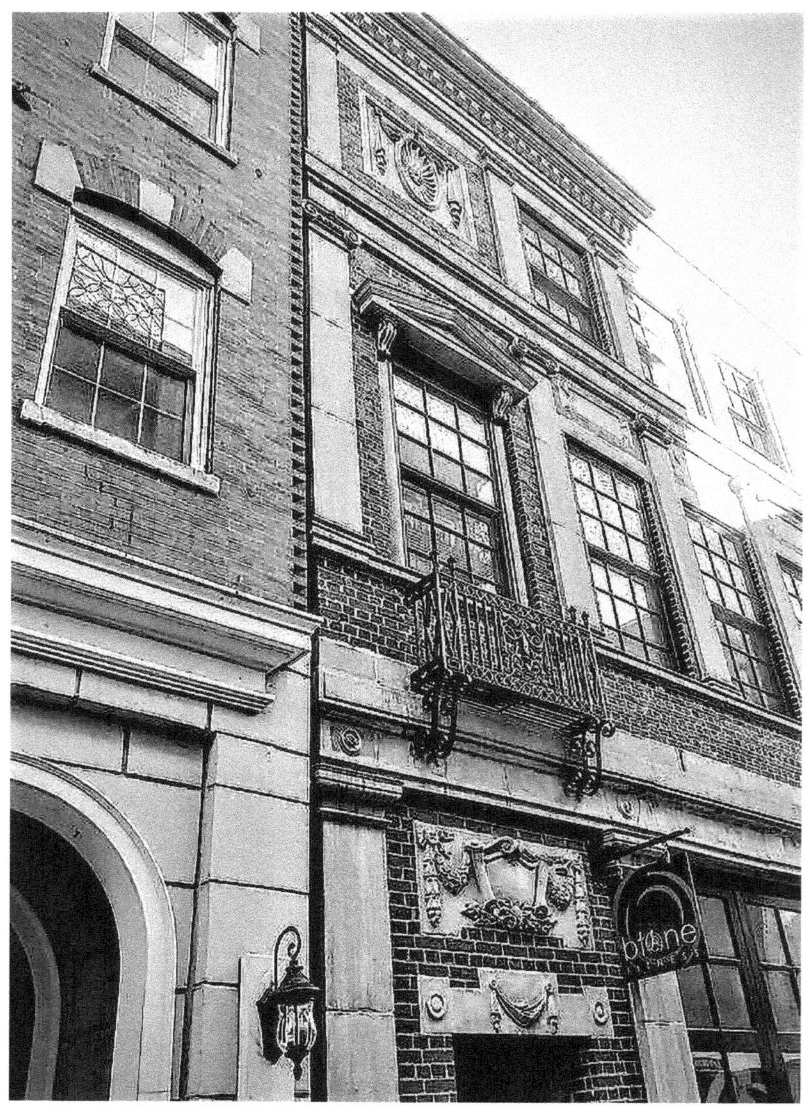

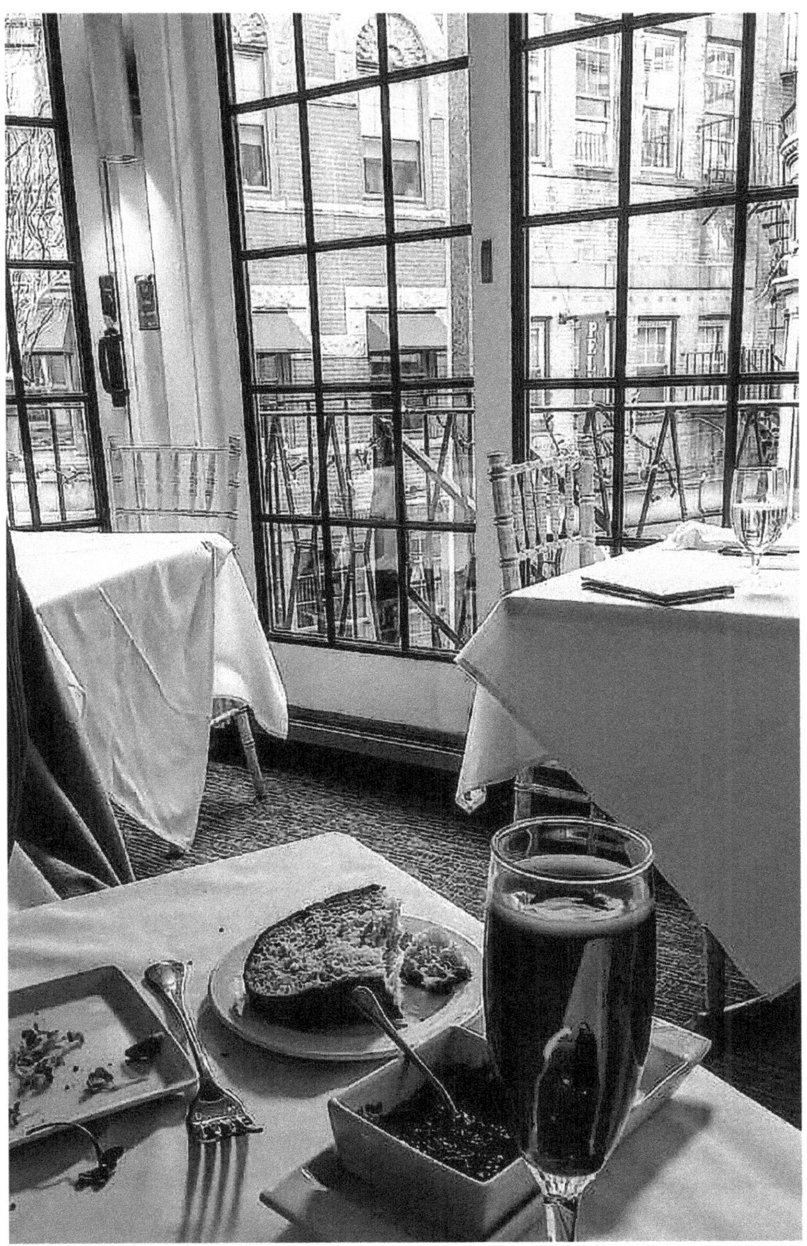

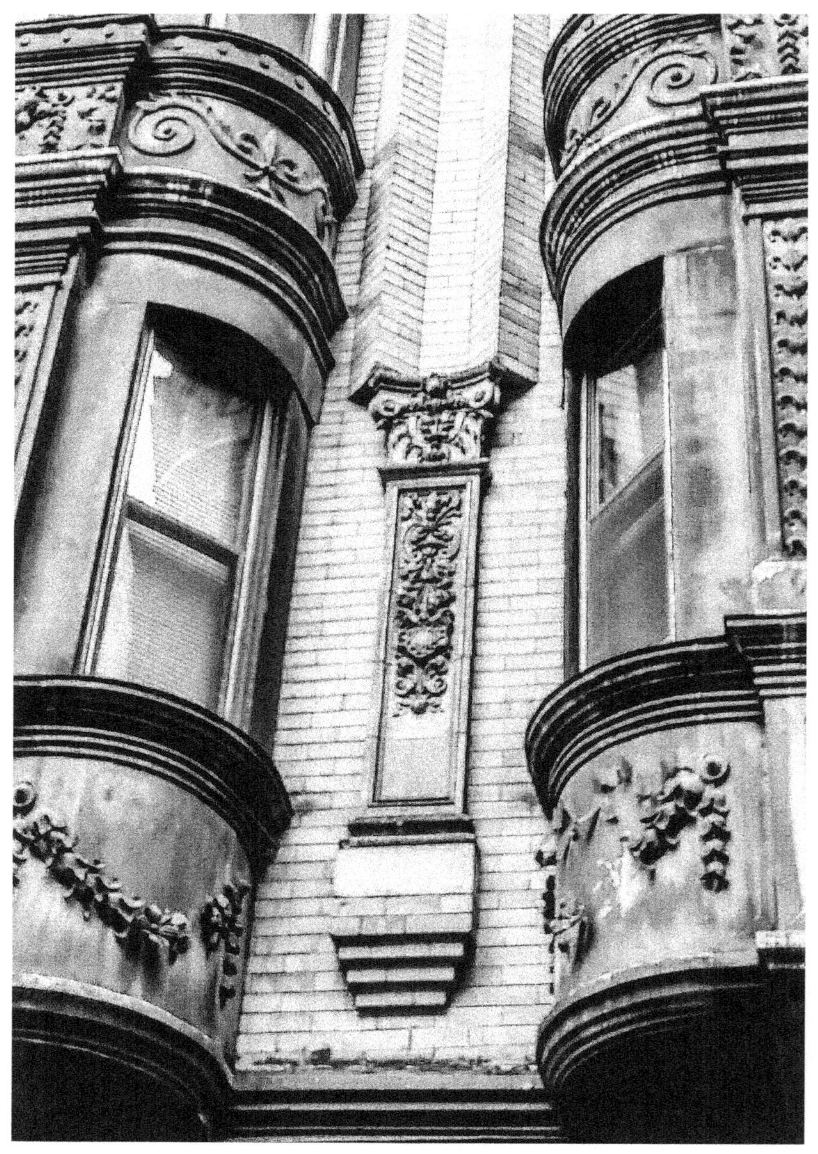

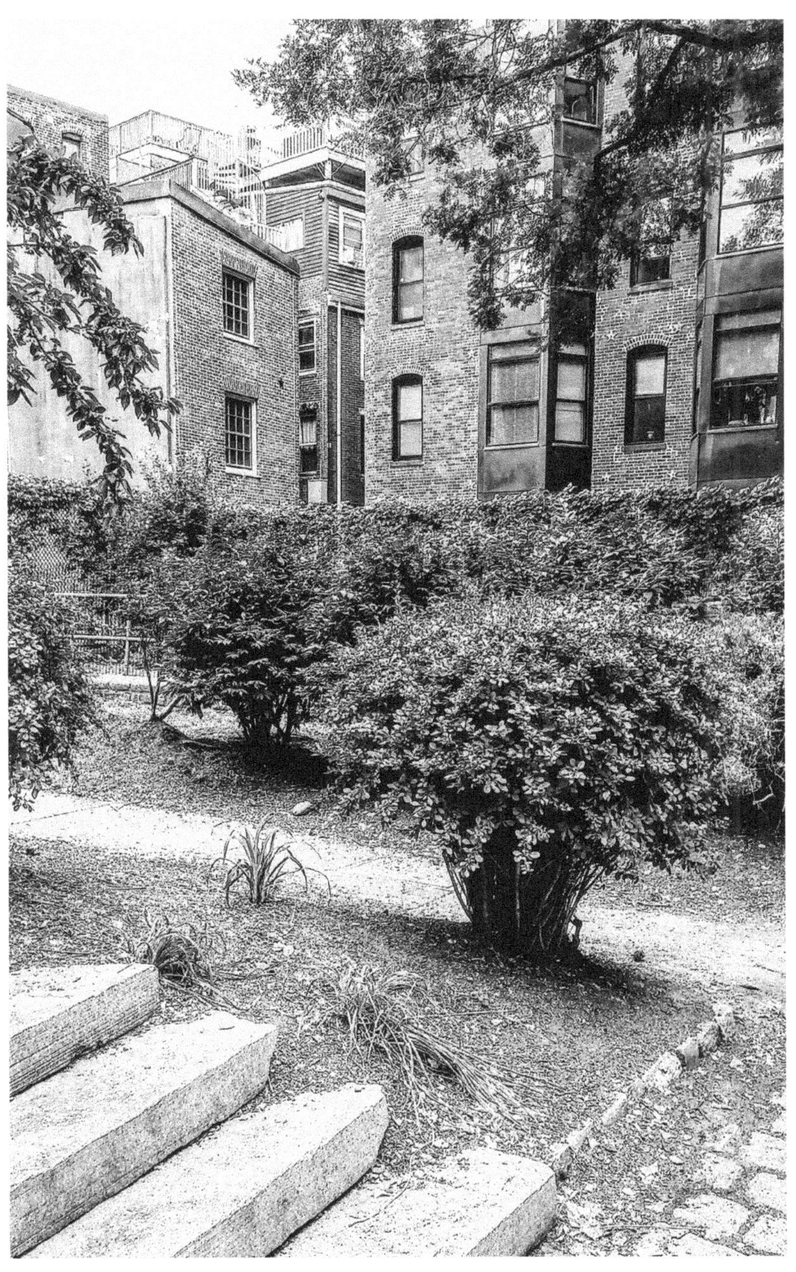

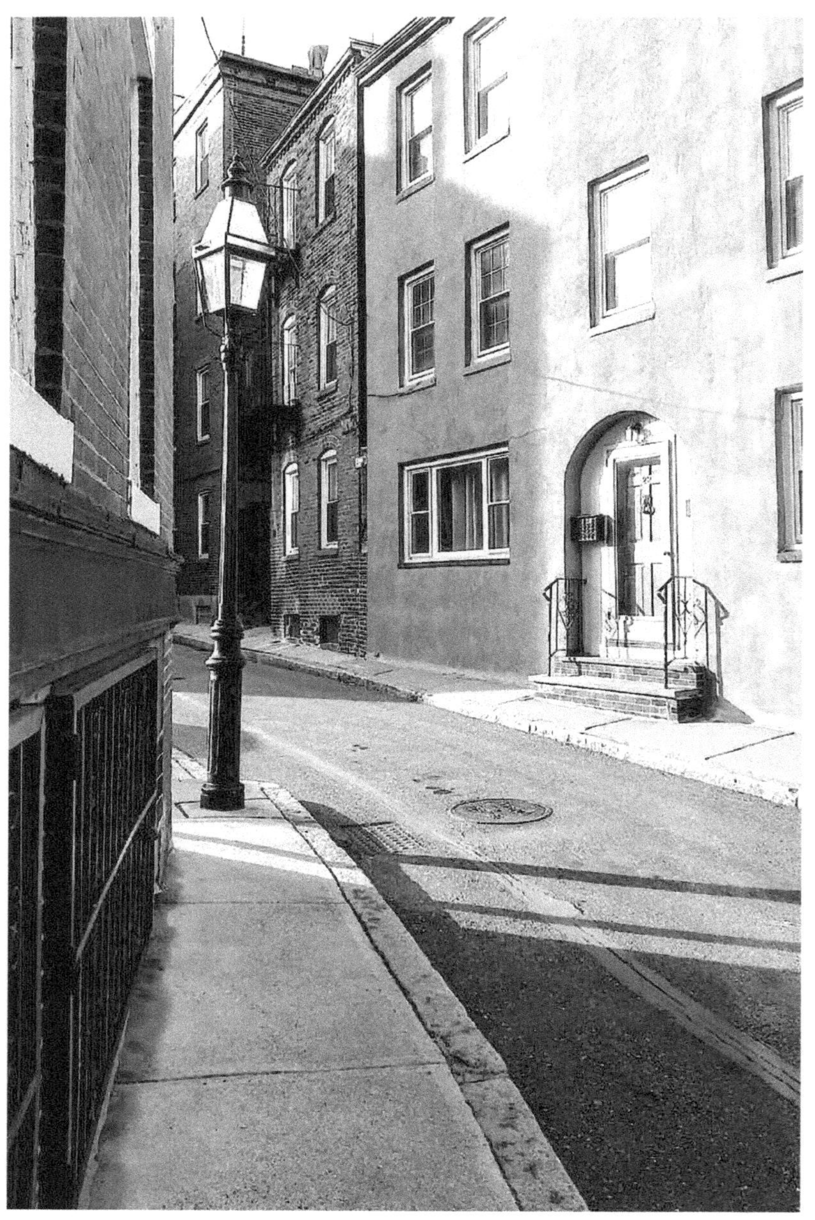

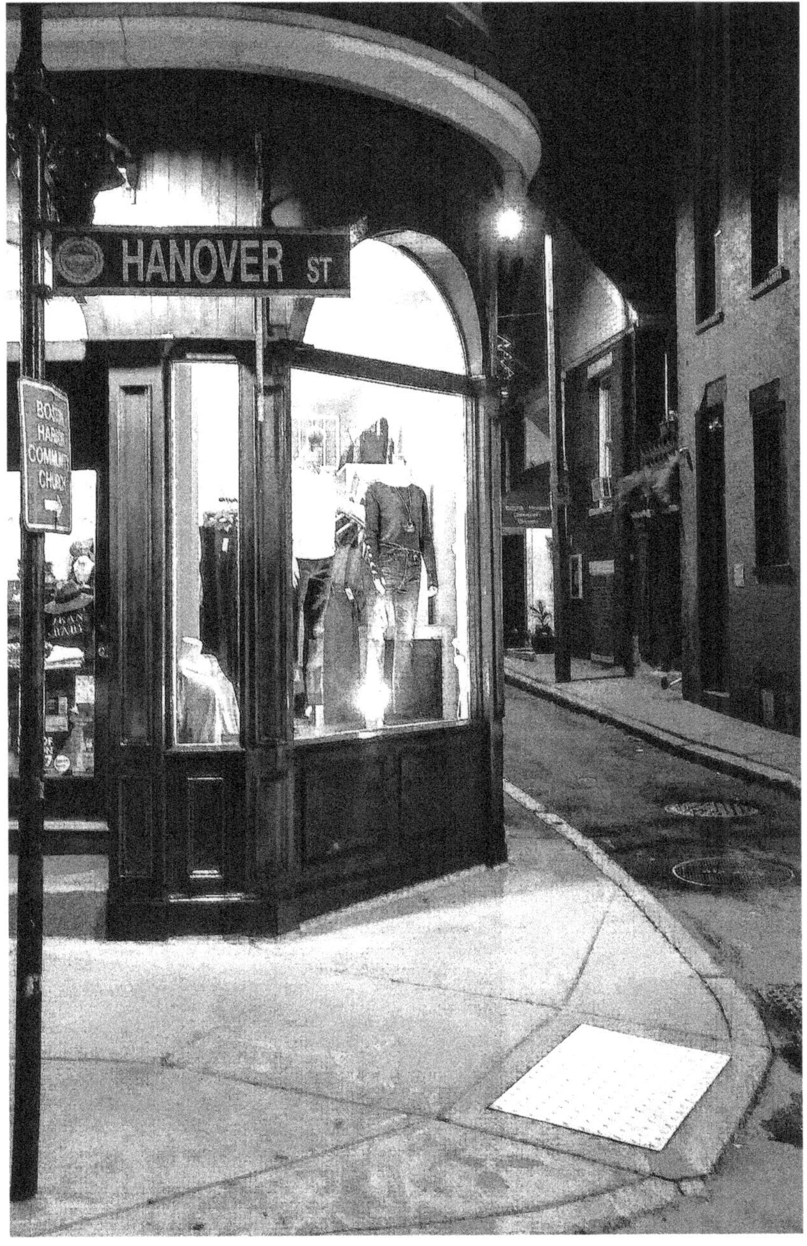
HANOVER ST
BOSTON
HARBOR
COMMUNITY
CHURCH

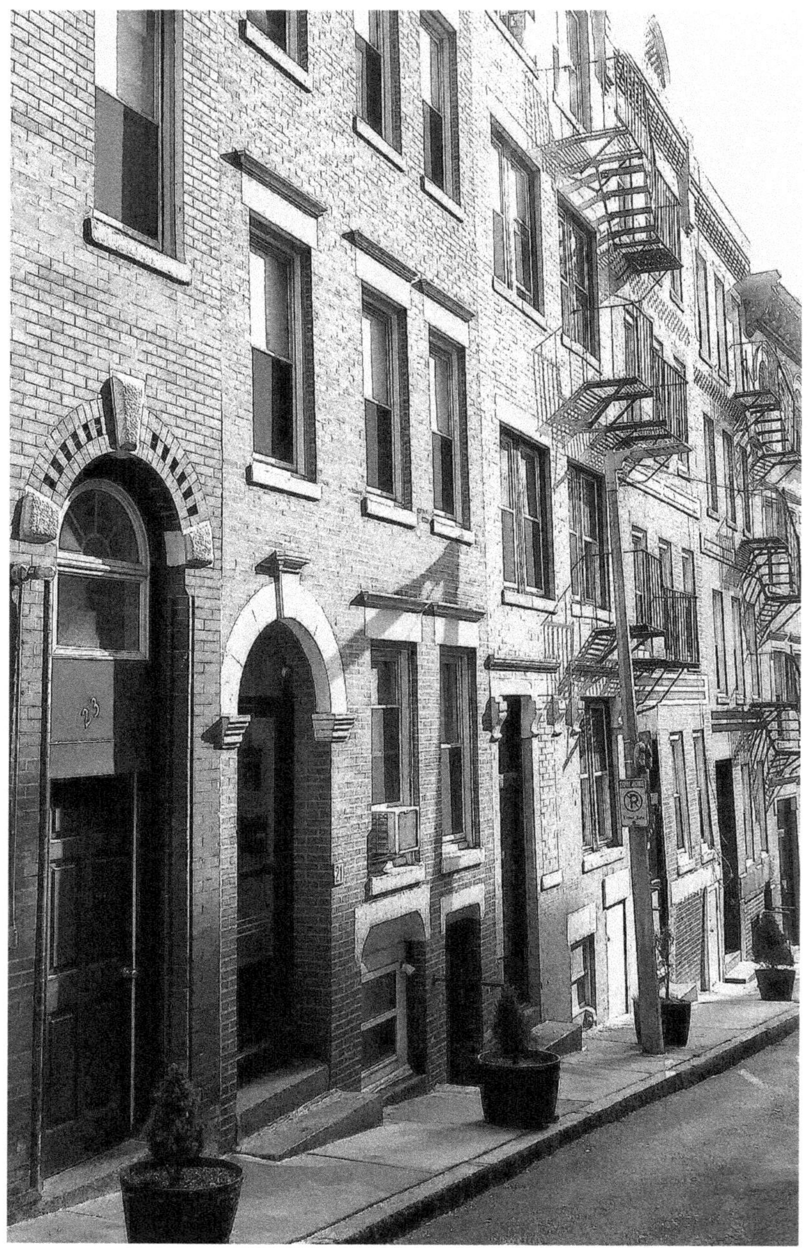

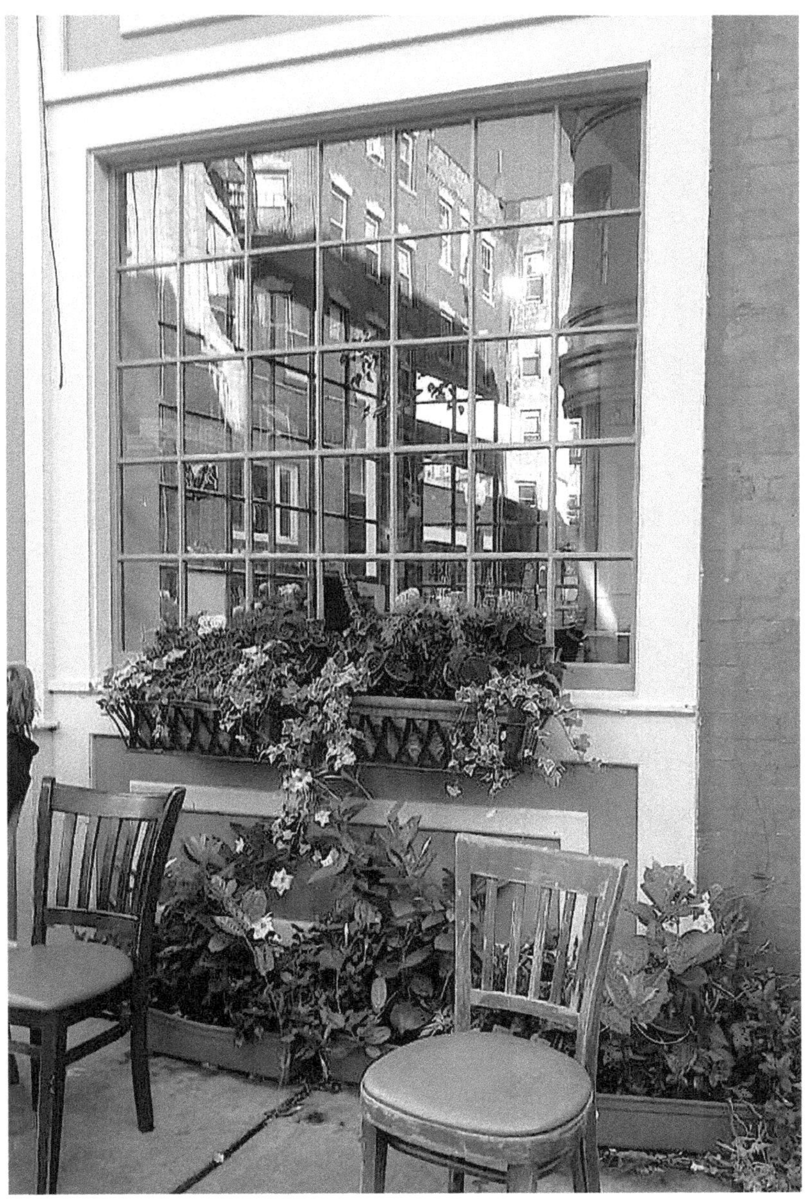

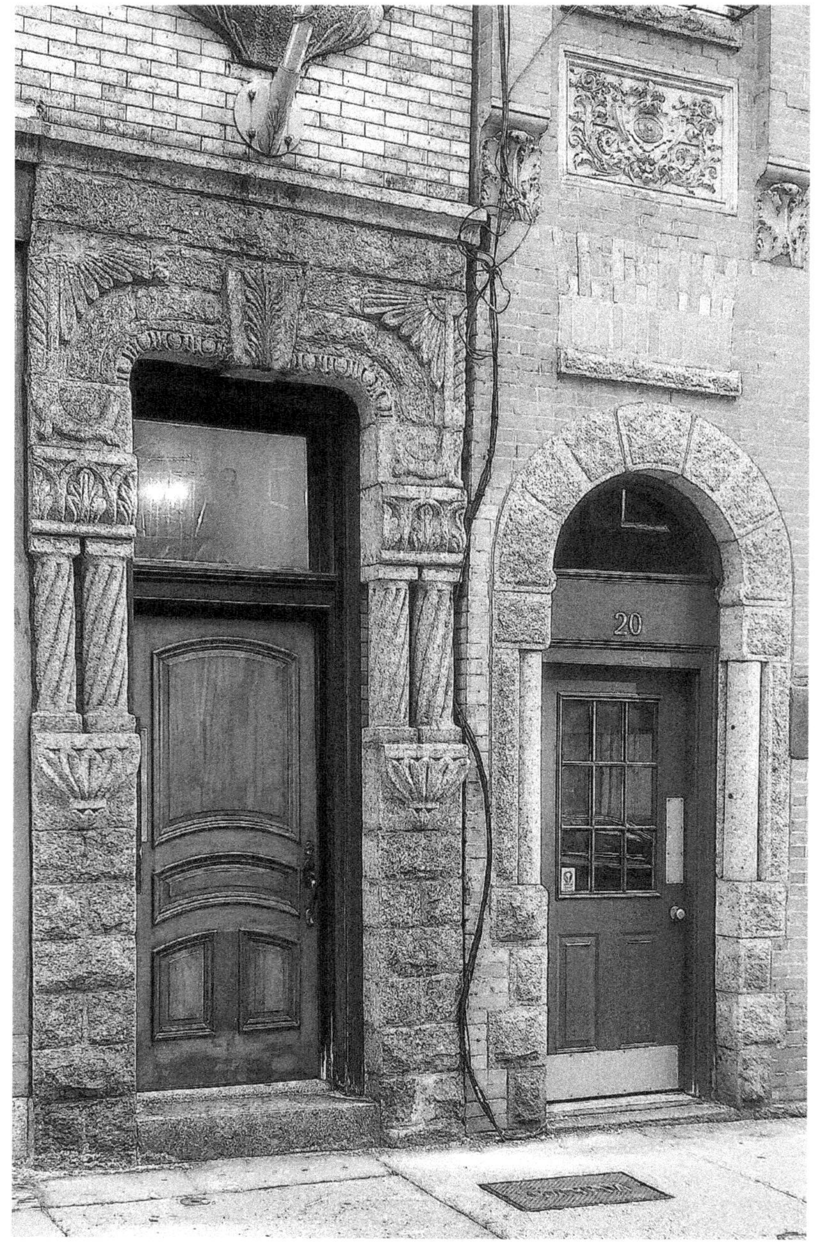

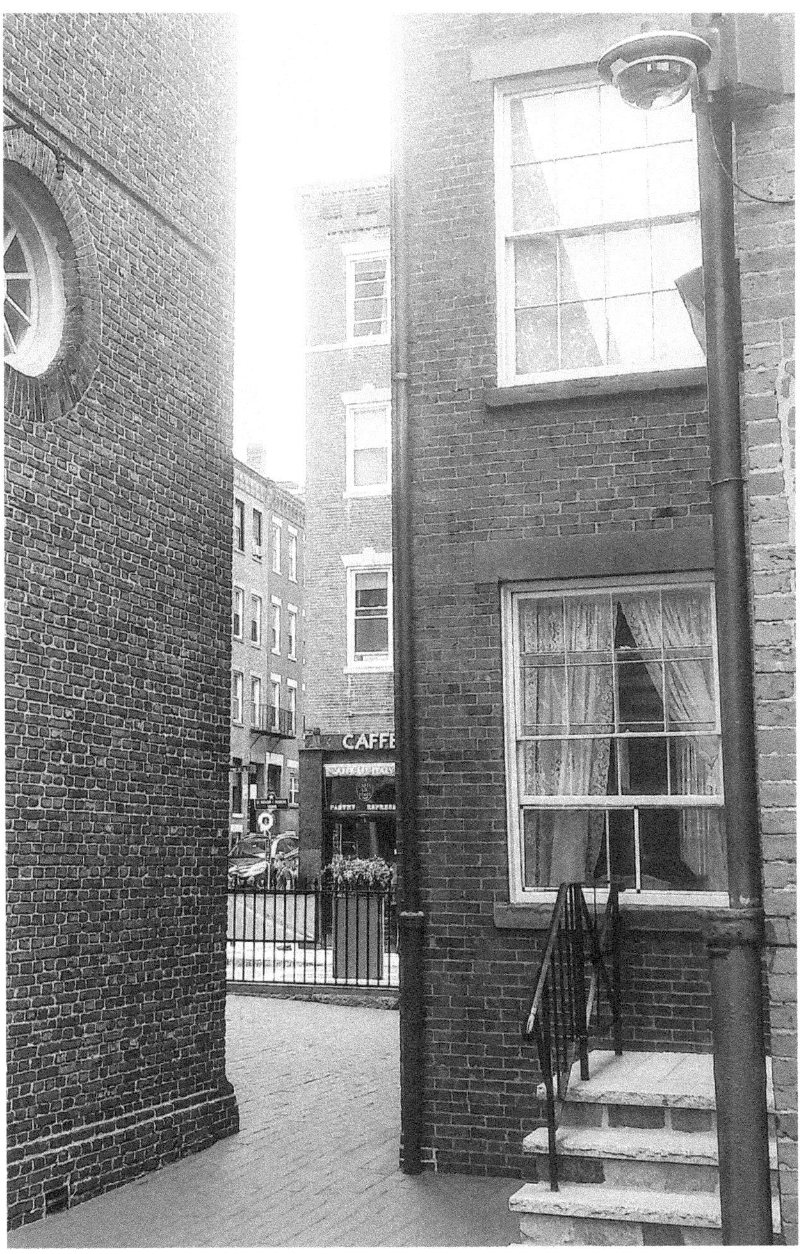

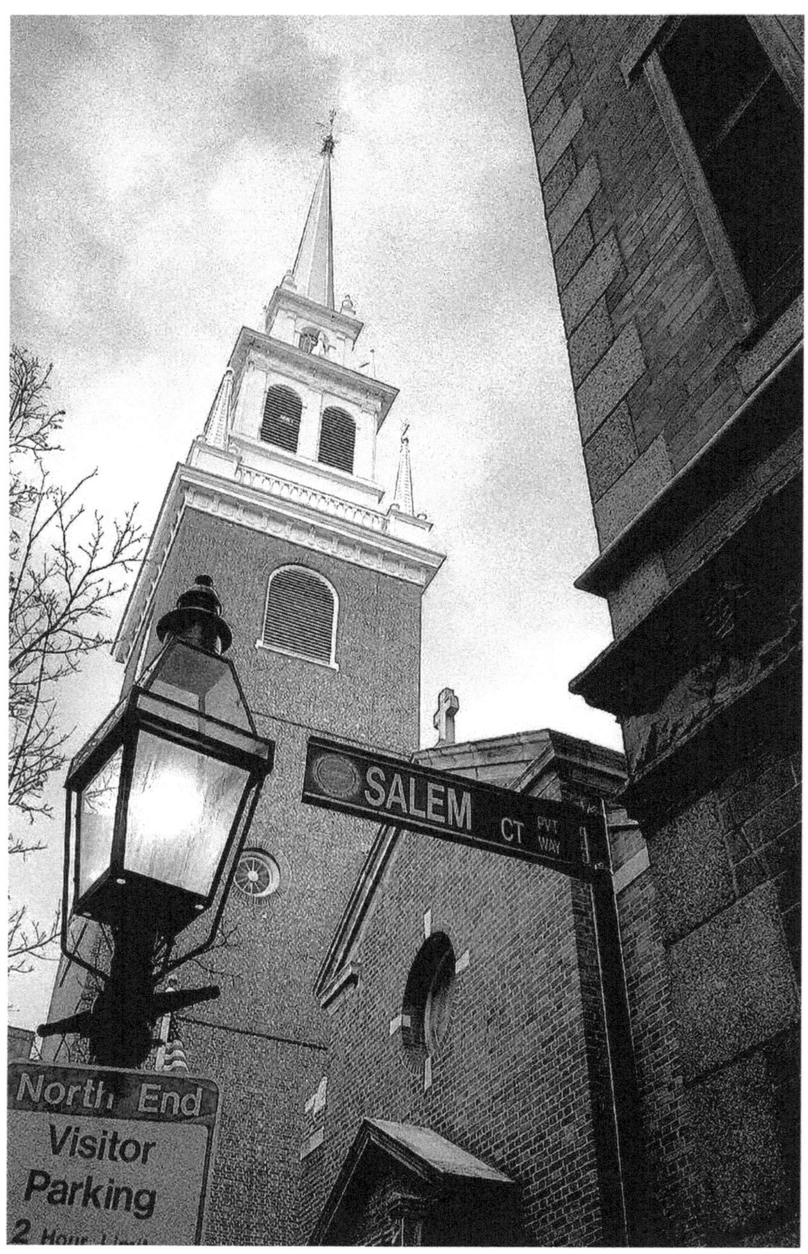
SALEM CT PVT WAY
North End
Visitor
Parking
2 Hour Limit

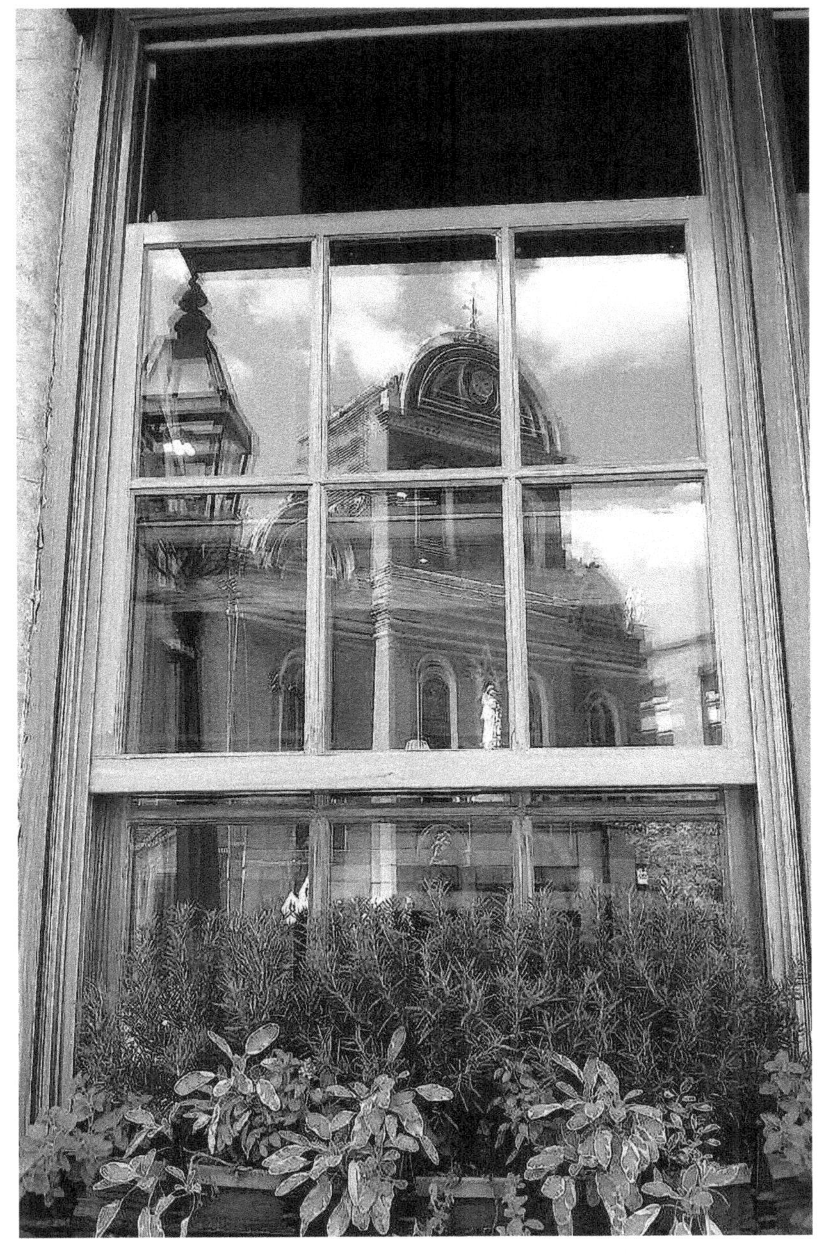

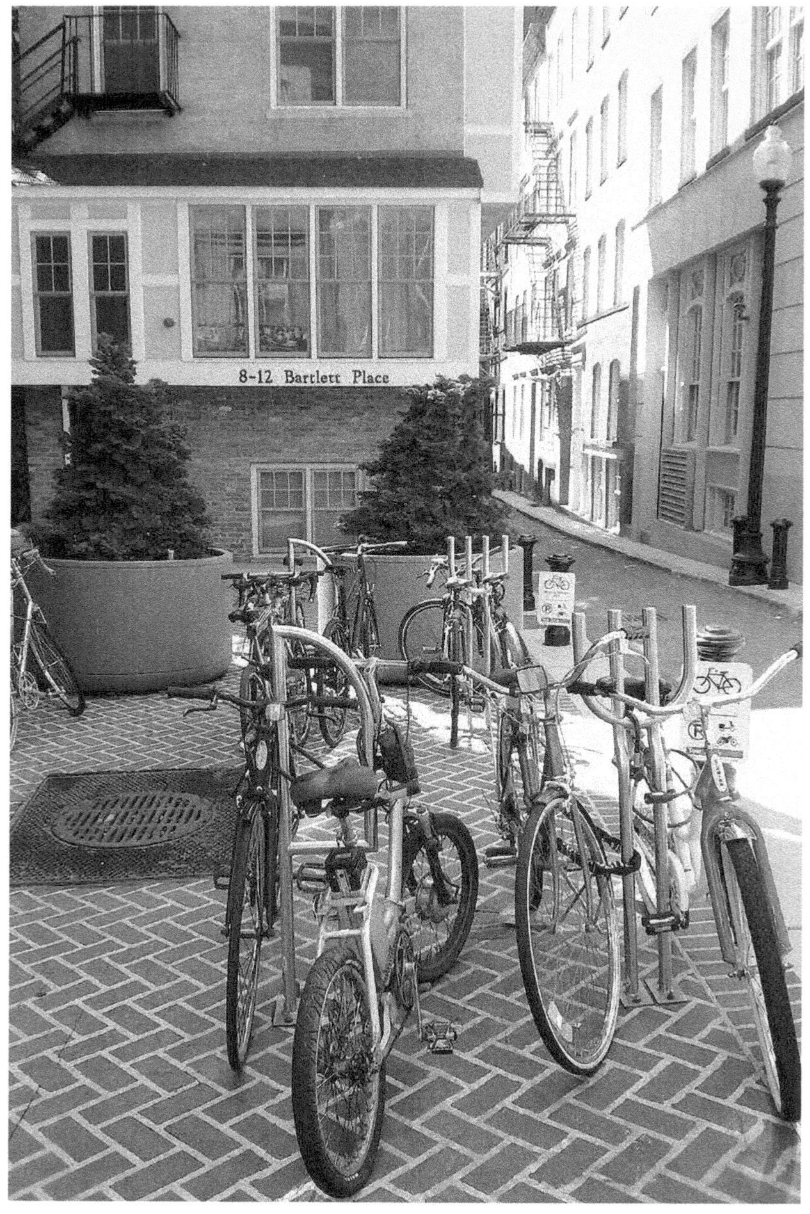
8-12 Bartlett Place

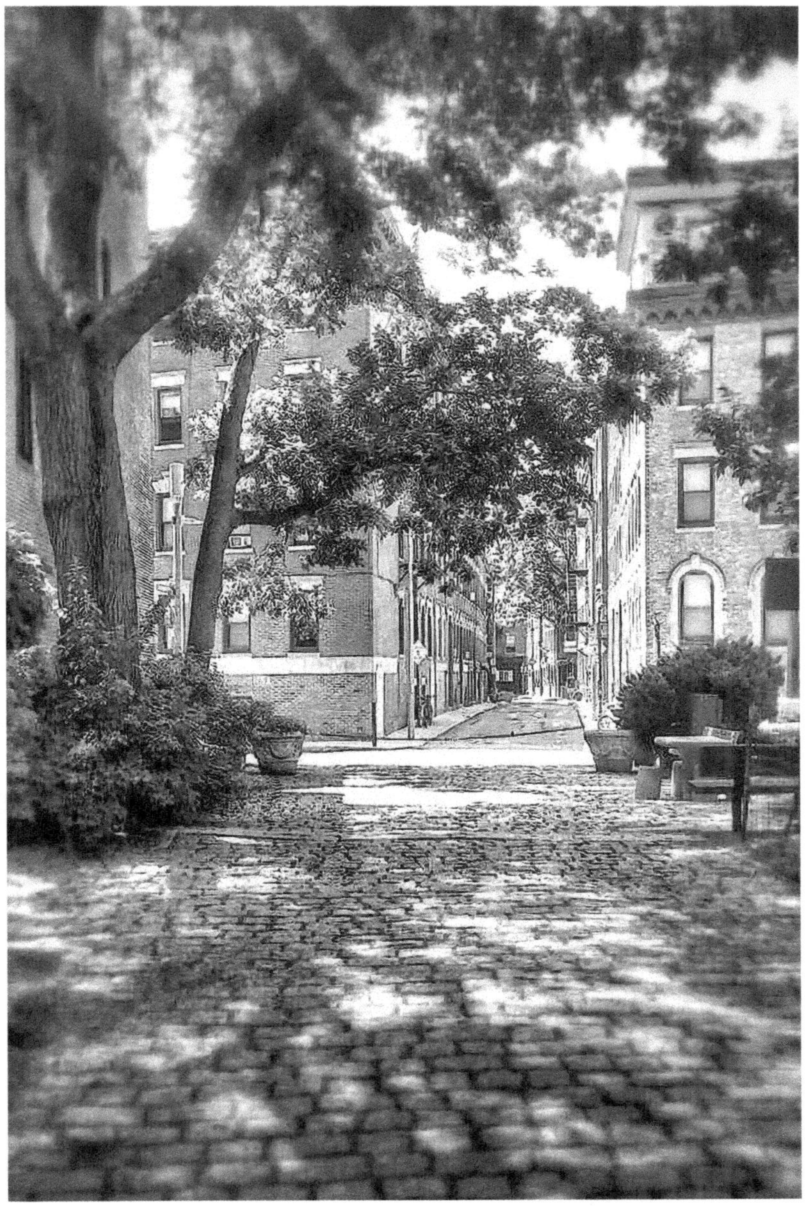

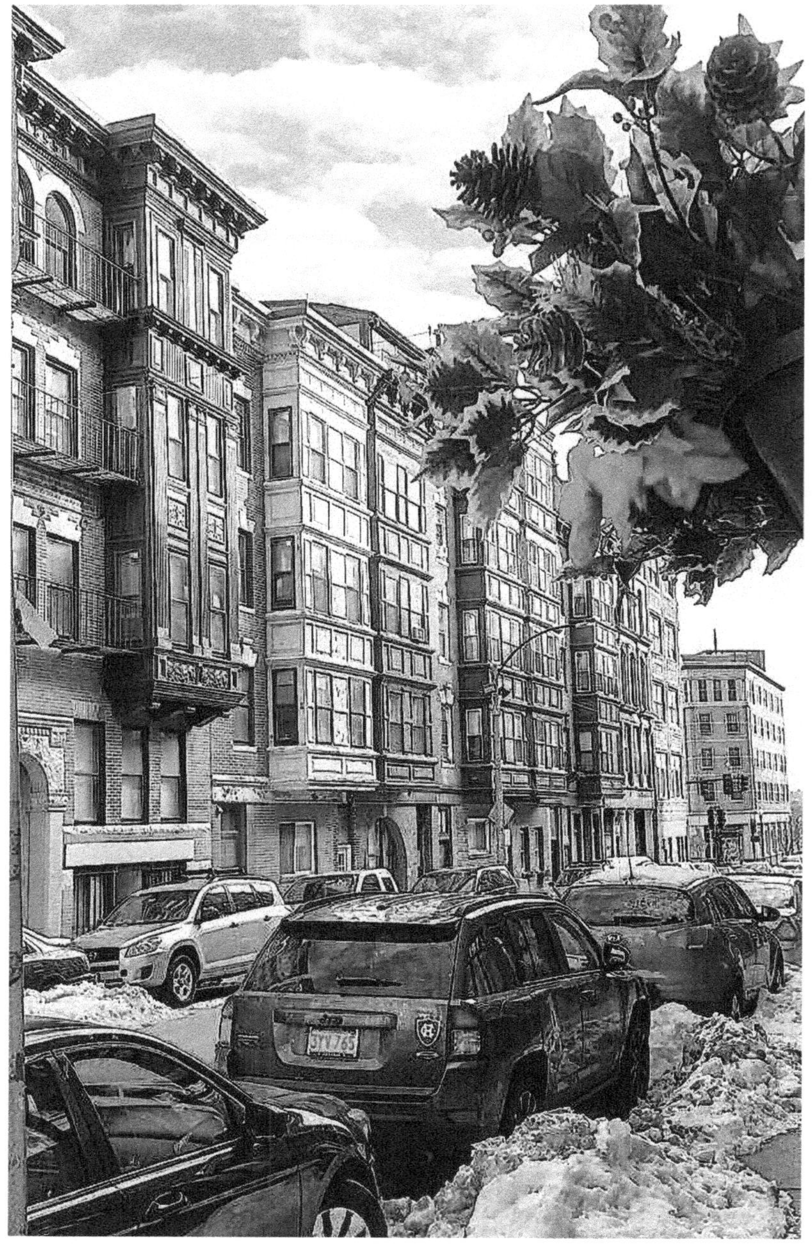

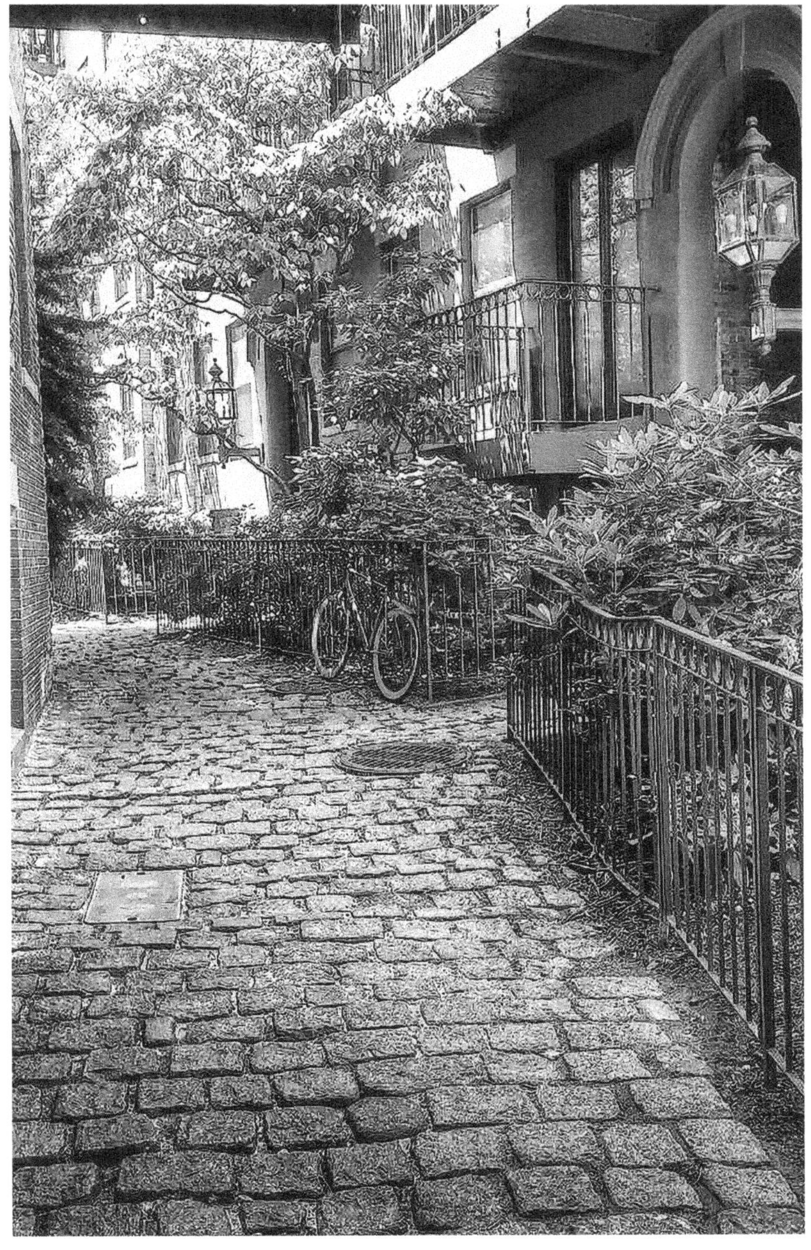

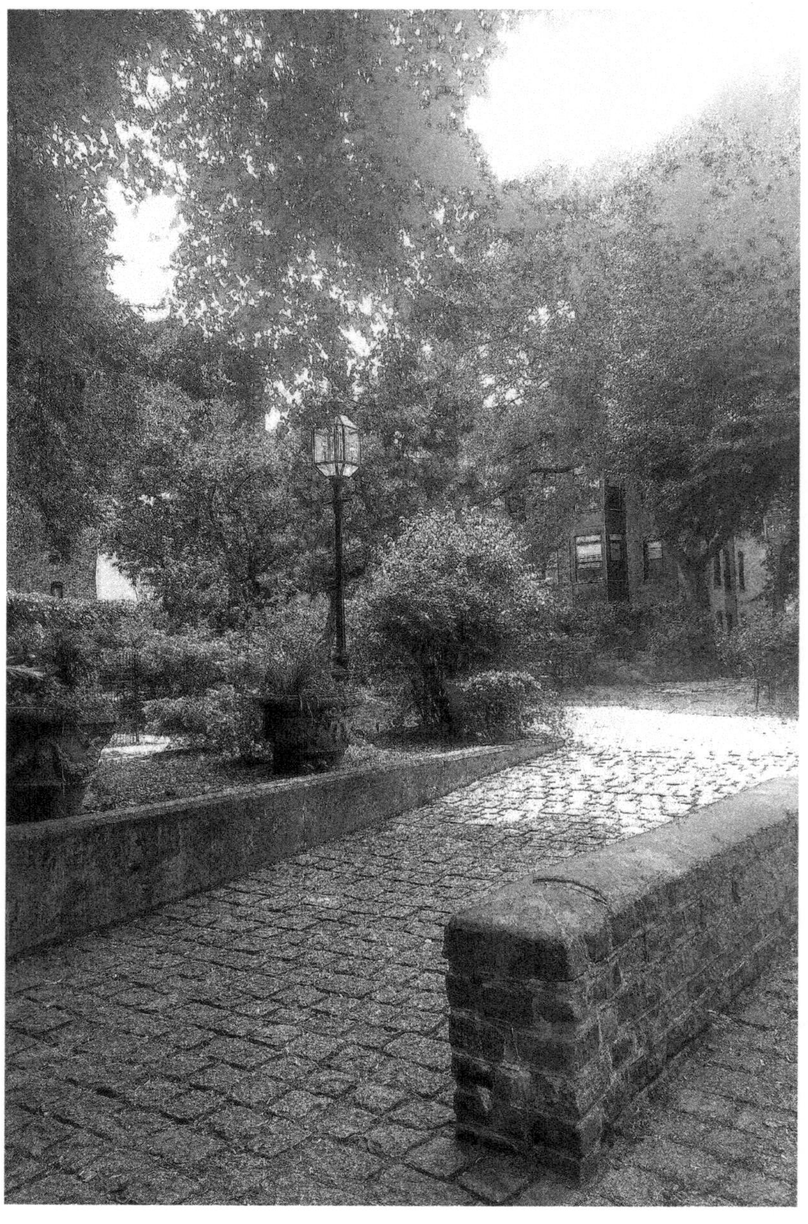

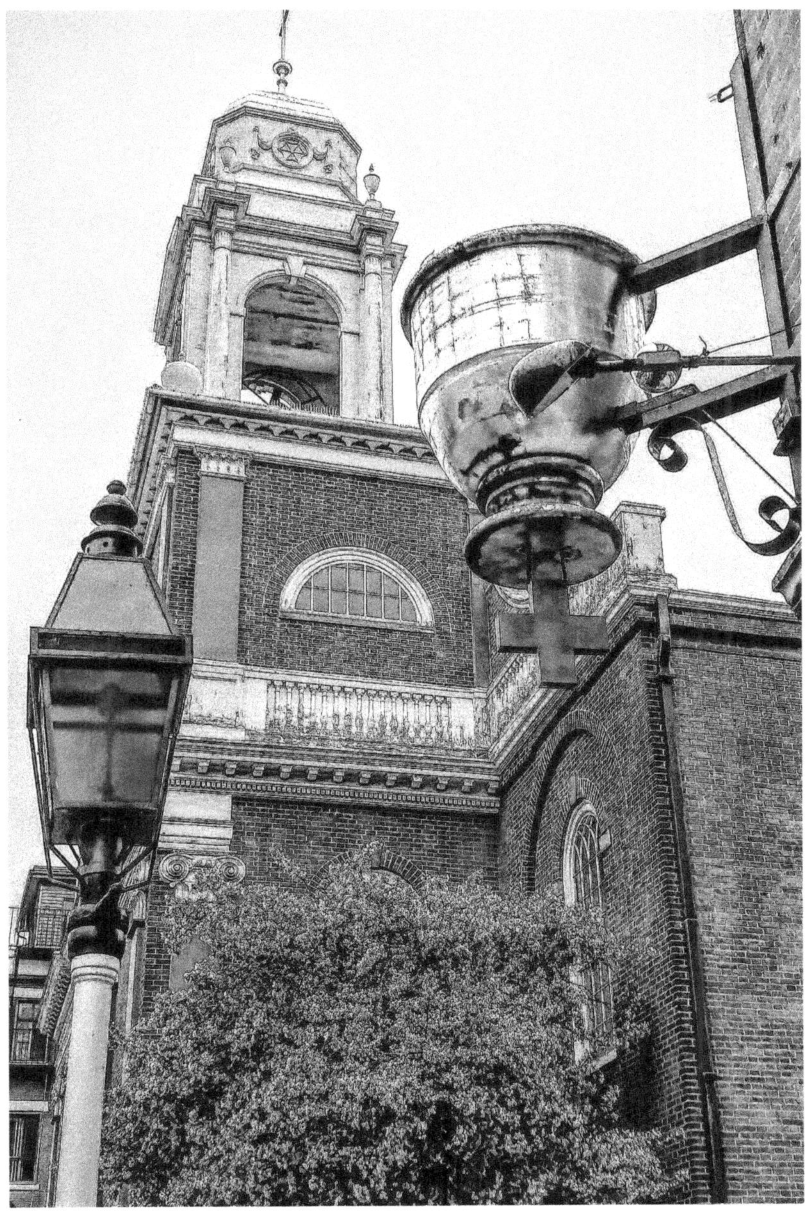

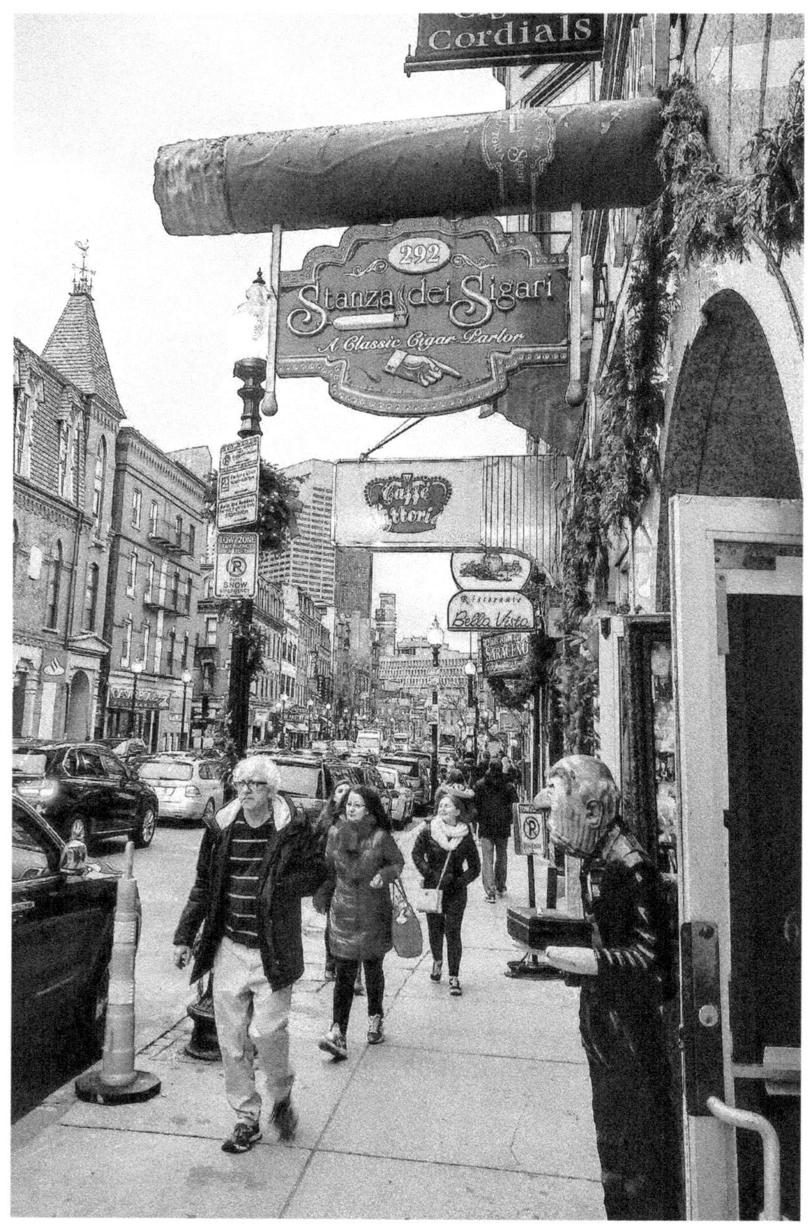
Cordials
292
Stanza dei Sigari
A Classic Cigar Parlor
Caffè Vittoria
Ristorante
Bella Vista
SARACENO
TOW ZONE
SNOW
EMERGENCY

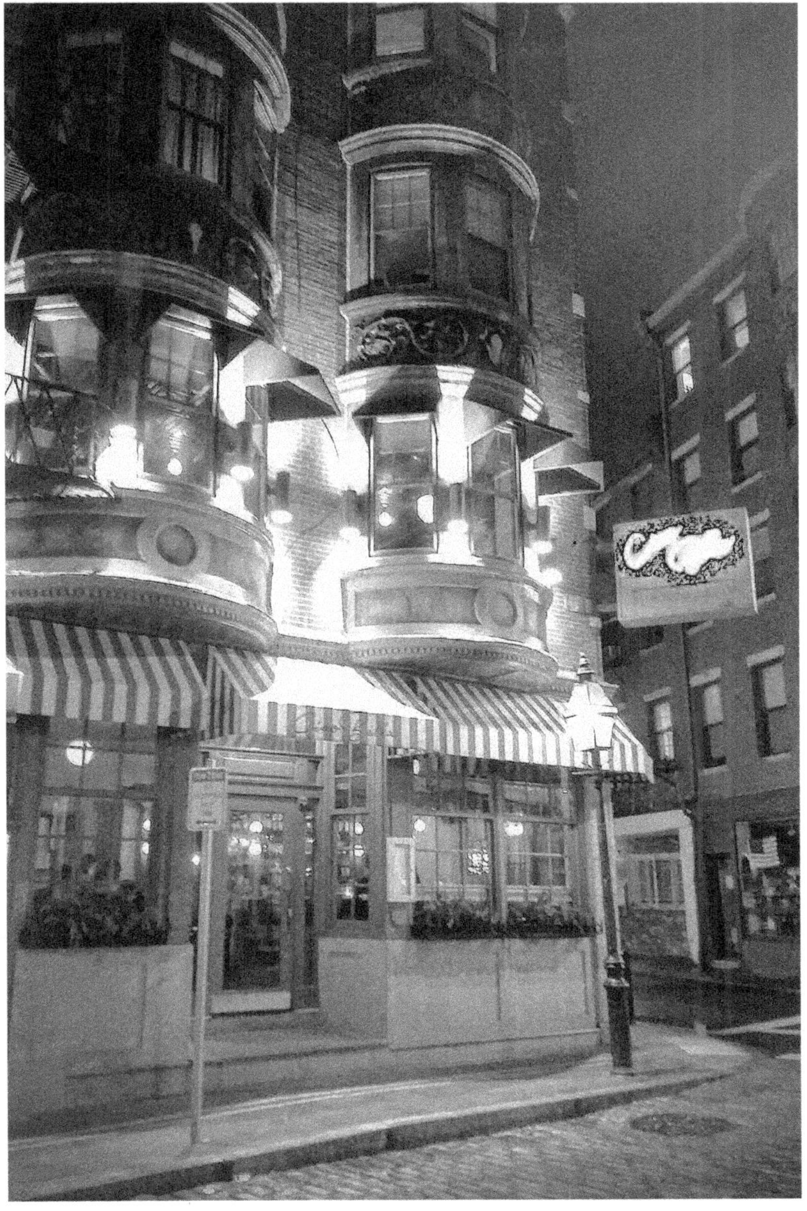

Beacon Hill

When I got into the streets upon this Sunday morning, the air was so clear, the houses were so bright and gay: the signboards were painted in such gaudy colours; the gilded letters were so very golden; the bricks were so very red, the stone was so very white, the blinds and area railings were so very green, the knobs and plates upon the street doors so marvellously bright and twinkling; and all so slight and unsubstantial in appearance — that every thoroughfare in the city looked exactly like a scene in a pantomime.

Charles Dickens (1812 – 1870)
English novelist, journalist and social critic

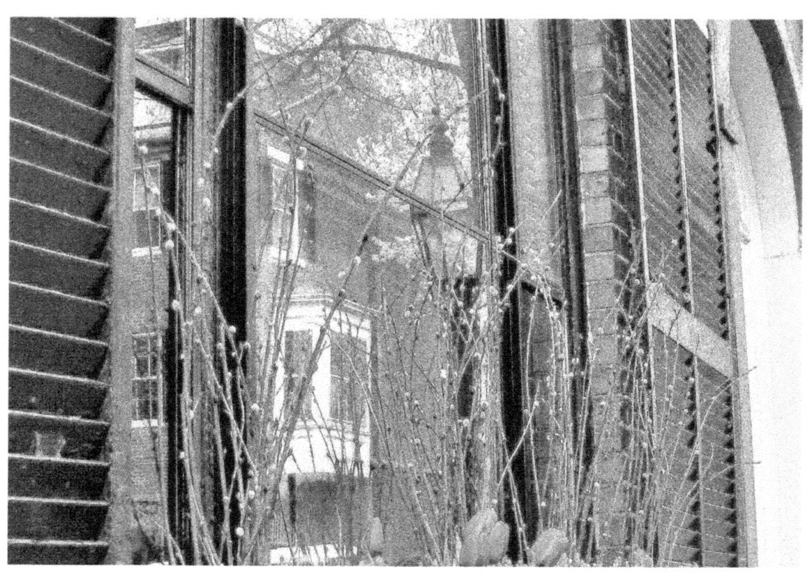

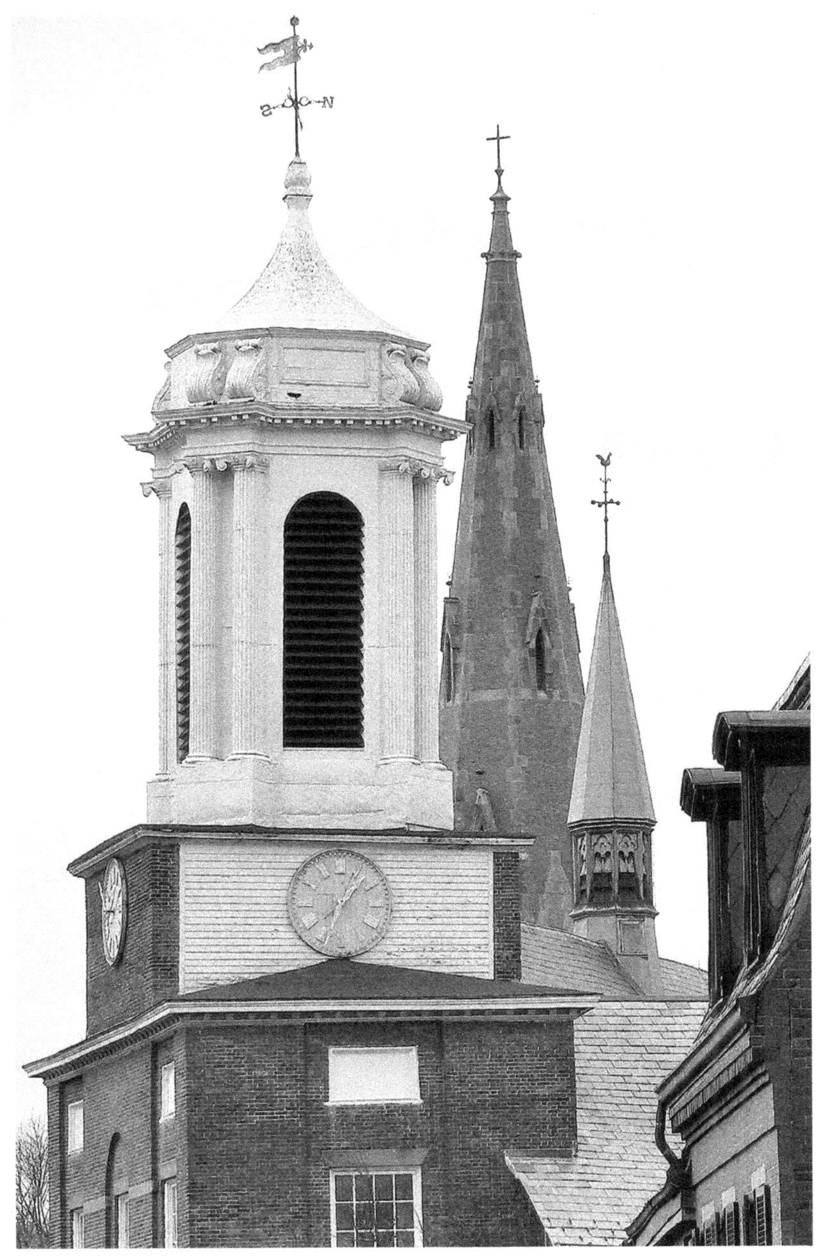

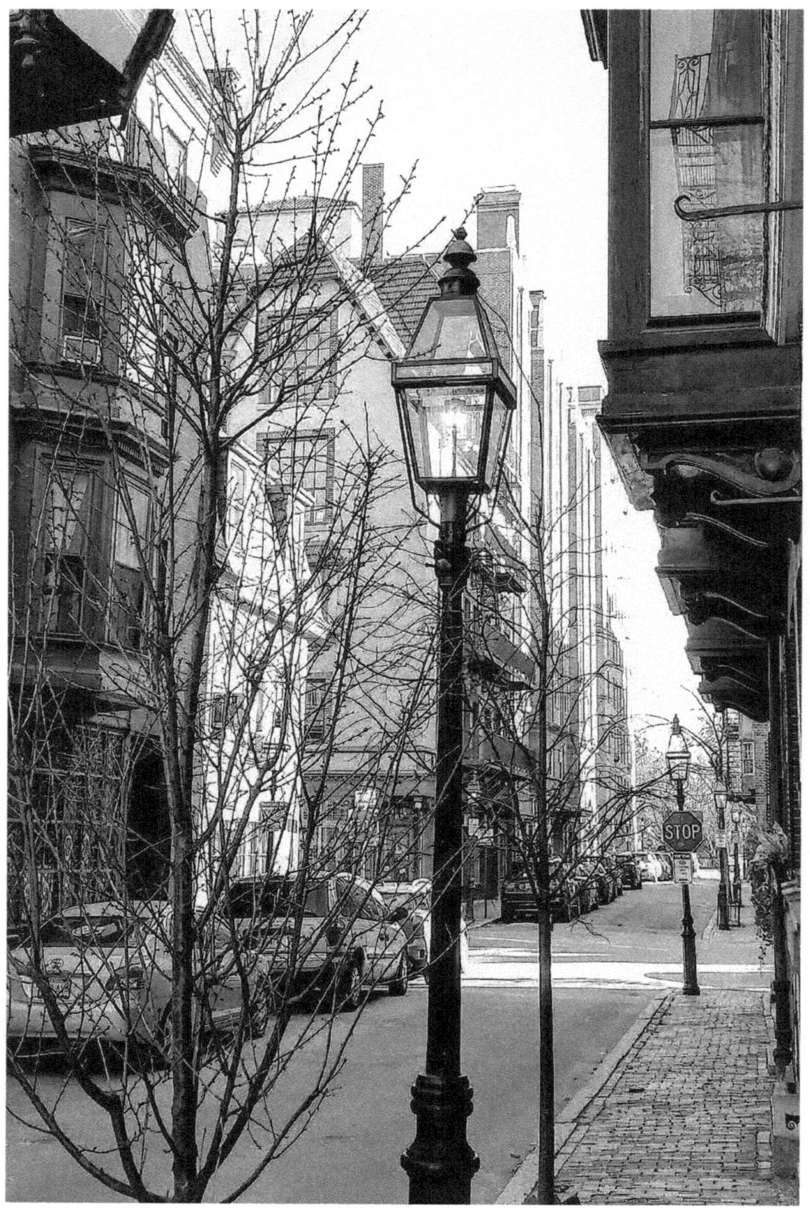

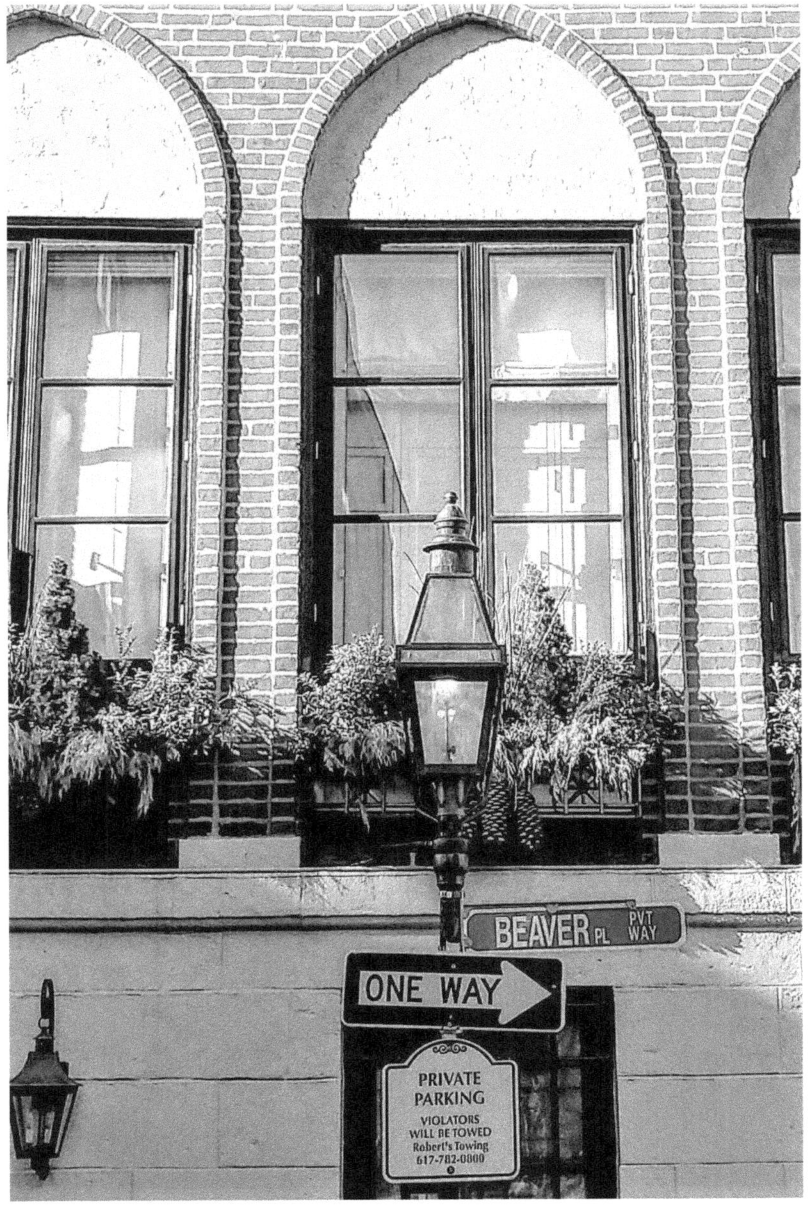
BEAVER PL PVT WAY
ONE WAY
PRIVATE
PARKING
VIOLATORS
WILL BE TOWED
Robert's Towing
617-782-0000

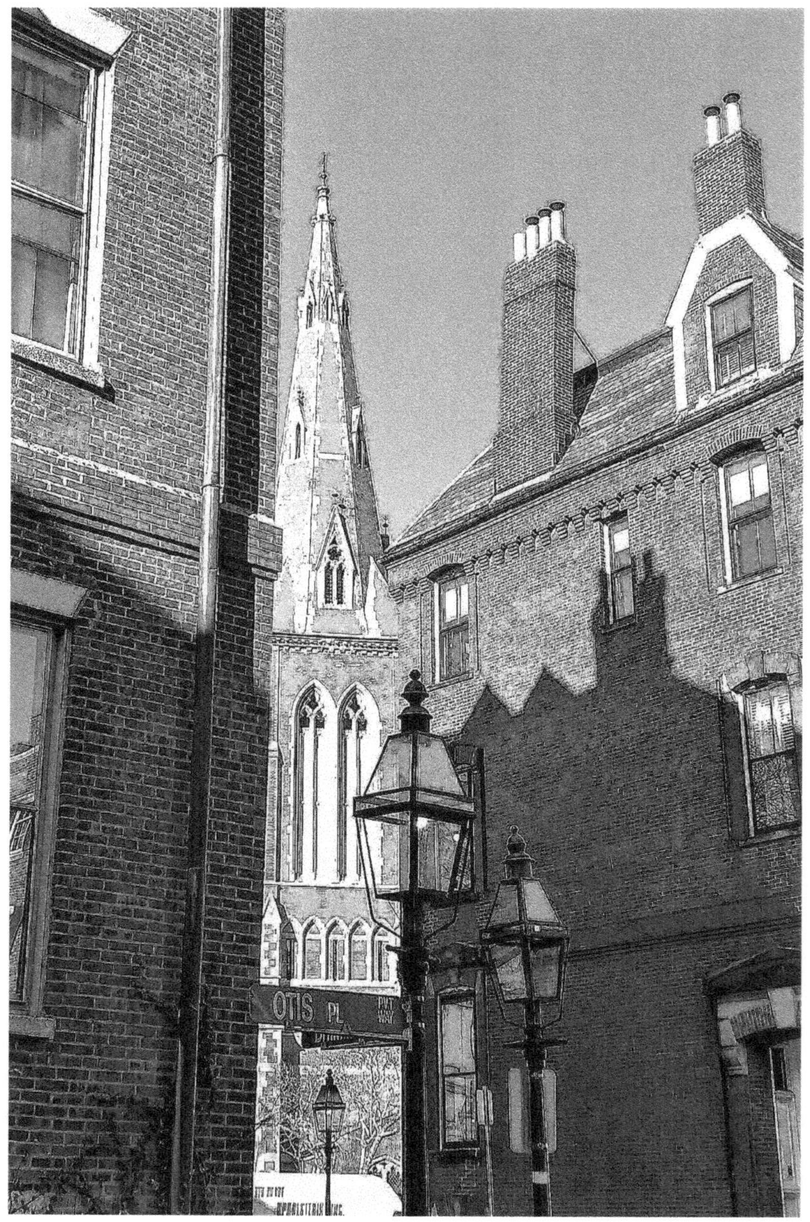
OTIS PL
PVT WAY

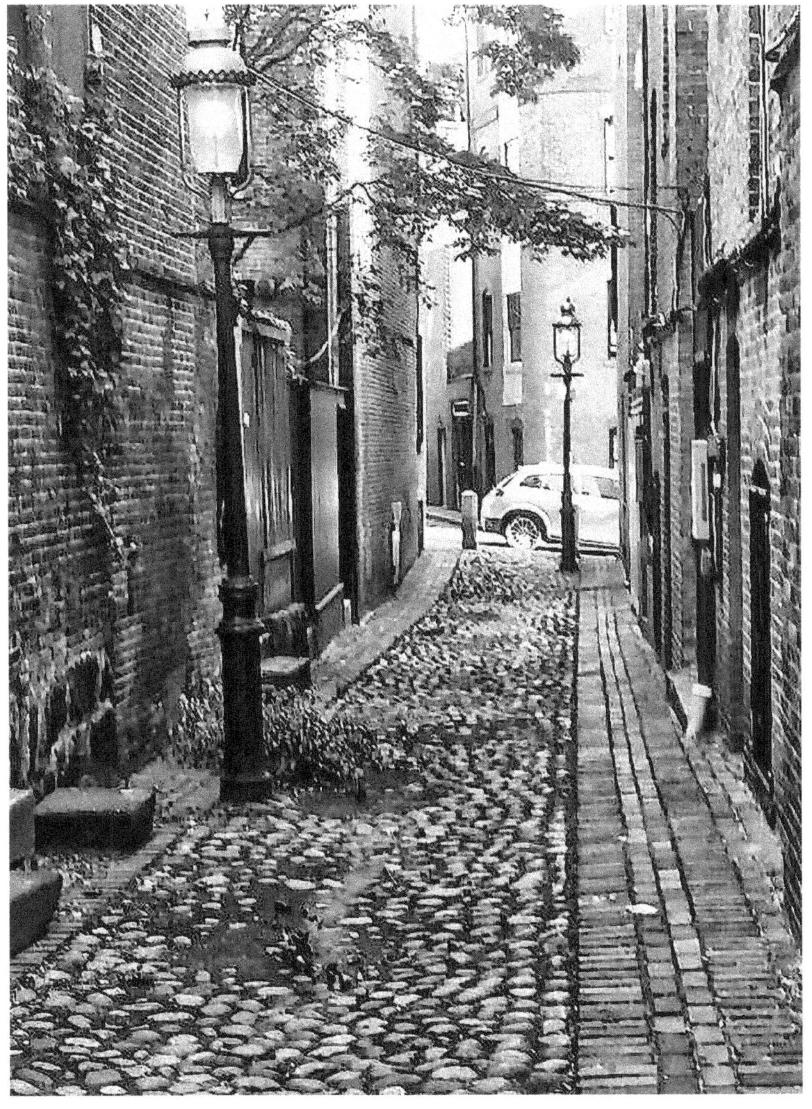

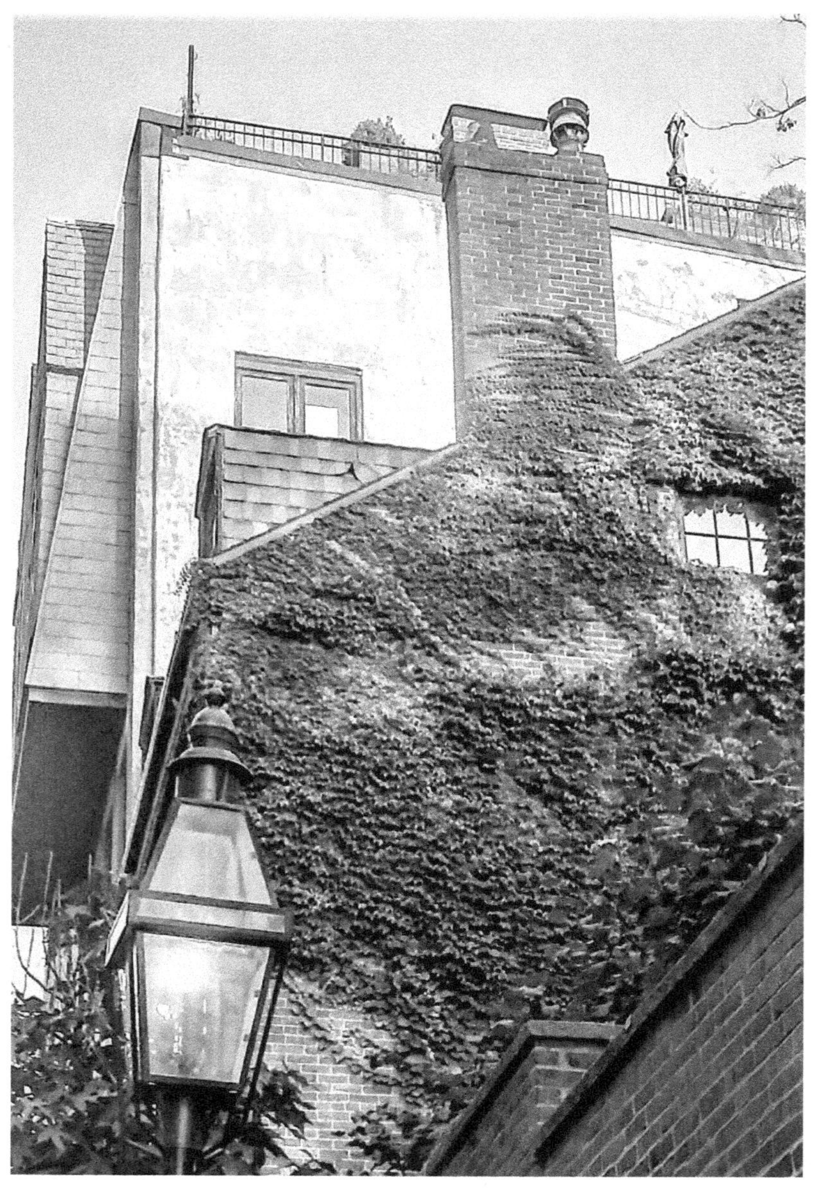

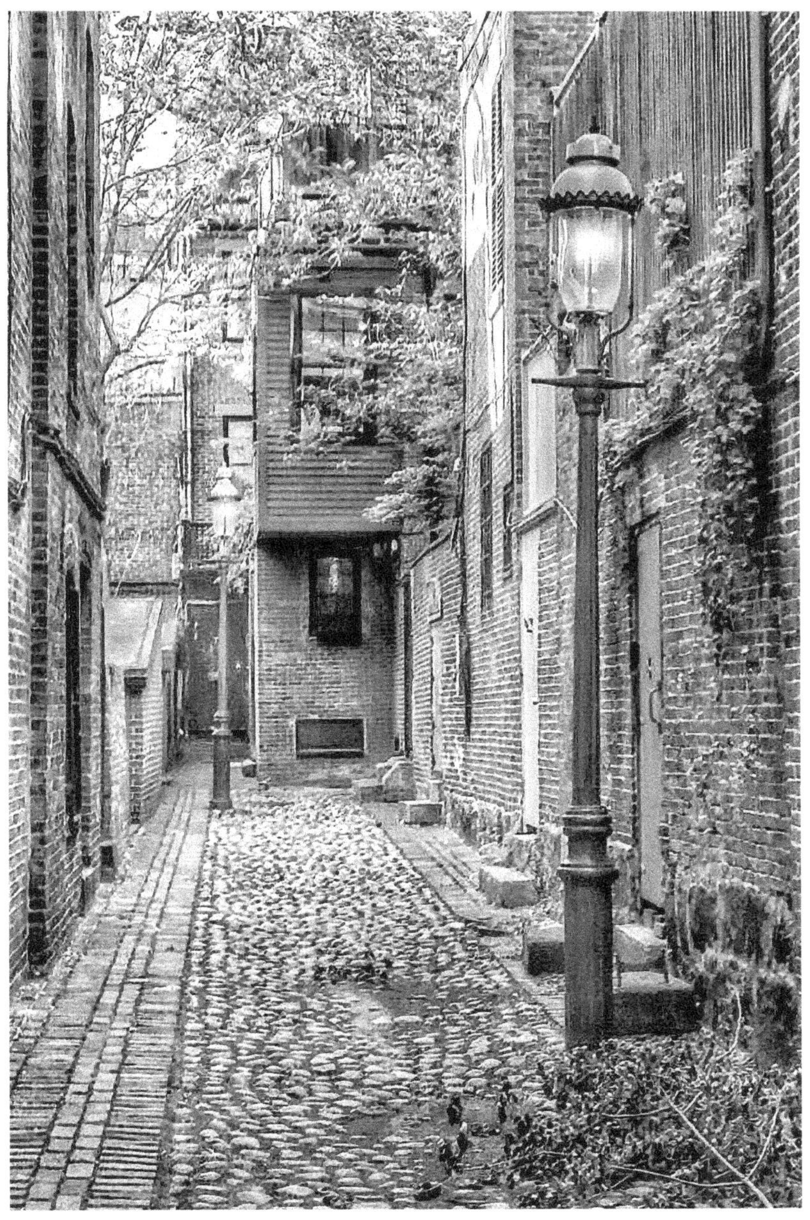

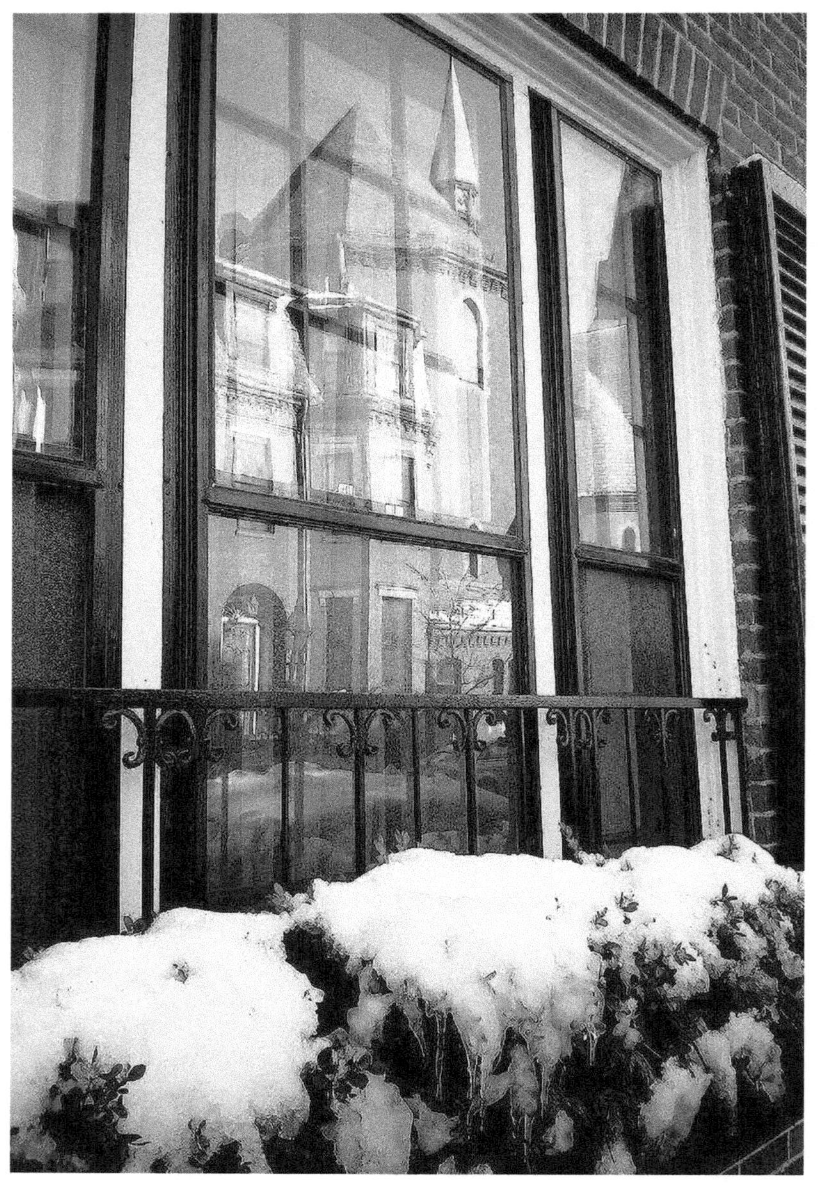

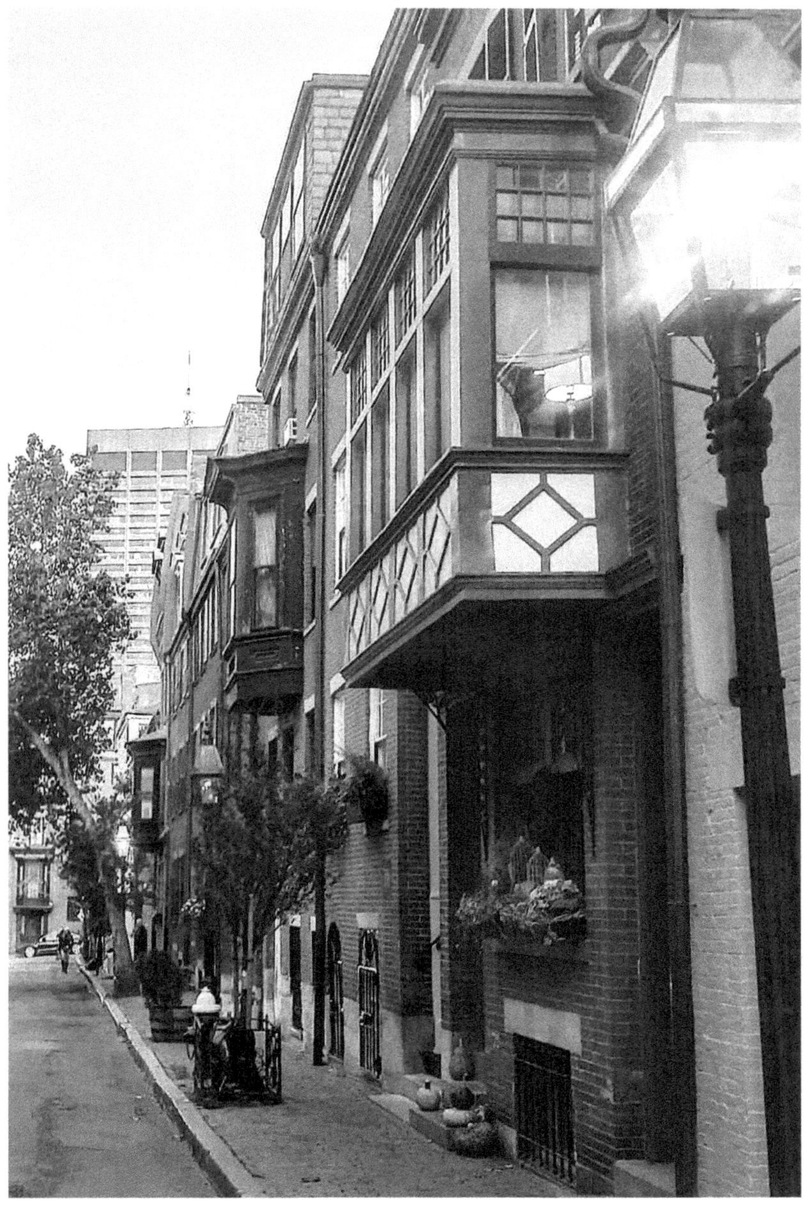

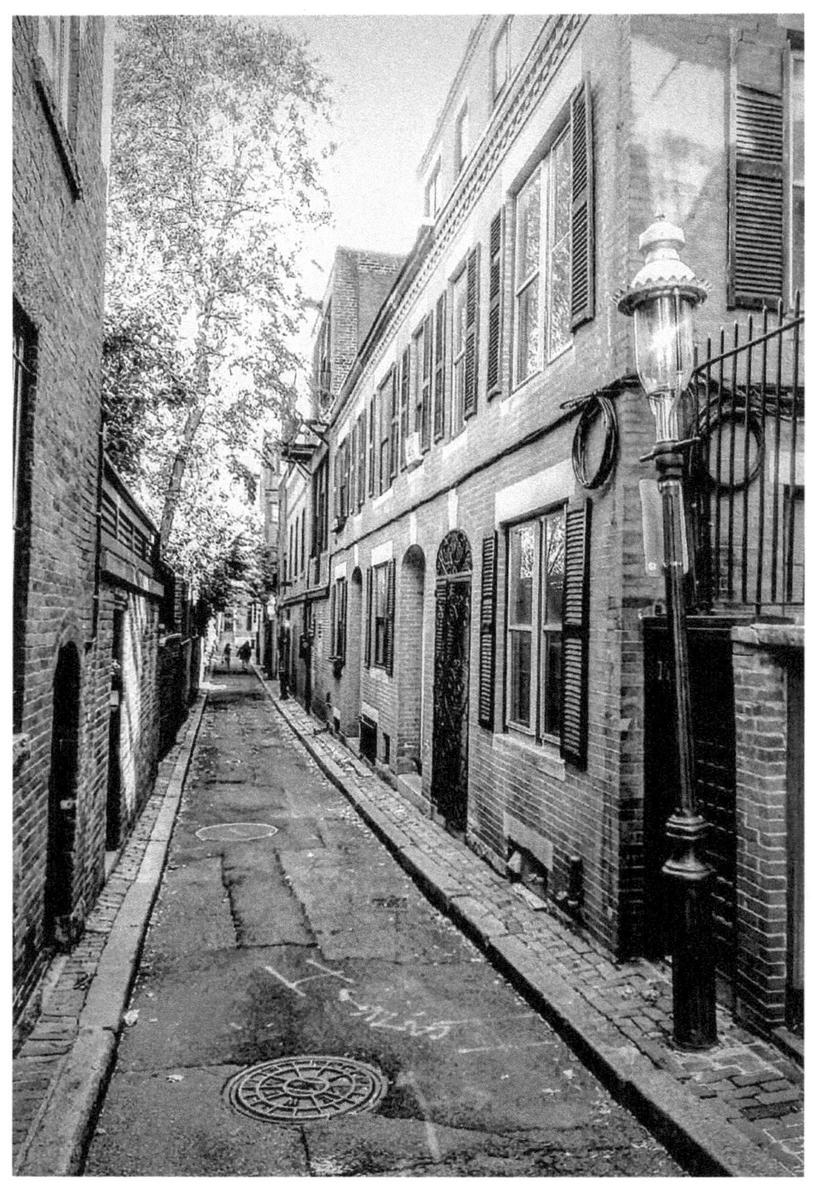

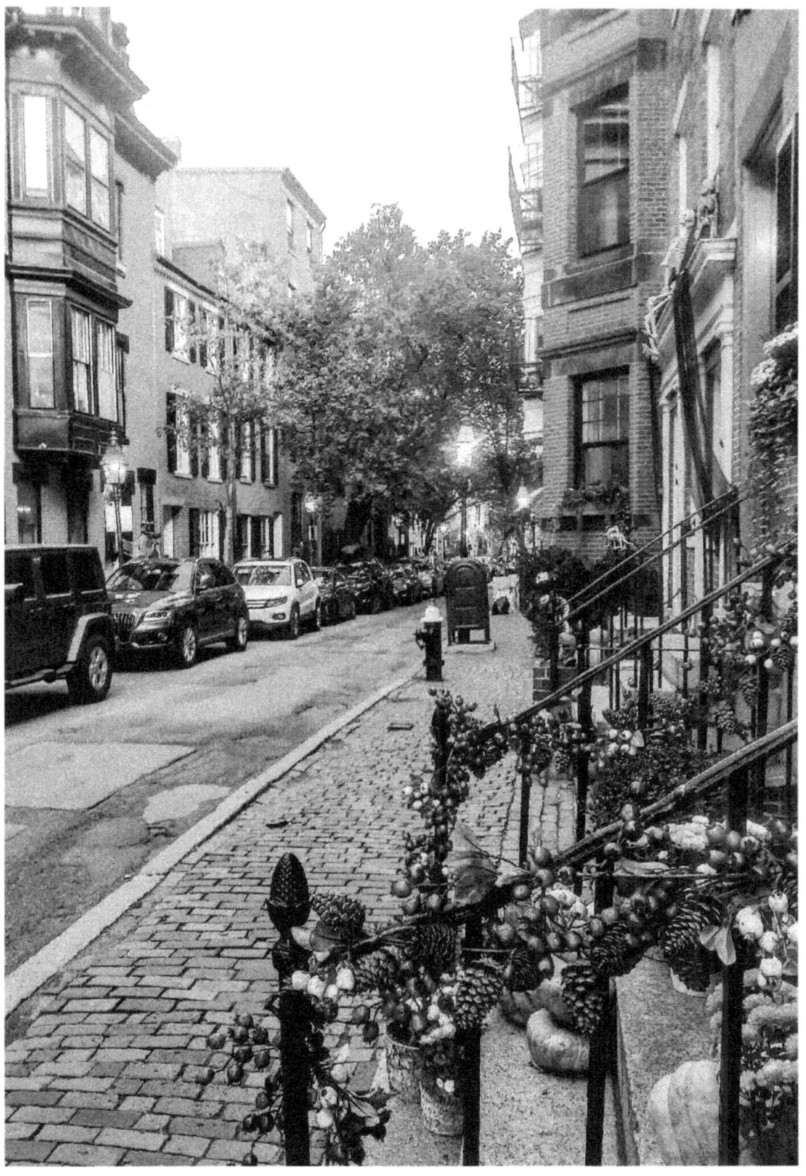

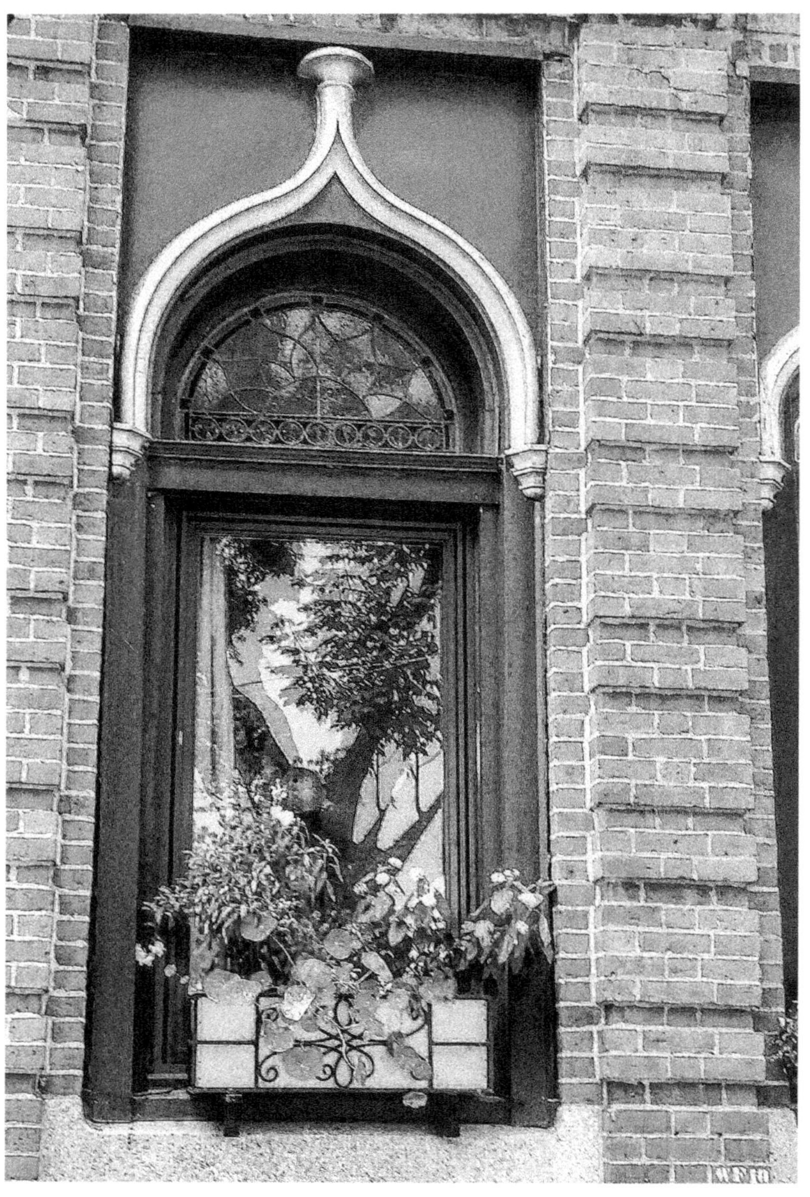

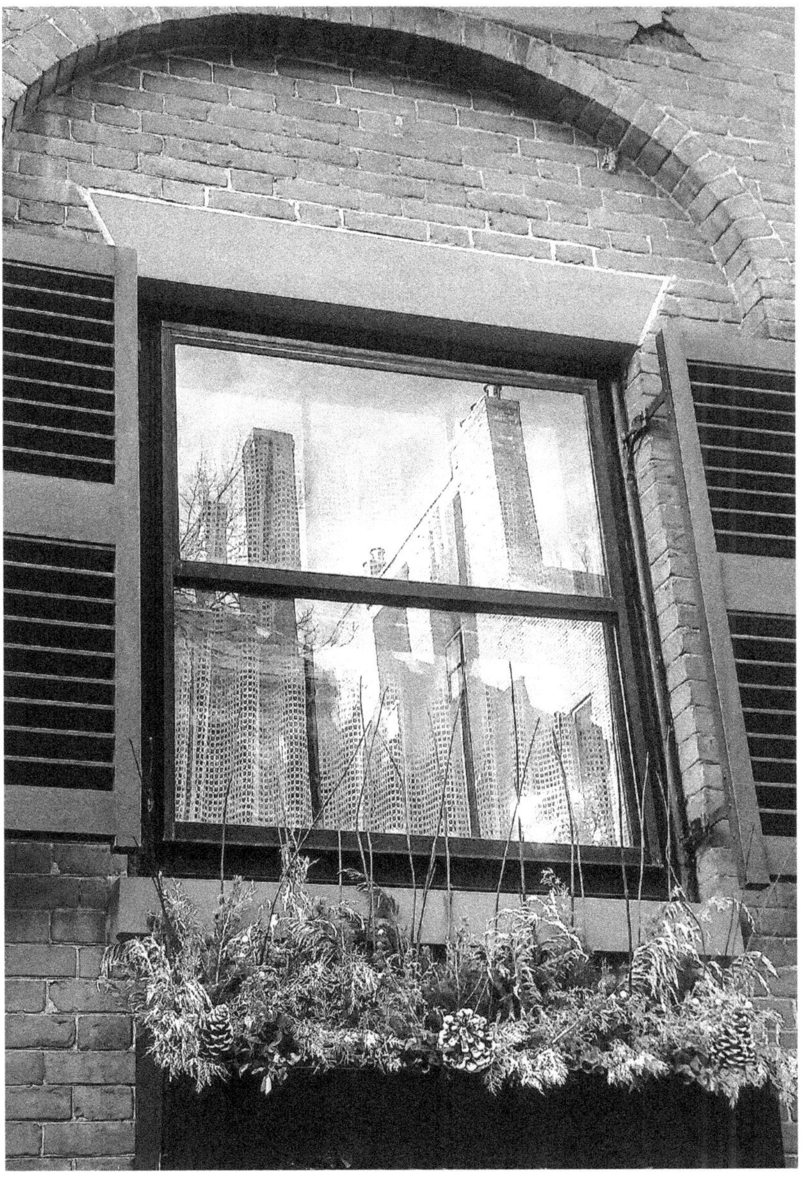

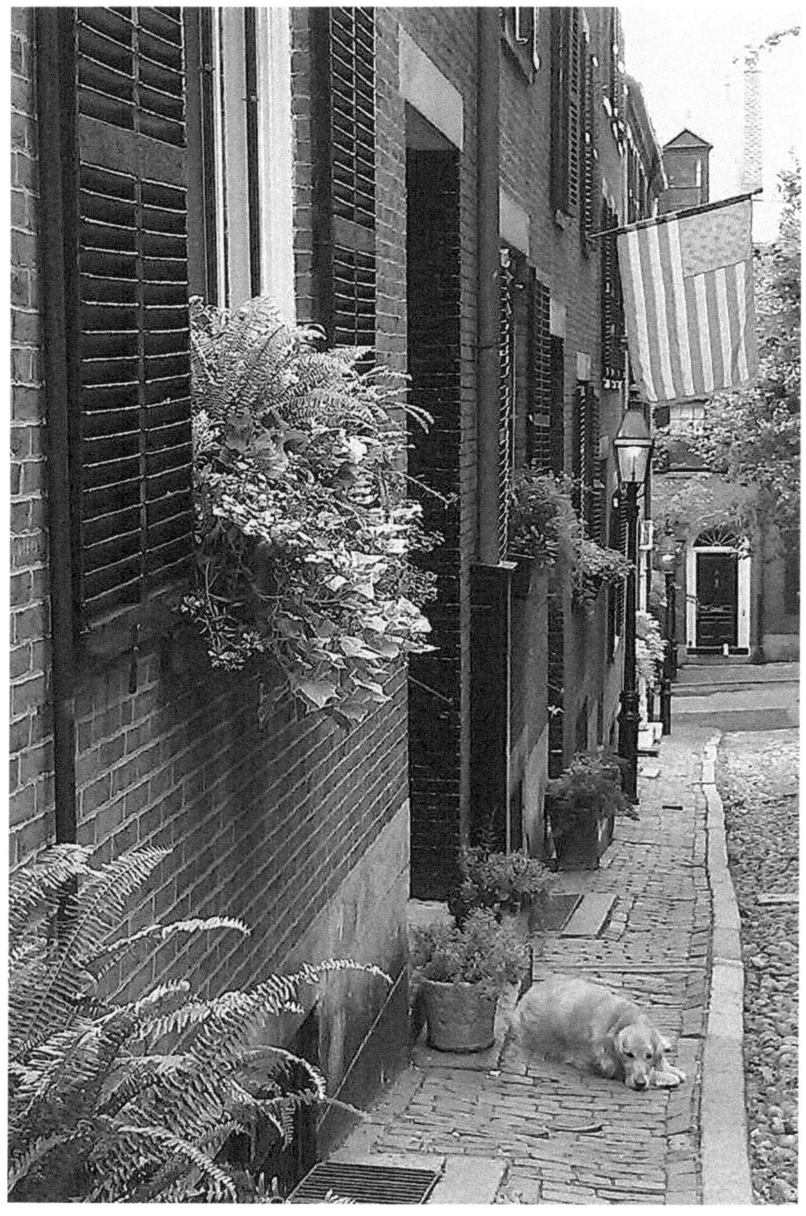

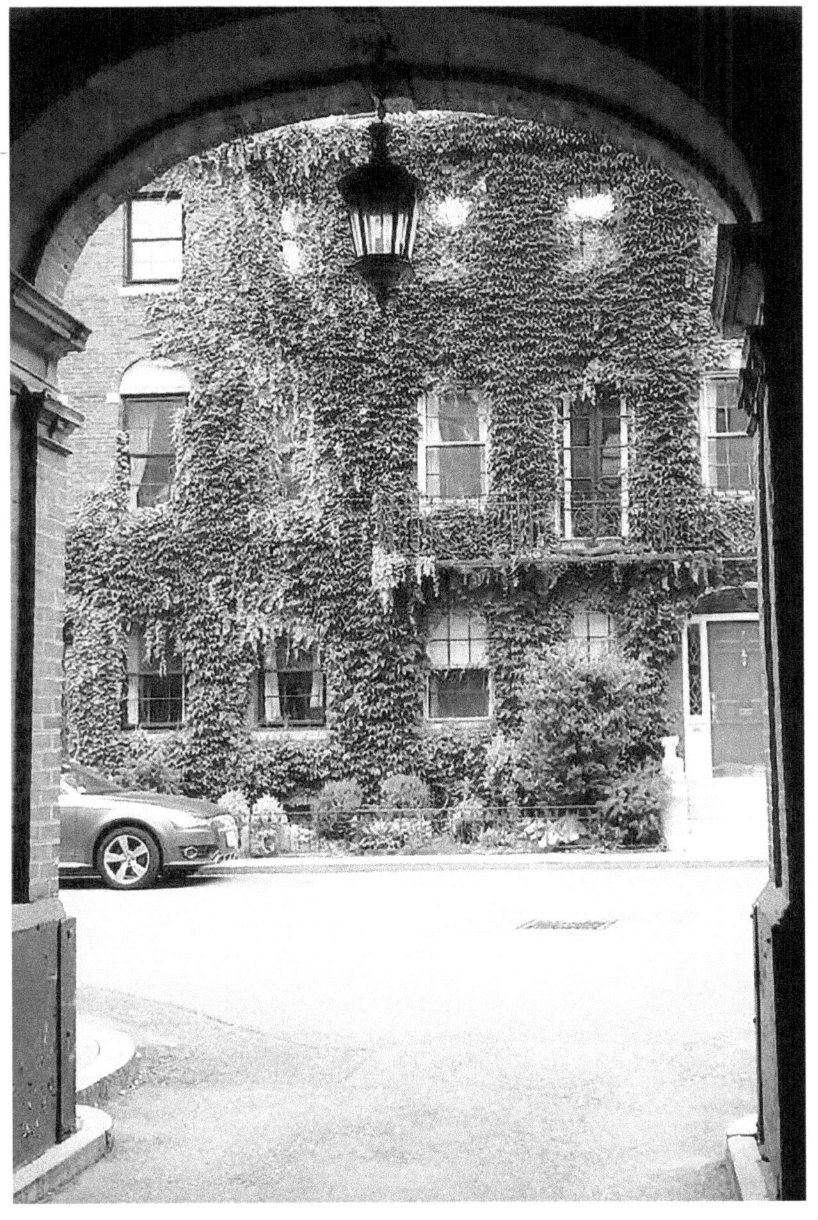

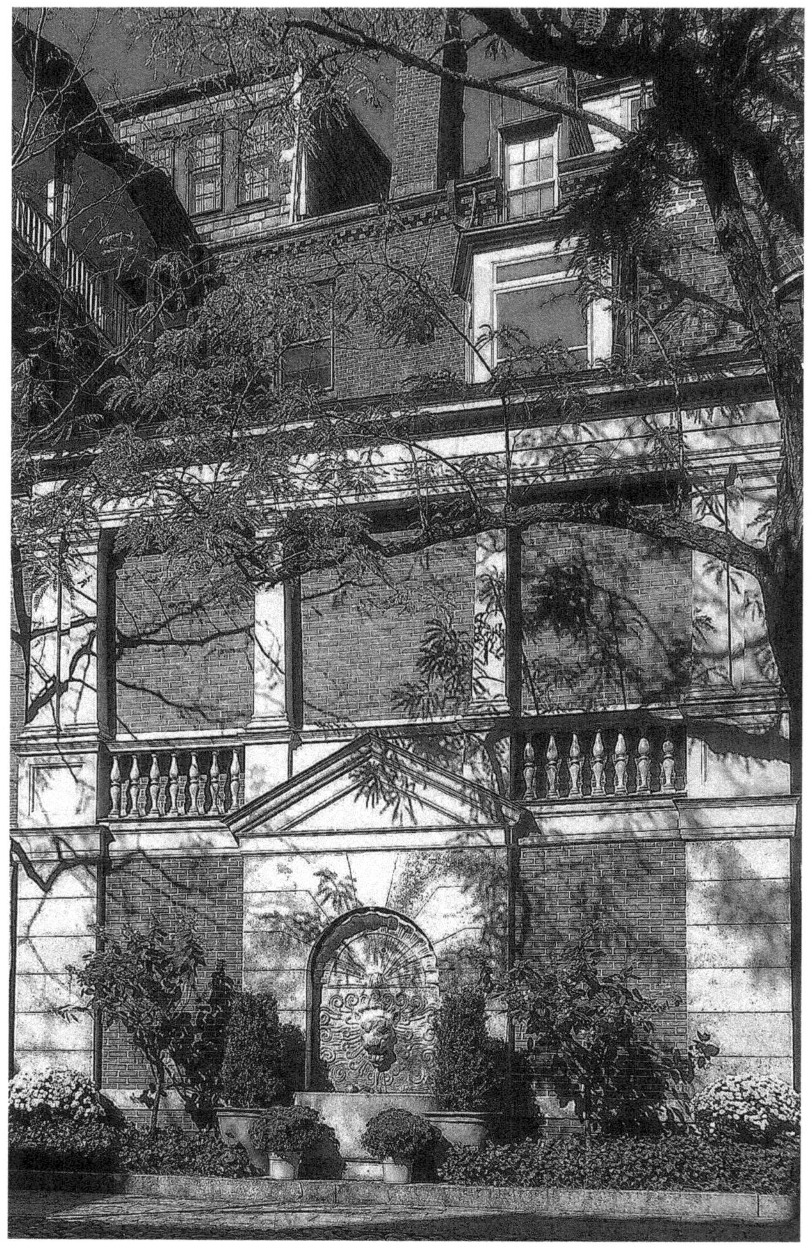

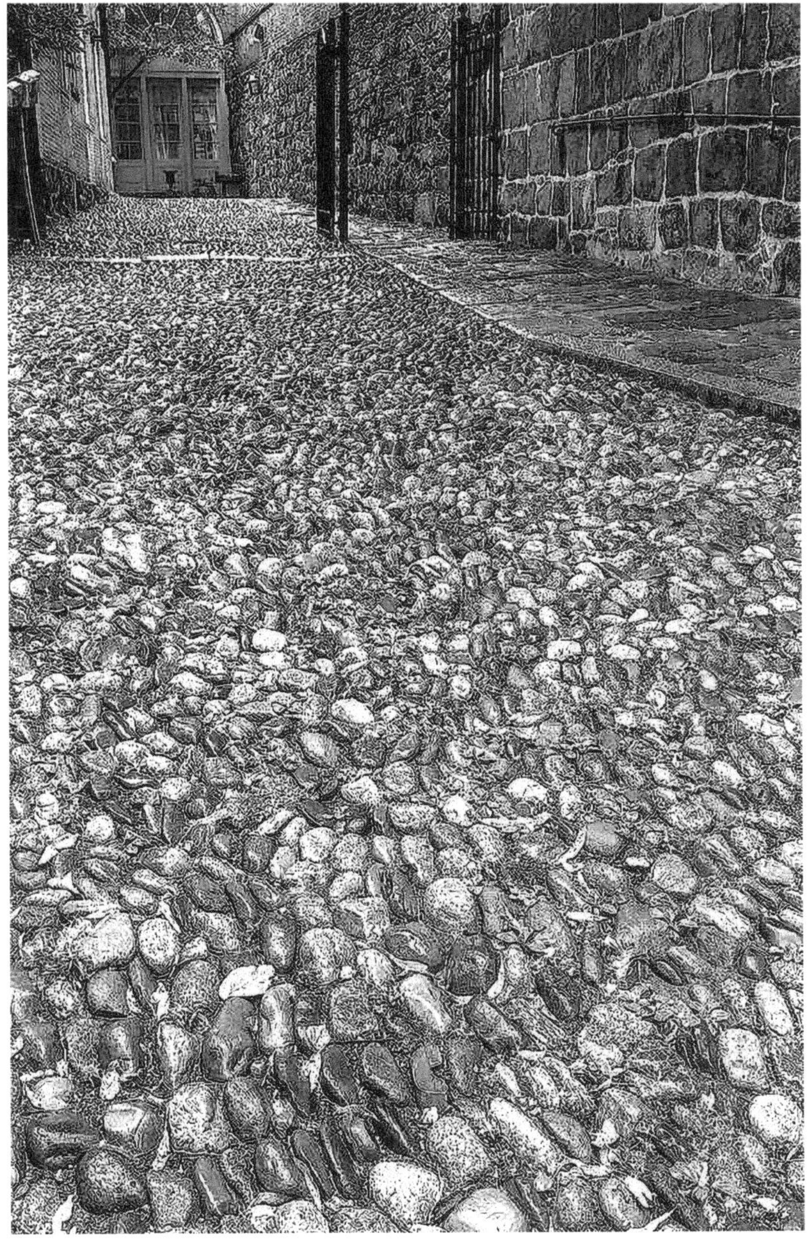

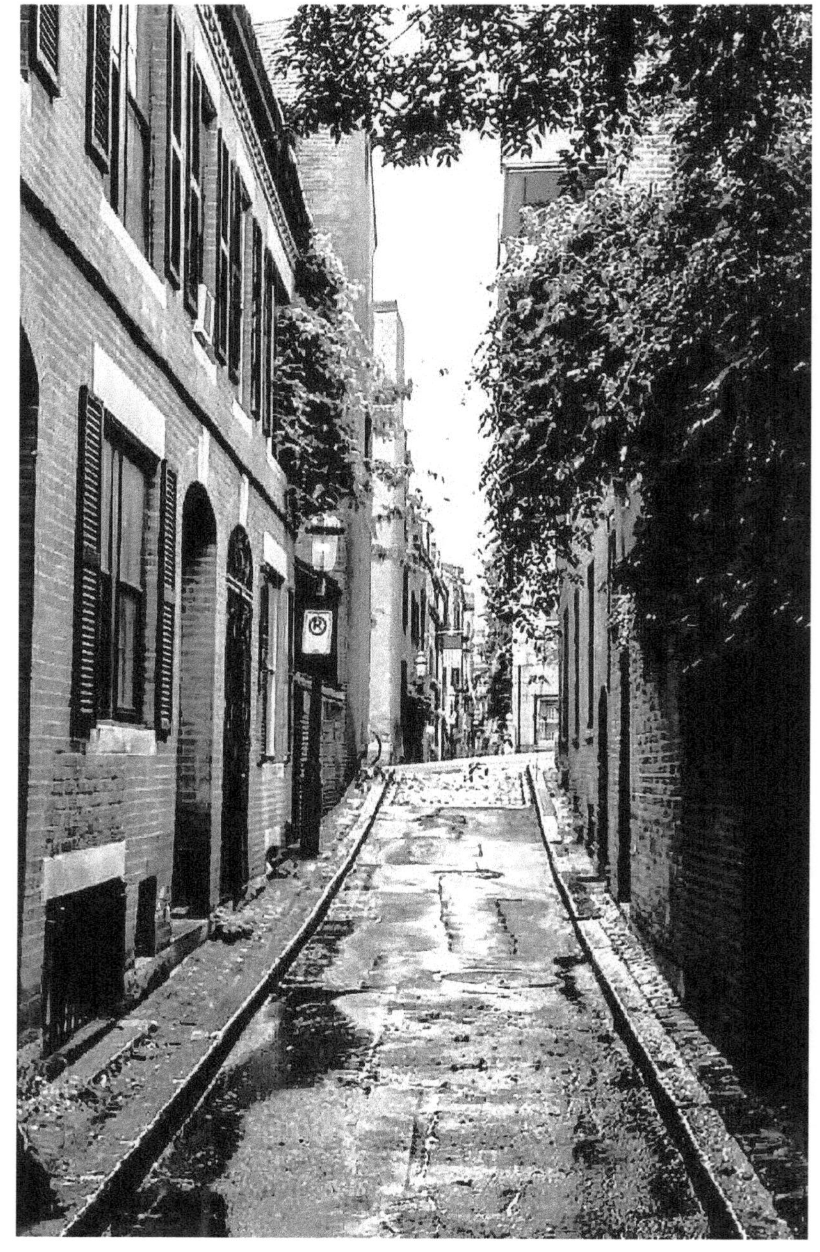

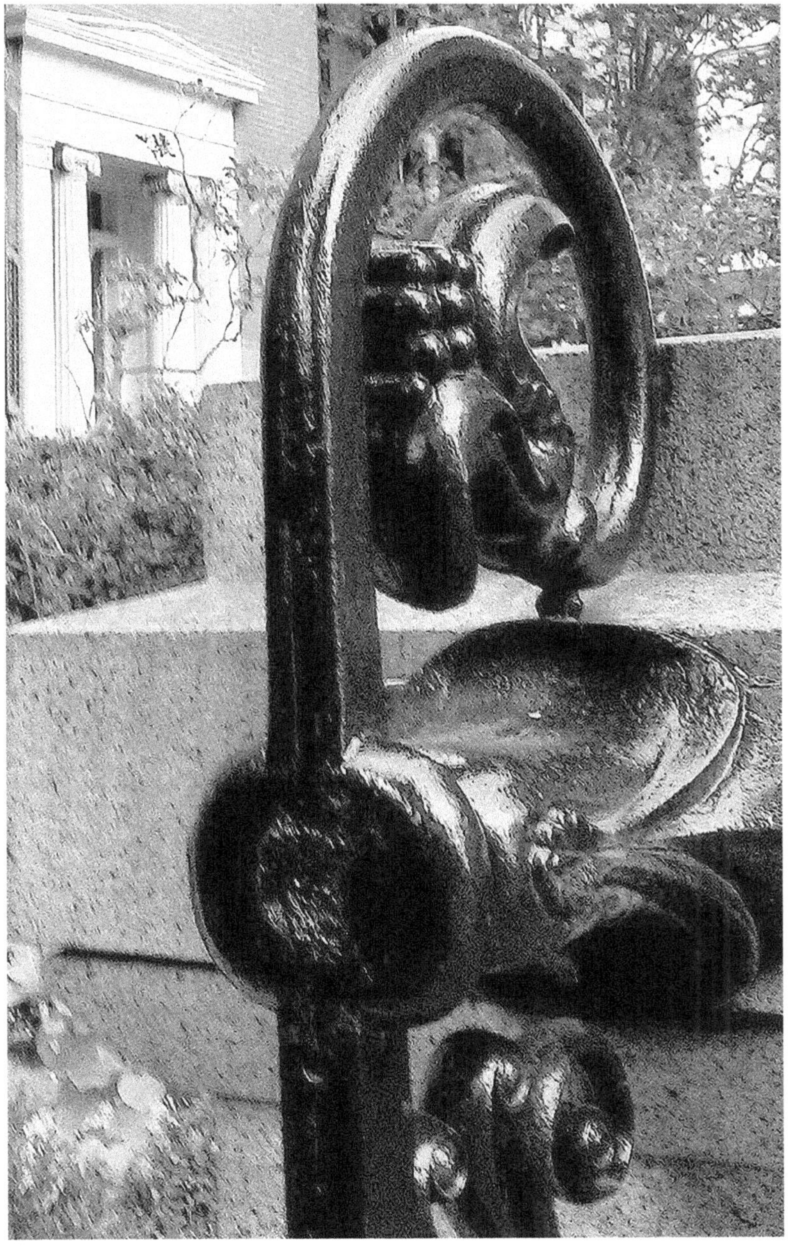

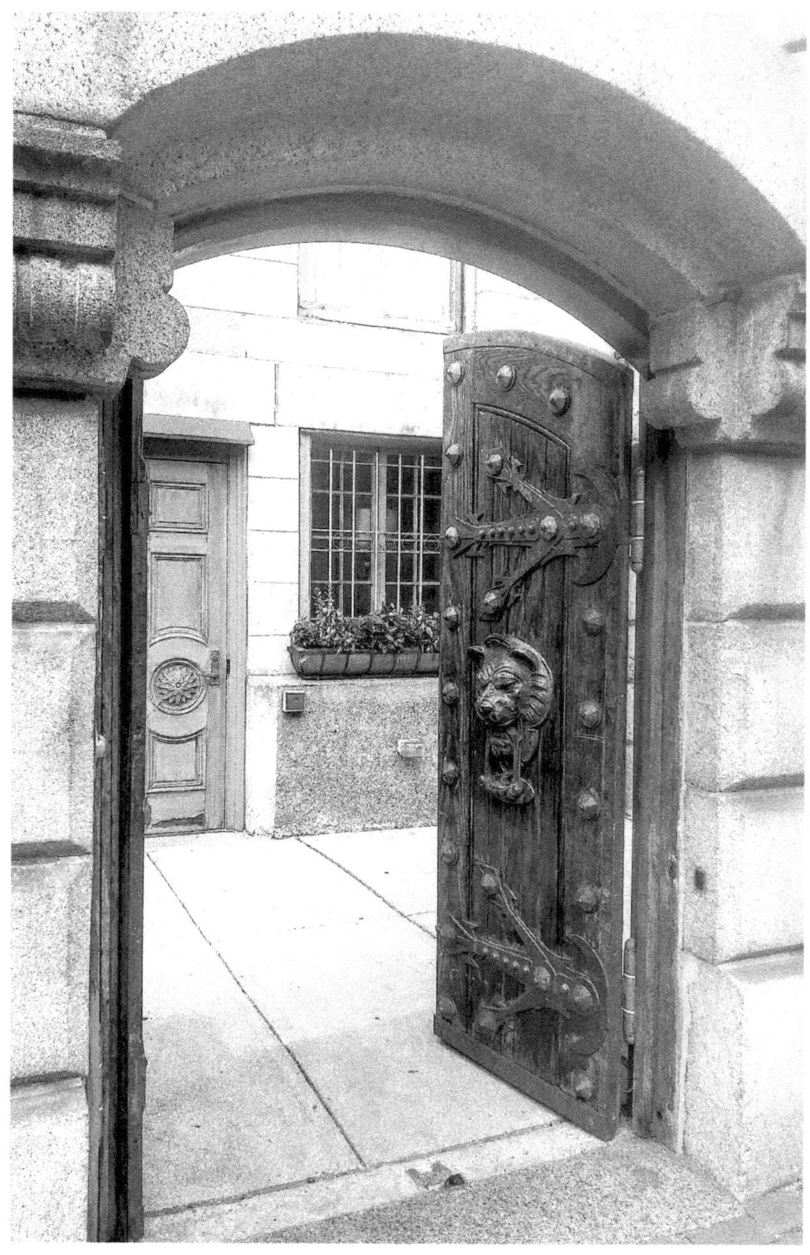

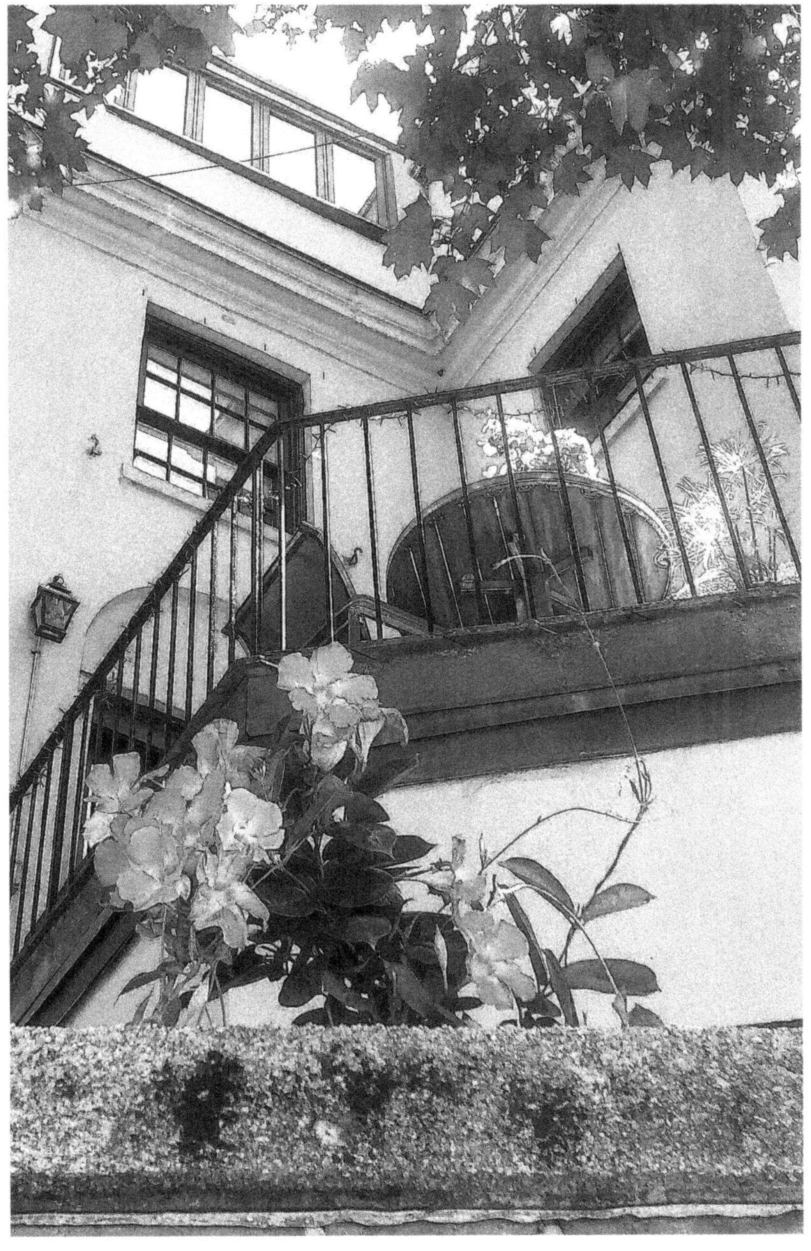

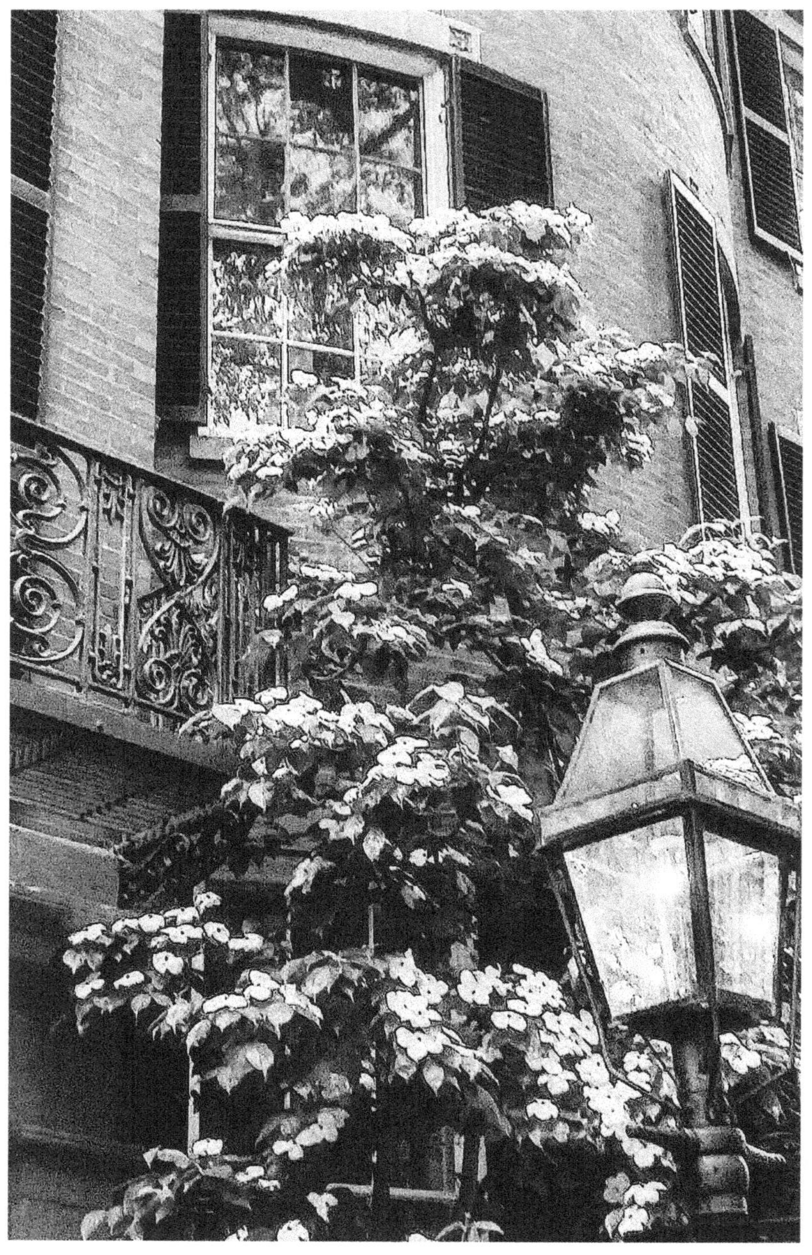

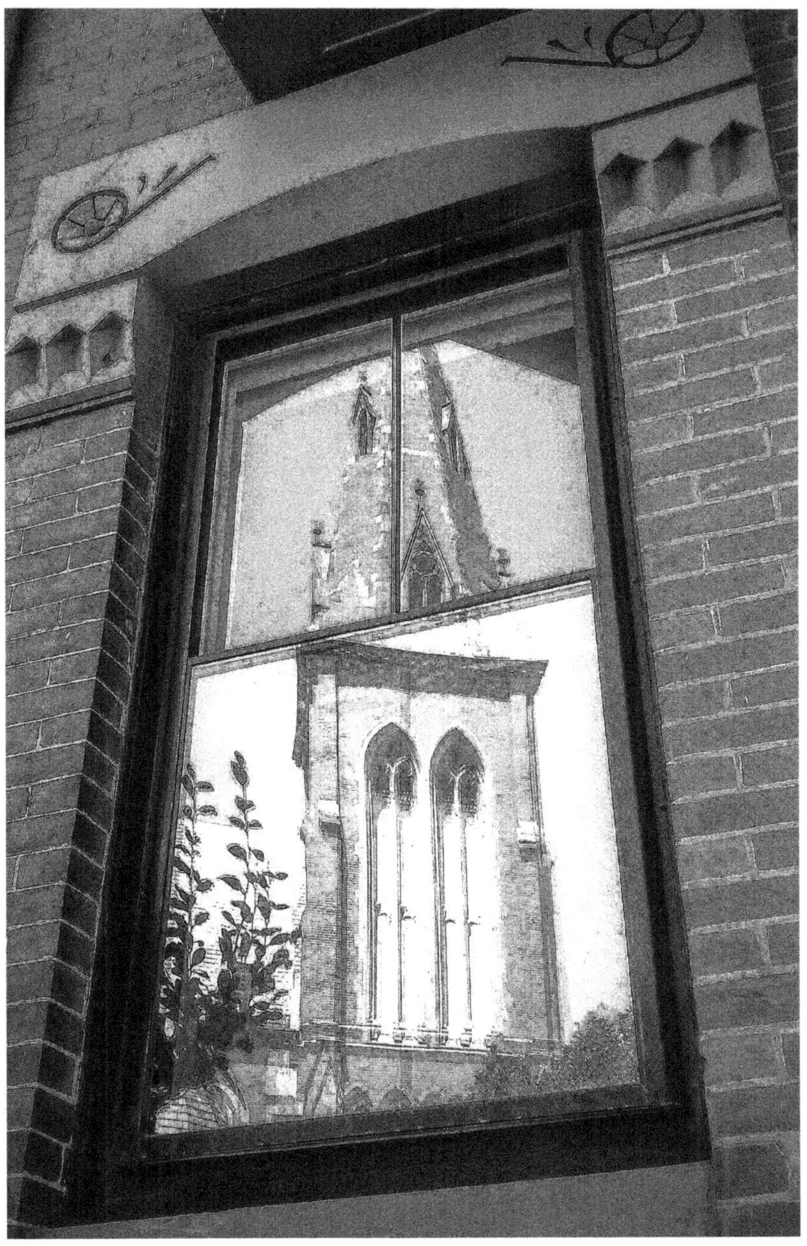

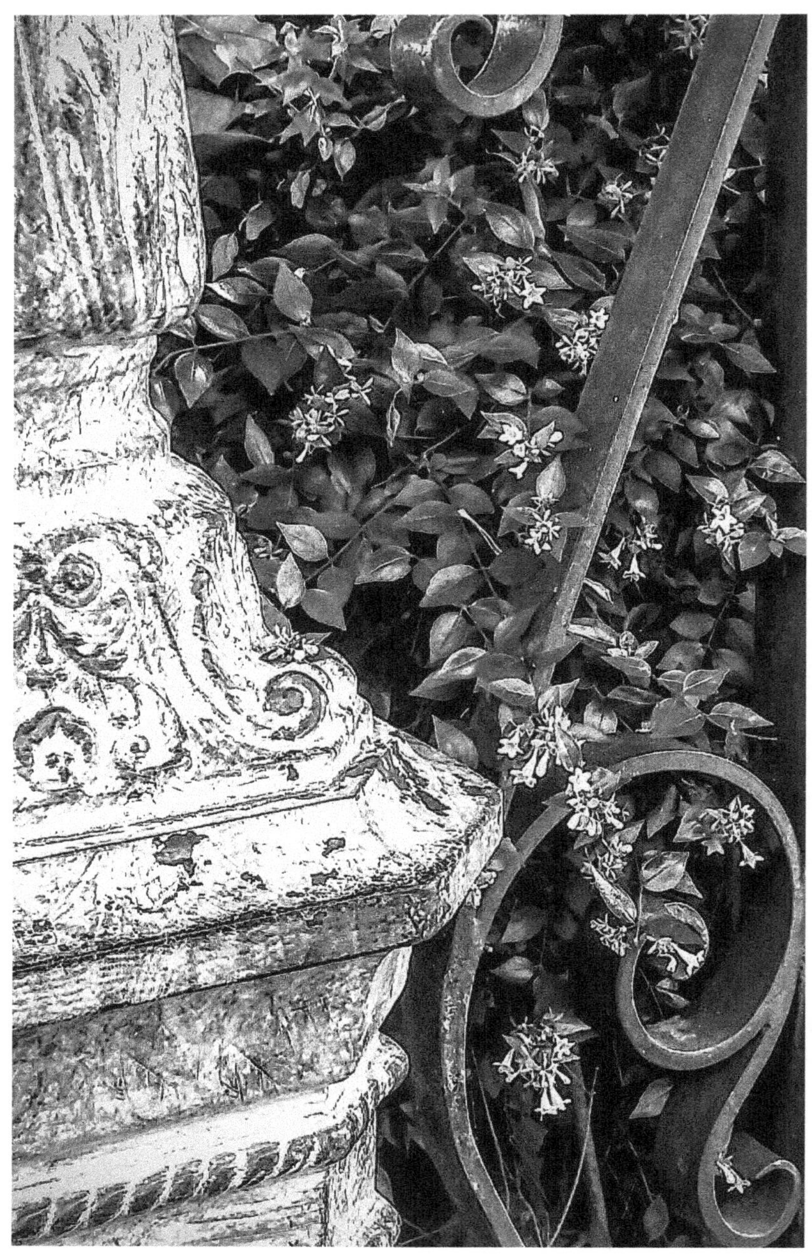

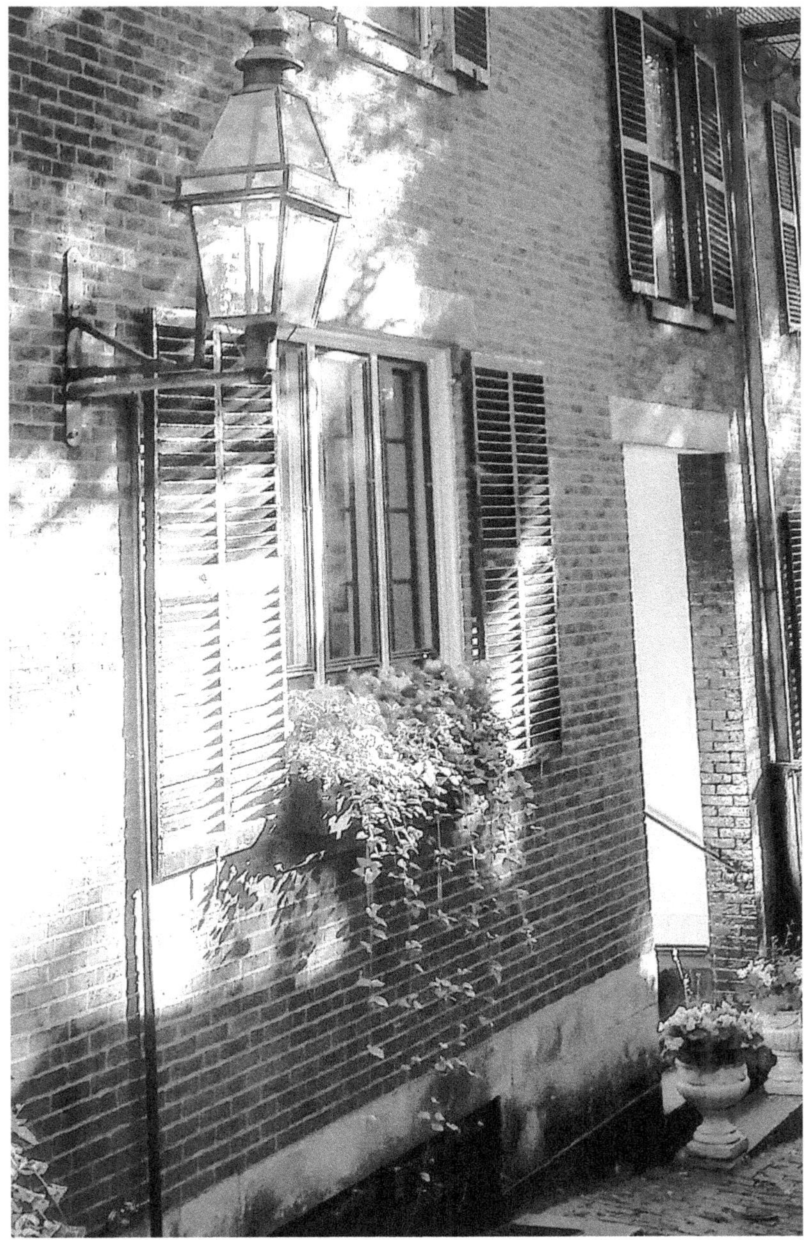

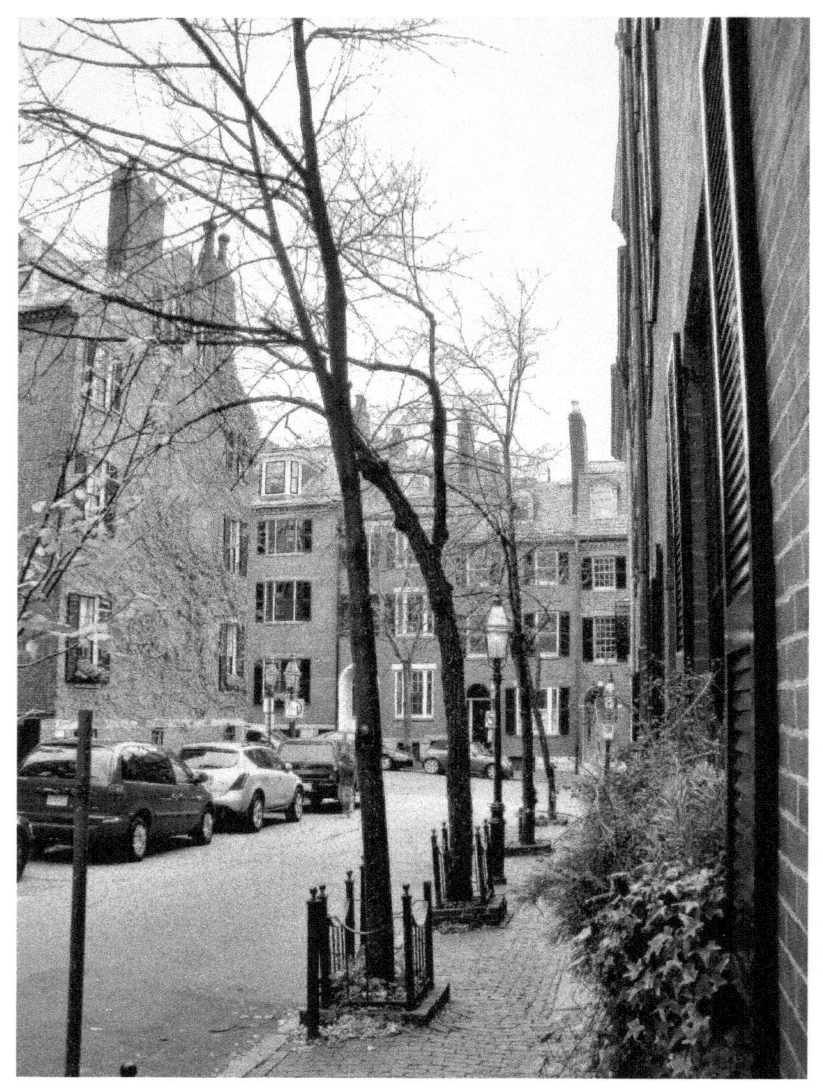

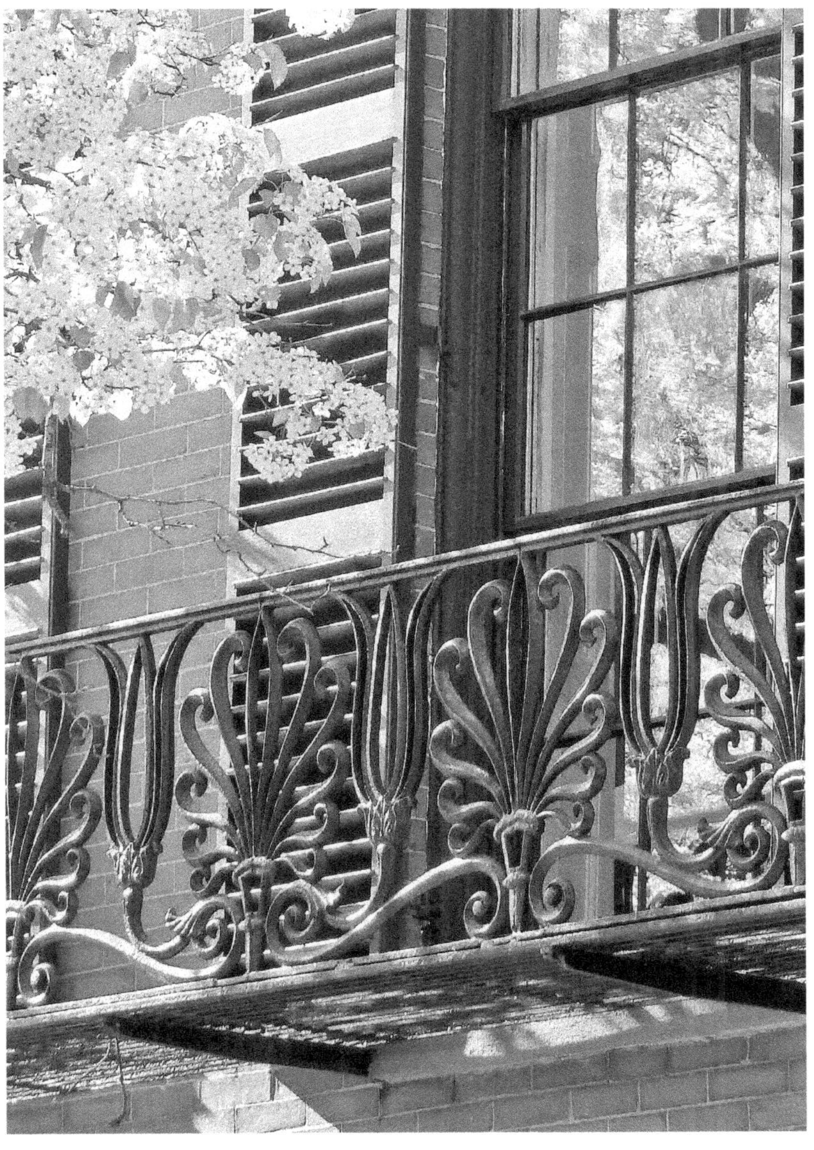

Back Bay

A solid man of Boston; A comfortable man with dividends, And the first salmon and the first green peas.

Henry Wadsworth Longfellow (1807 – 1882)
poet and educator

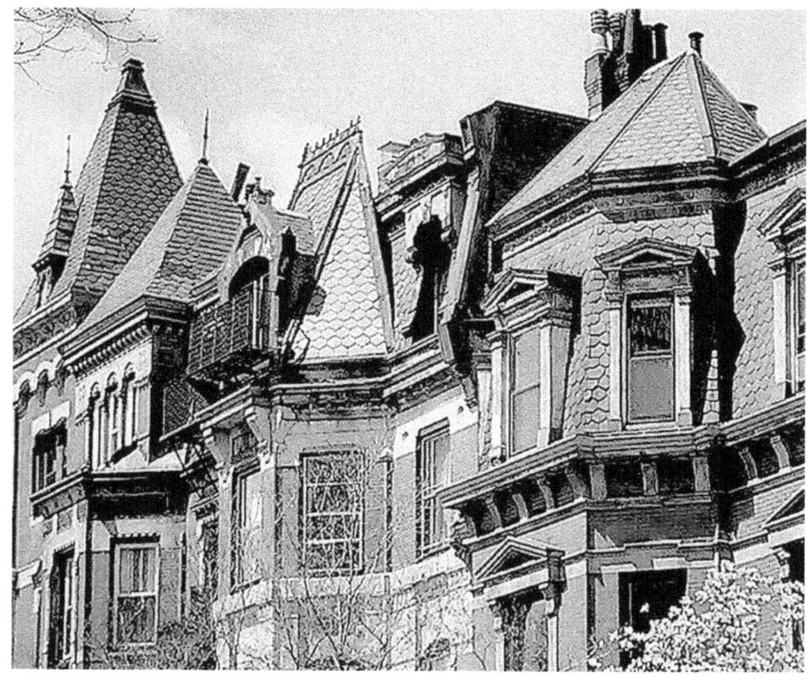

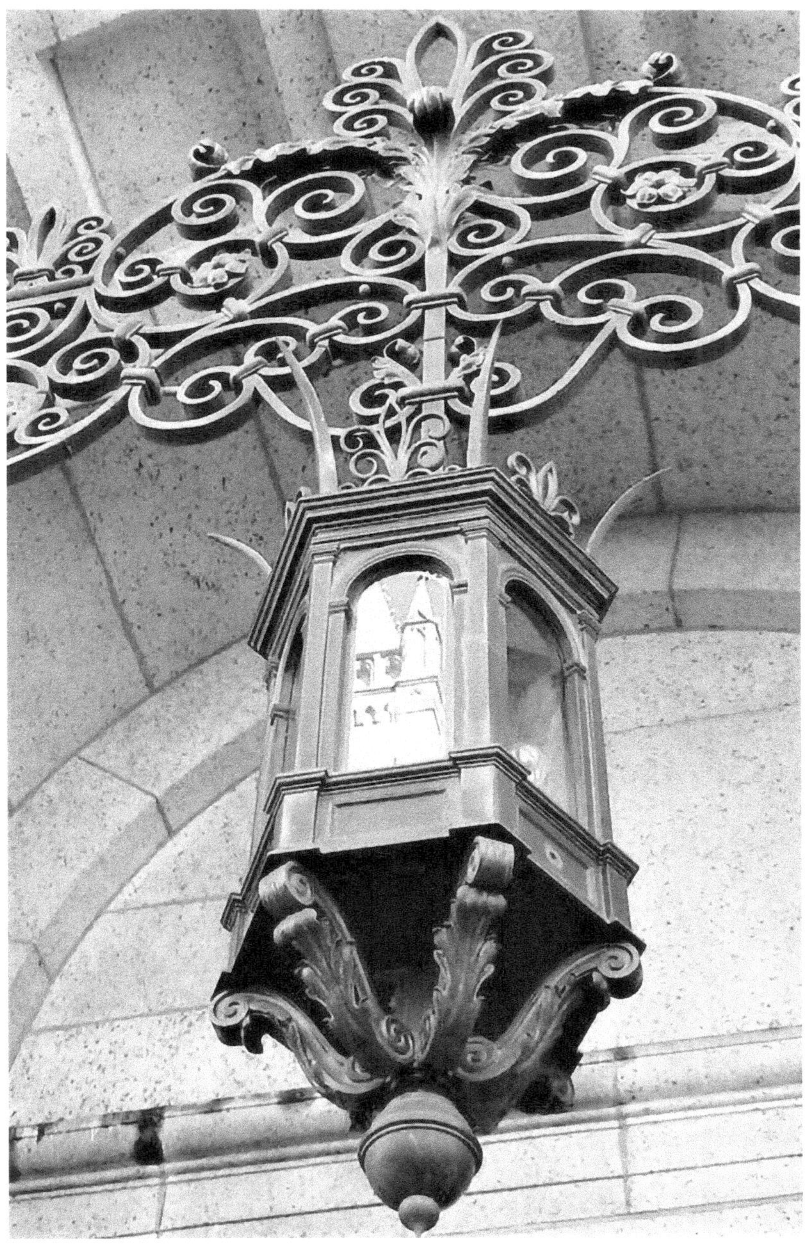

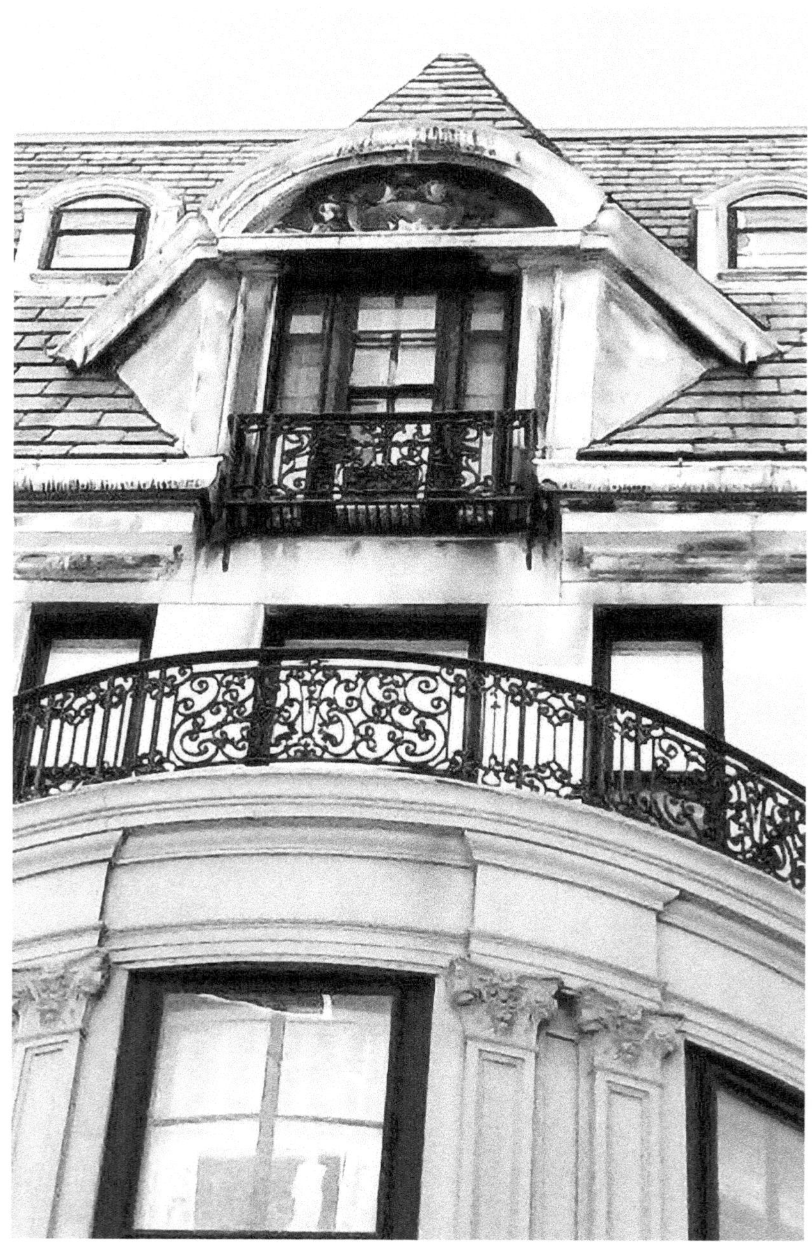

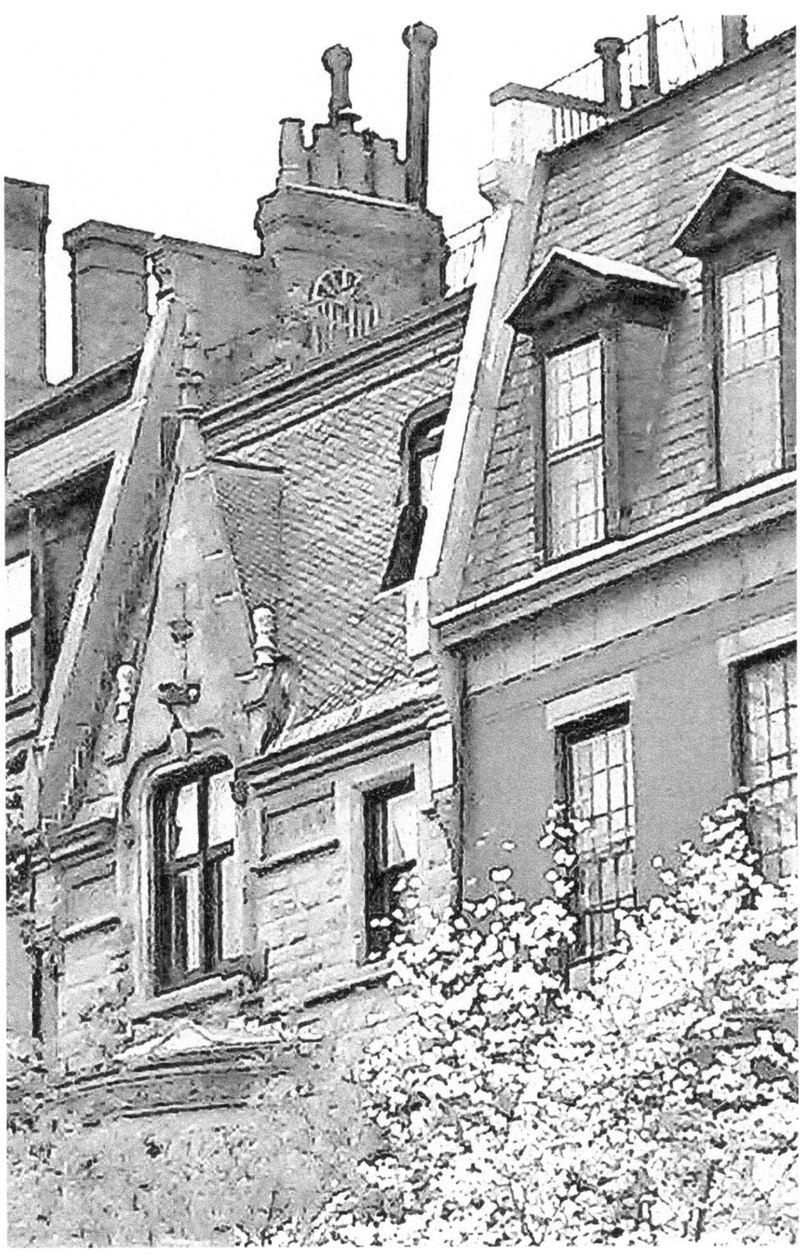

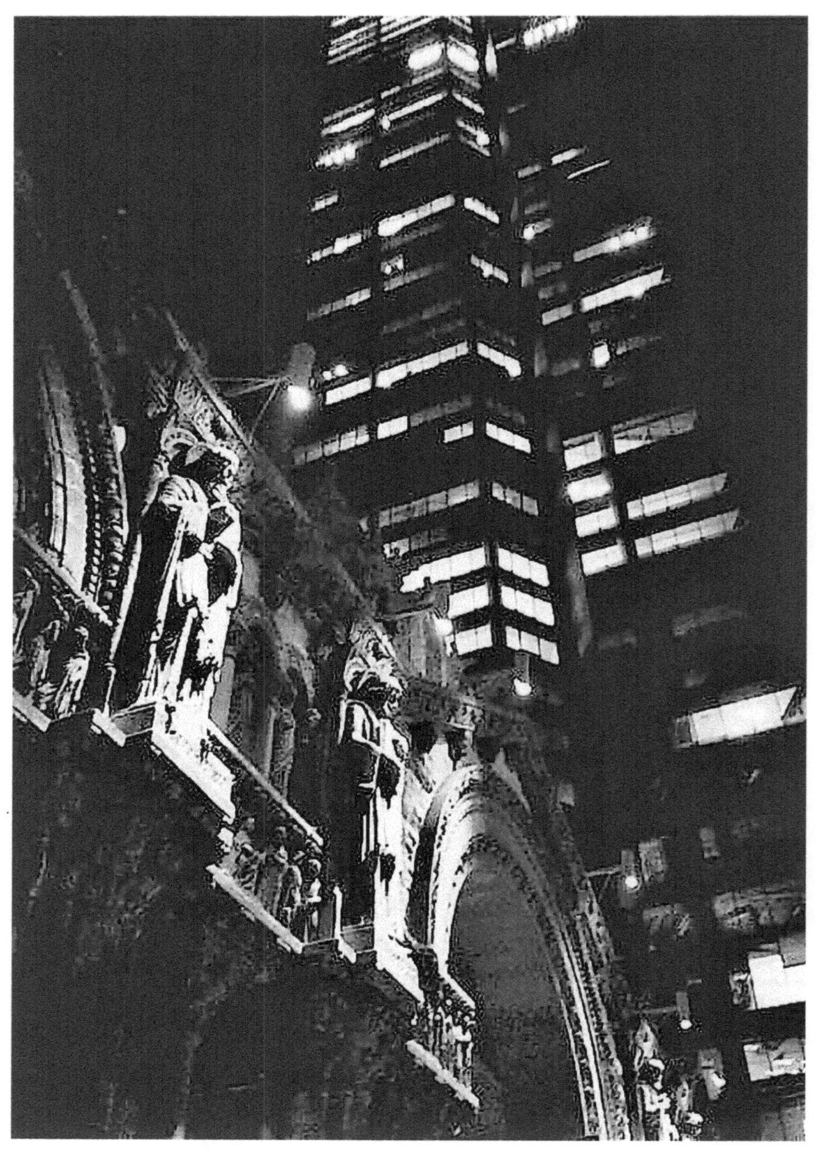

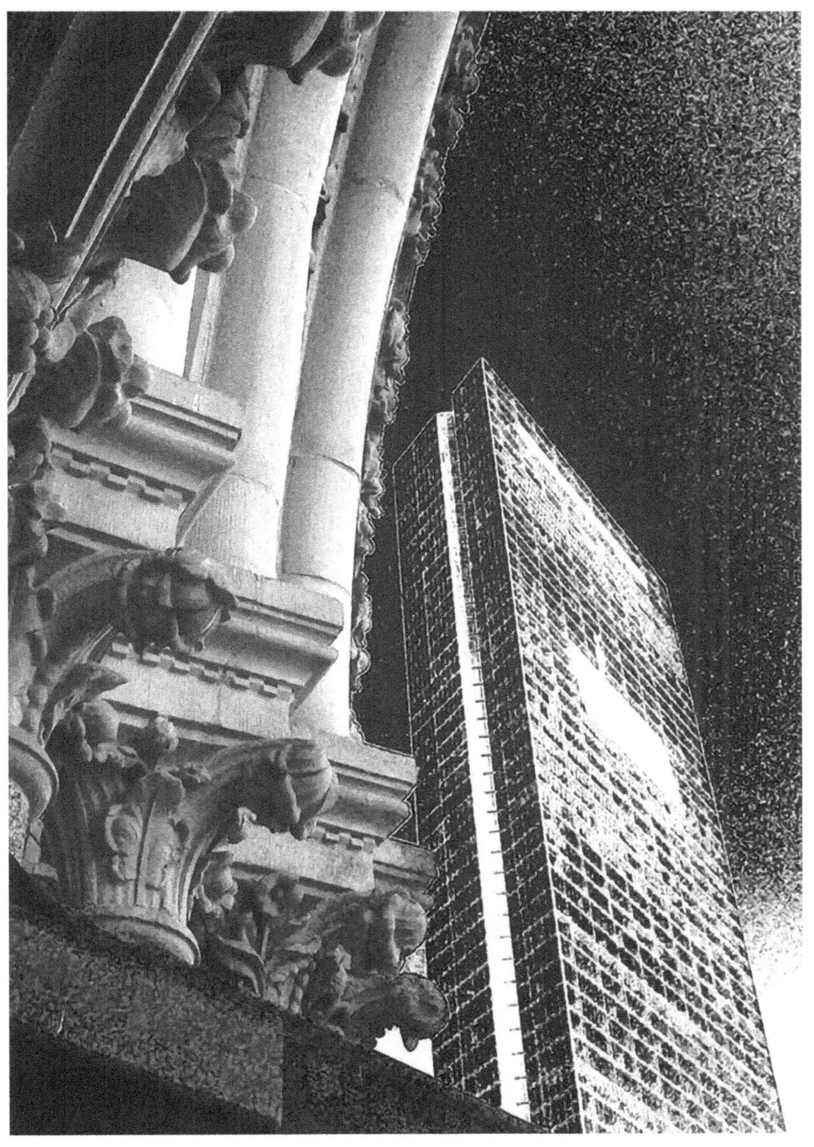

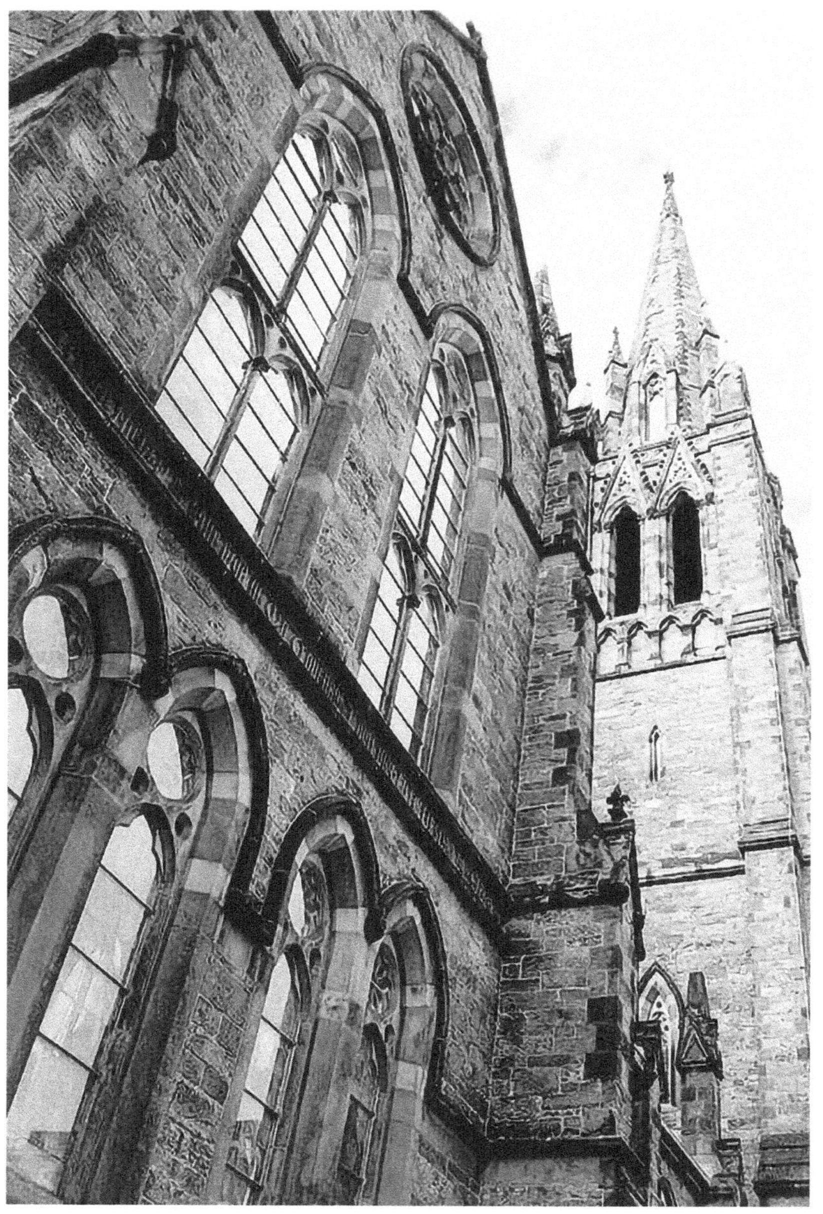

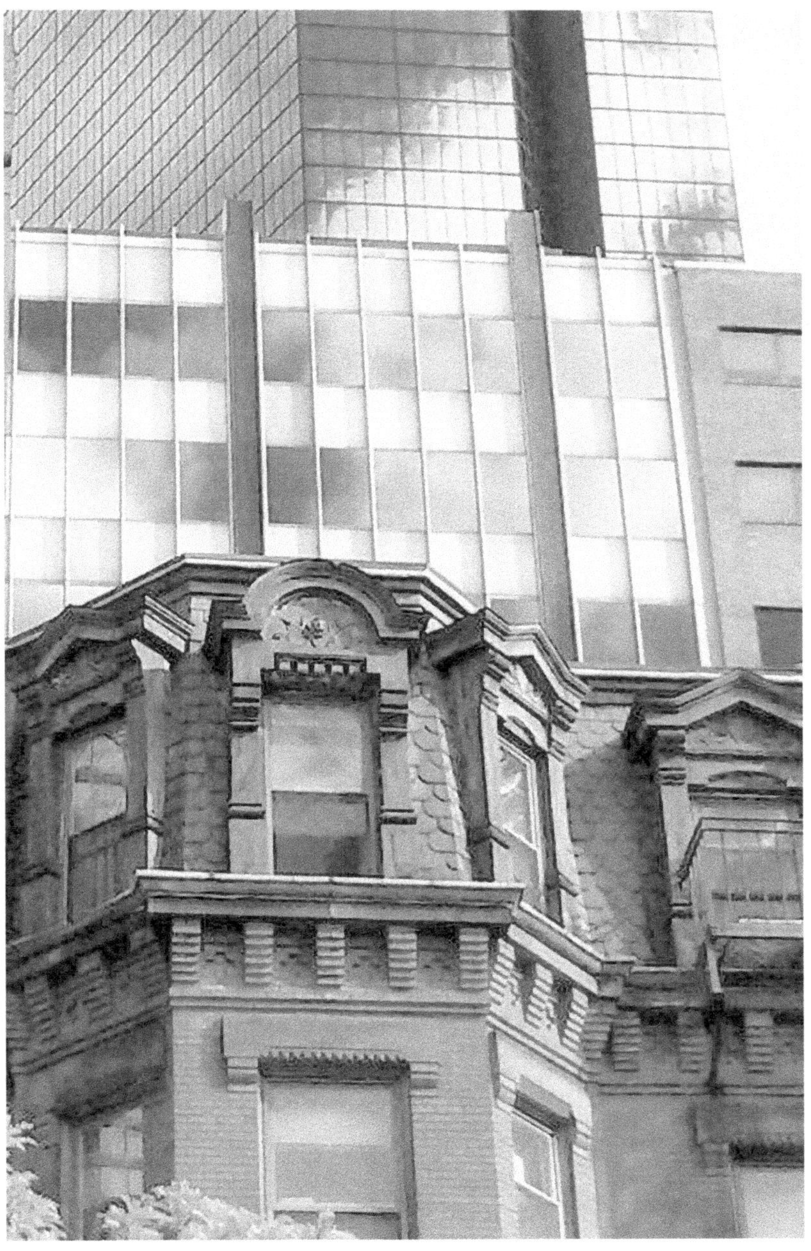

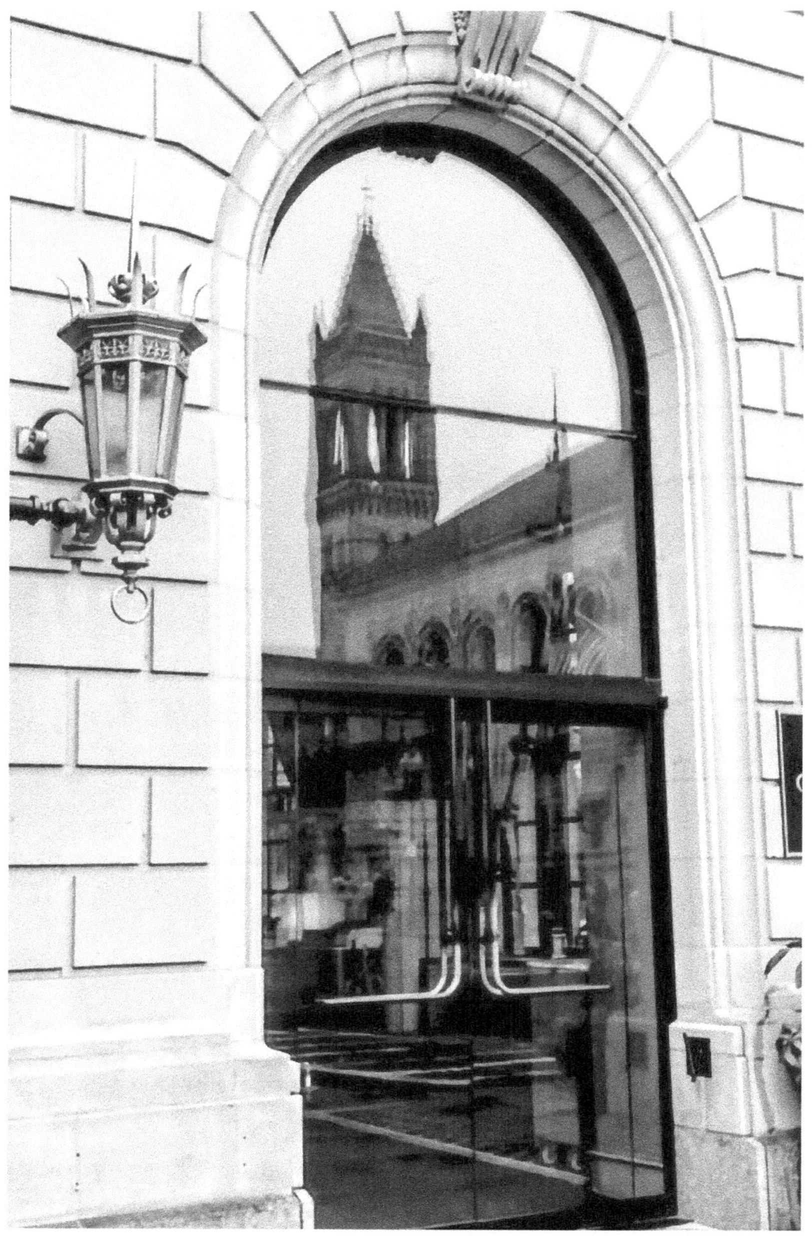

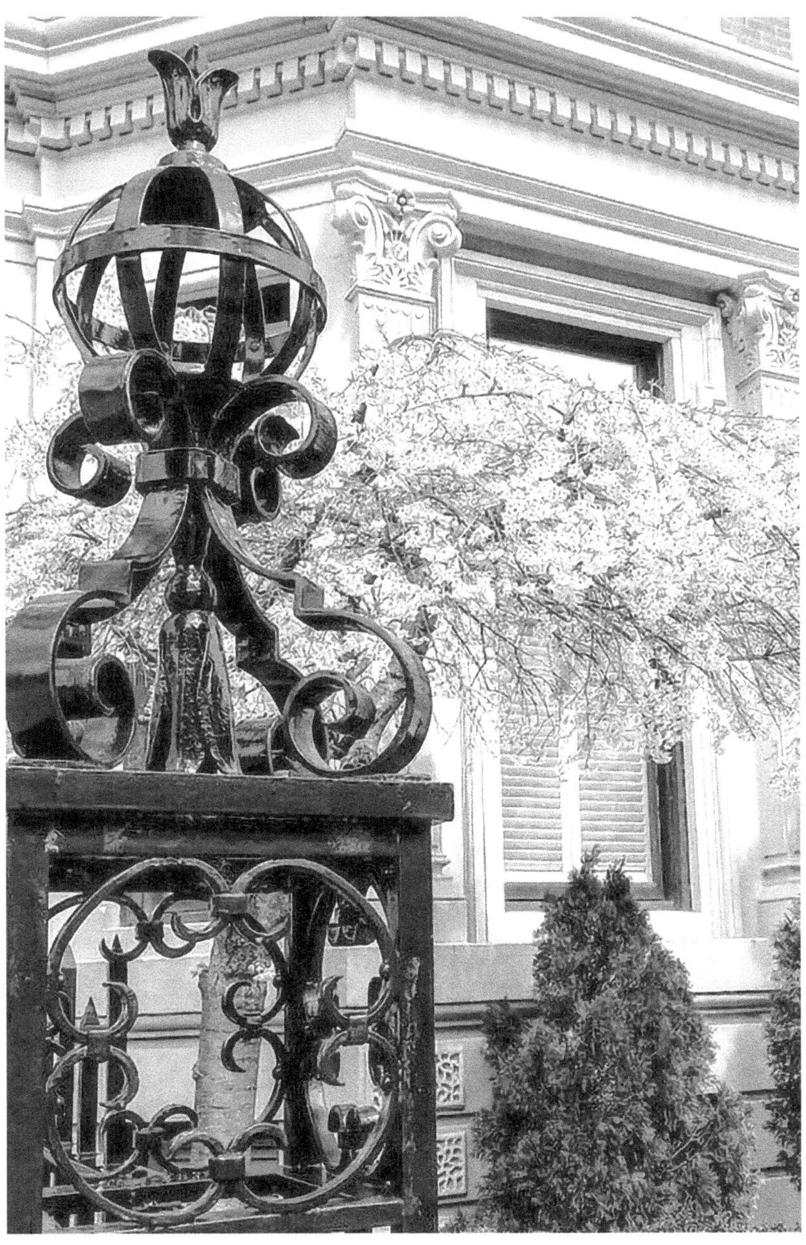

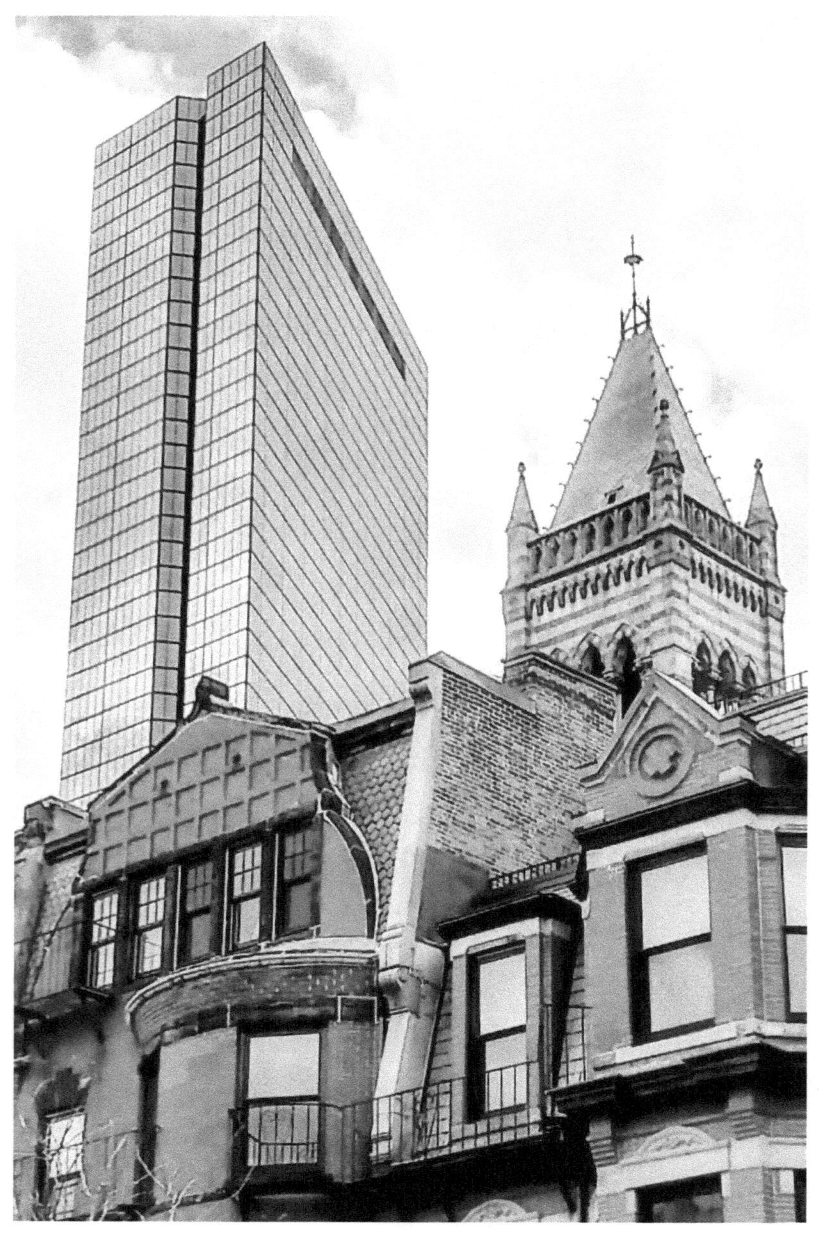

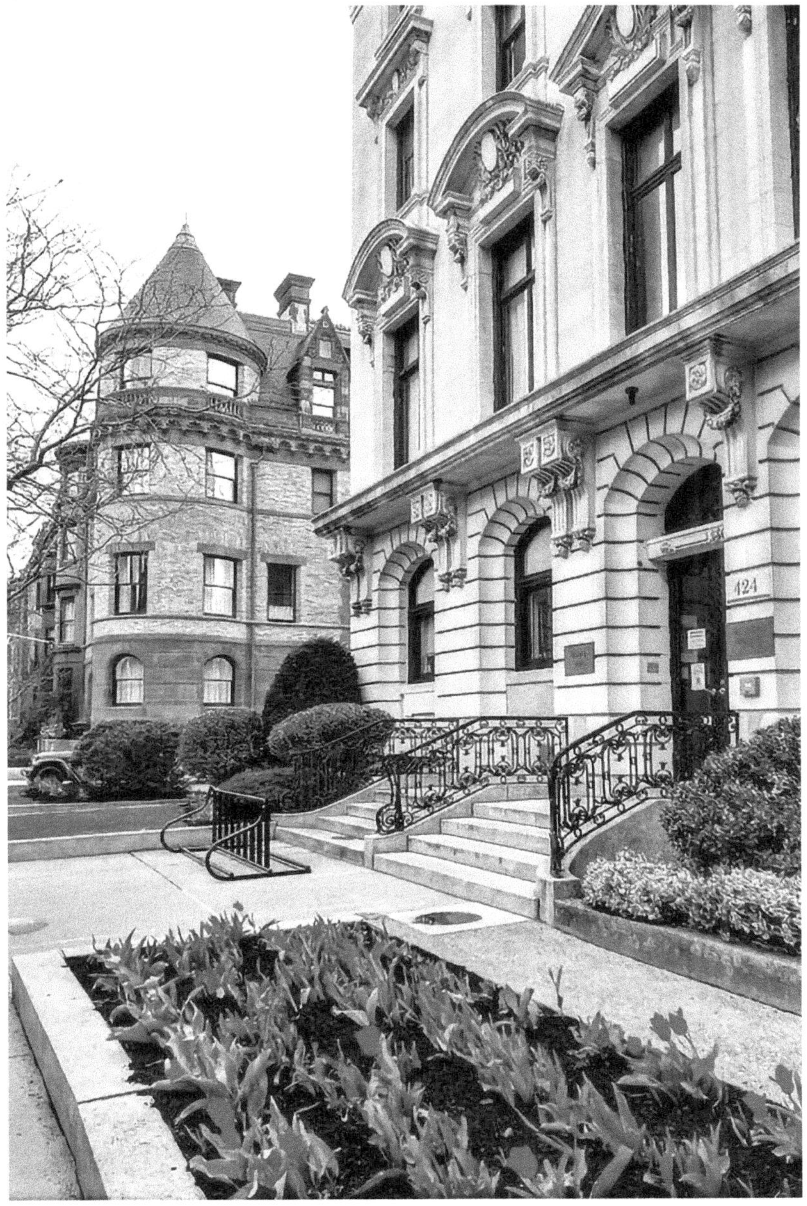

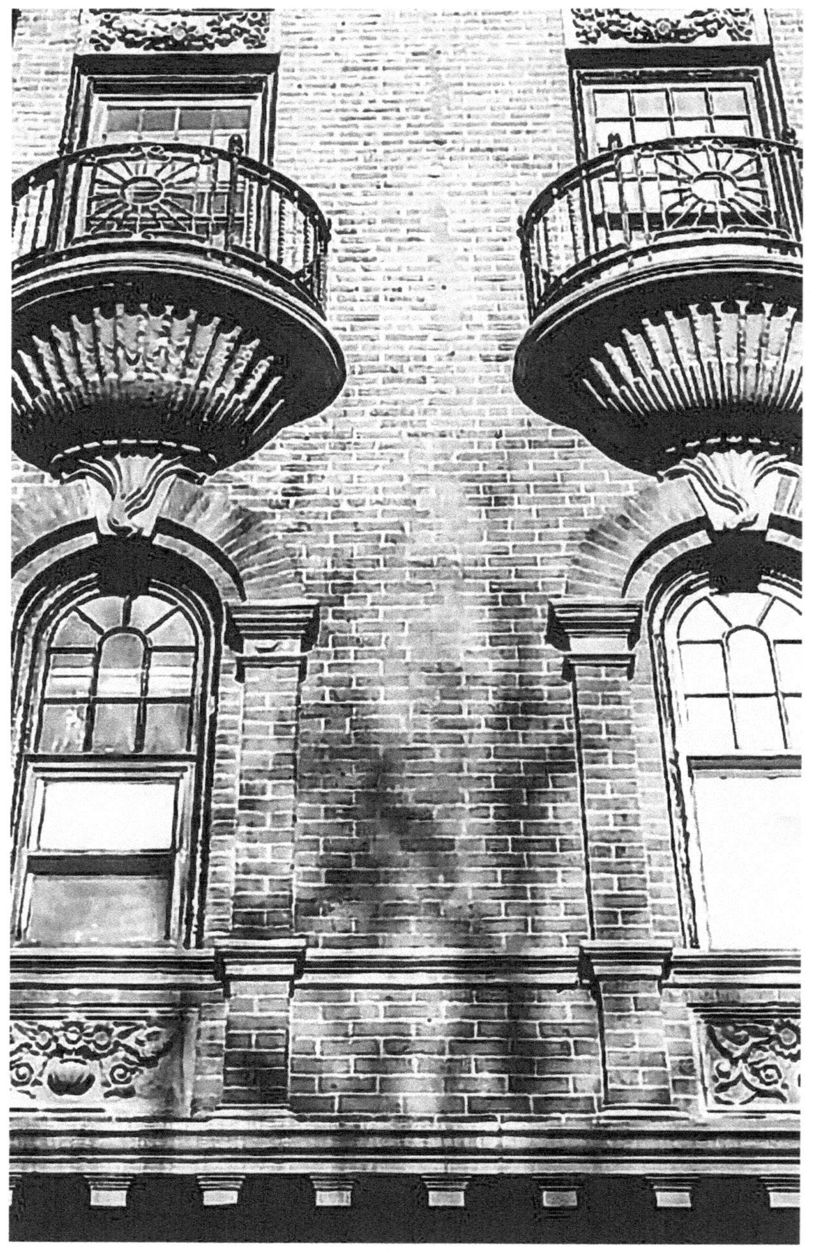

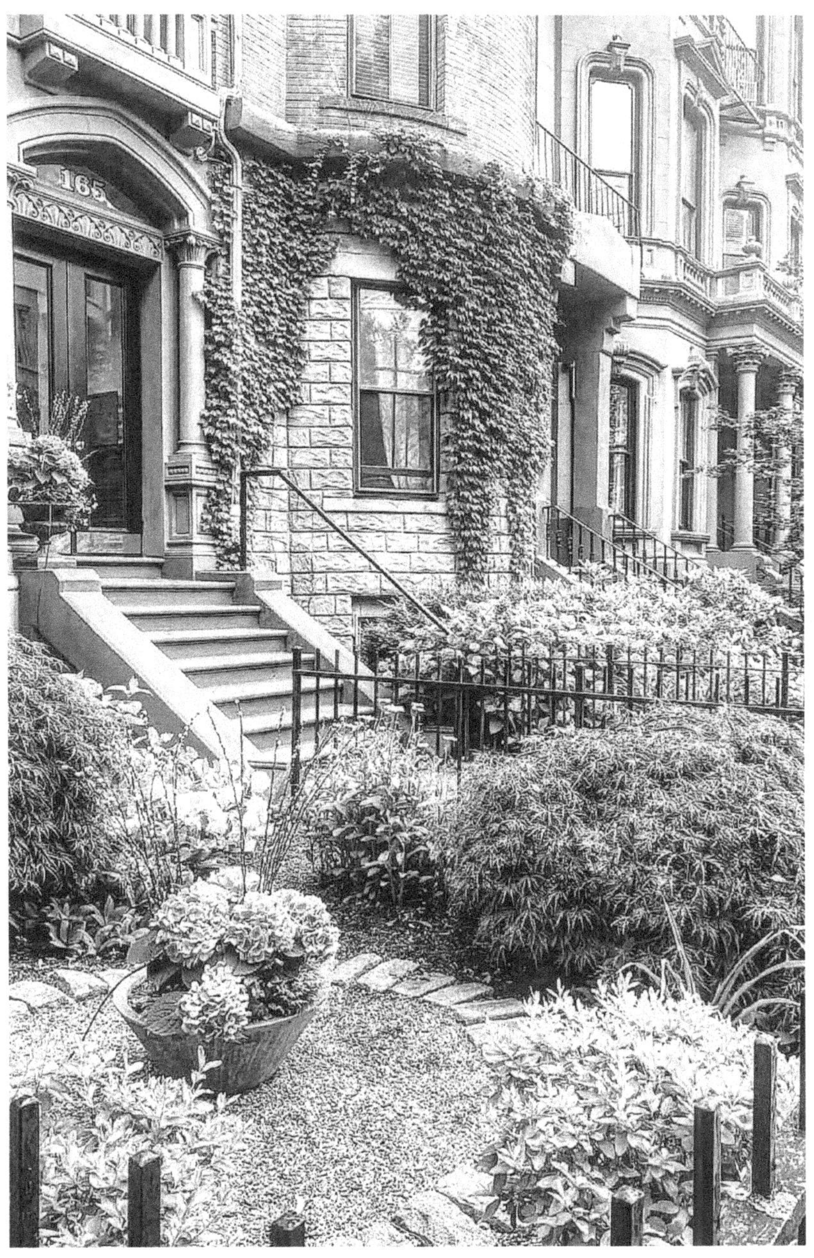

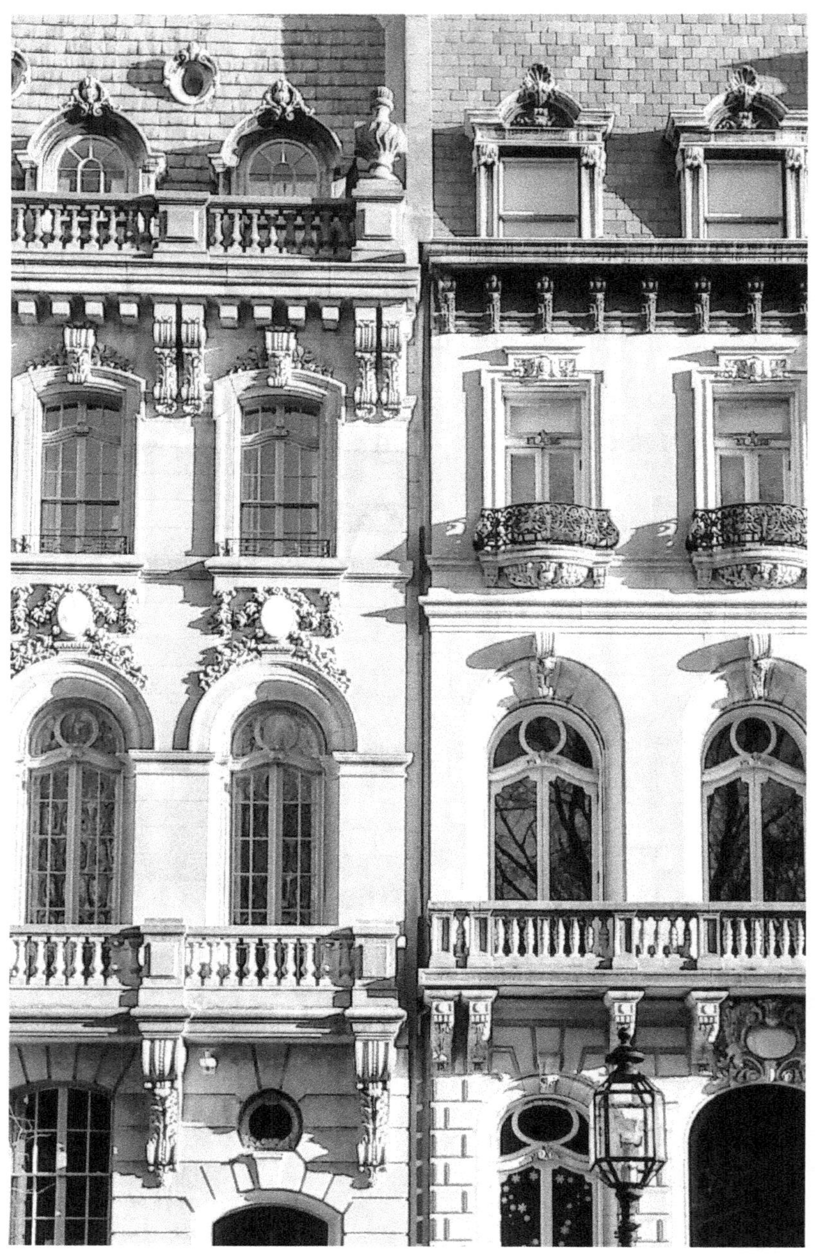

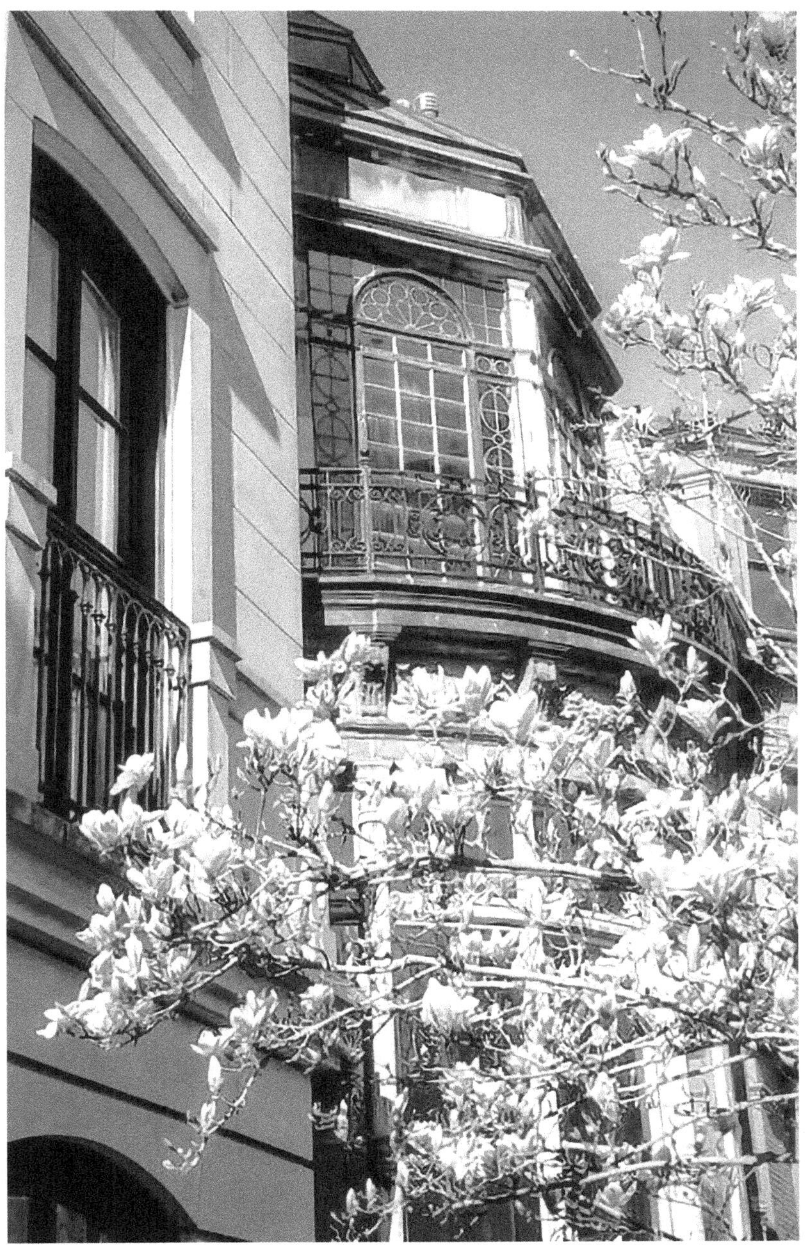

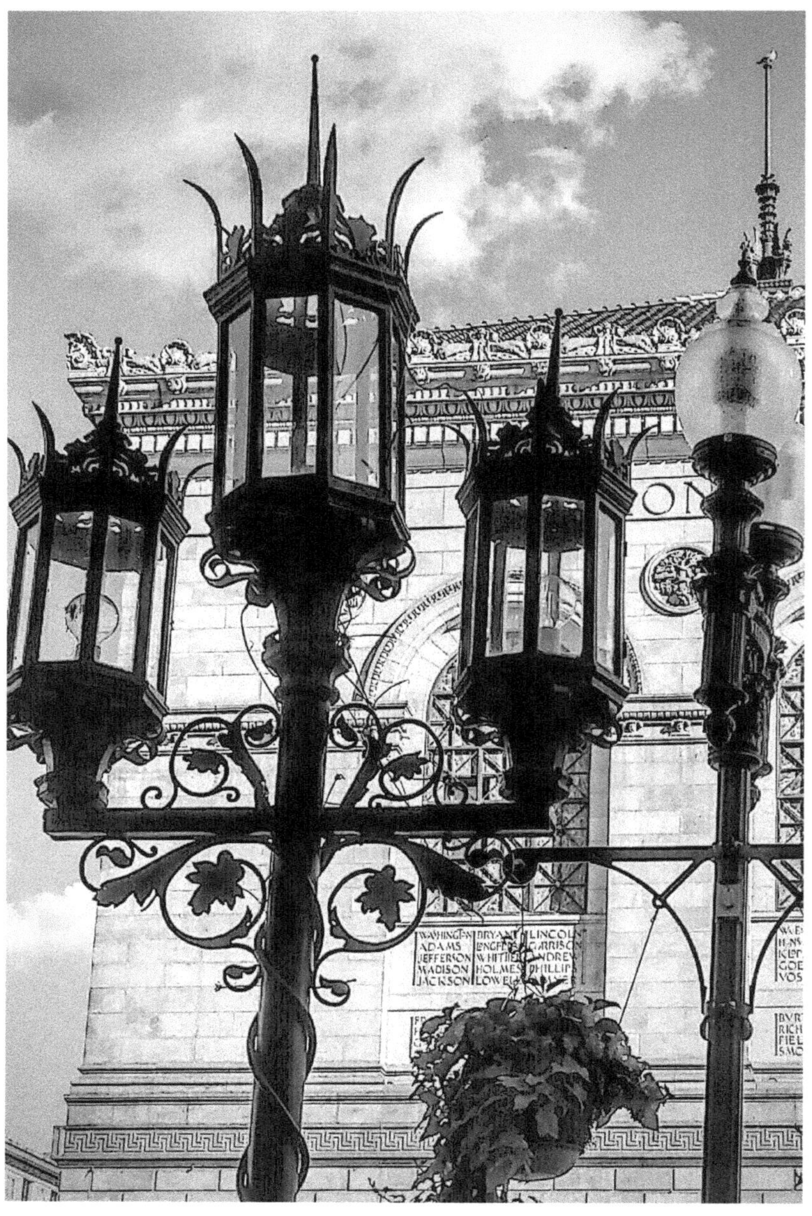

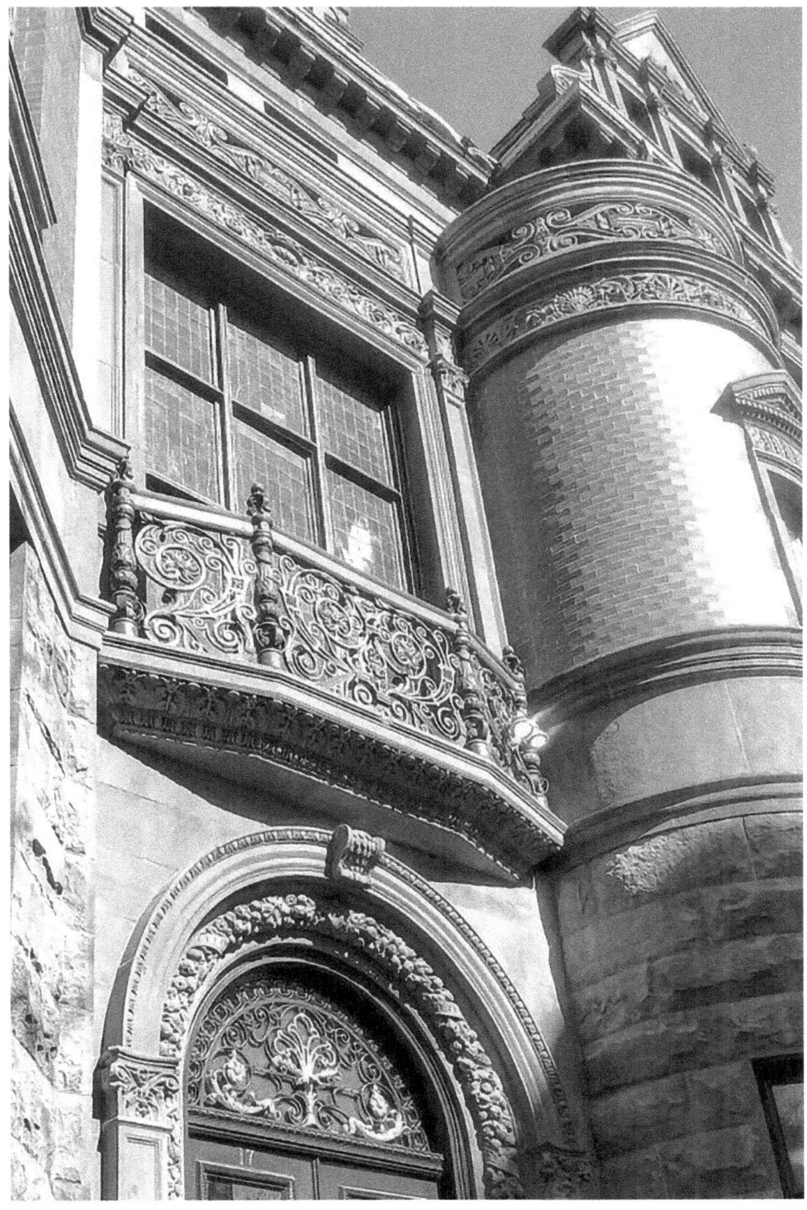

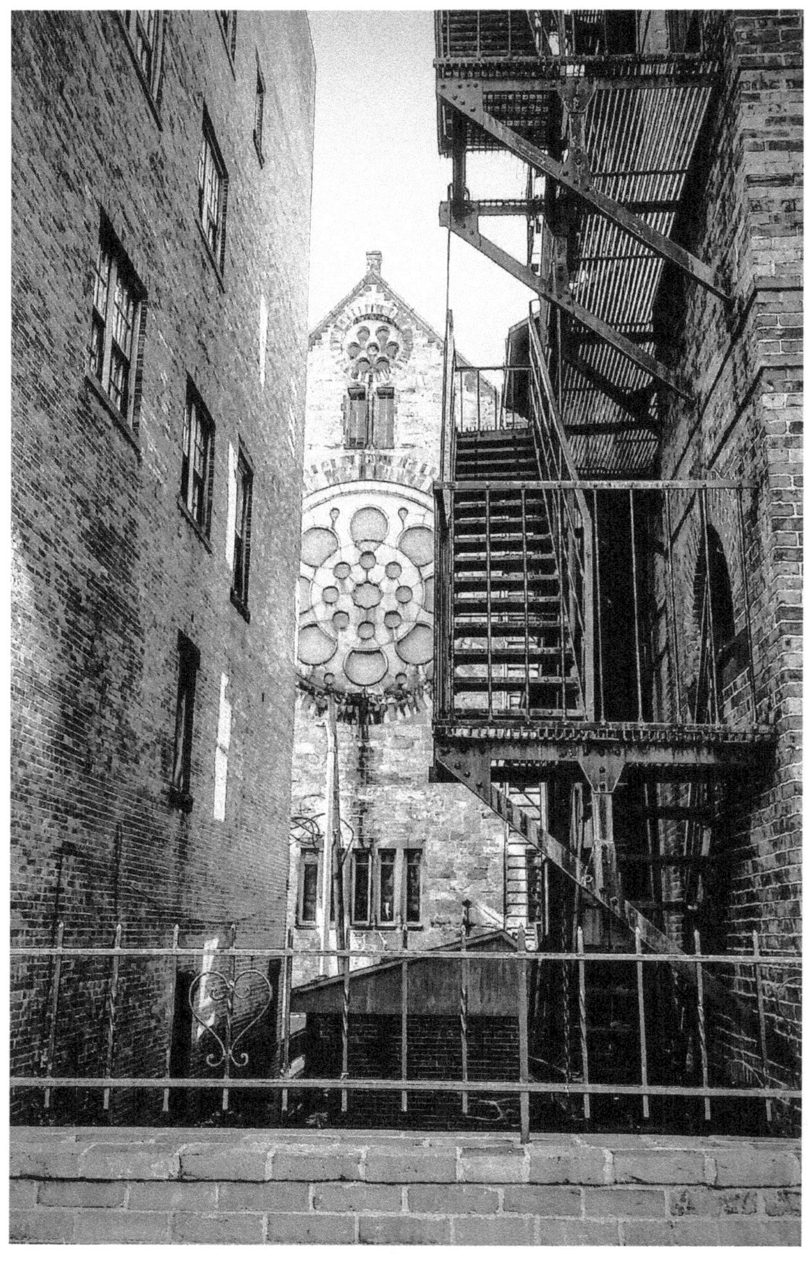

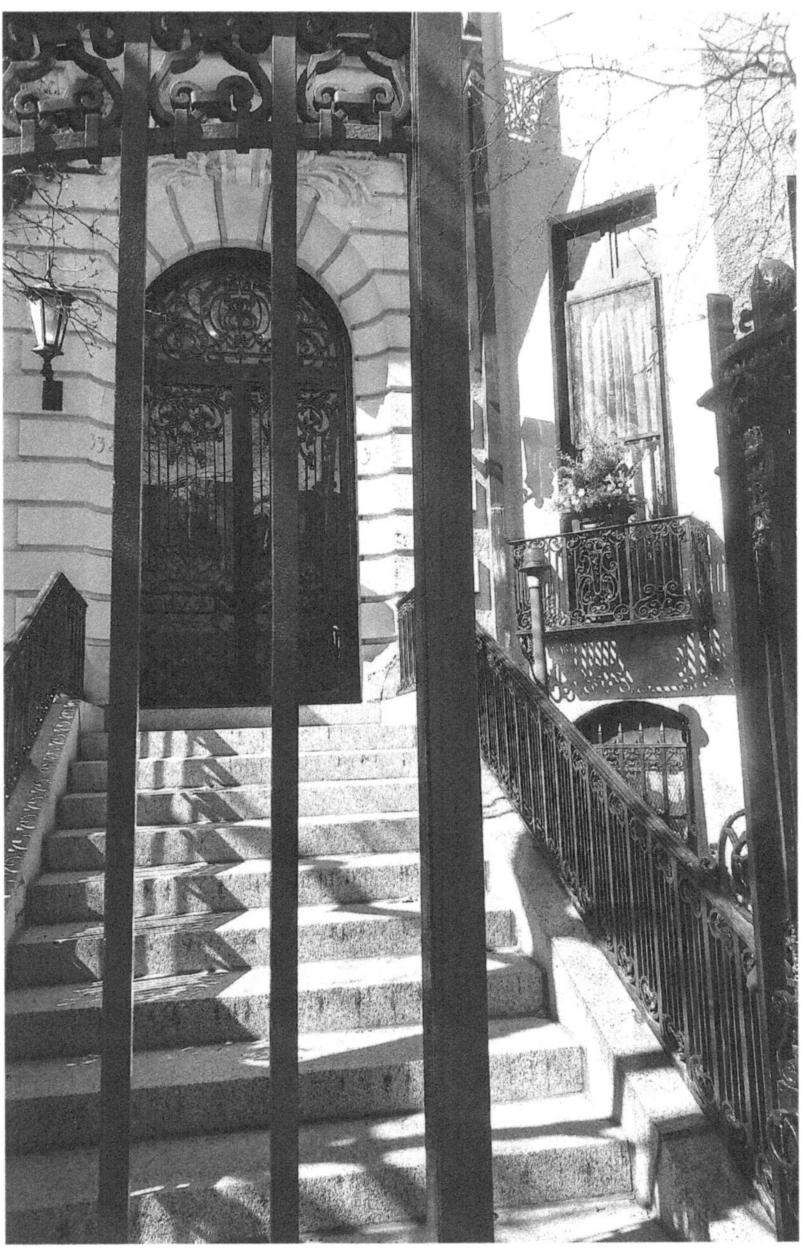

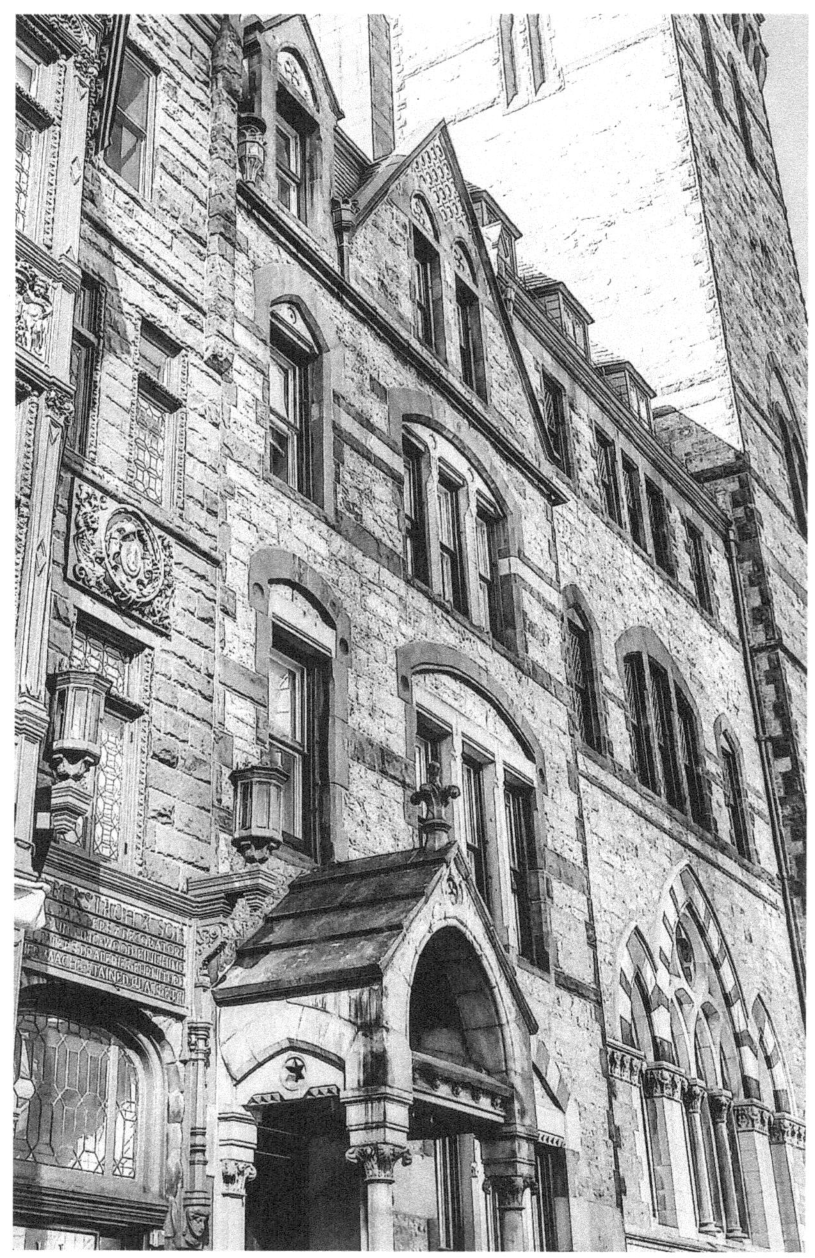

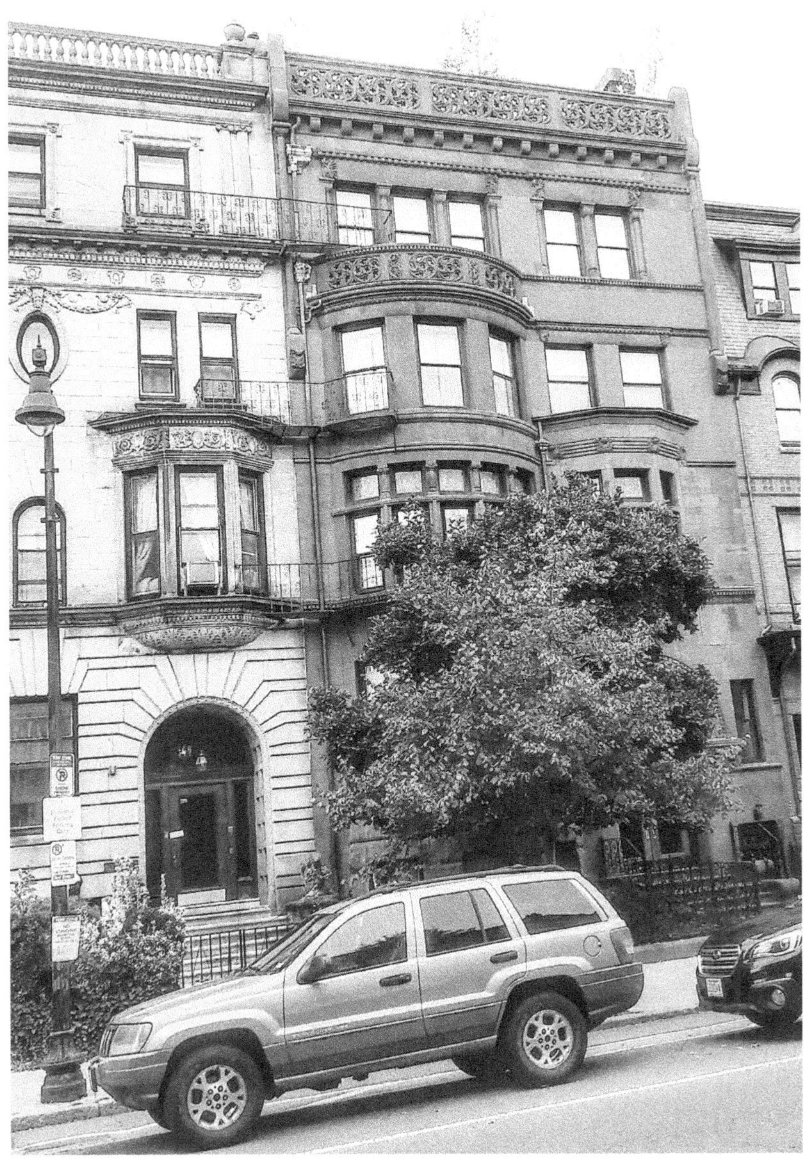

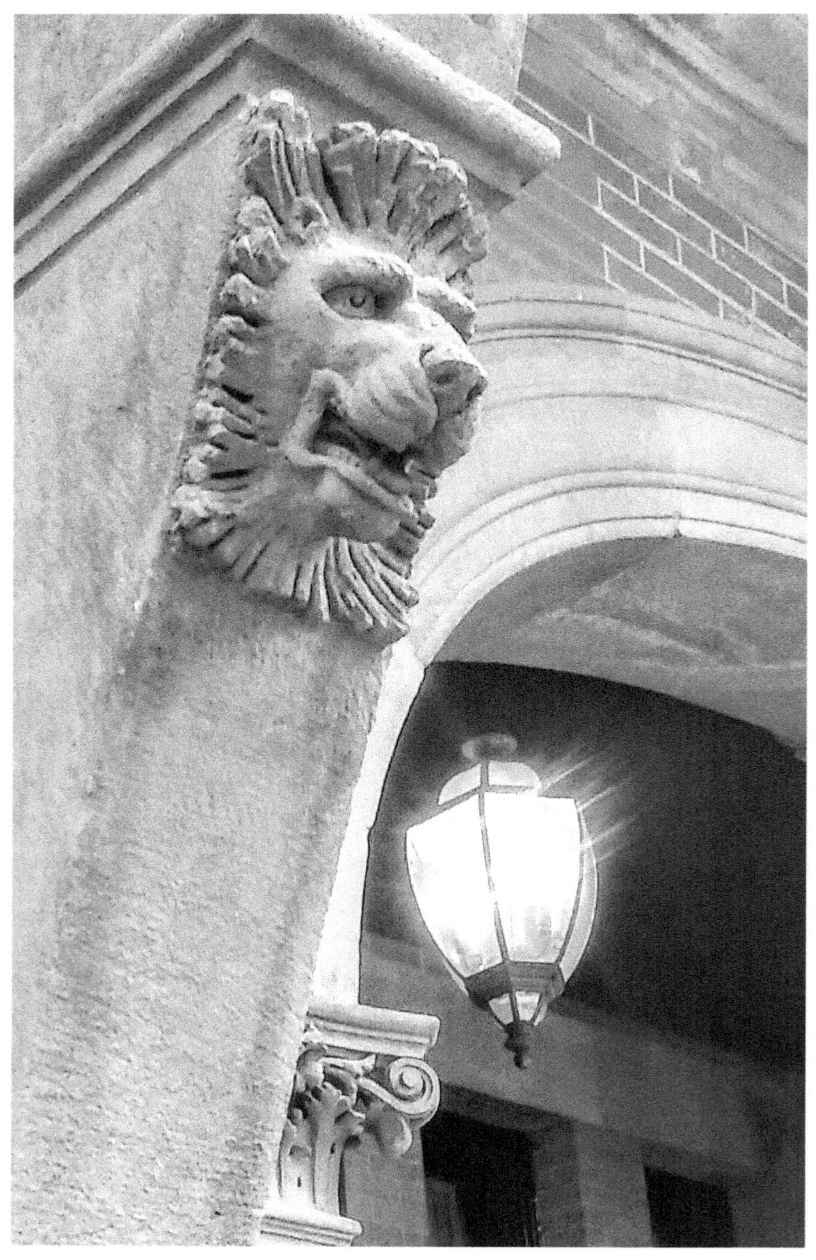

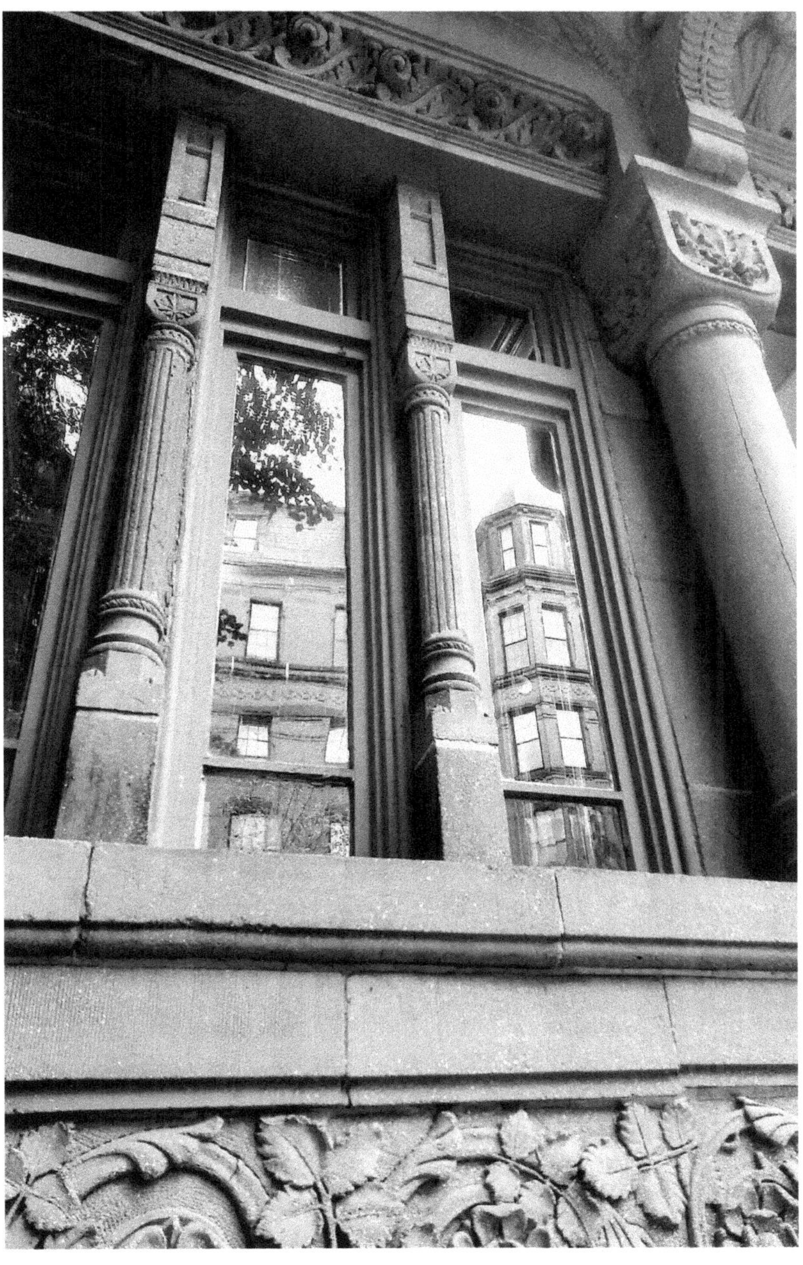

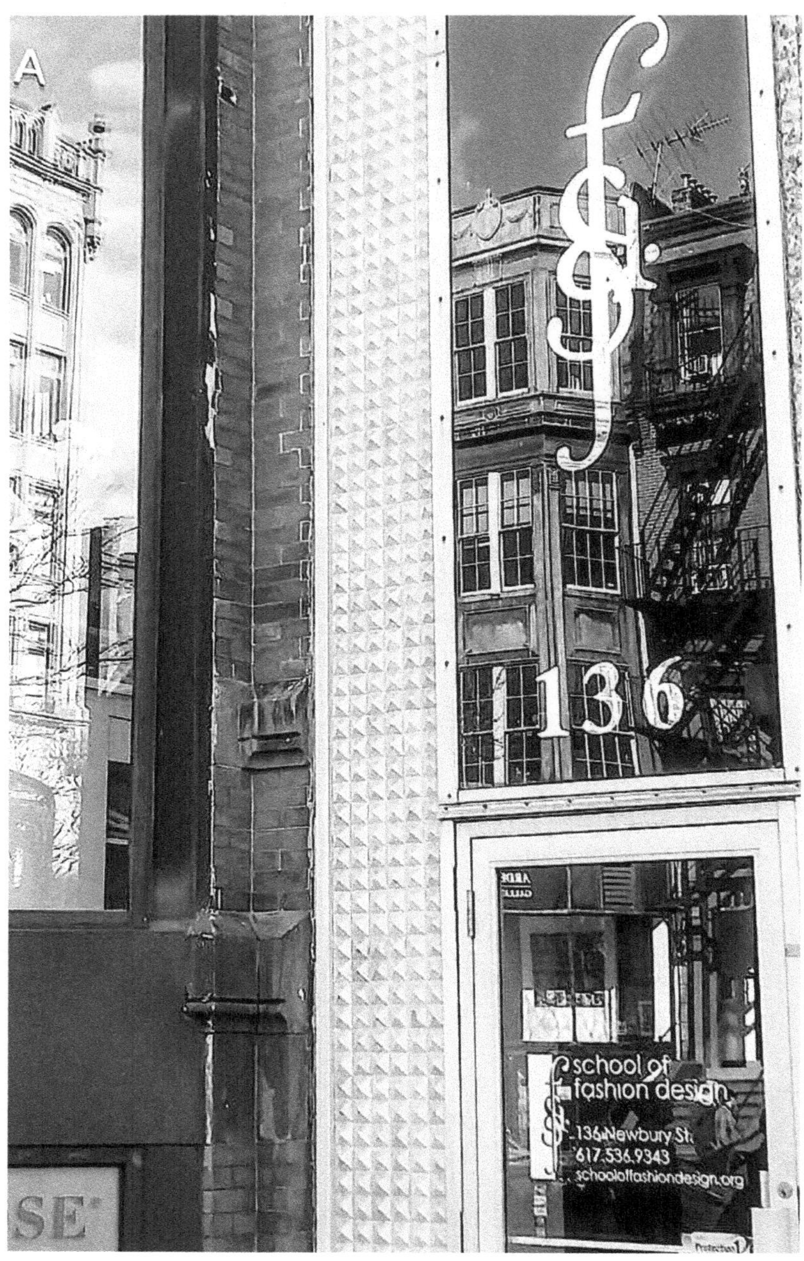
136
school of
fashion design
136 Newbury St.
617.536.9343
schooloffashiondesign.org

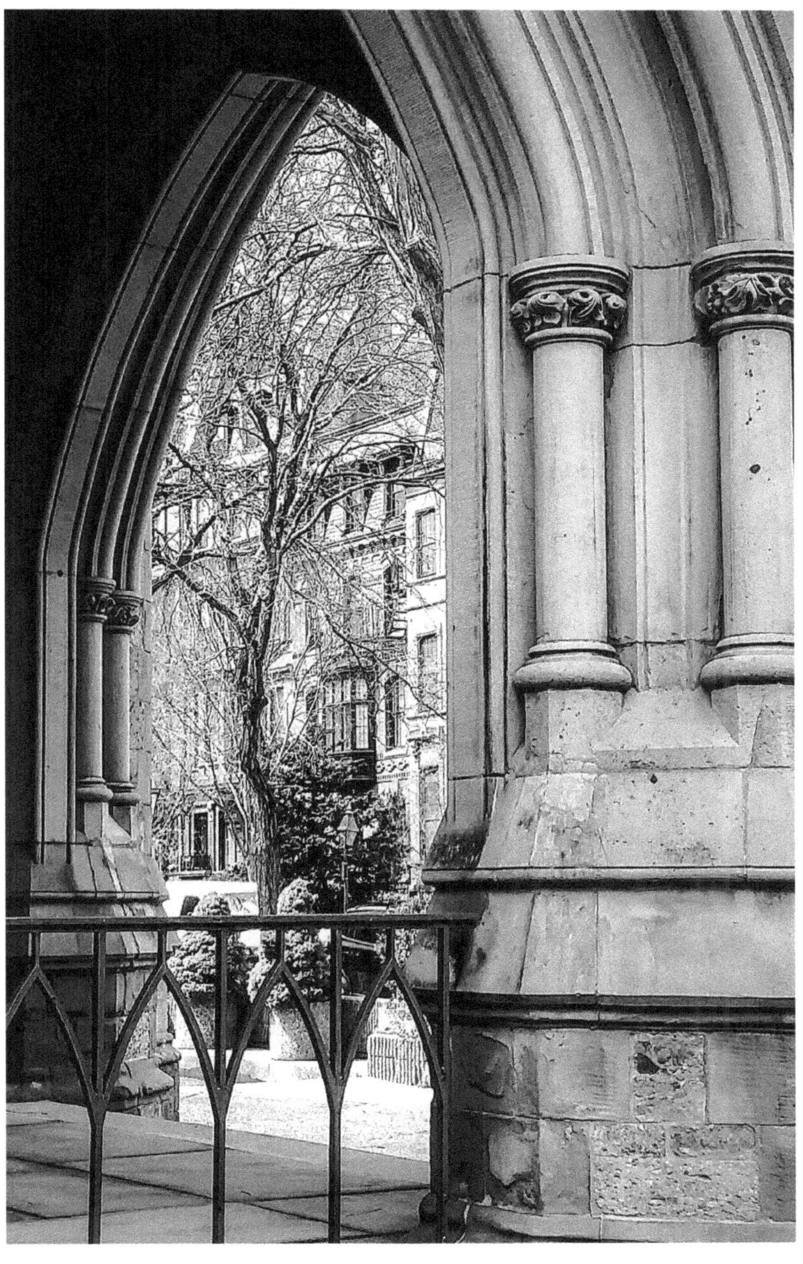

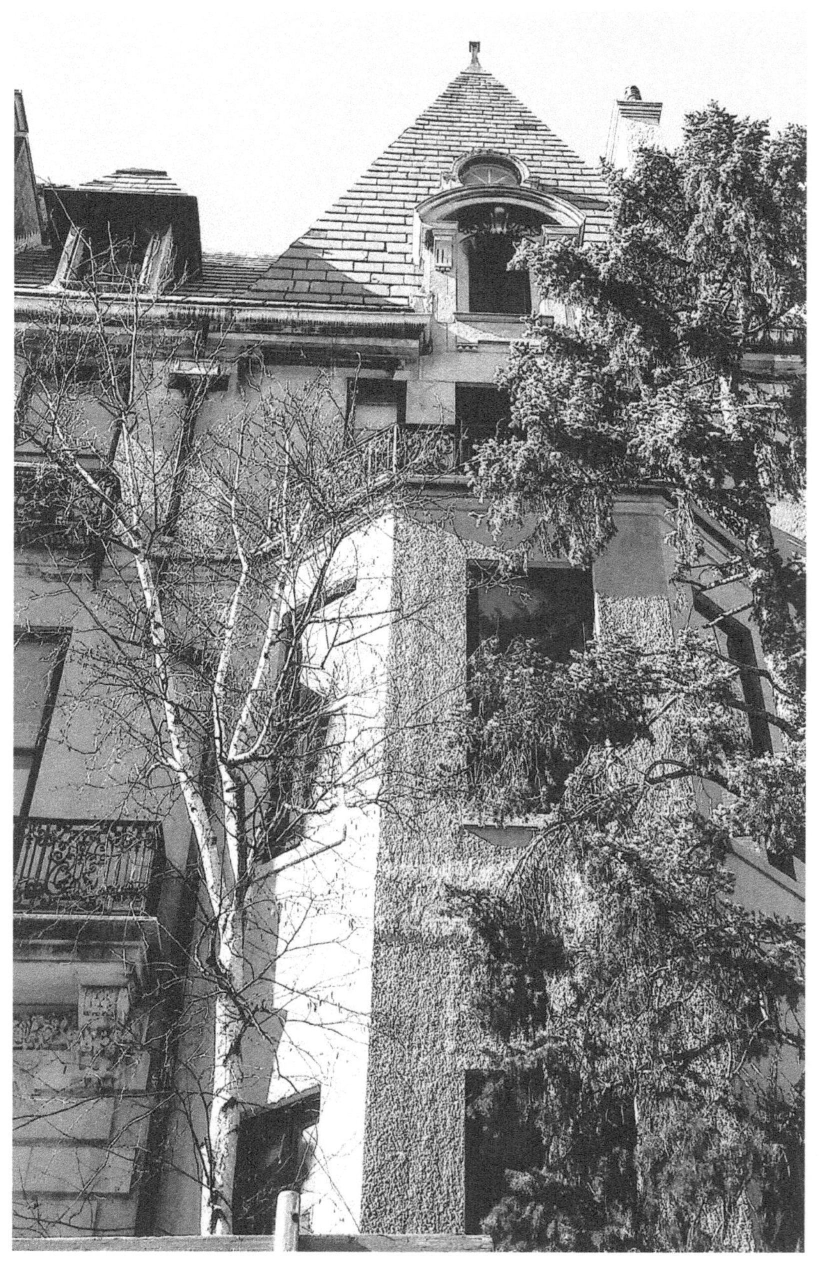

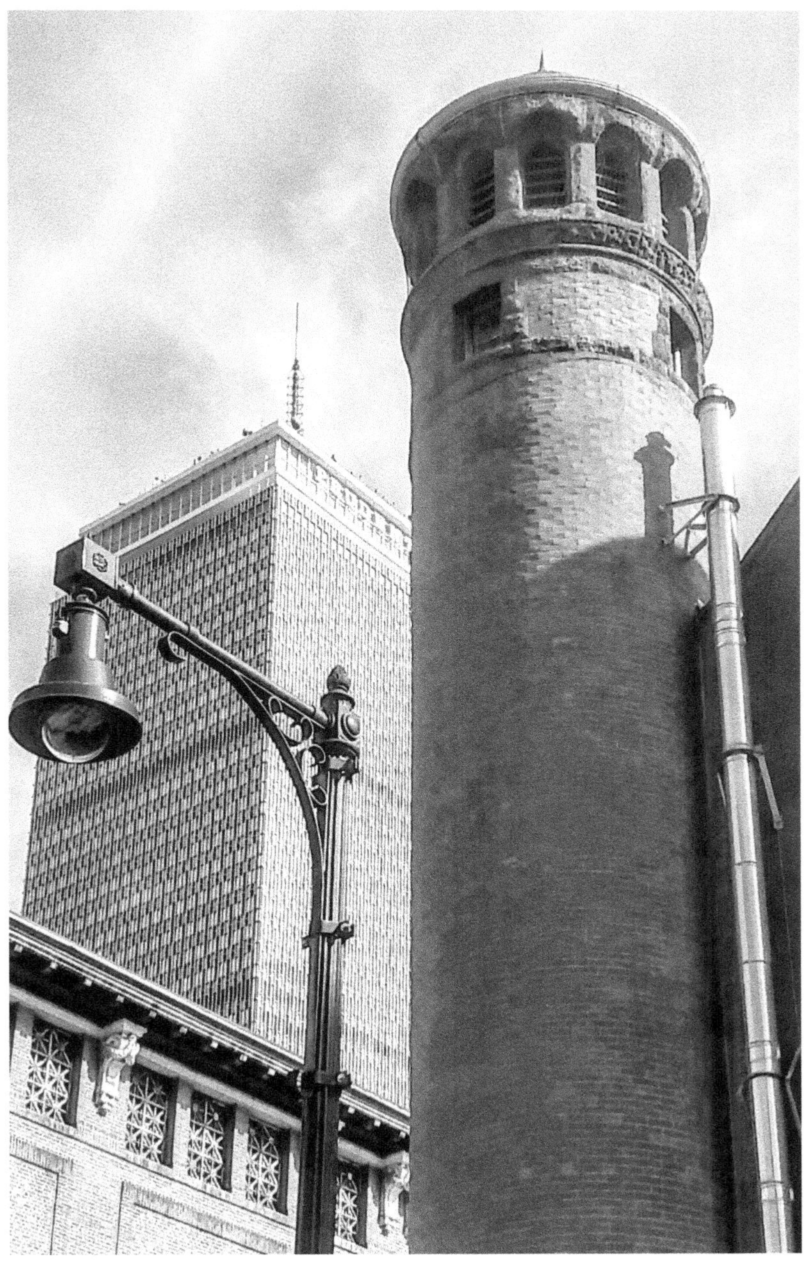

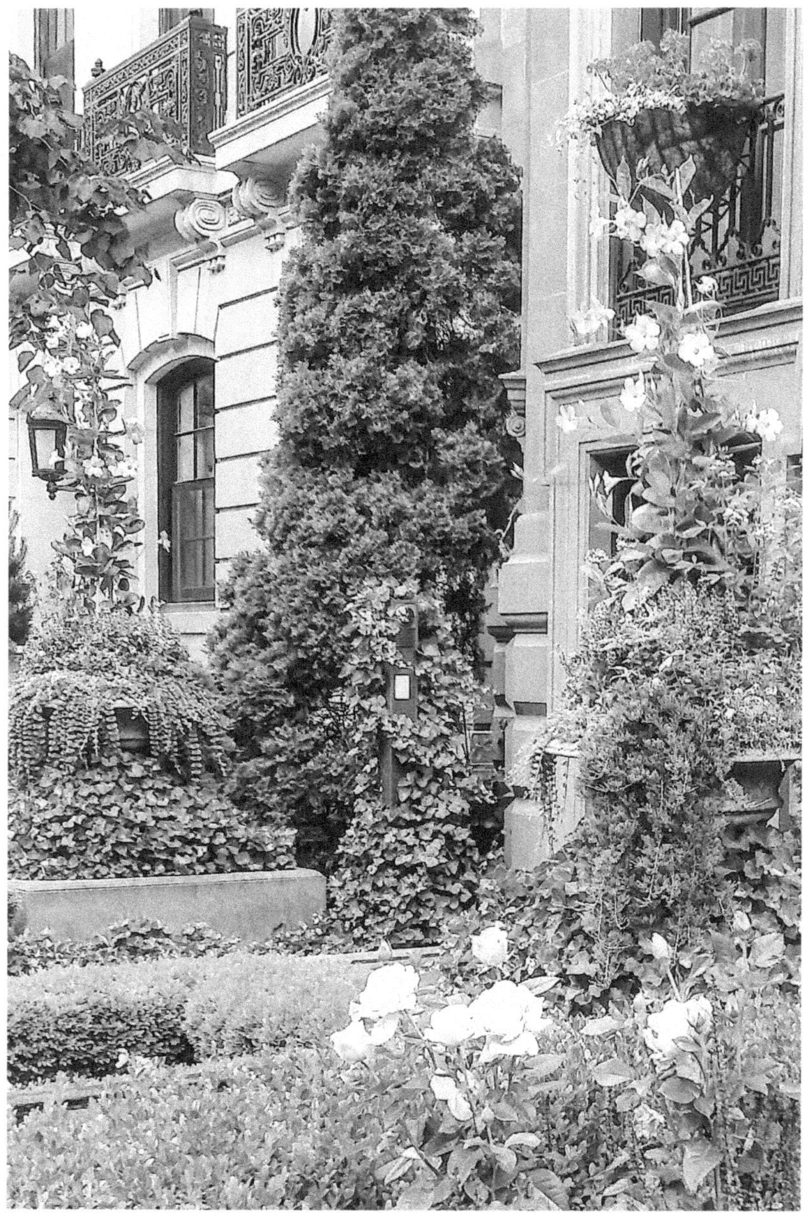

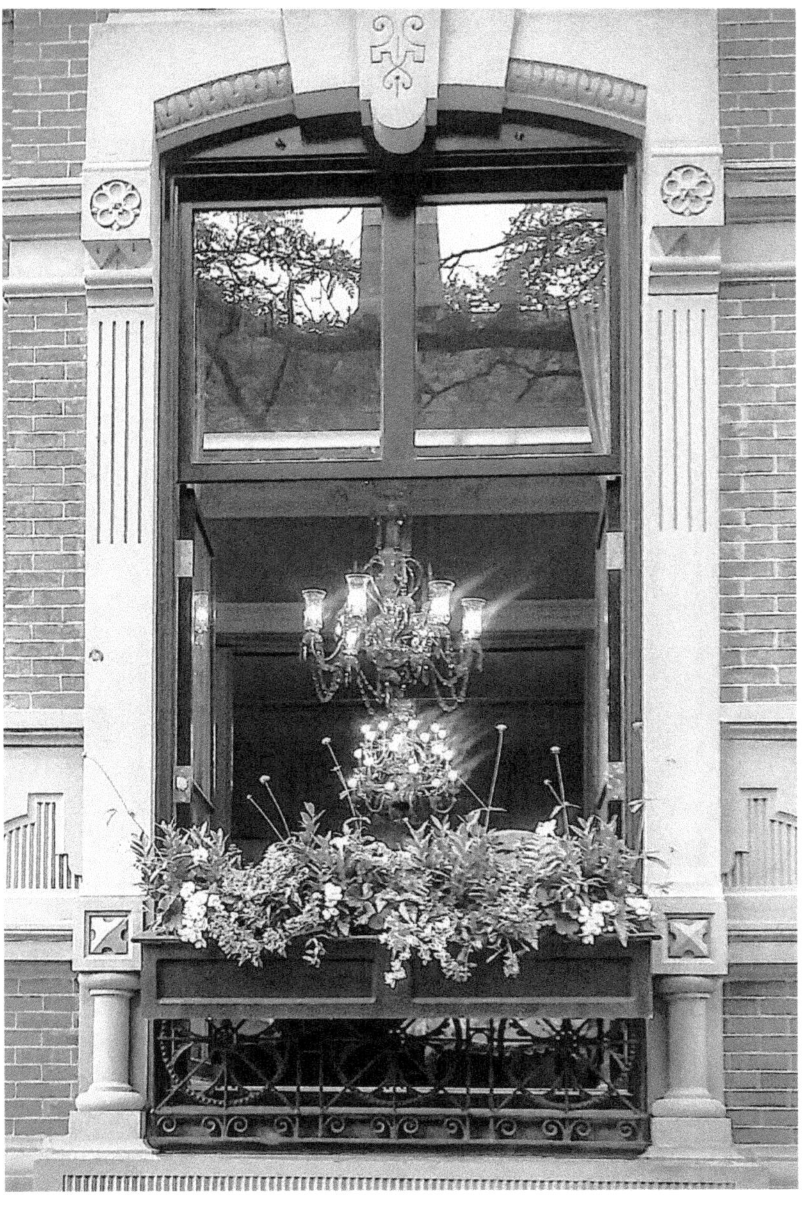

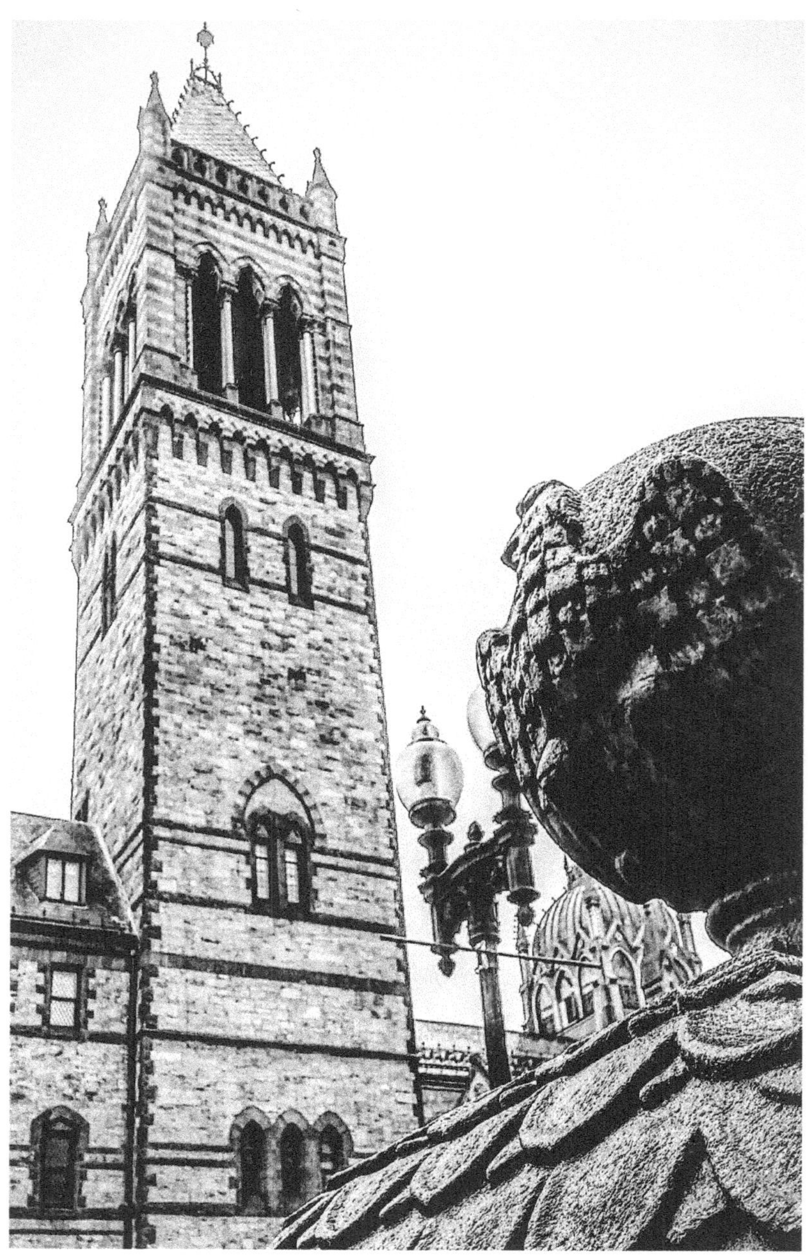

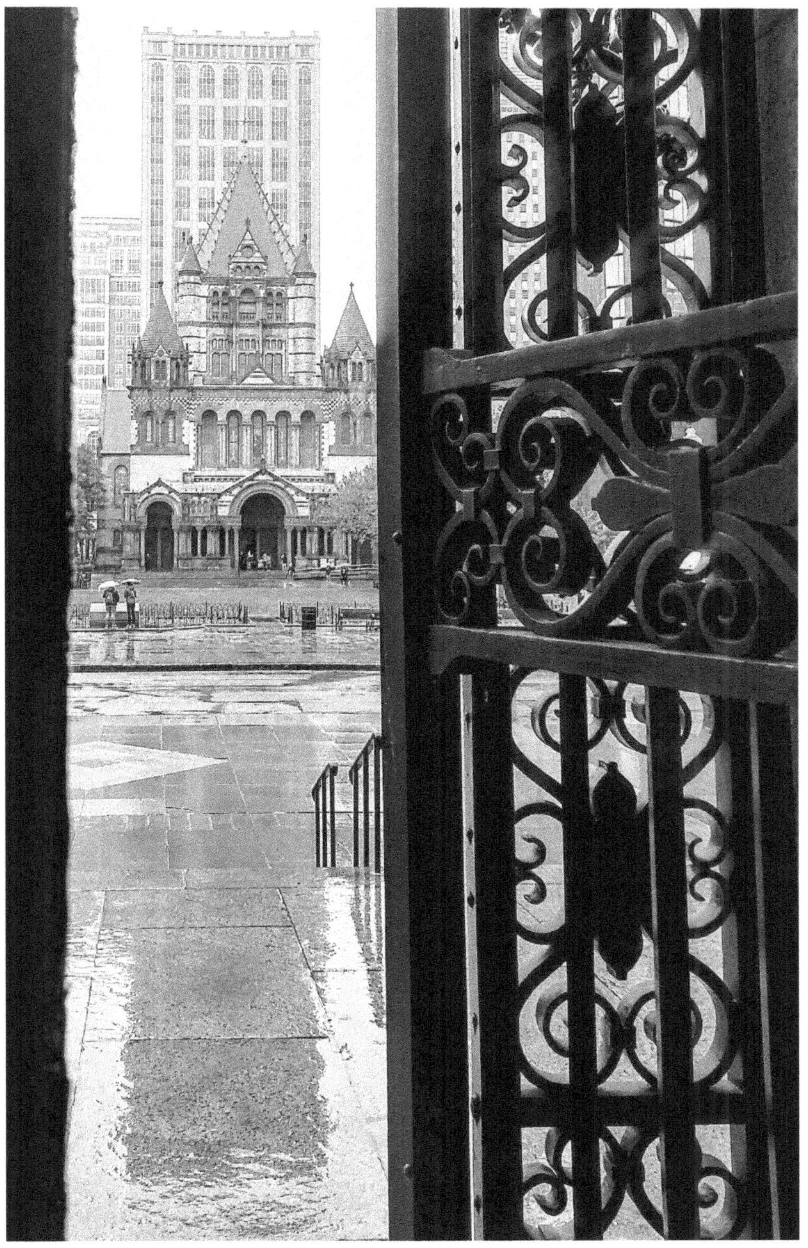

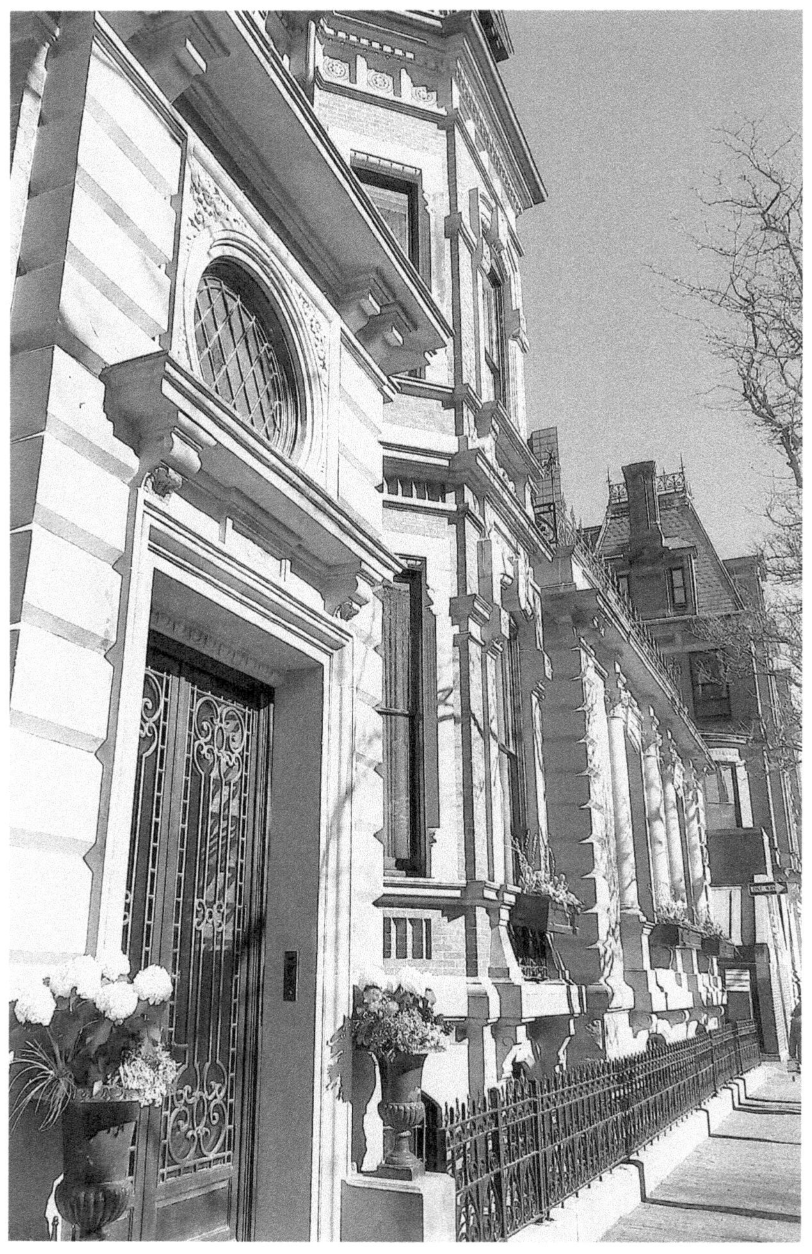

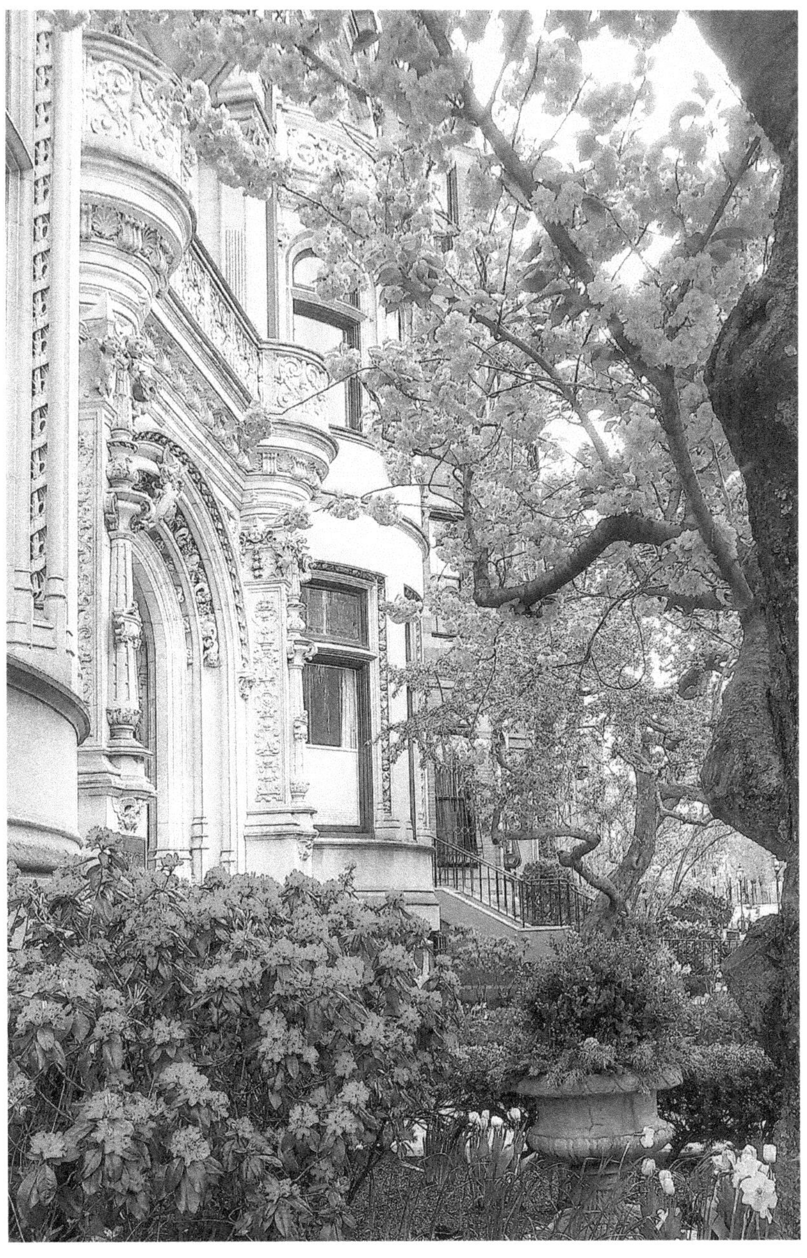

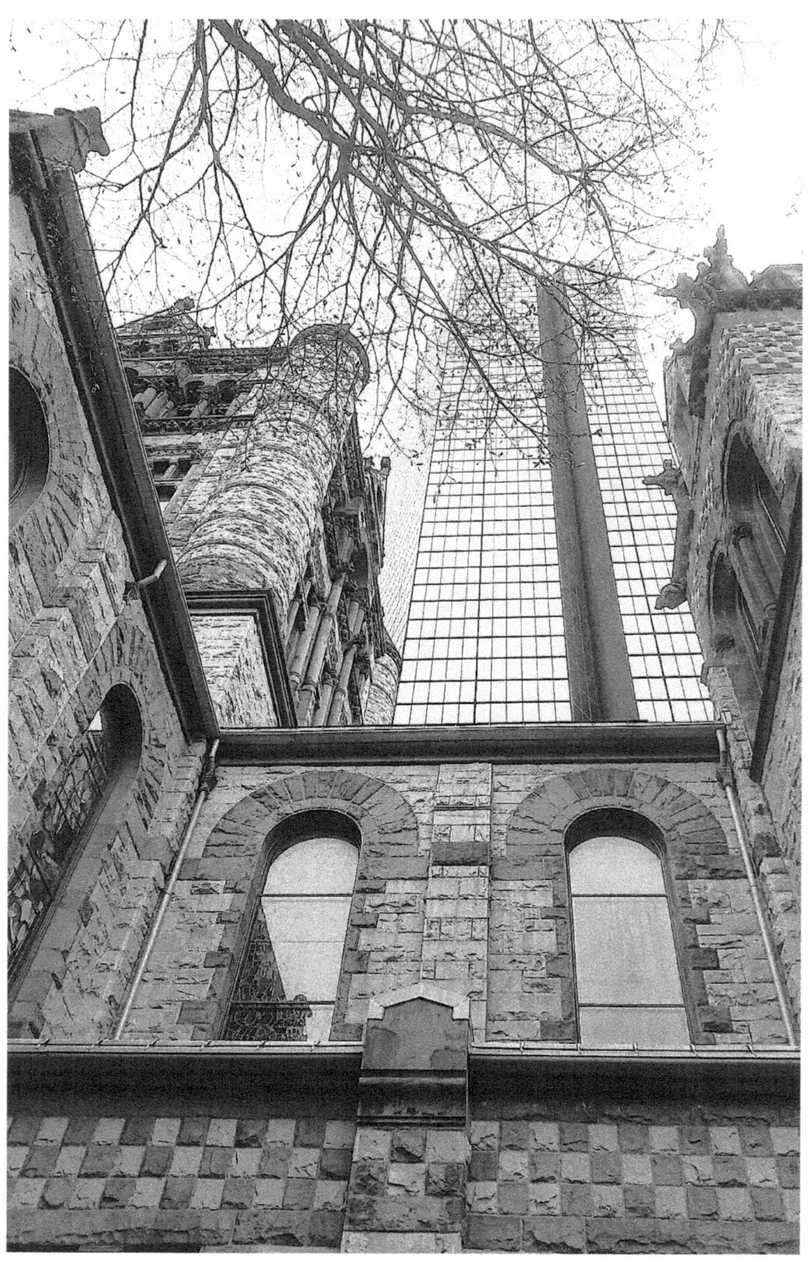

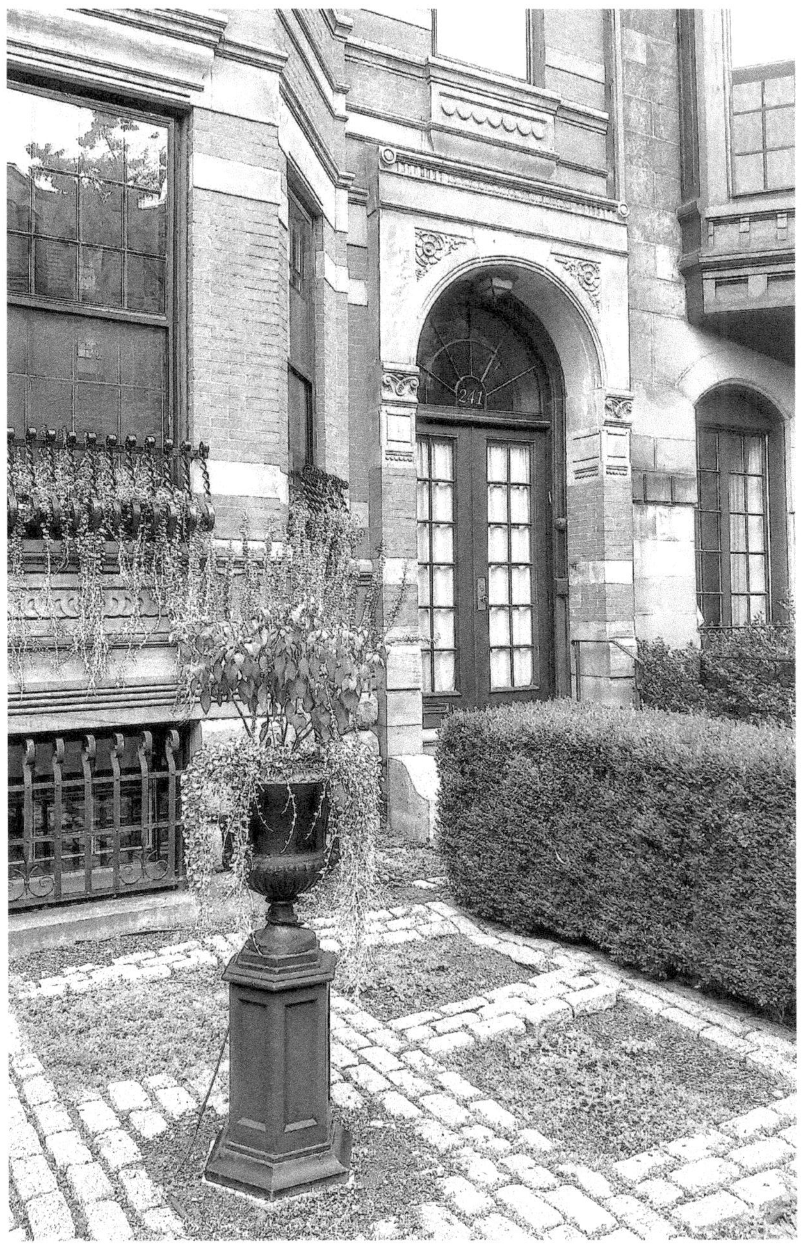

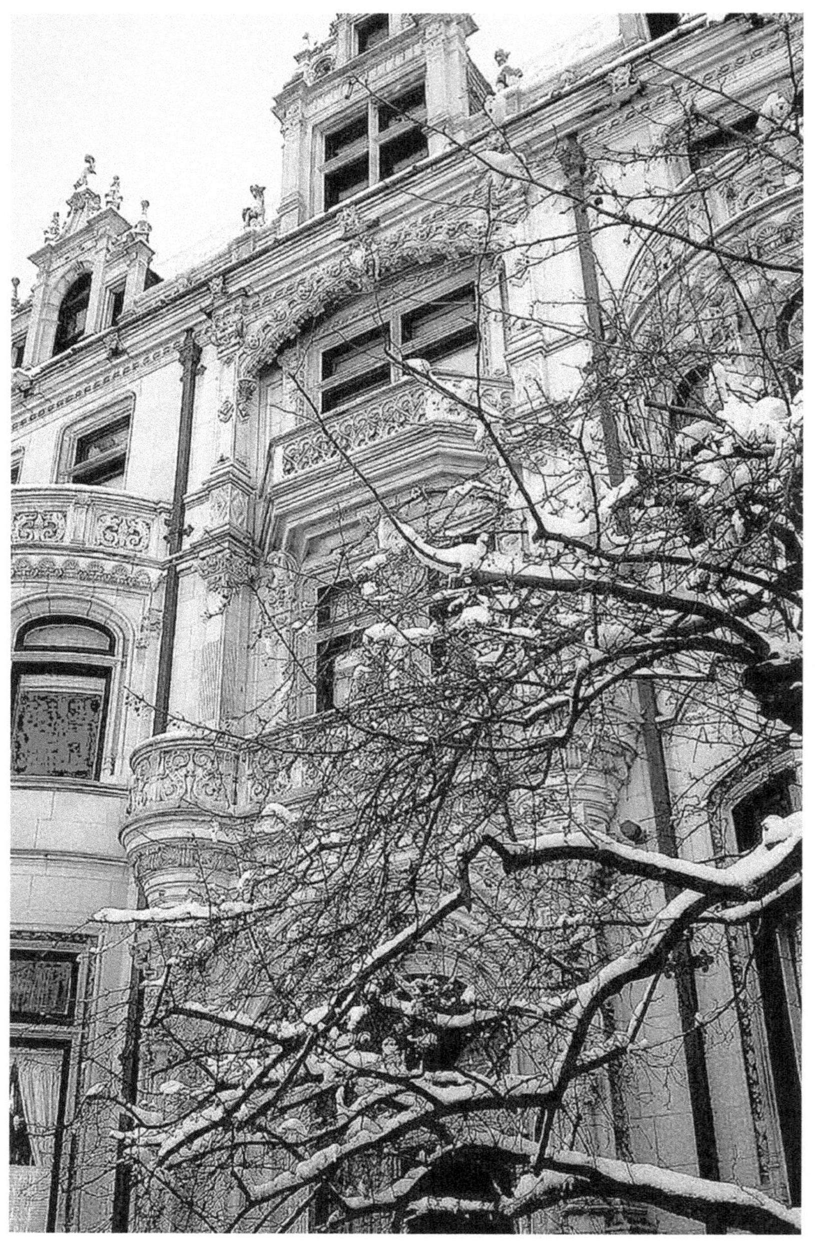

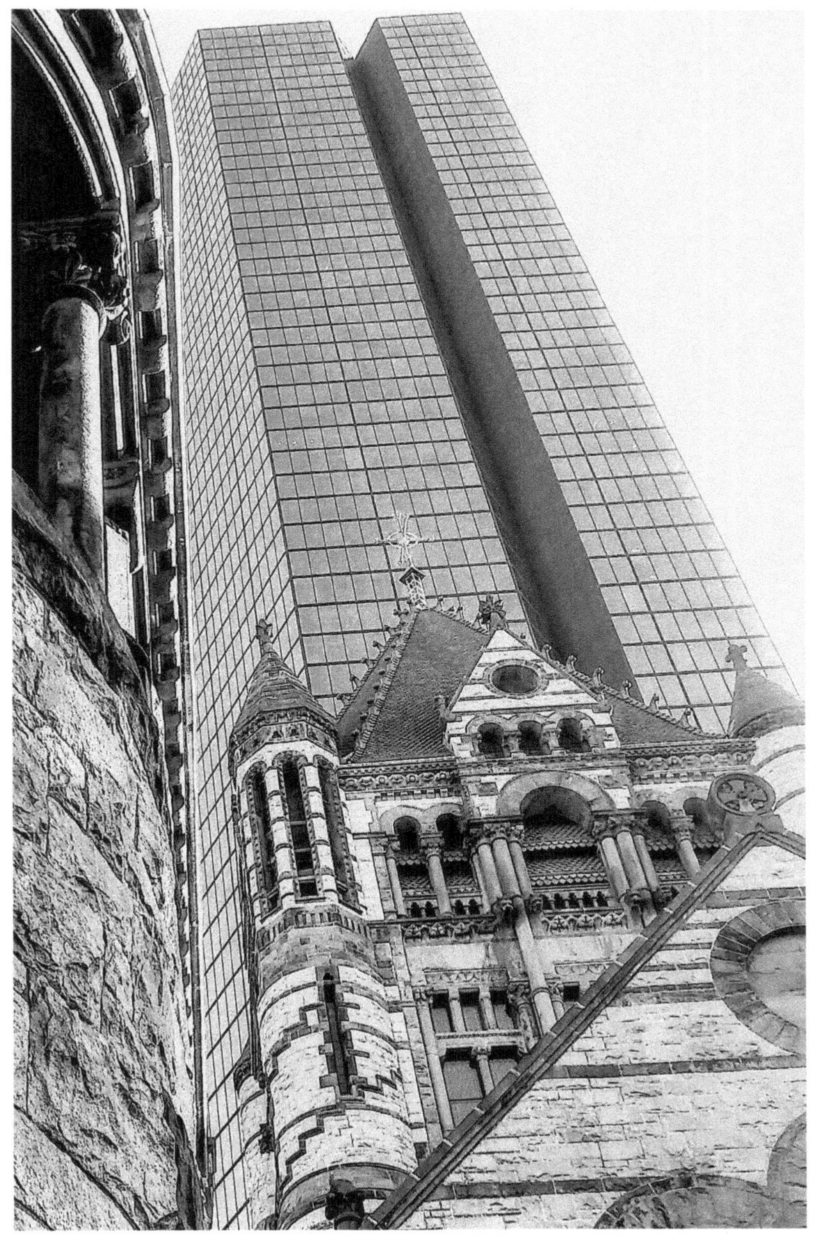

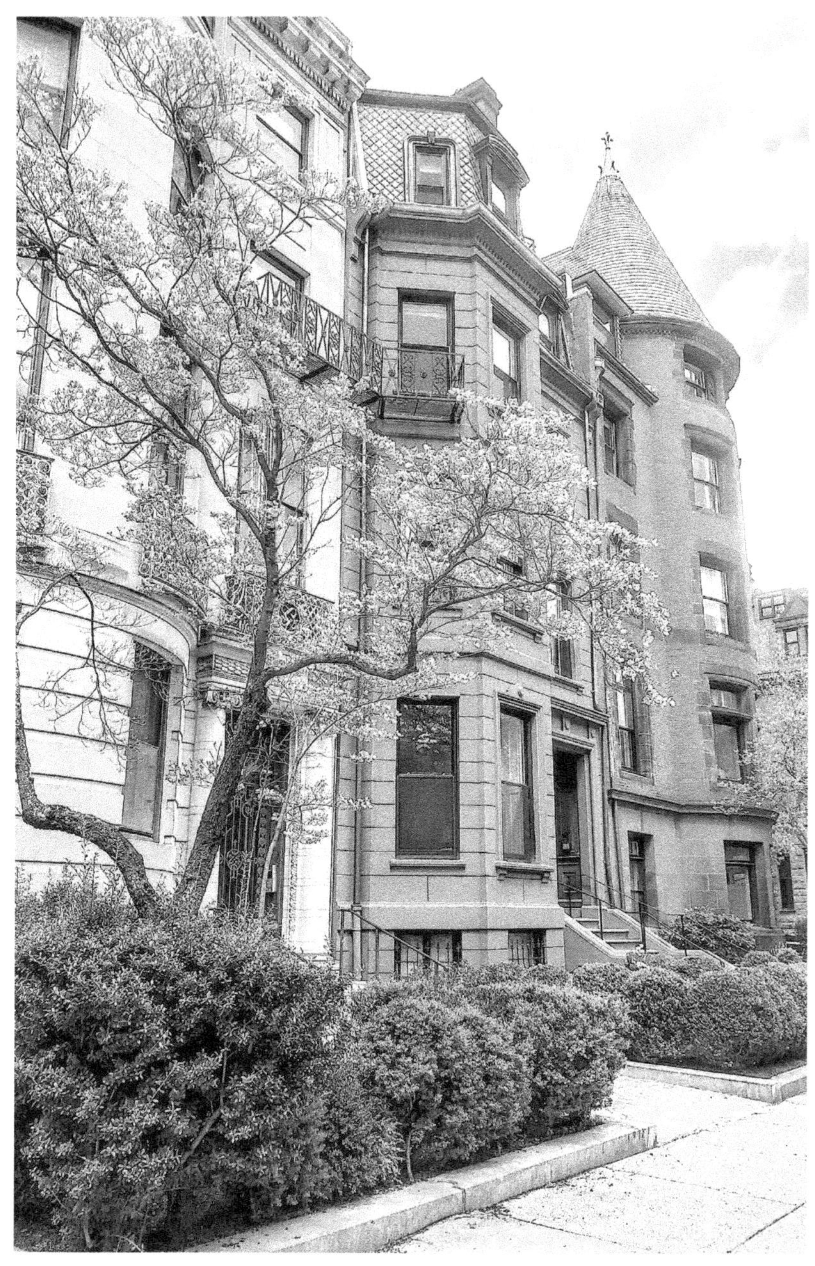

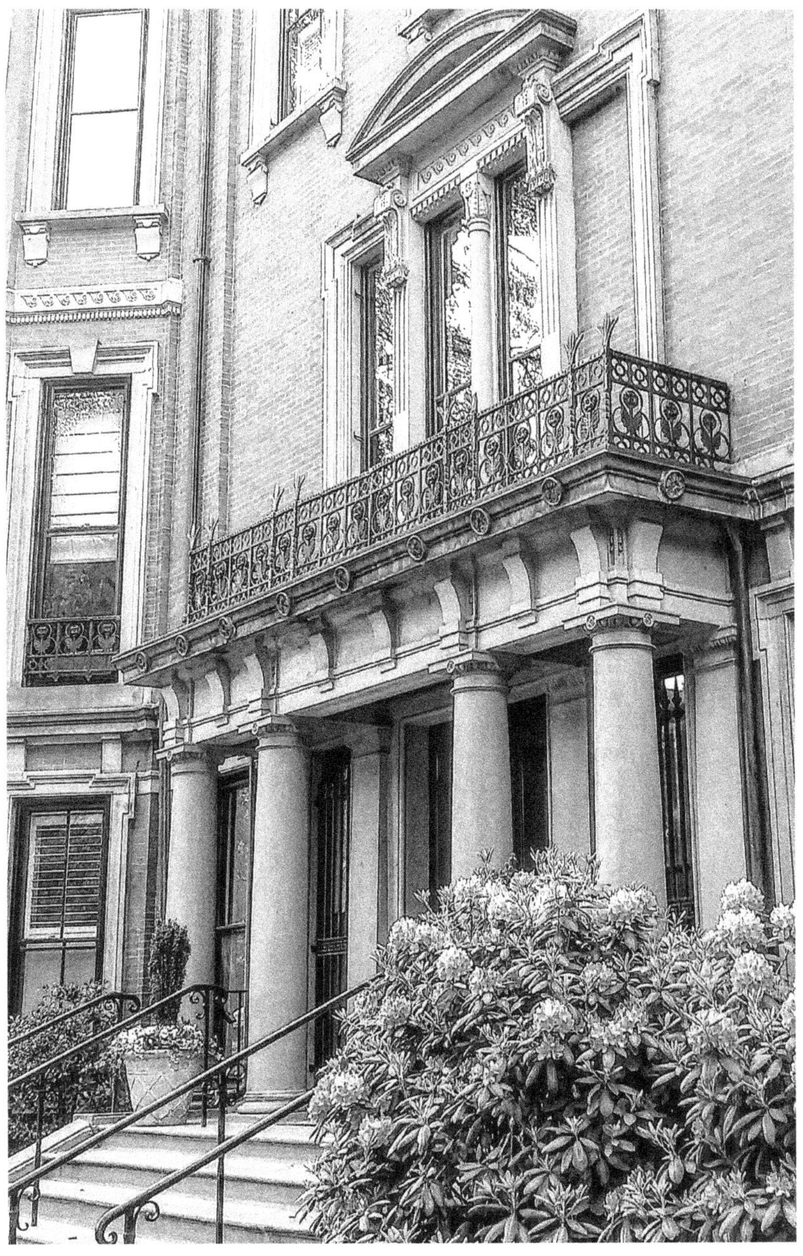

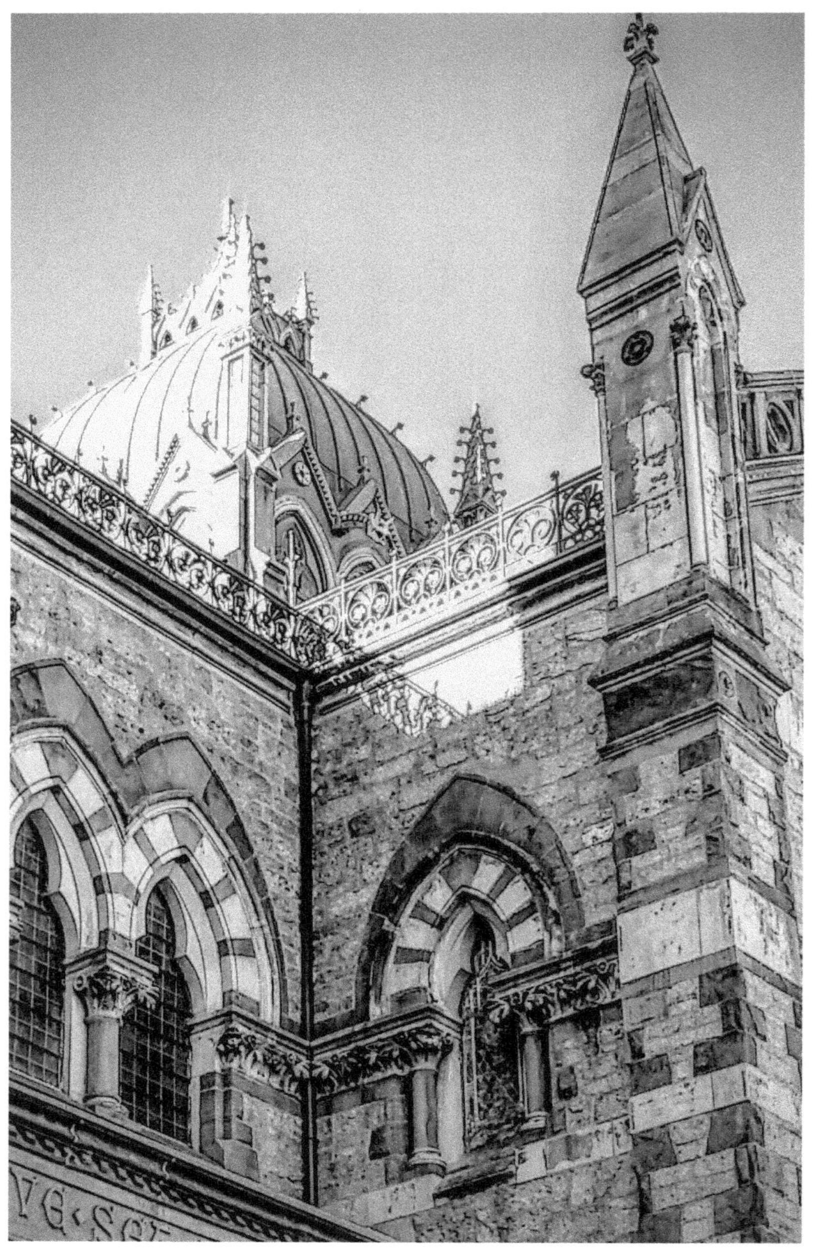

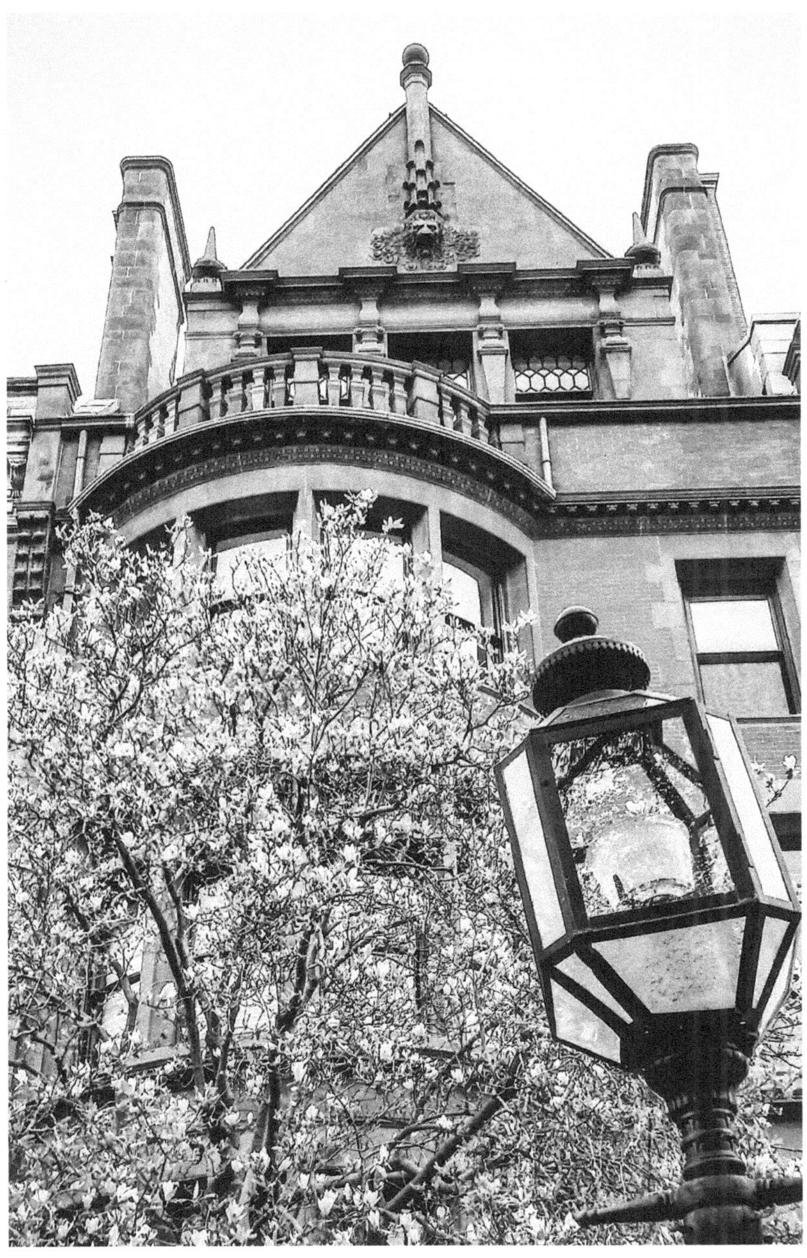

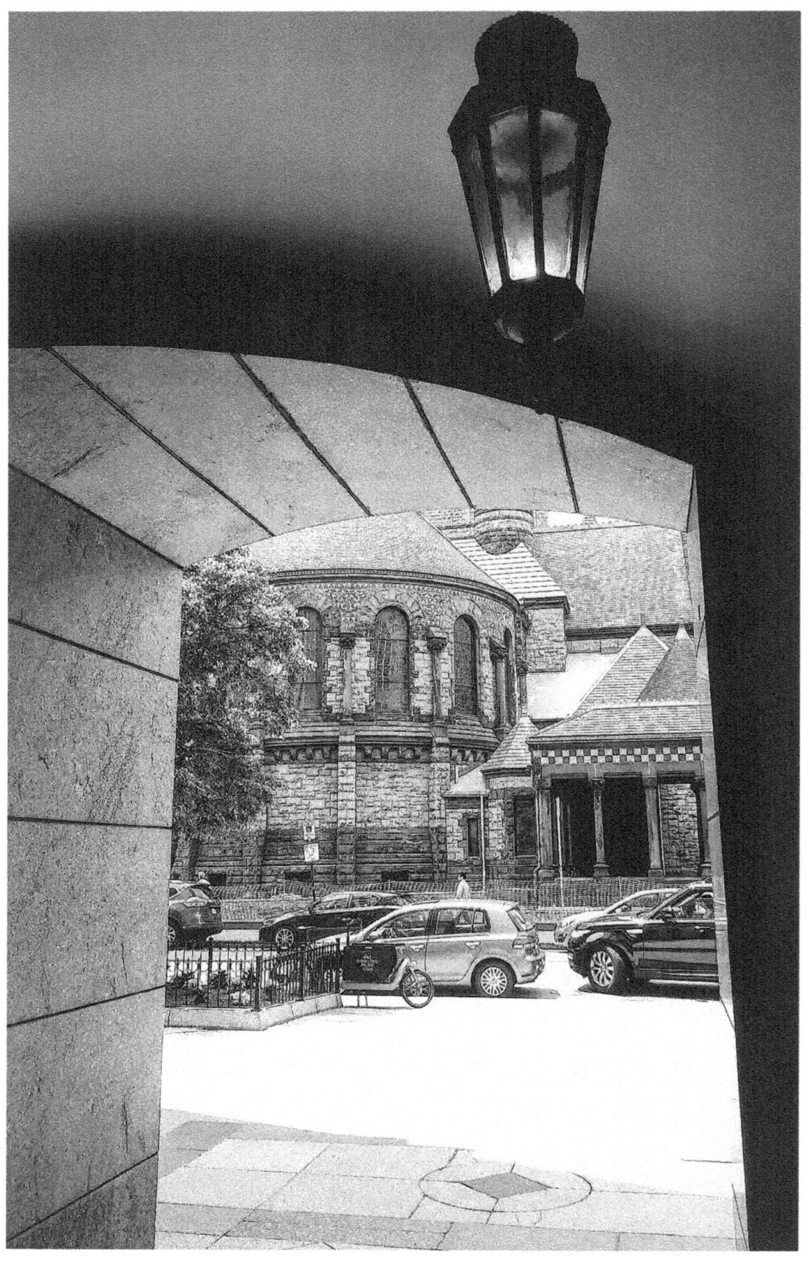

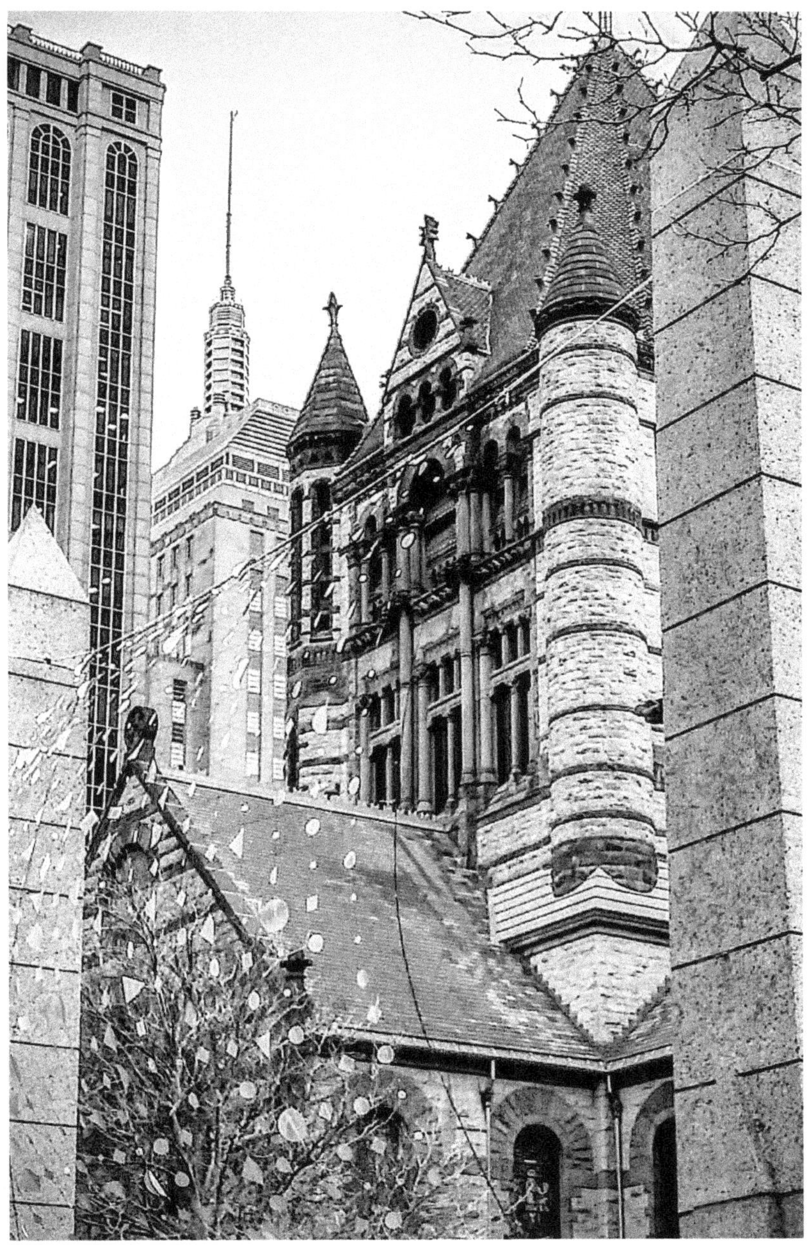

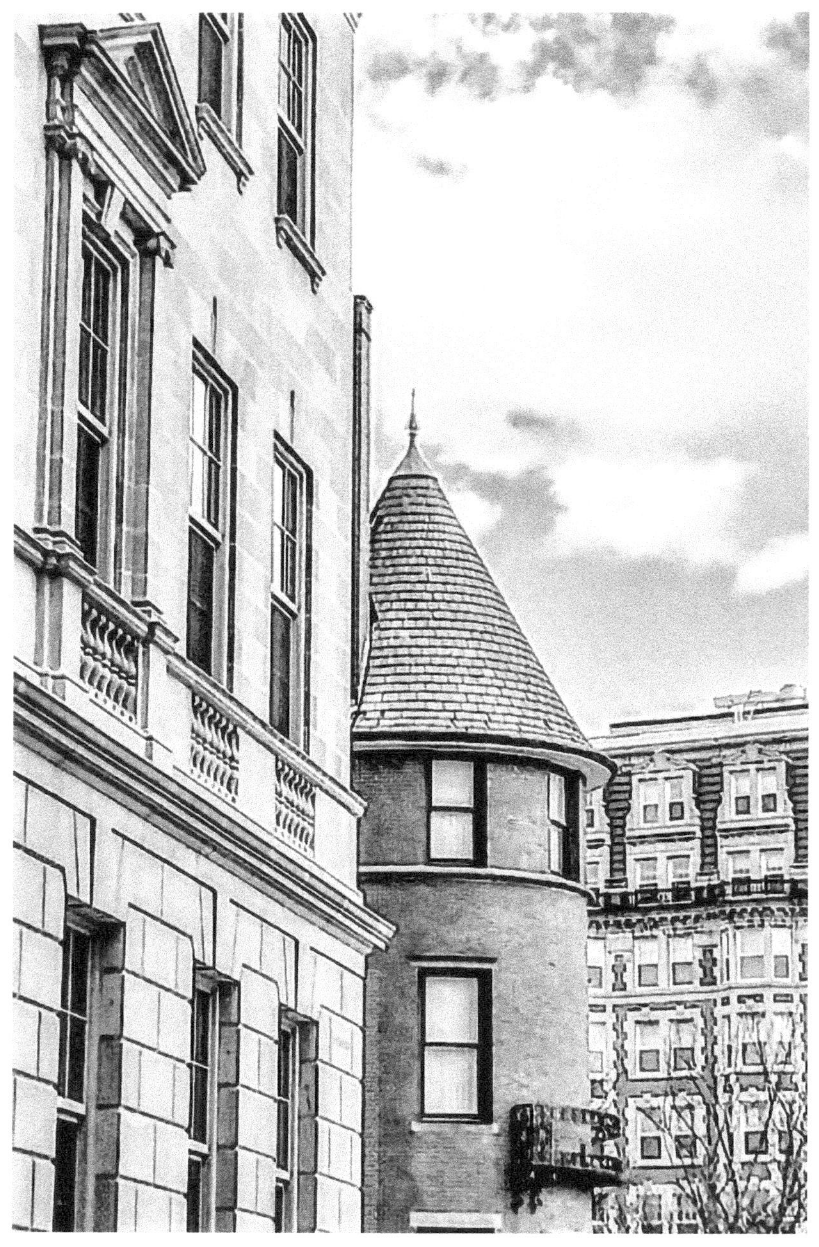

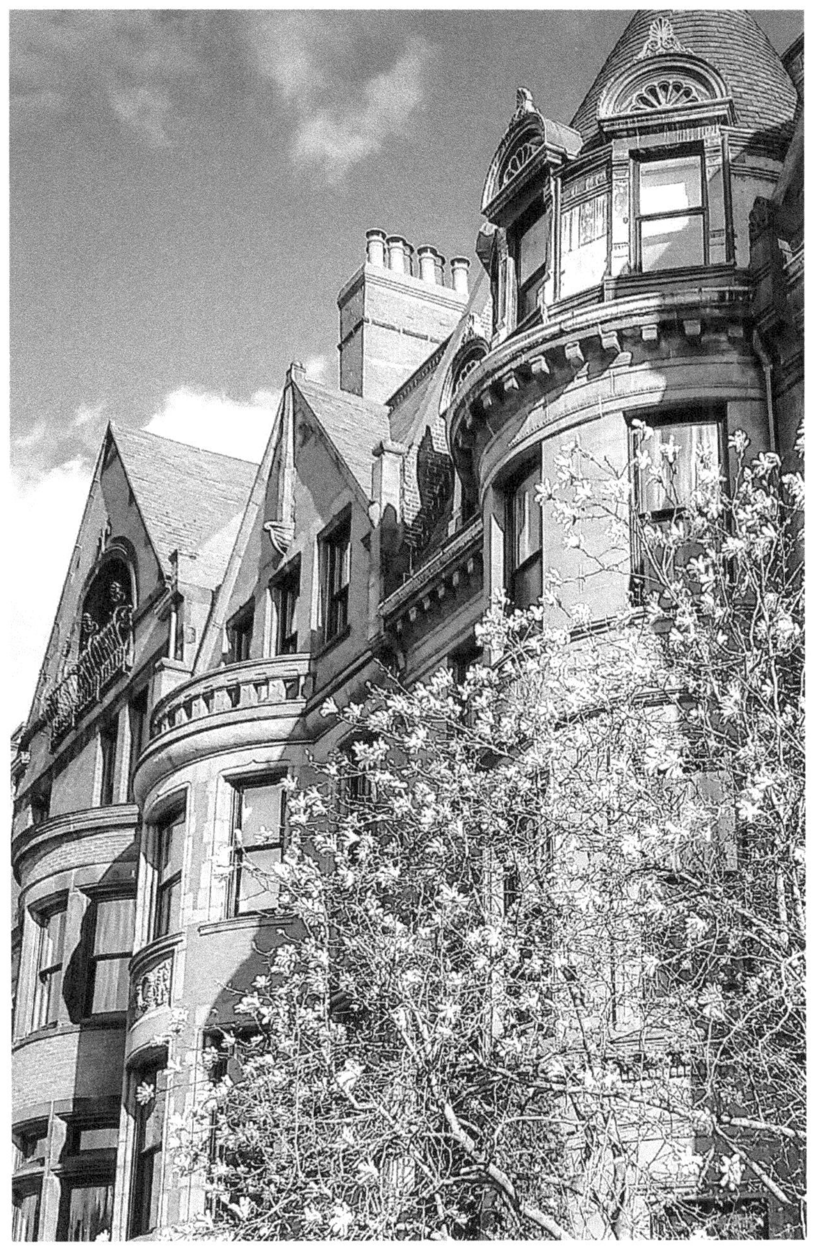

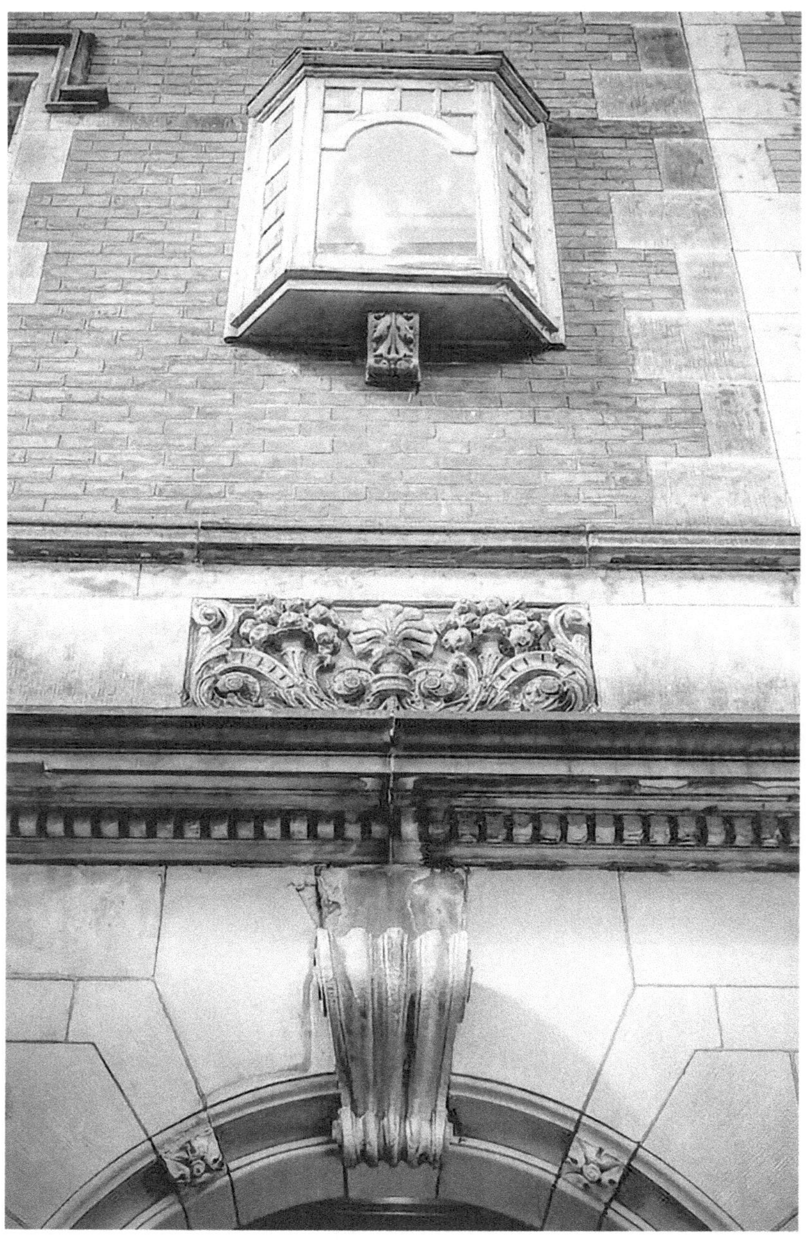

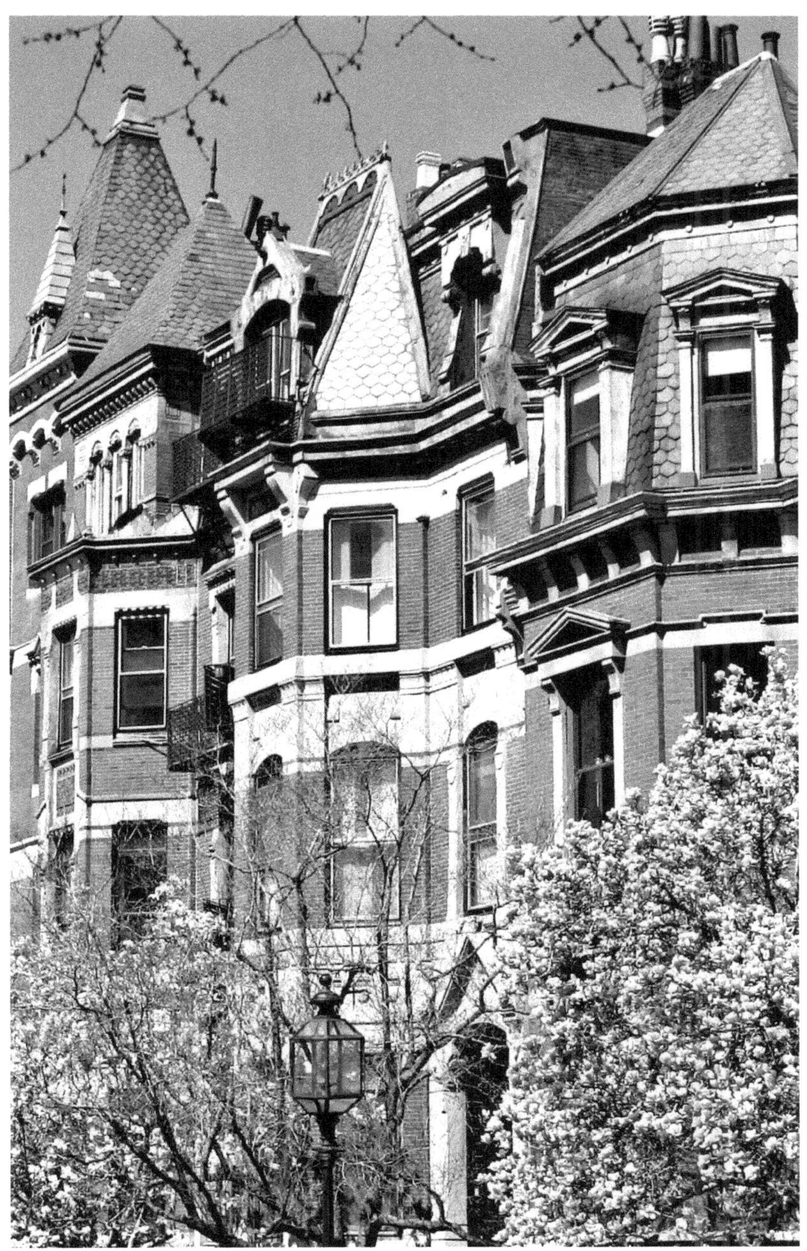

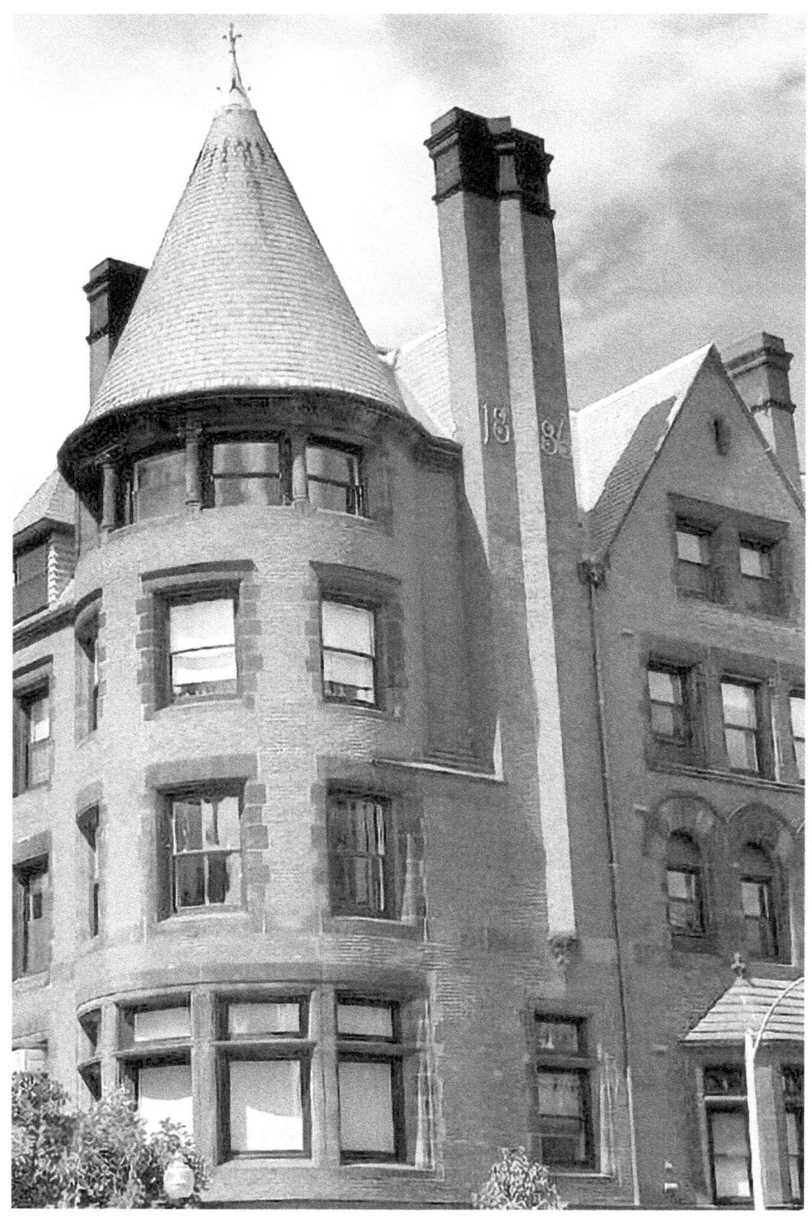

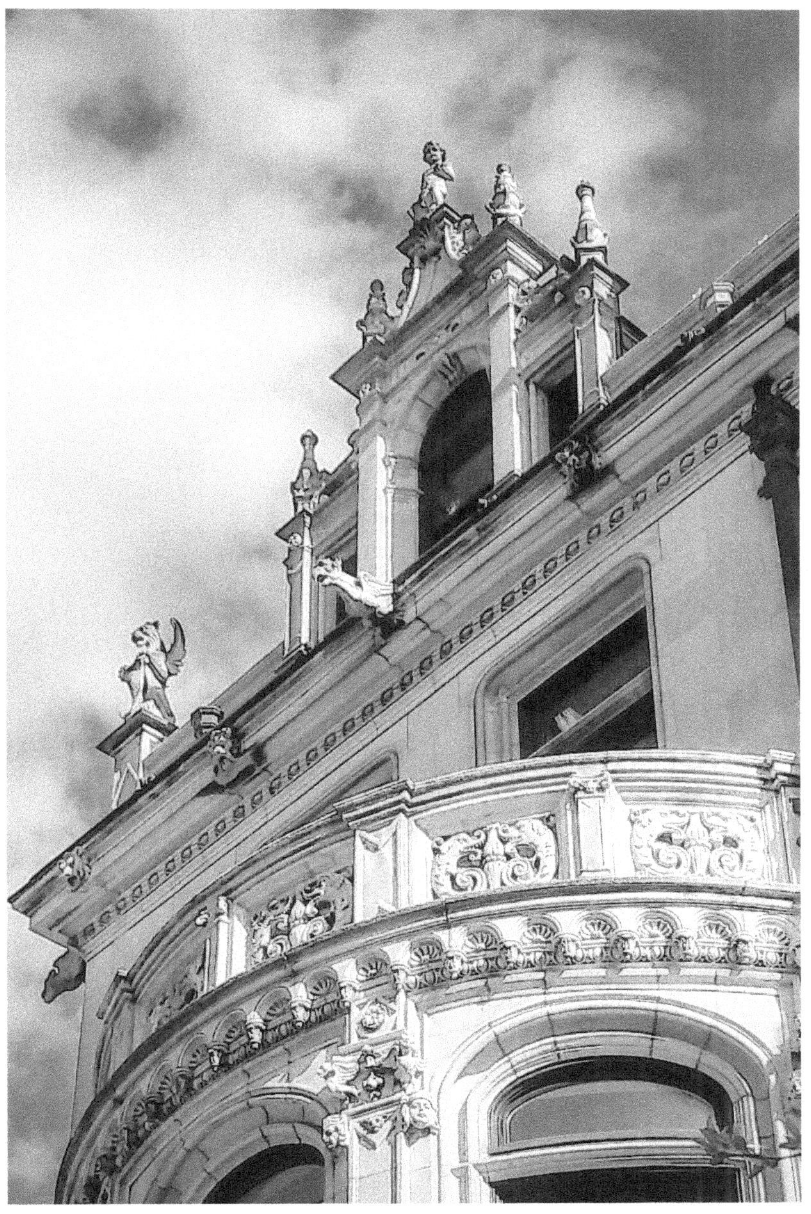

Cambridge

It takes me several days, after I get
back to Boston, to realize that the
reference "the president" refers to the
president of Harvard and not to
a minor official in Washington.

Oliver Wendell Holmes, Jr. (1841 – 1935)
Associate Justice of the U.S. Supreme Court

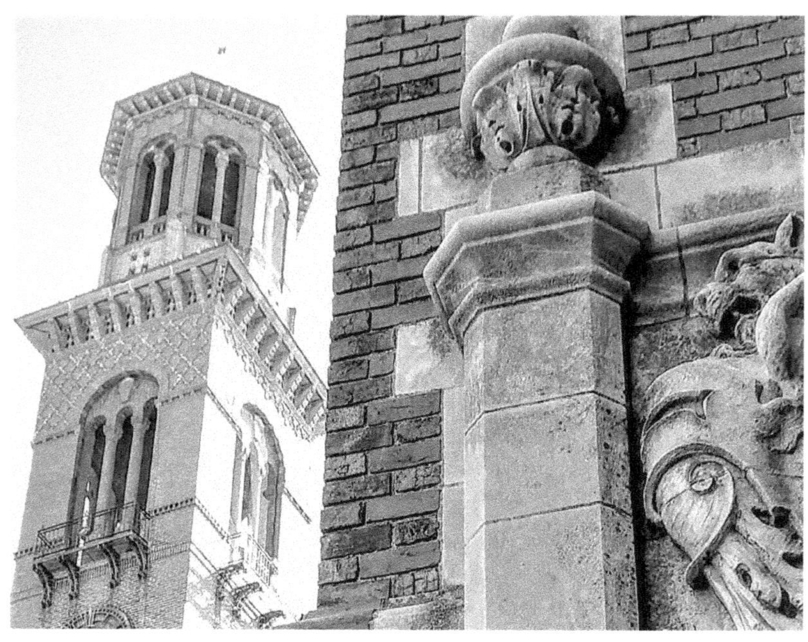

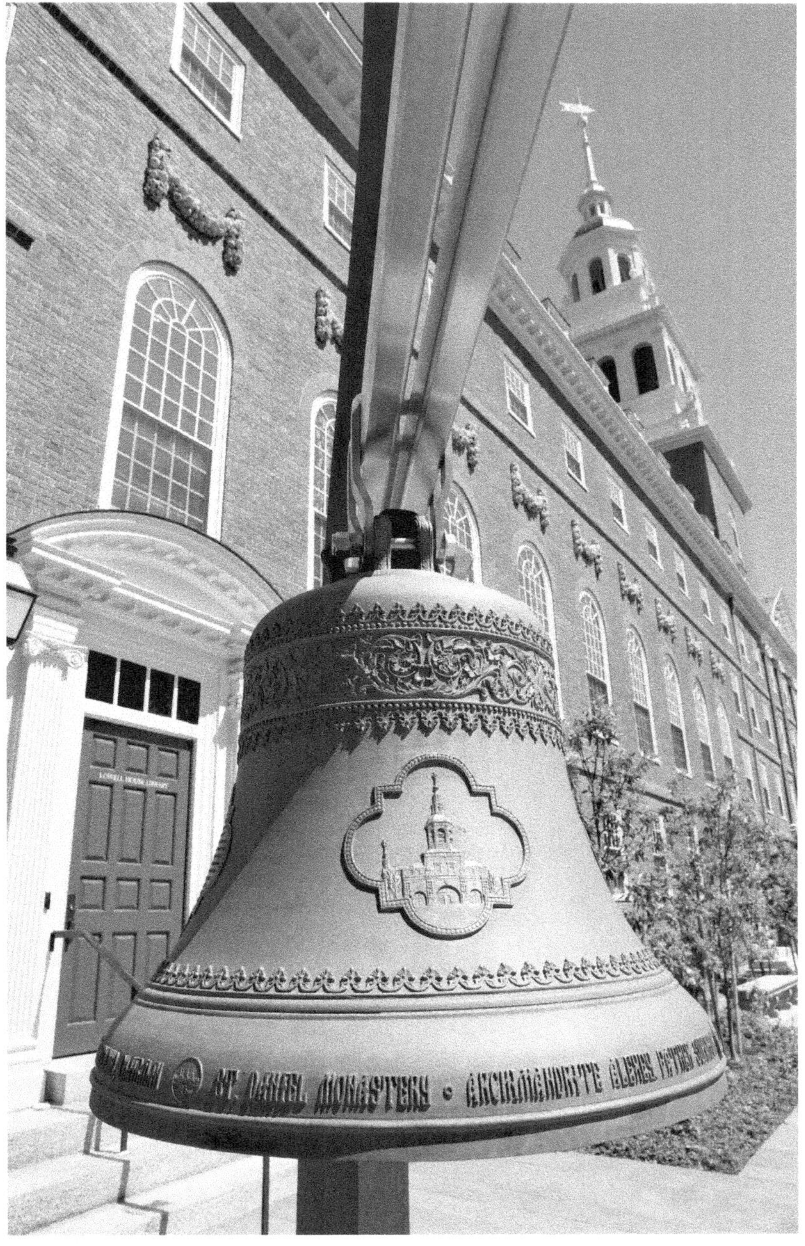

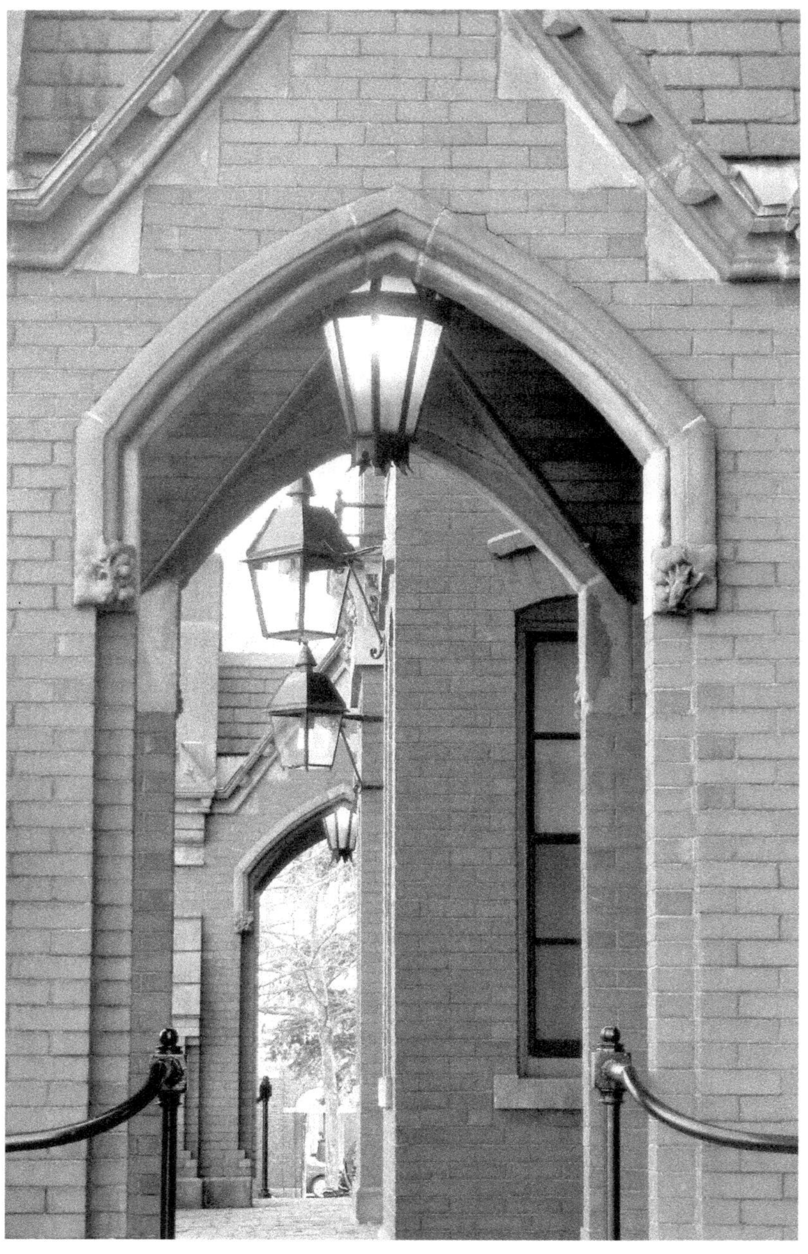

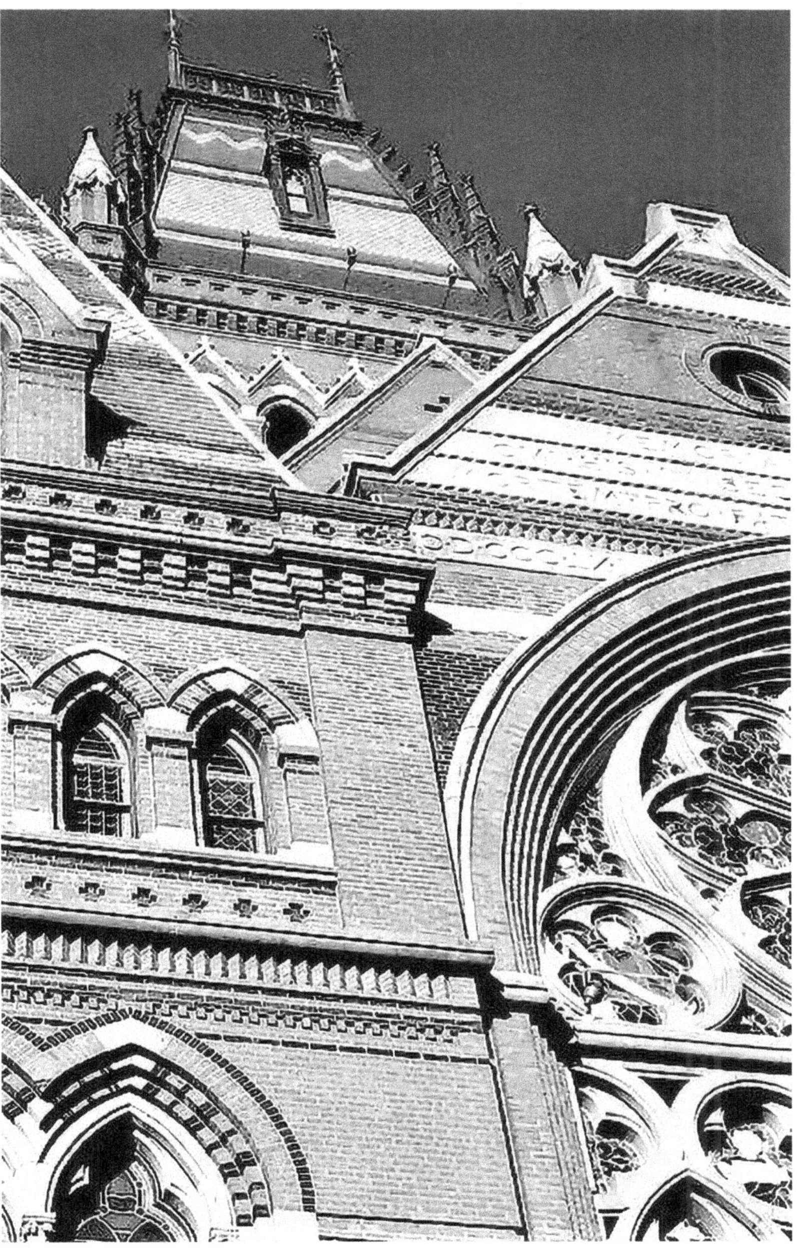

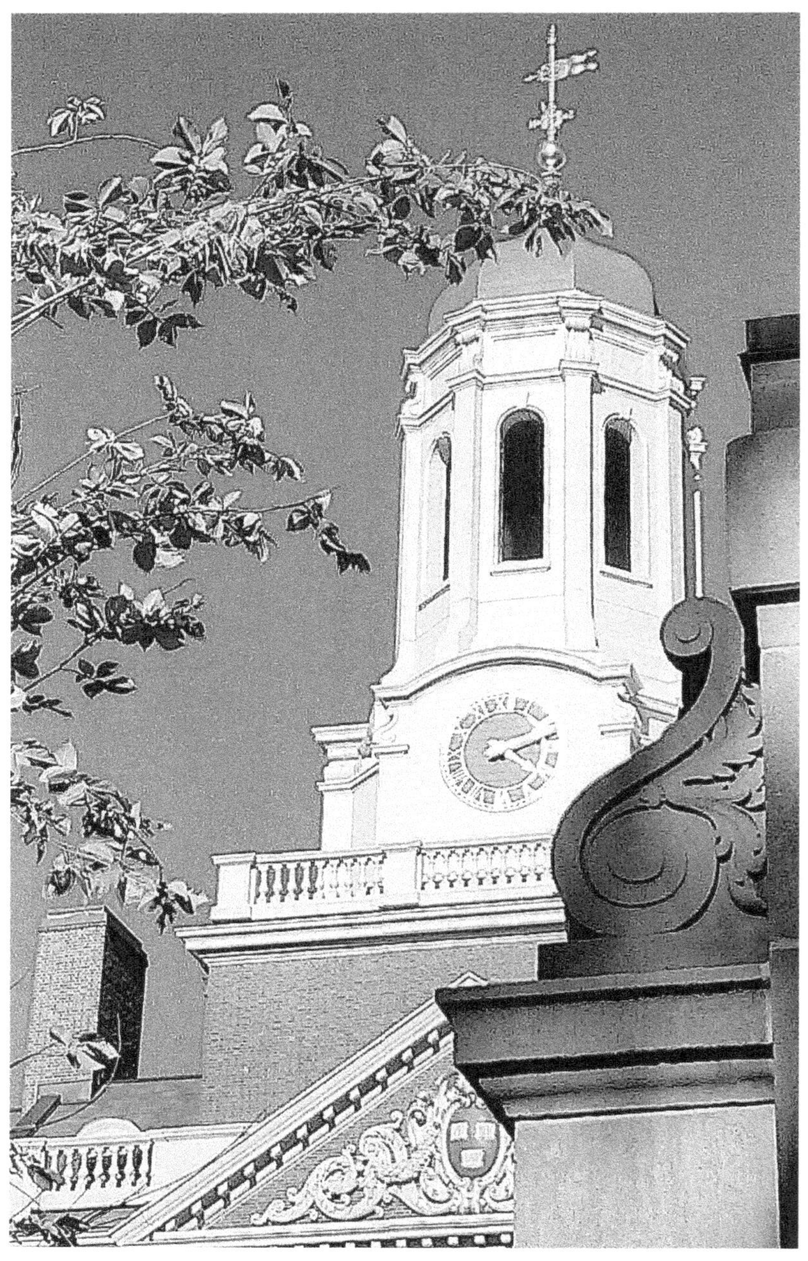

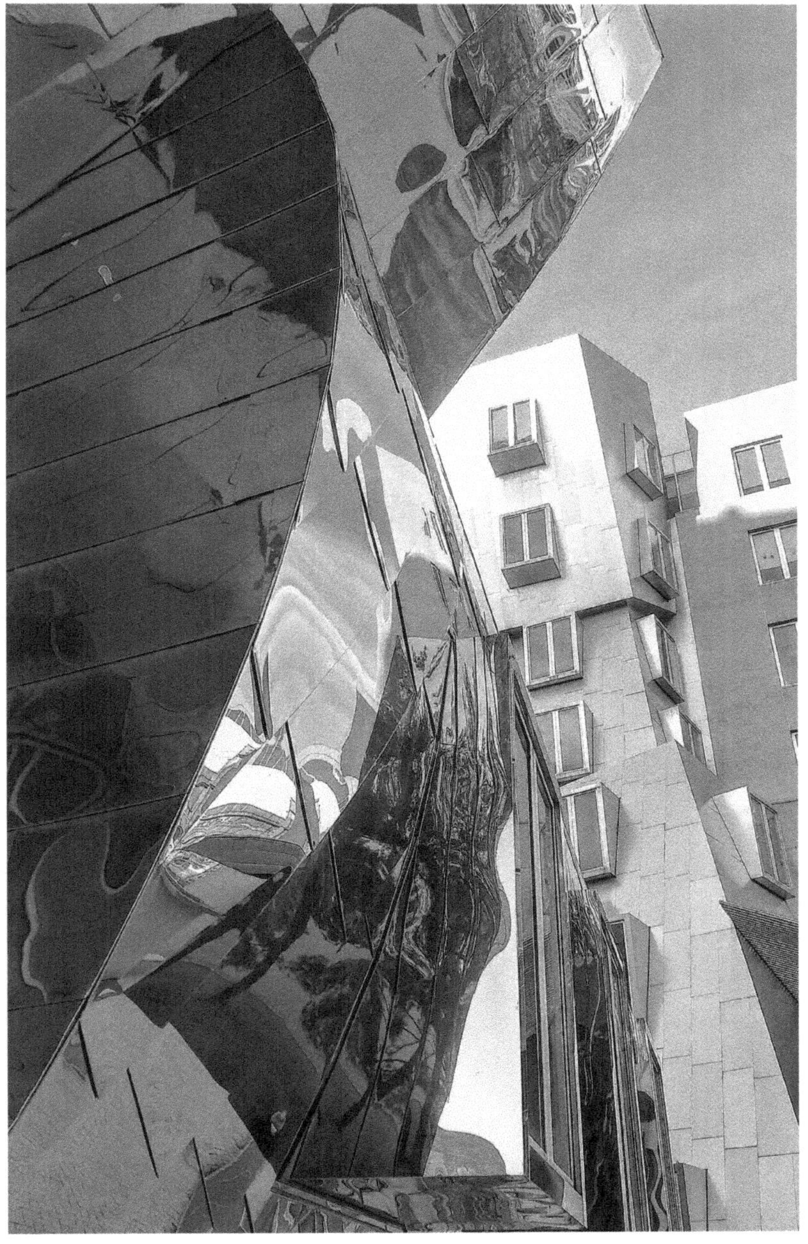

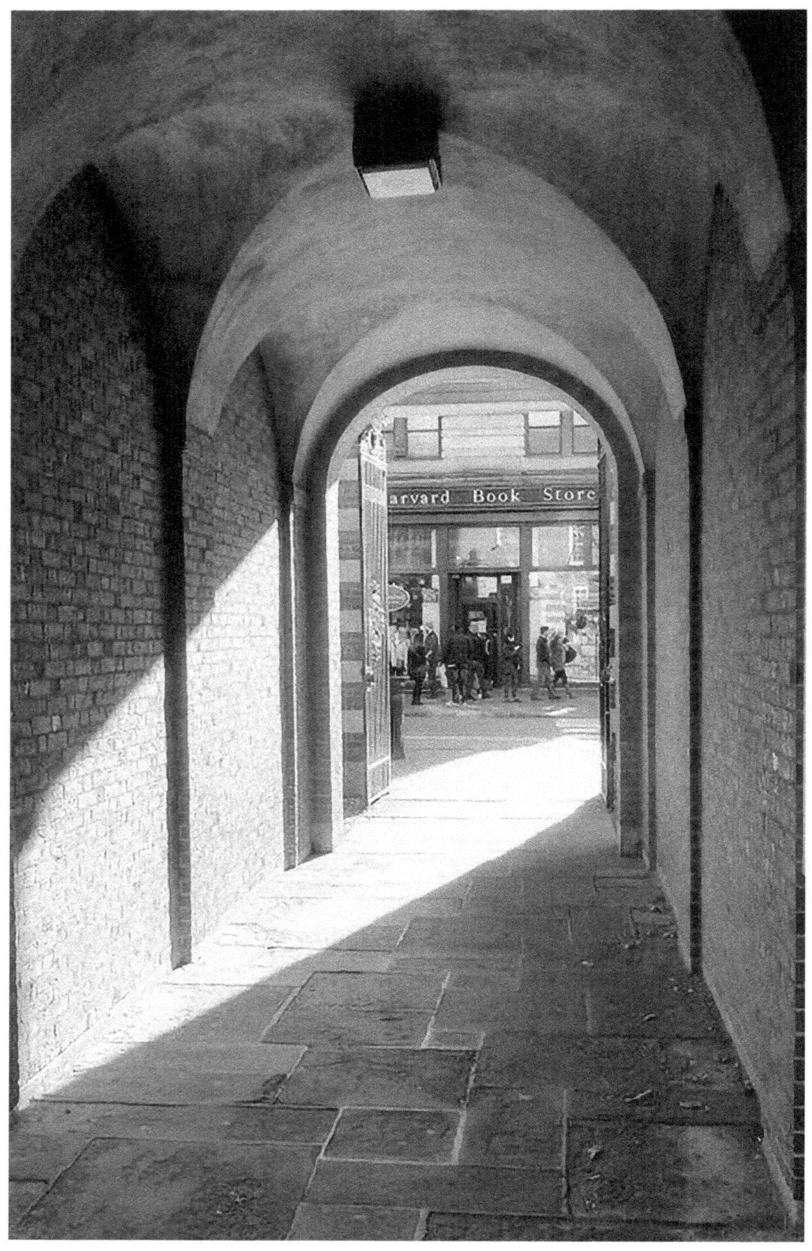
arvard Book Store

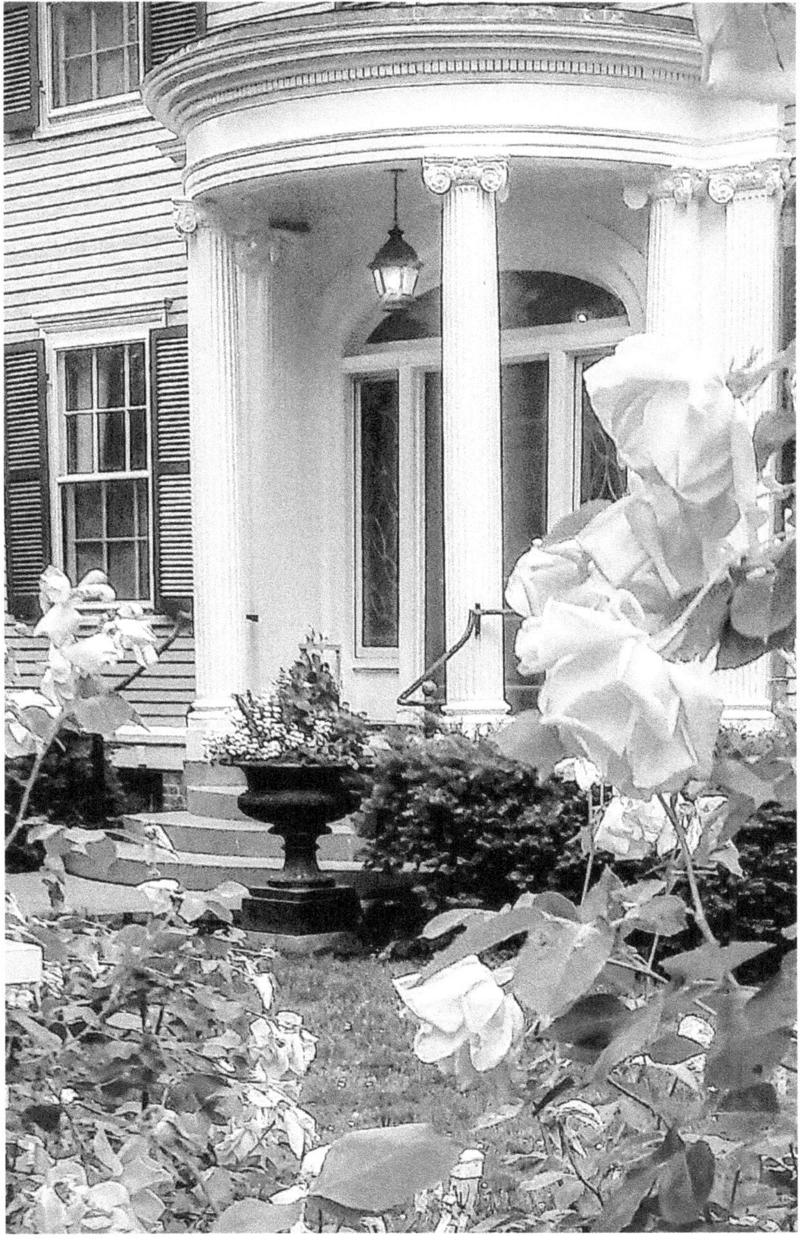

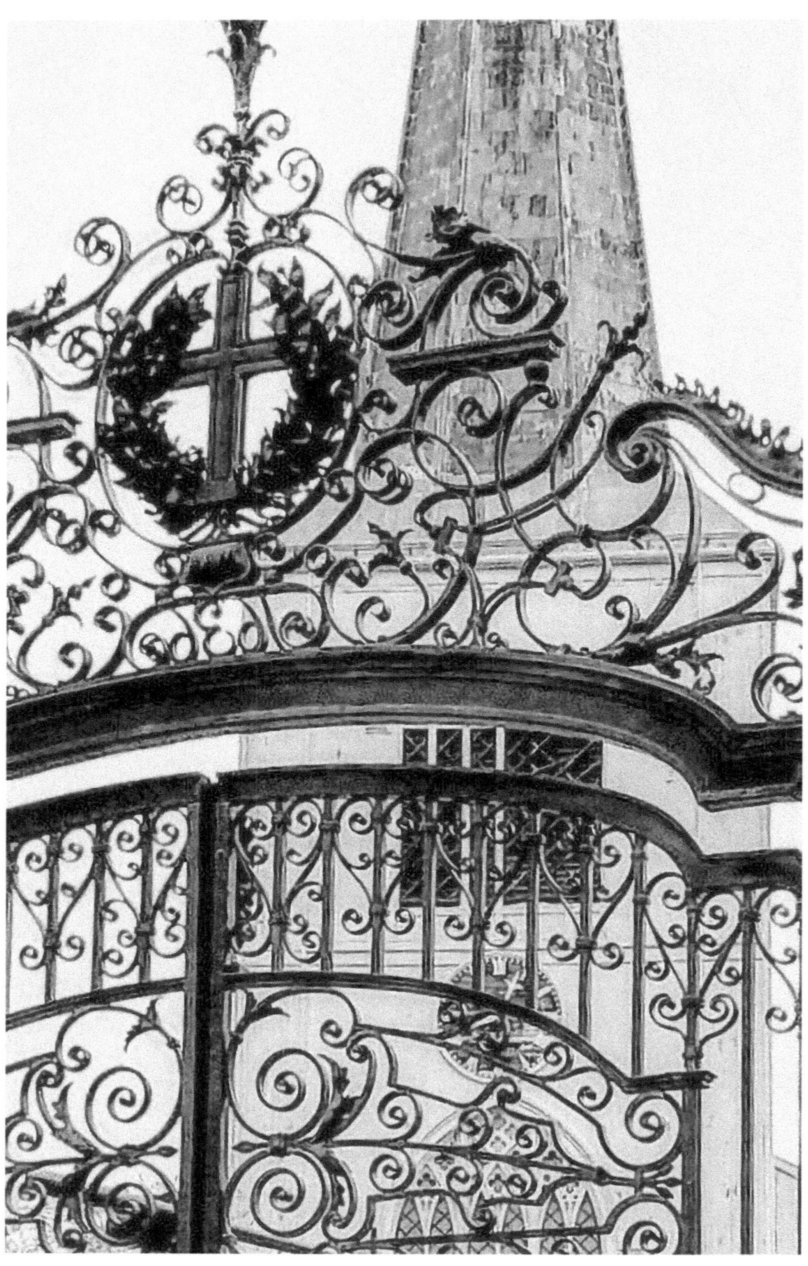

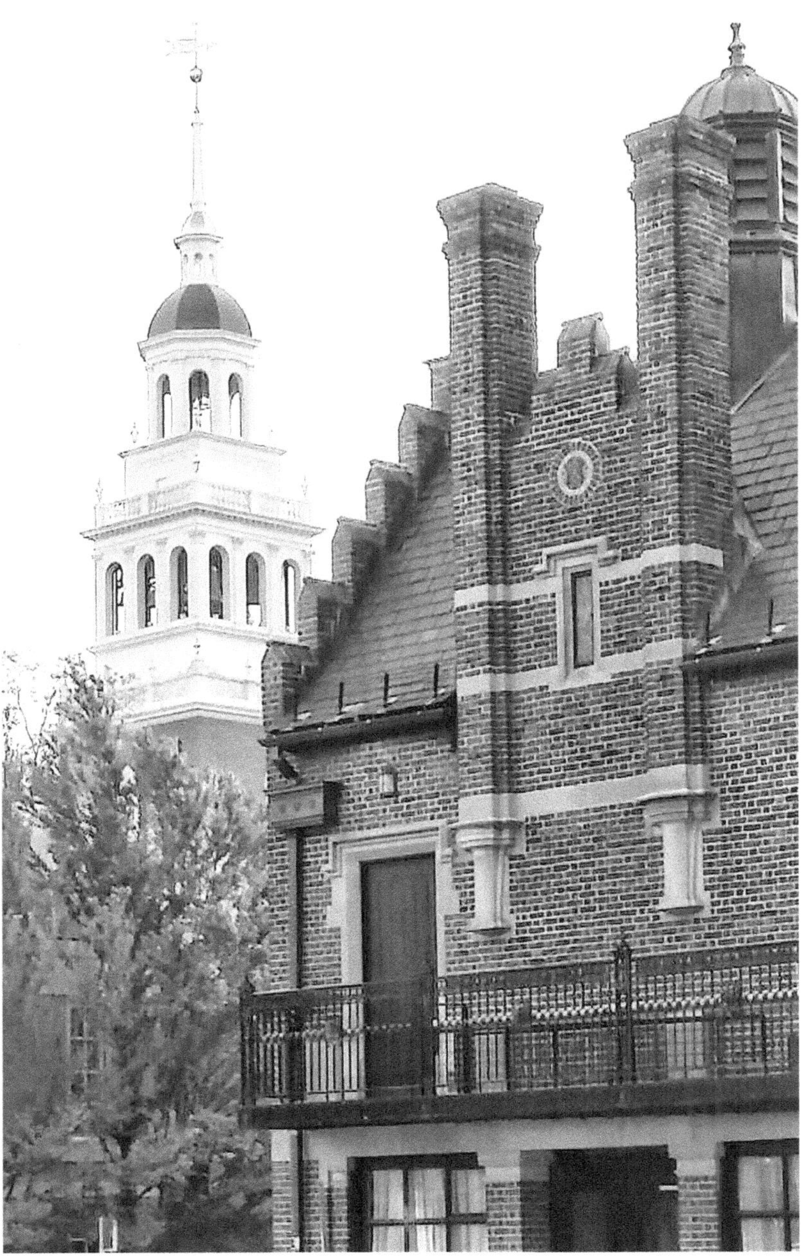

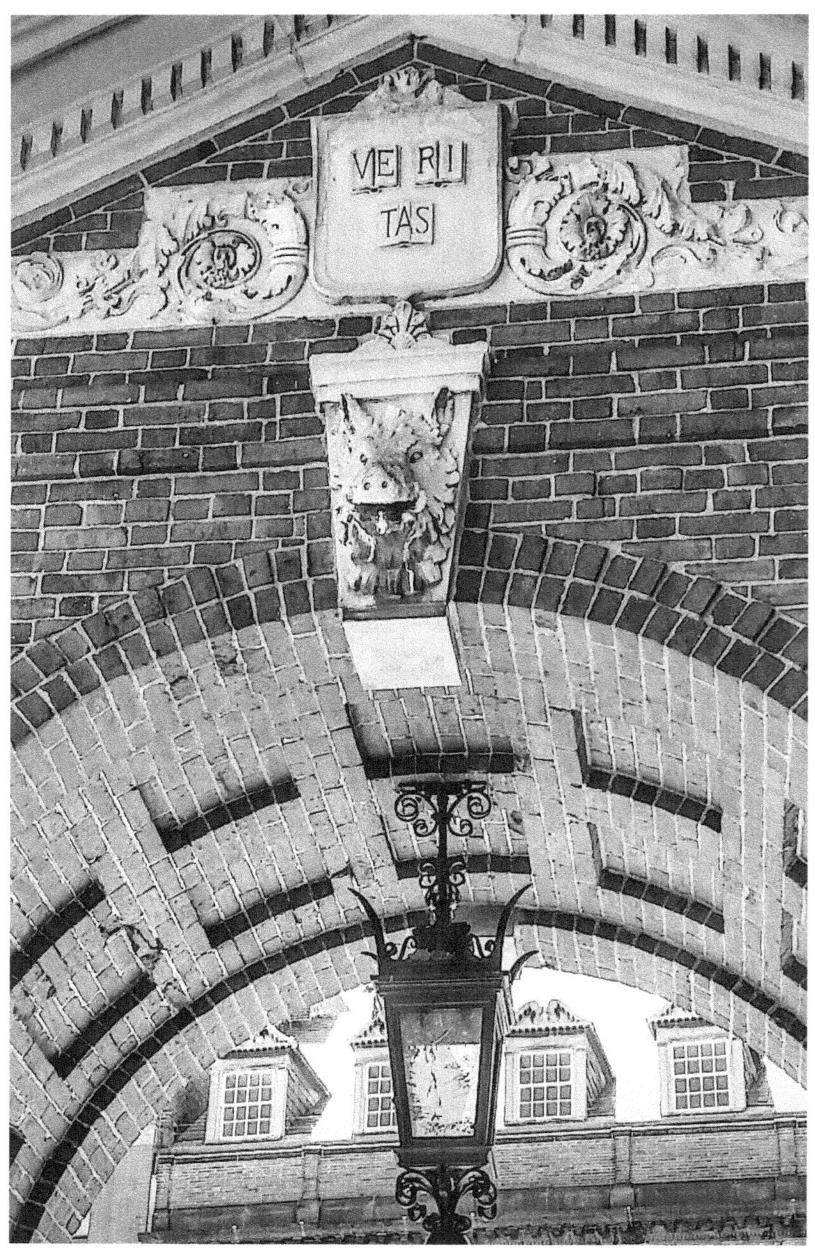
VE RI
TAS

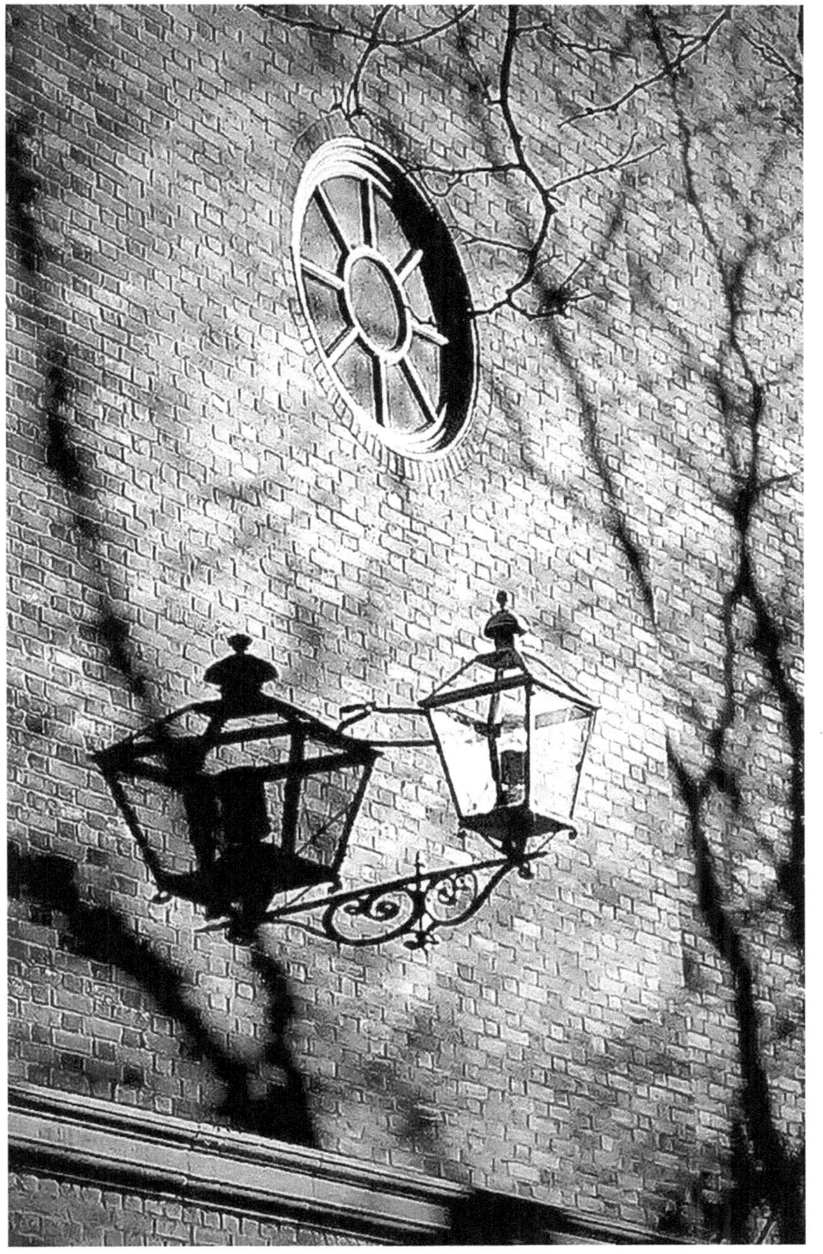

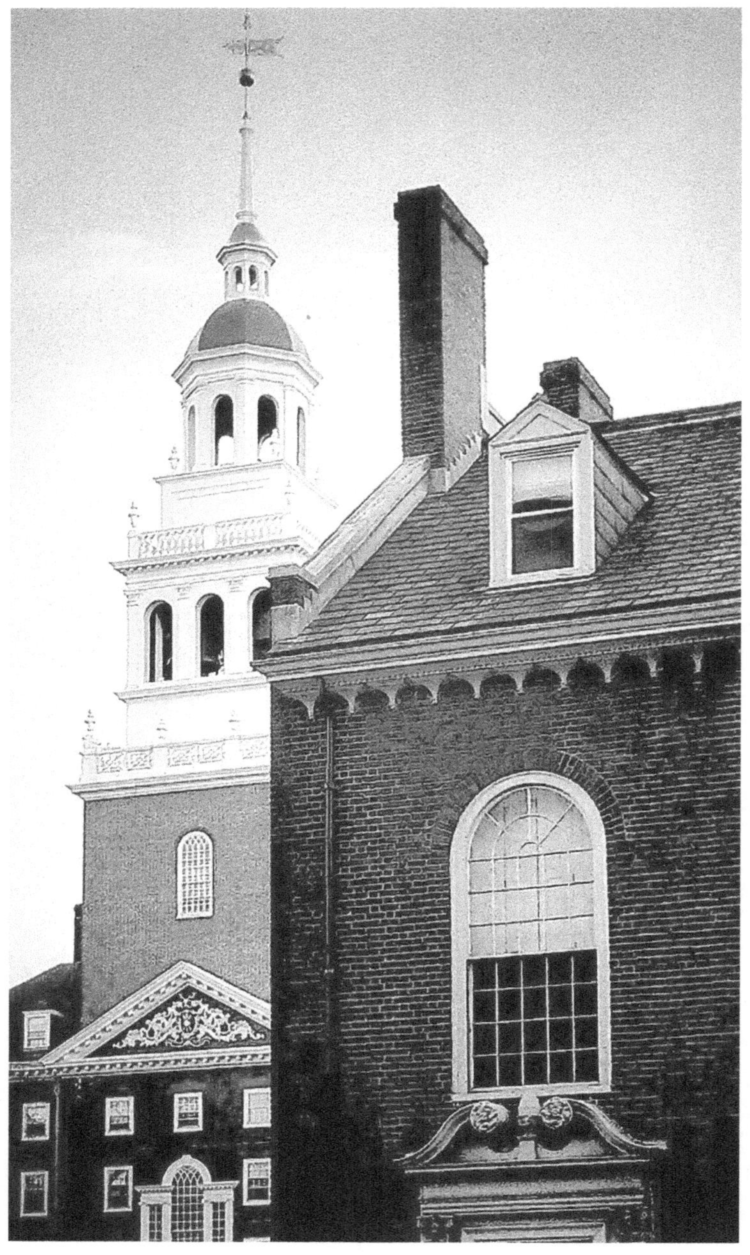

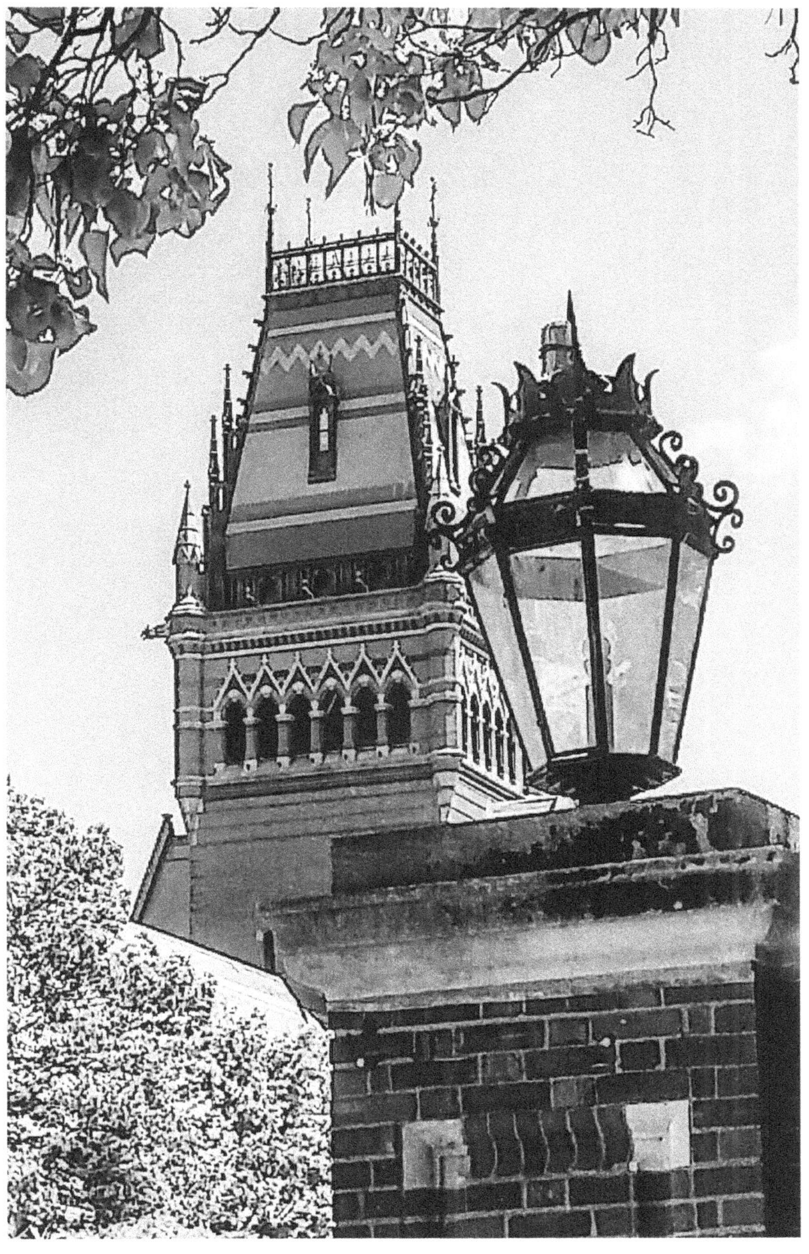

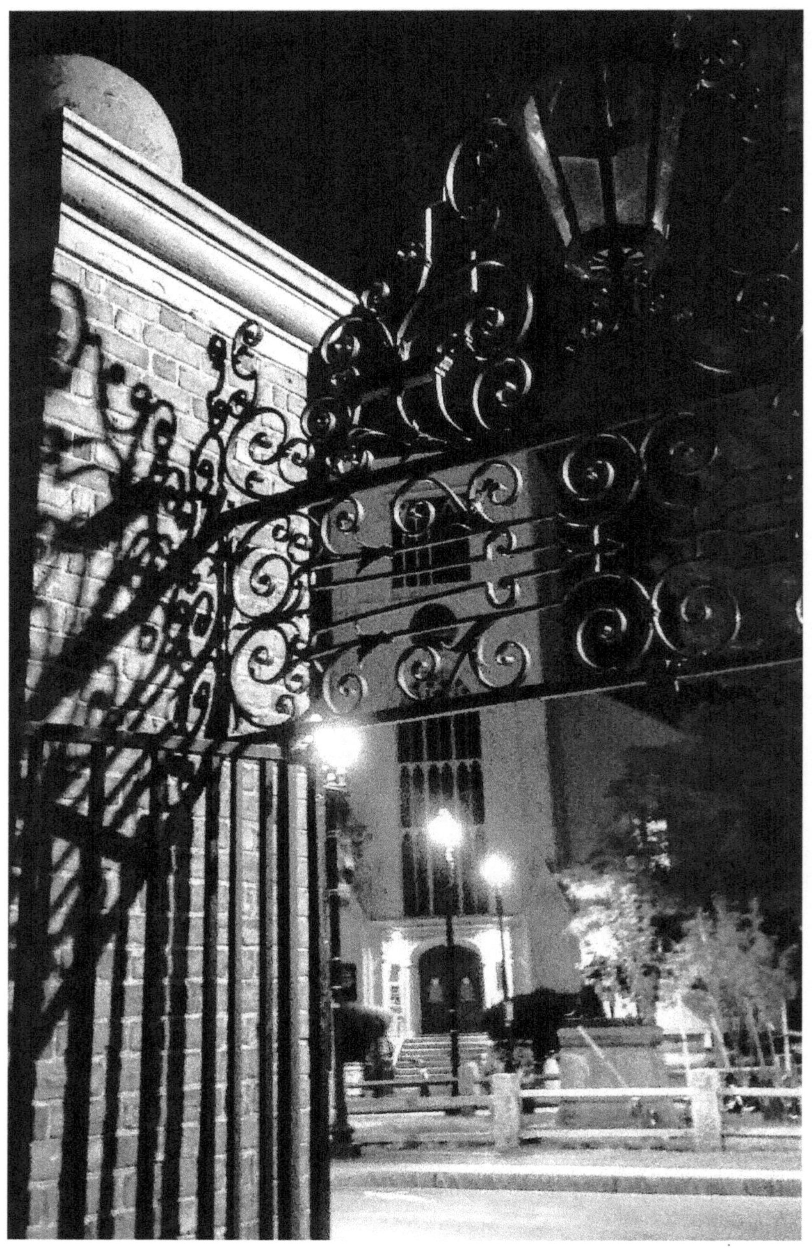

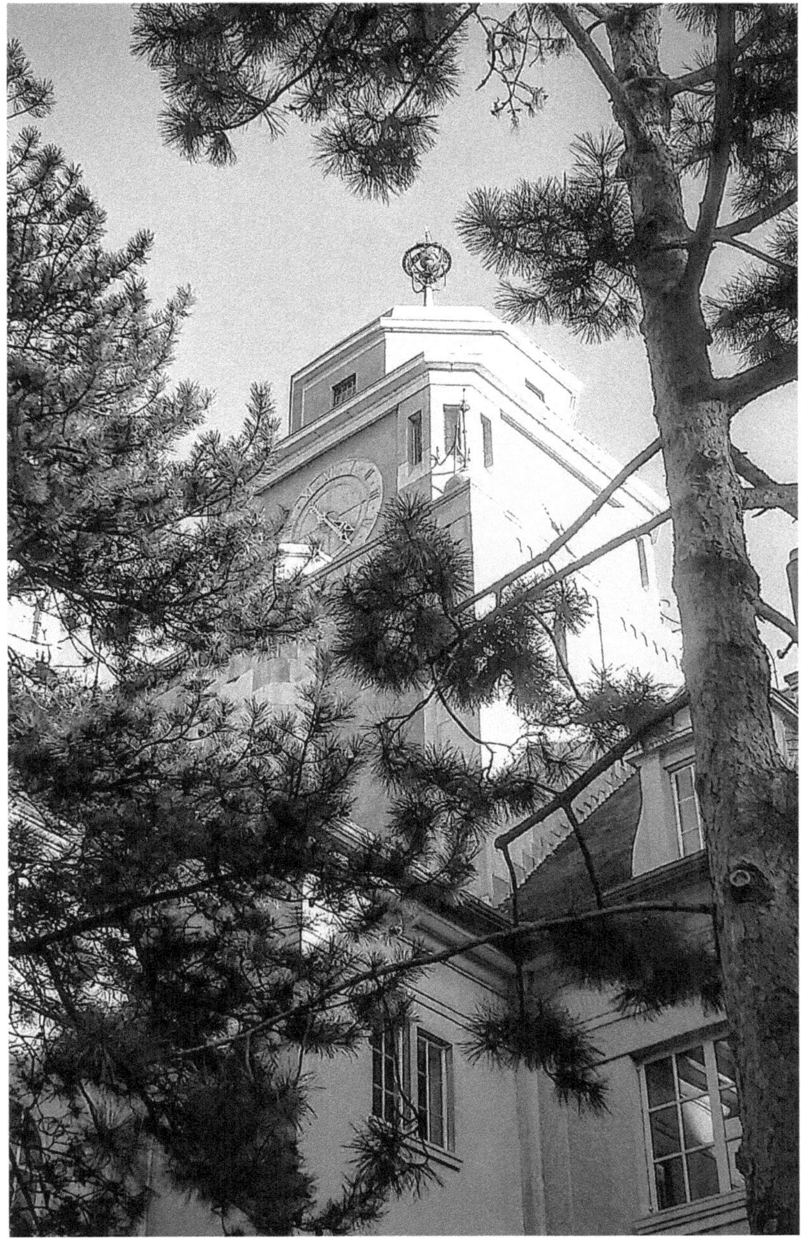

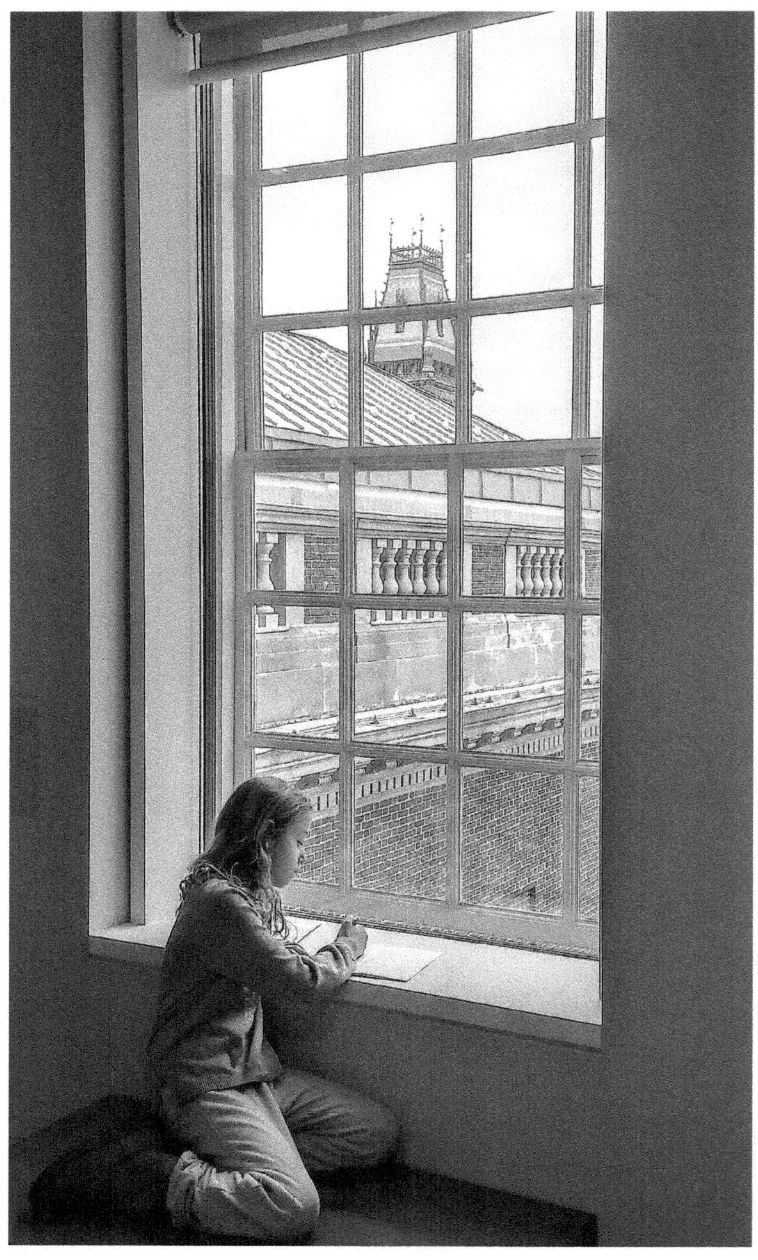

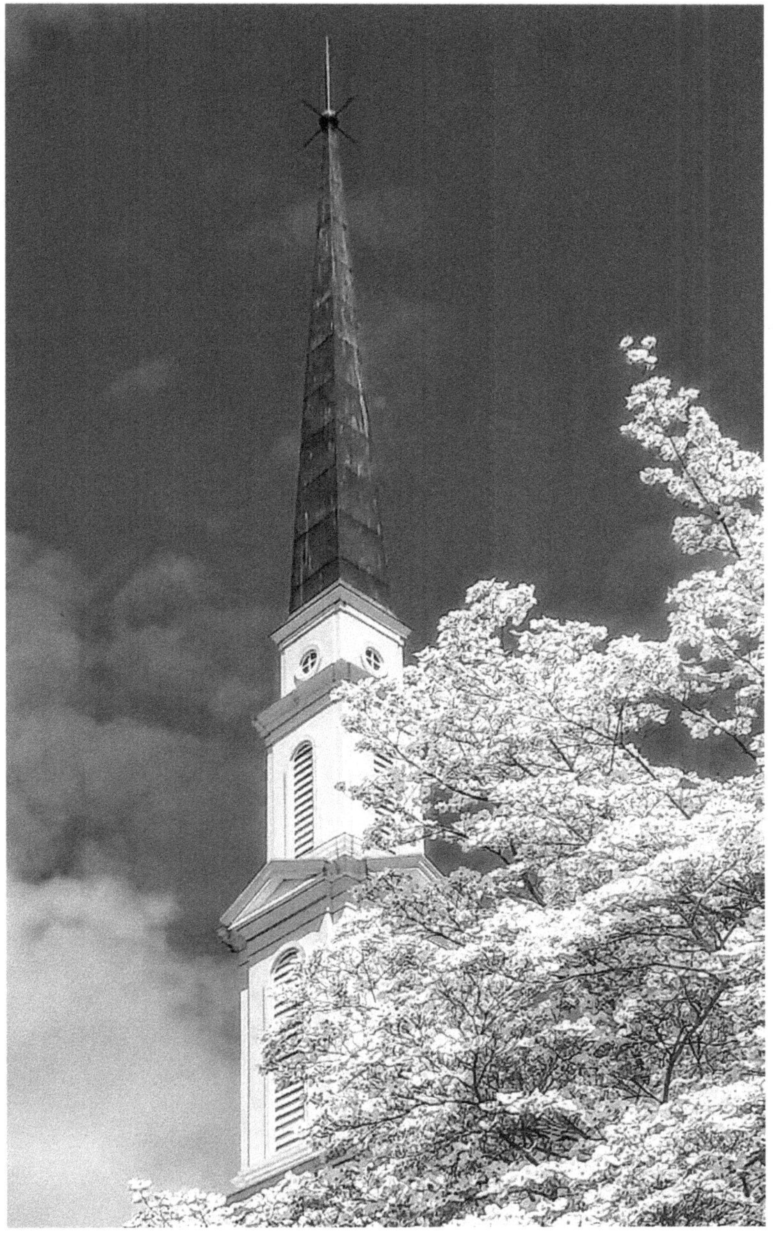

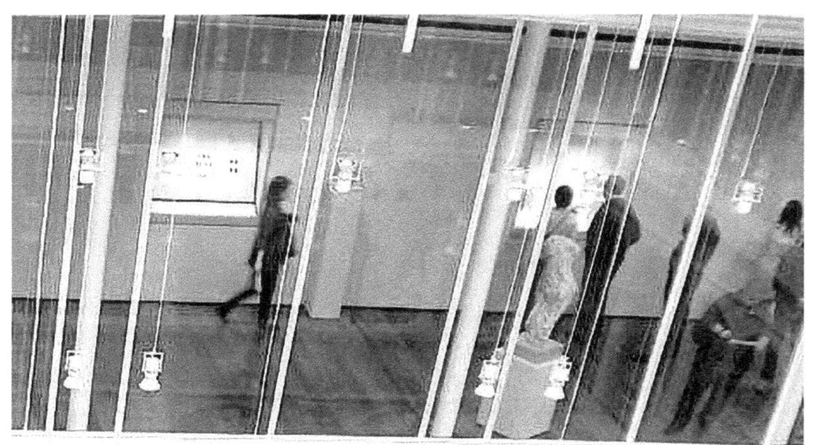

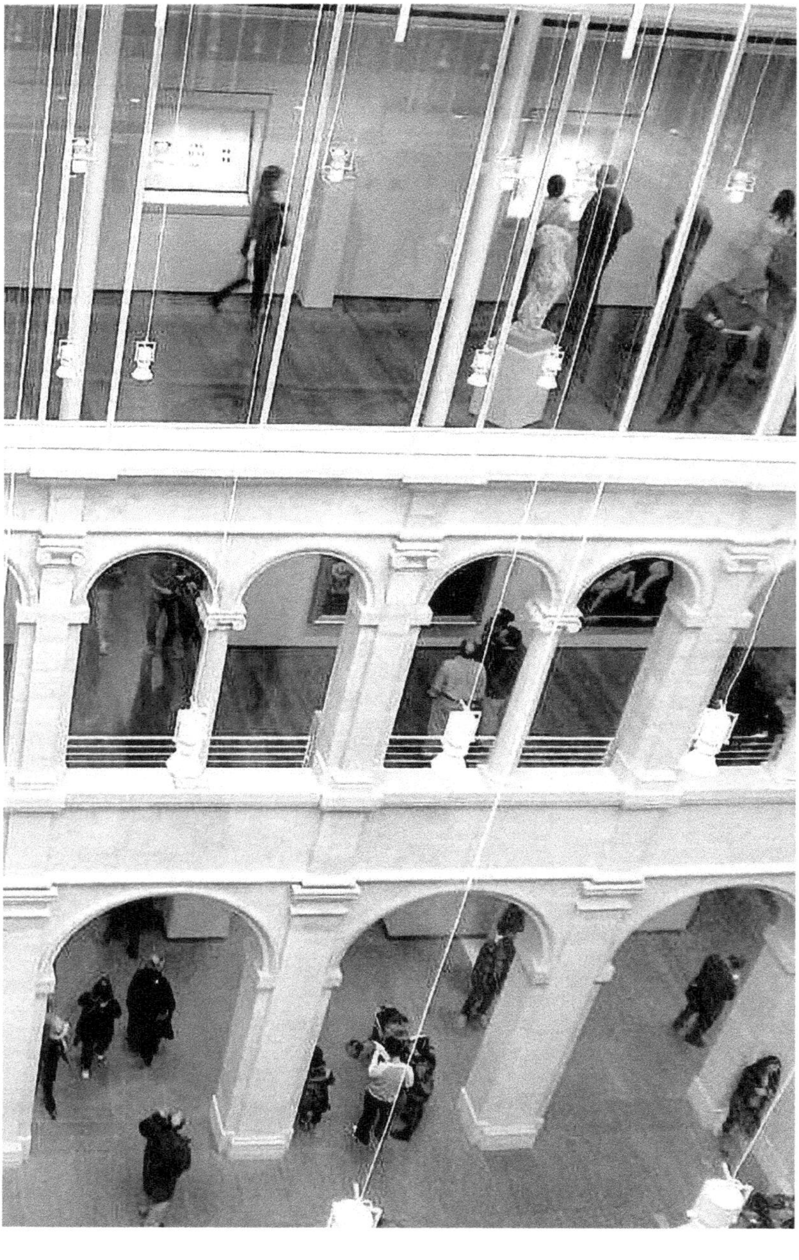

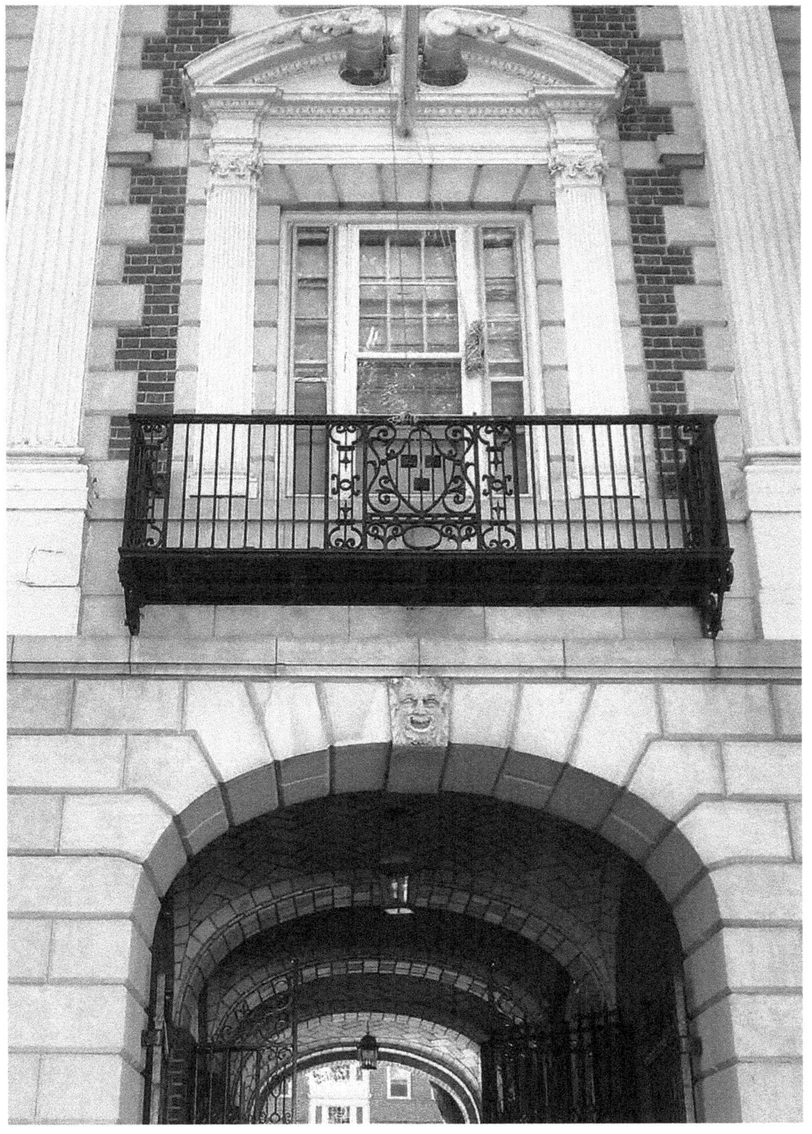

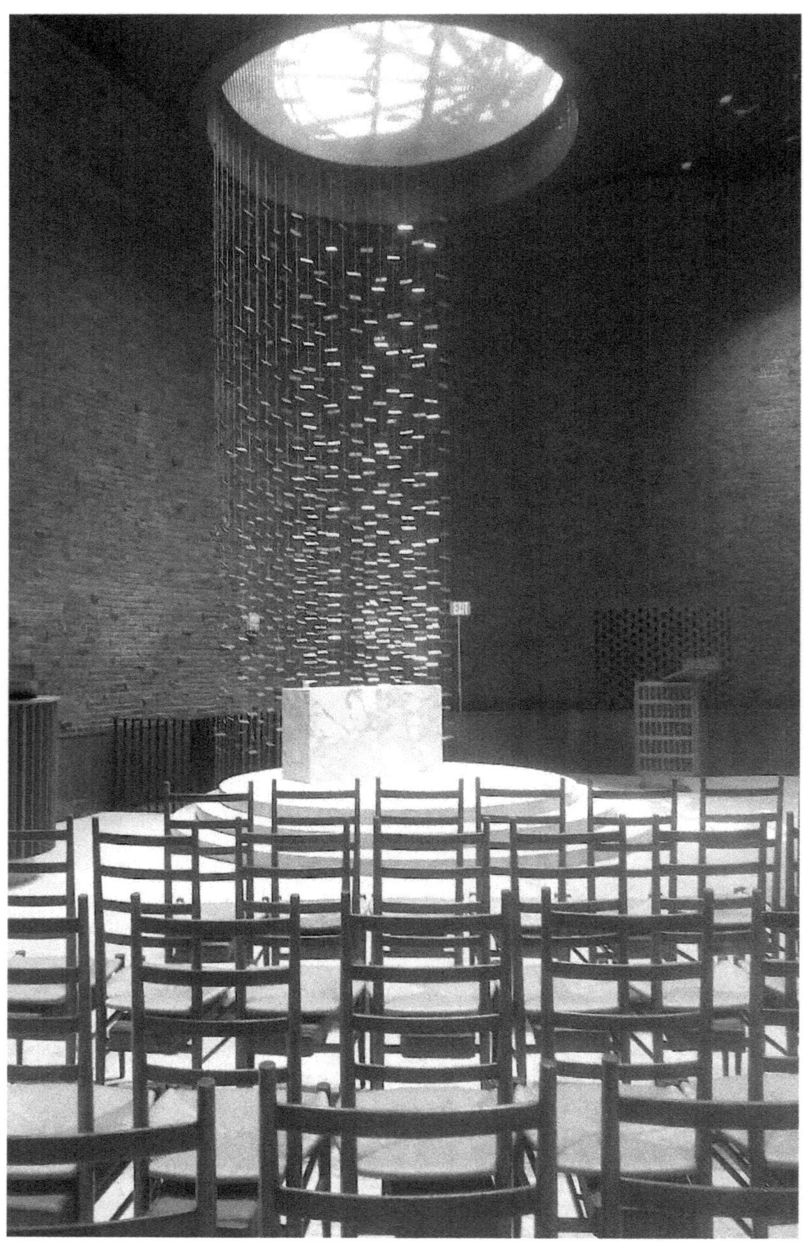

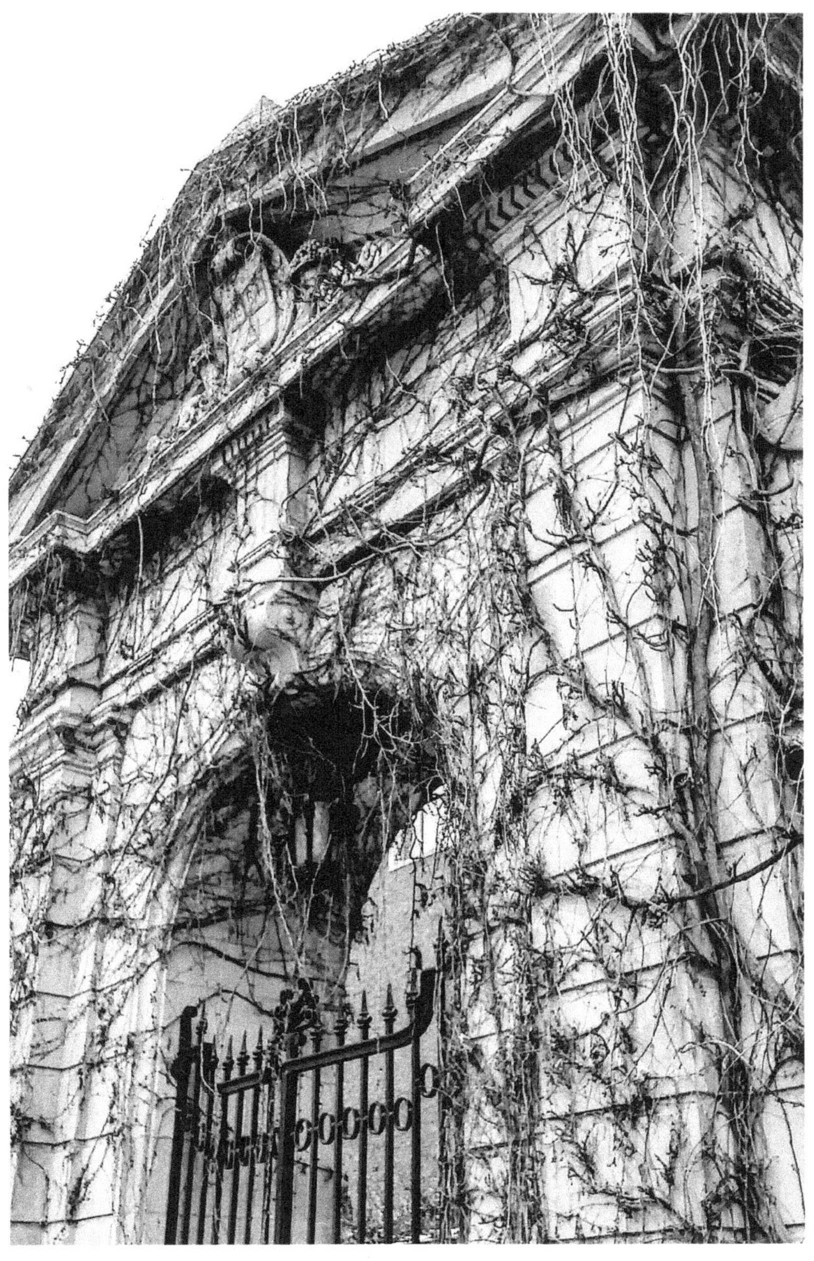

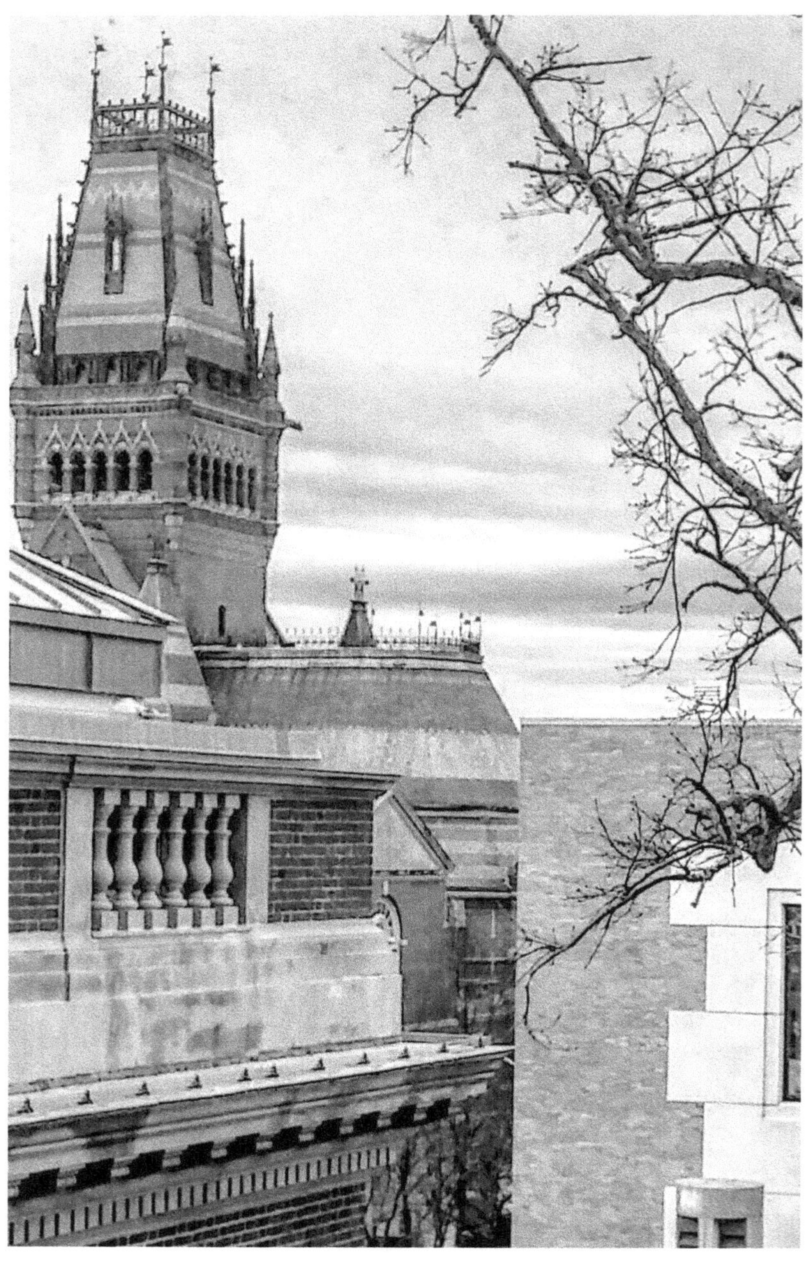

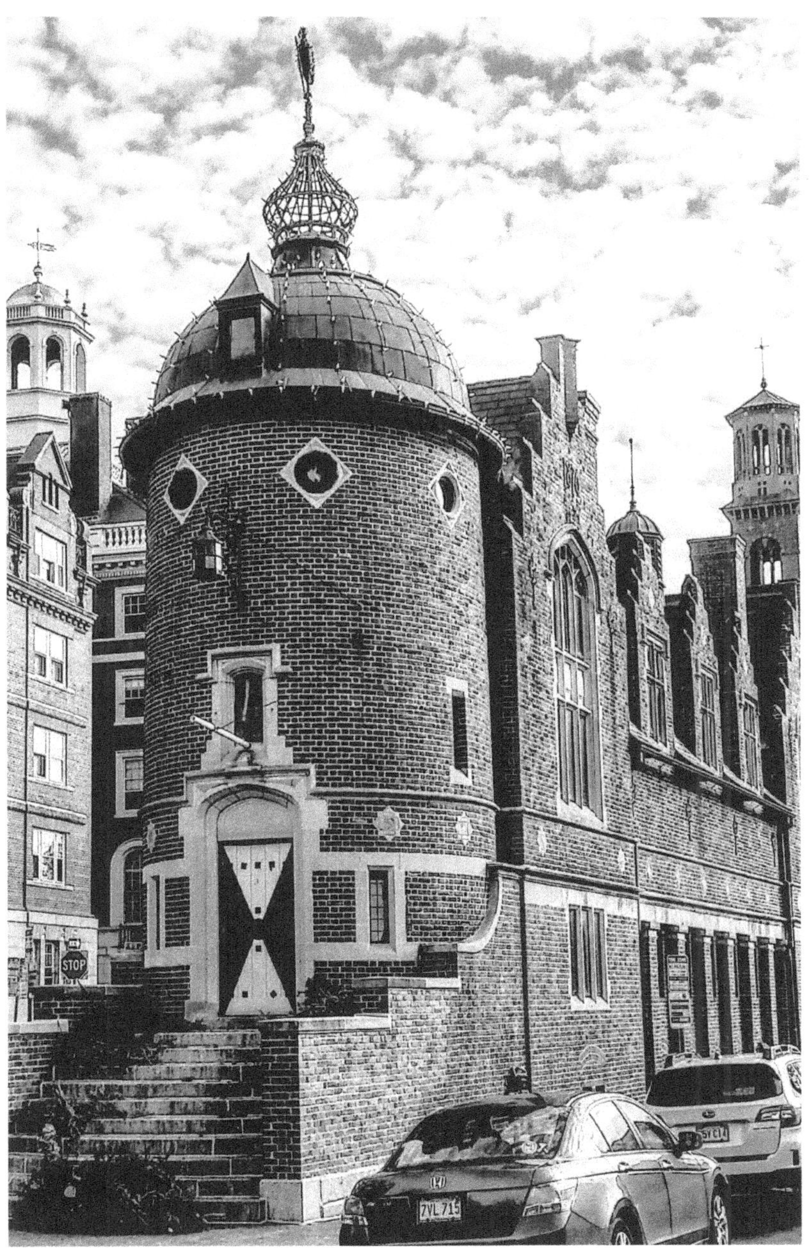

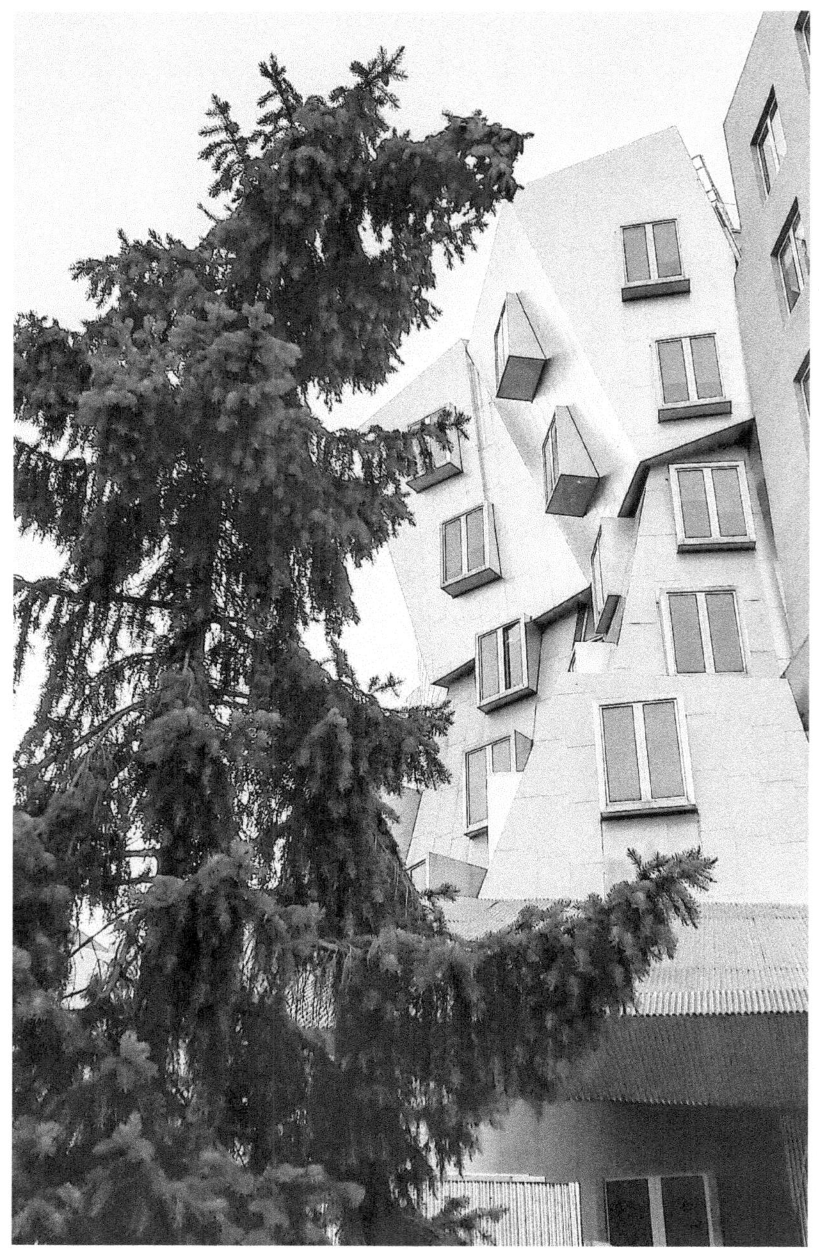

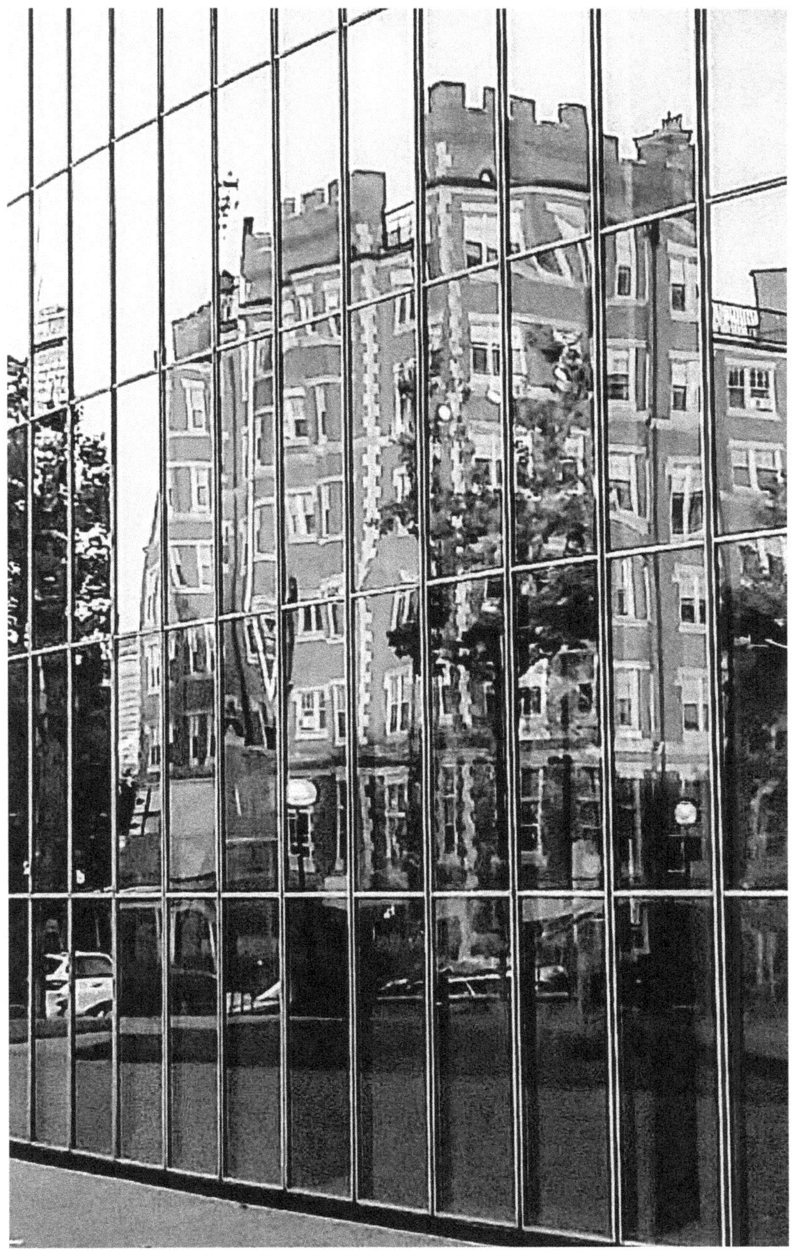

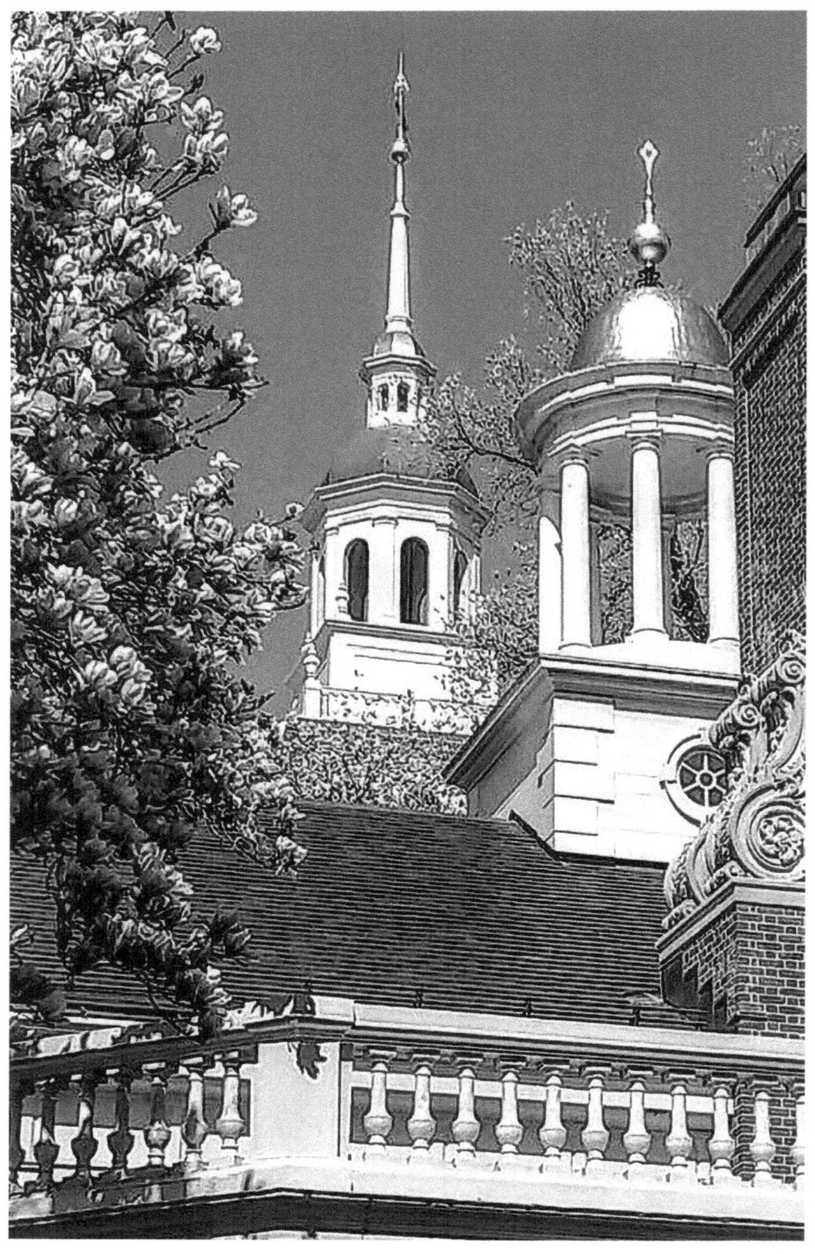

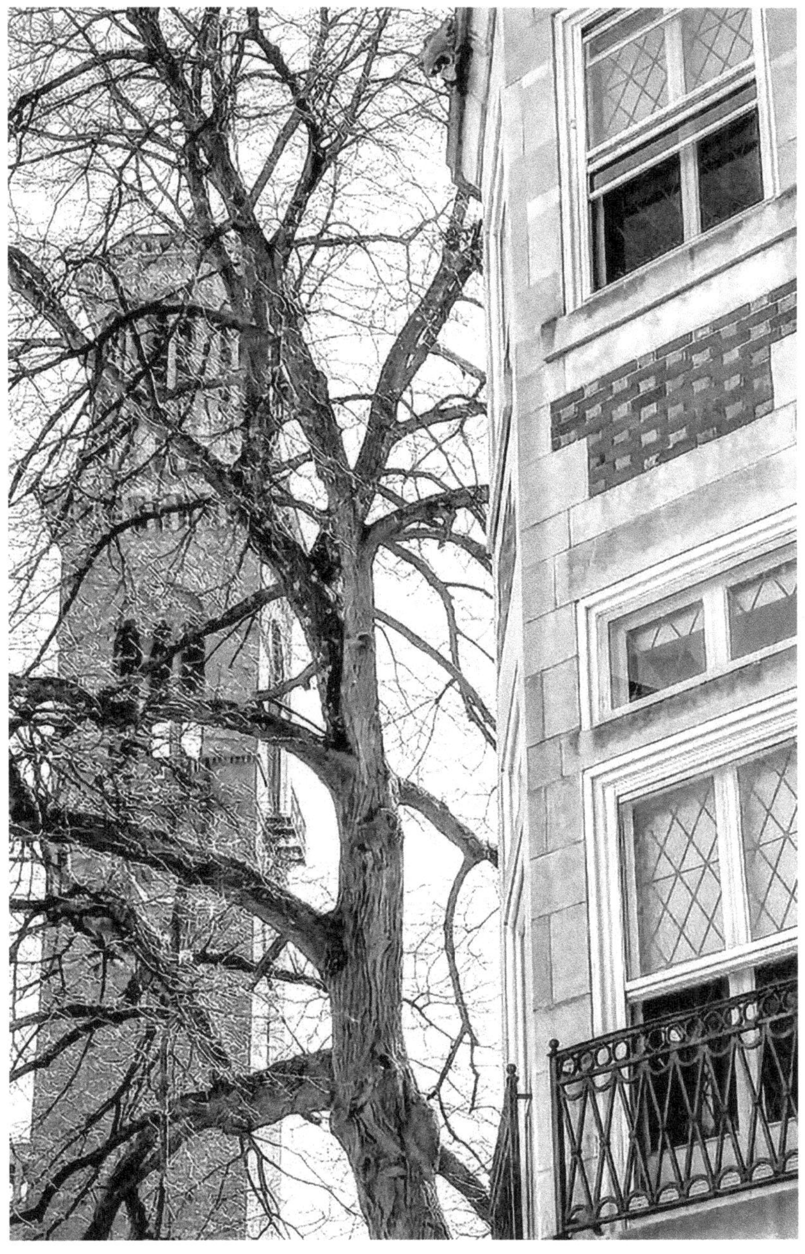

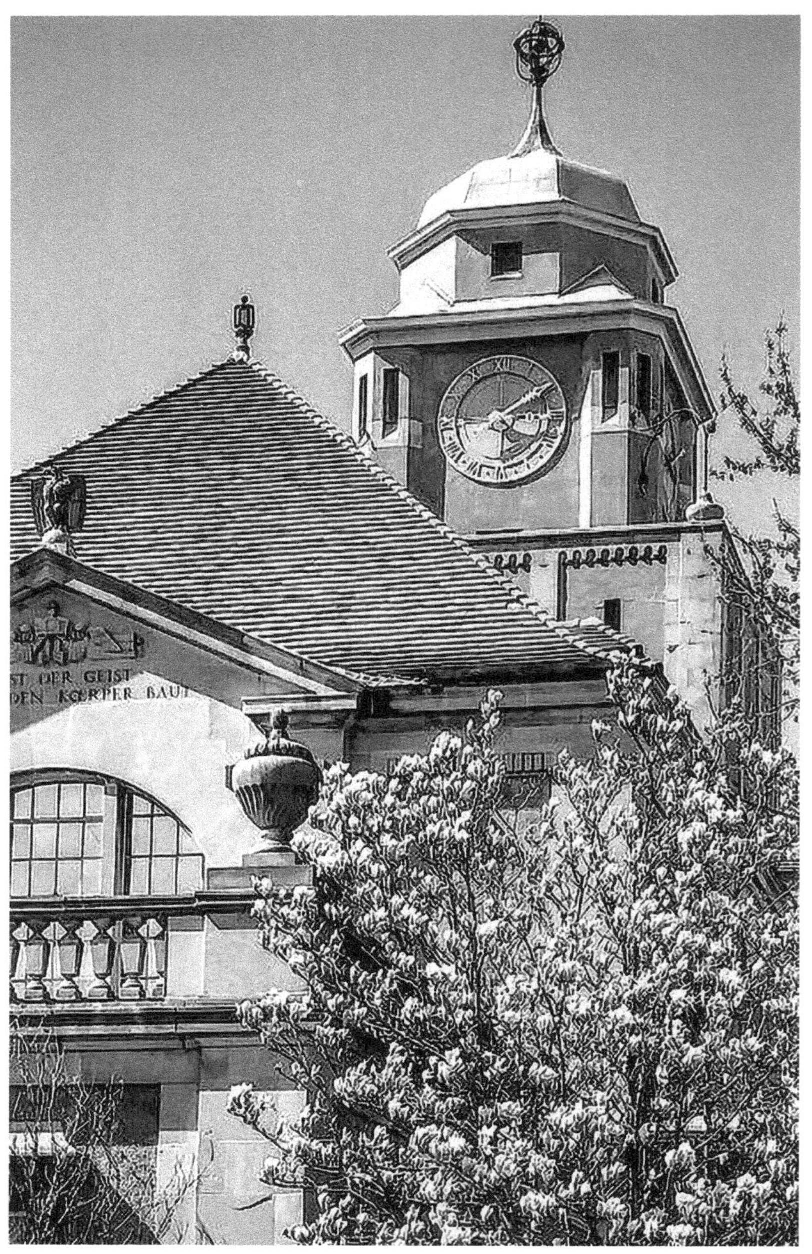

ST DER GEIST
DEN KOERPER BAUT

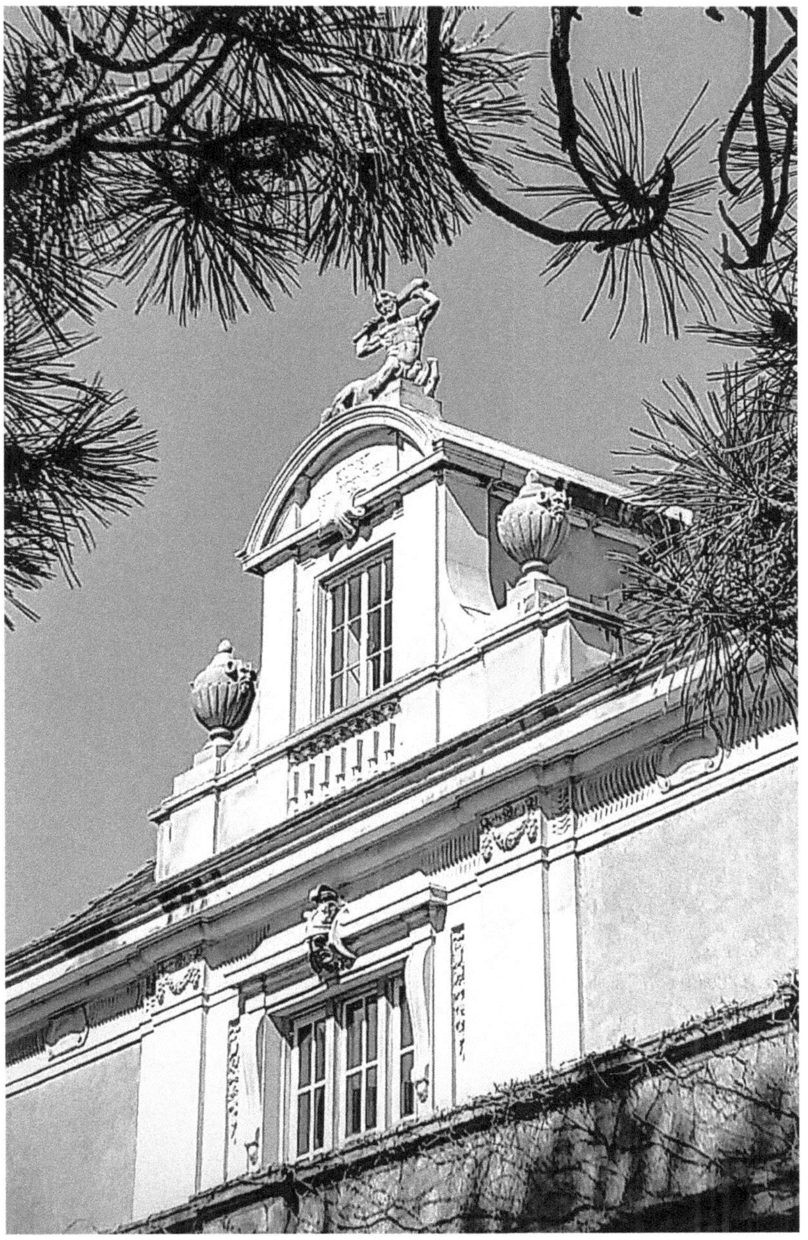

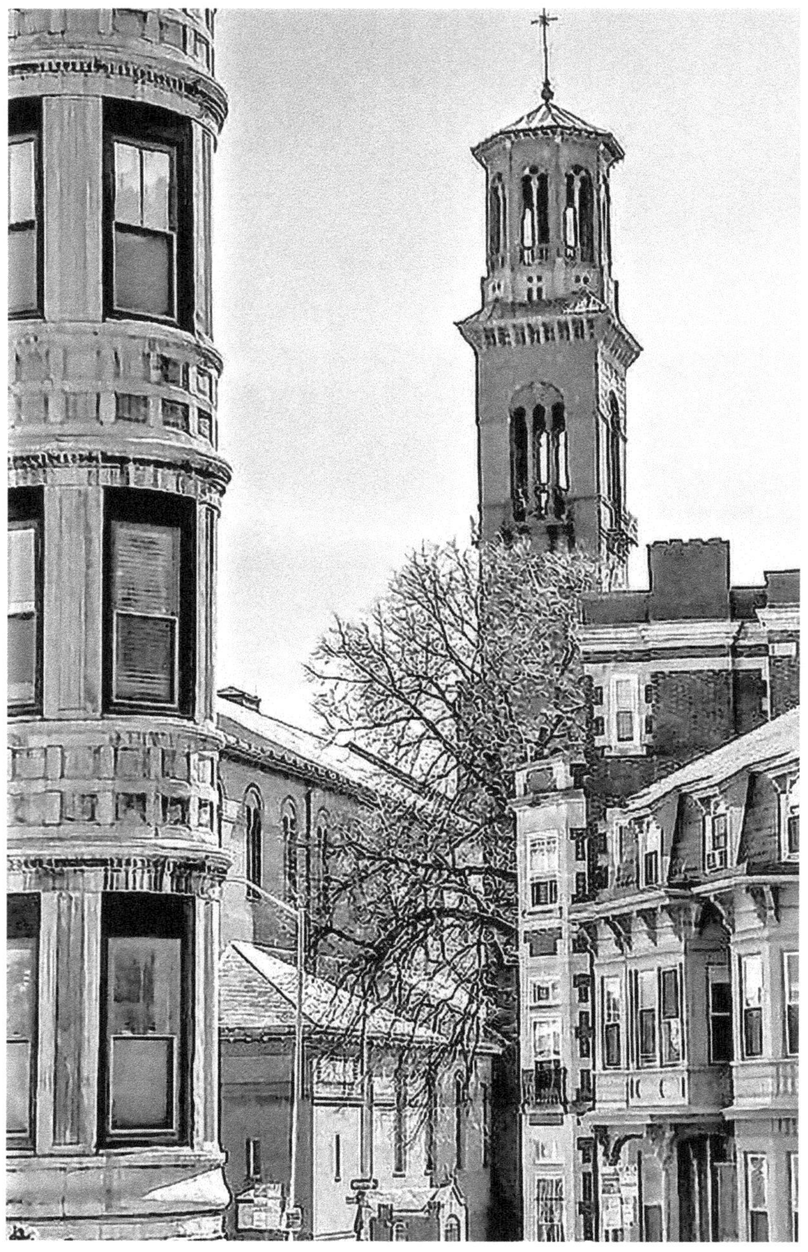

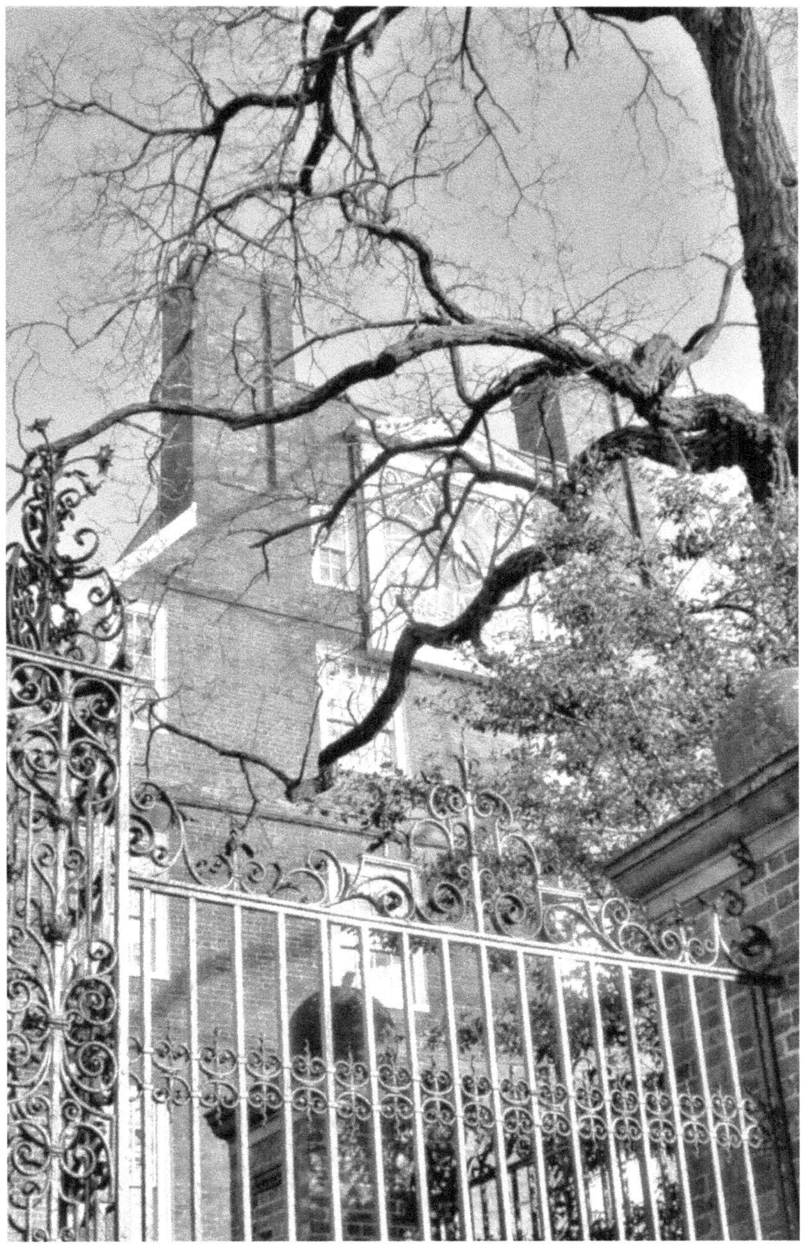

Brookline

The whole of this neighborhood of Brookline is a kind of landscape garden, and there is nothing in America of the sort, so inexpressibly charming as the lanes which lead from one cottage, or villa, to another... These lanes are clothed with a profusion of trees and wild shrubbery, often almost to the carriage tracks, and curve and wind about, in a manner quite bewildering to the stranger who attempts to thread them alone; and there are more hints here for the lover of the picturesque in lanes than we ever saw assembled together in so small a compass.

Andrew Jackson Downing (1815 – 1852)
writer, landscape designer and art critic

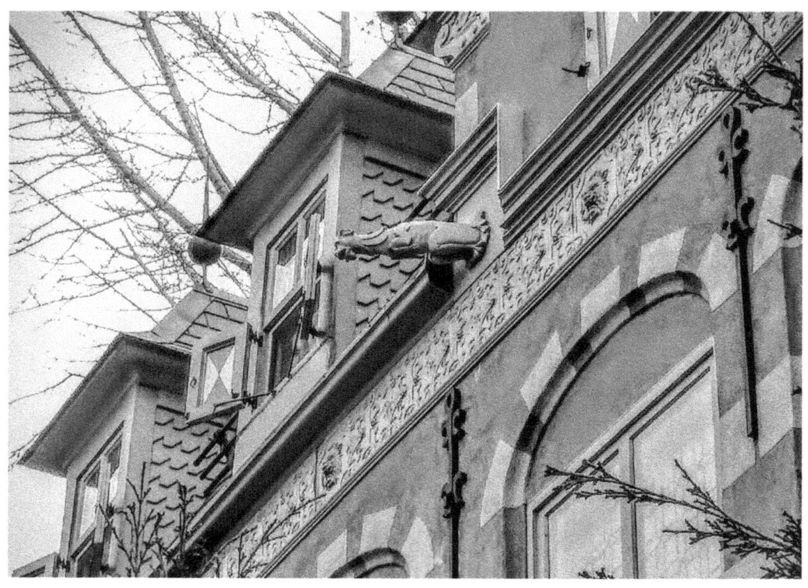

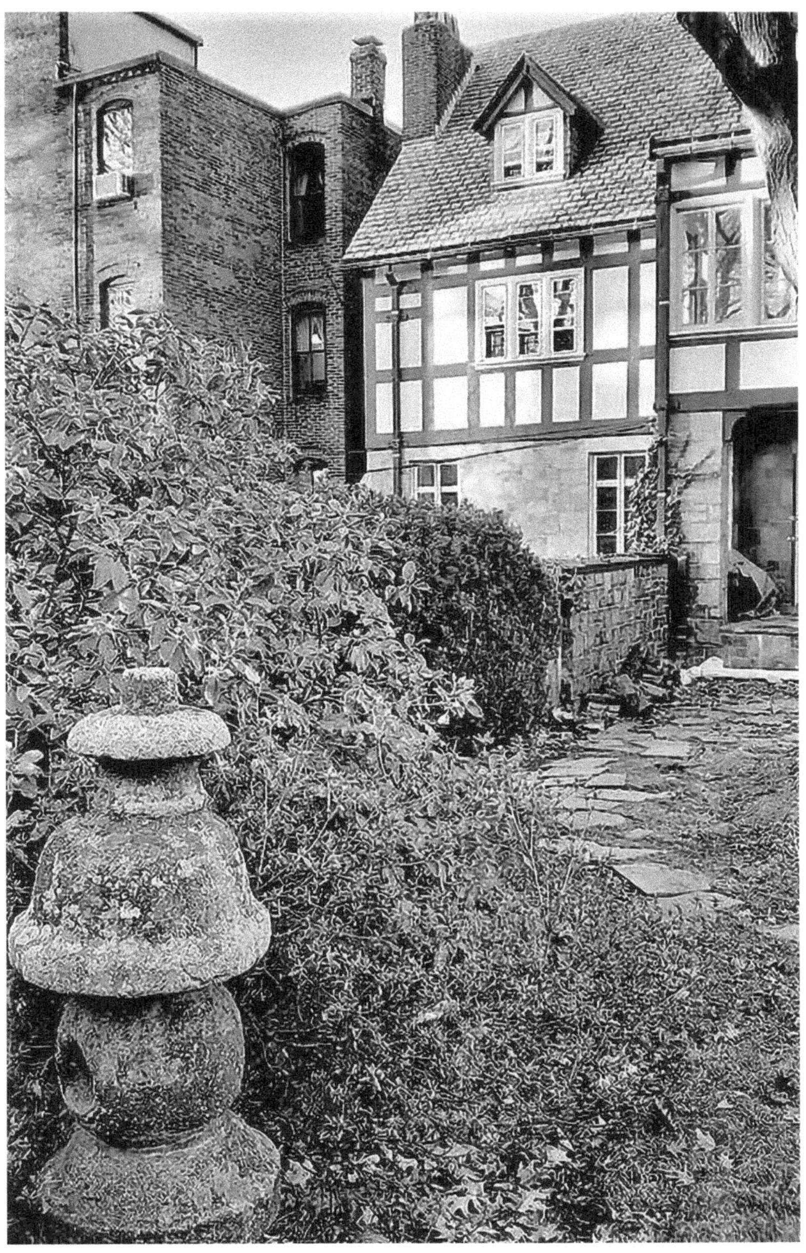

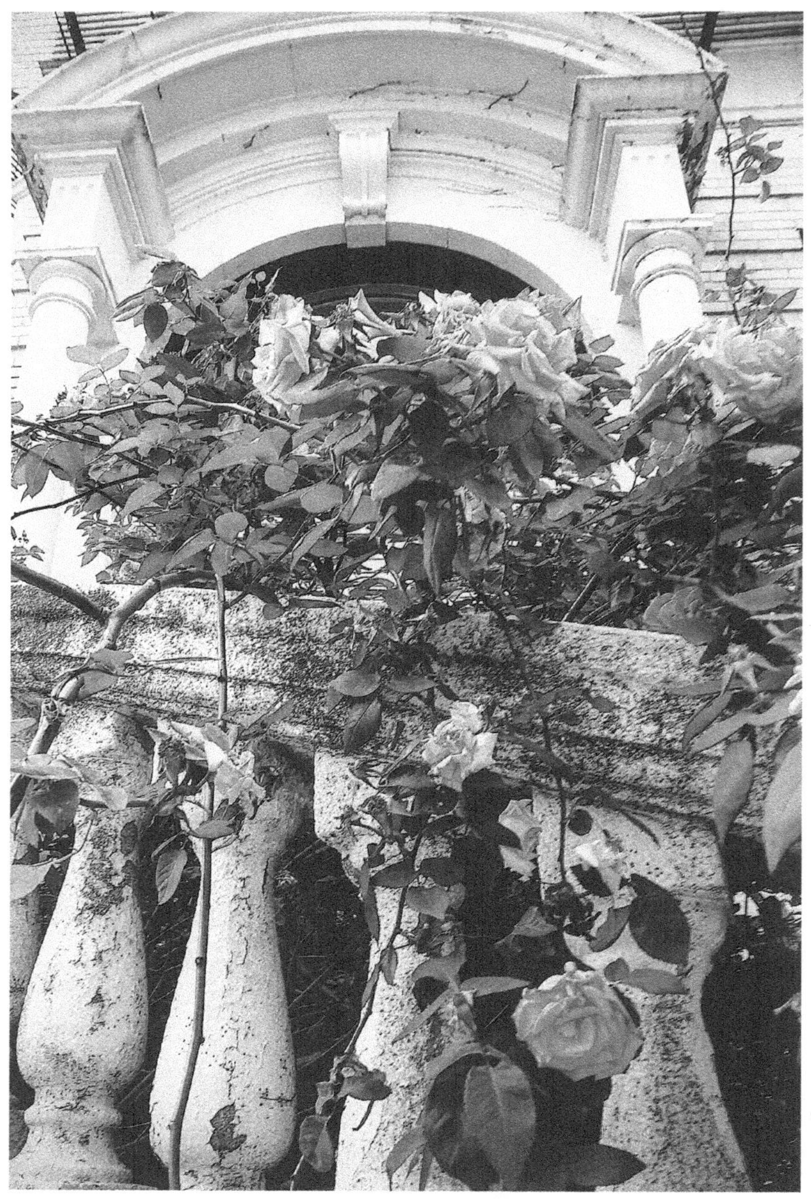

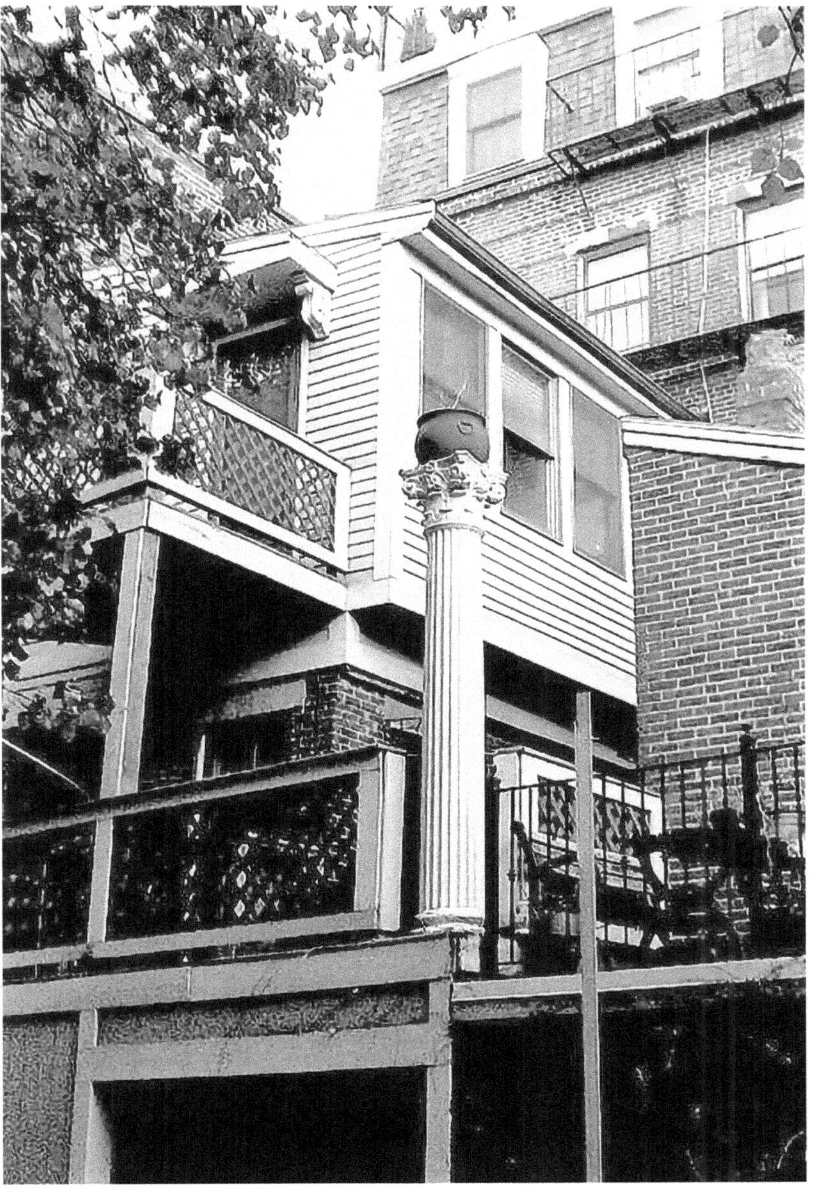

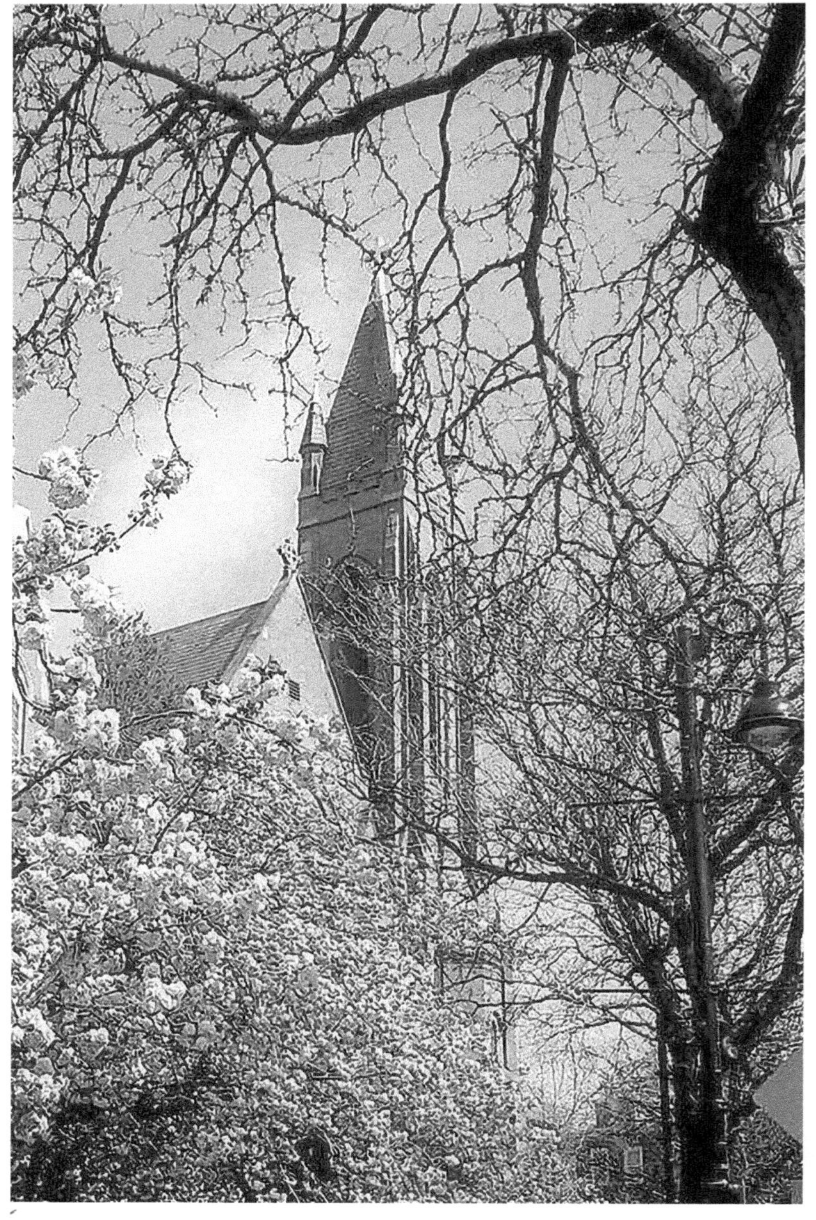

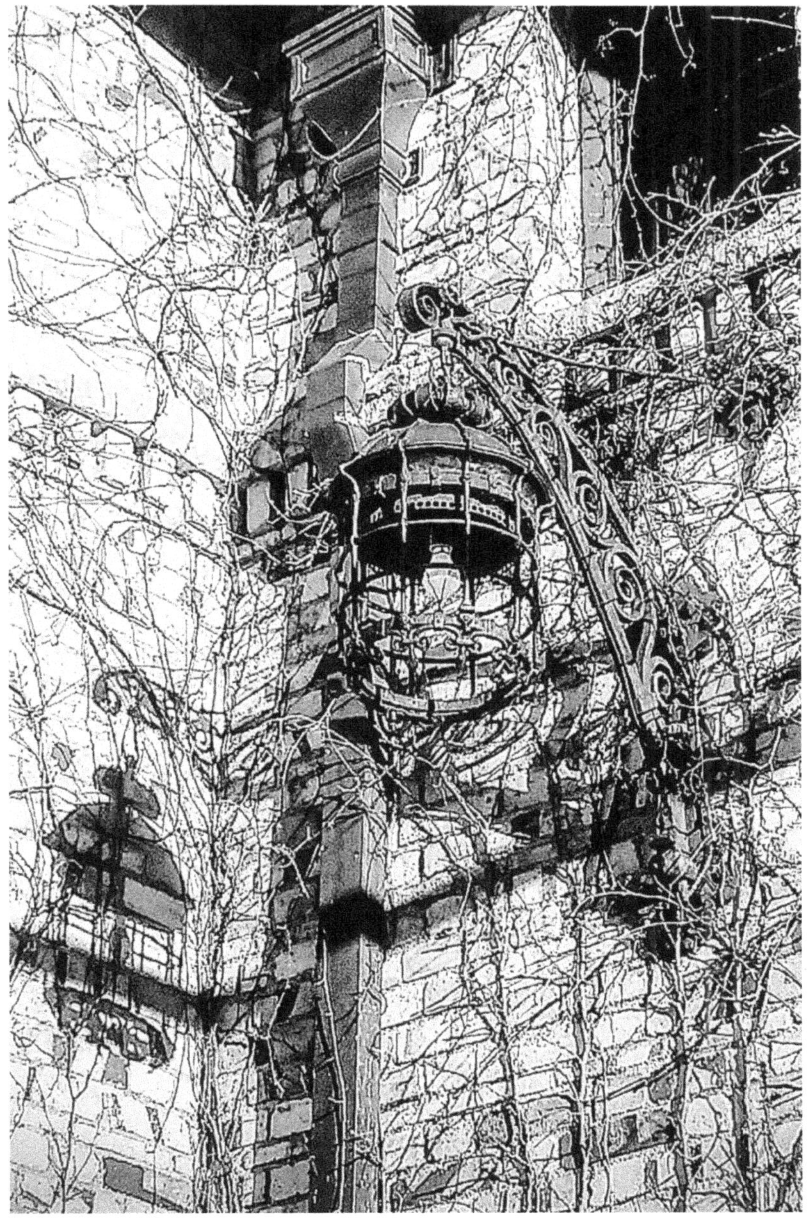

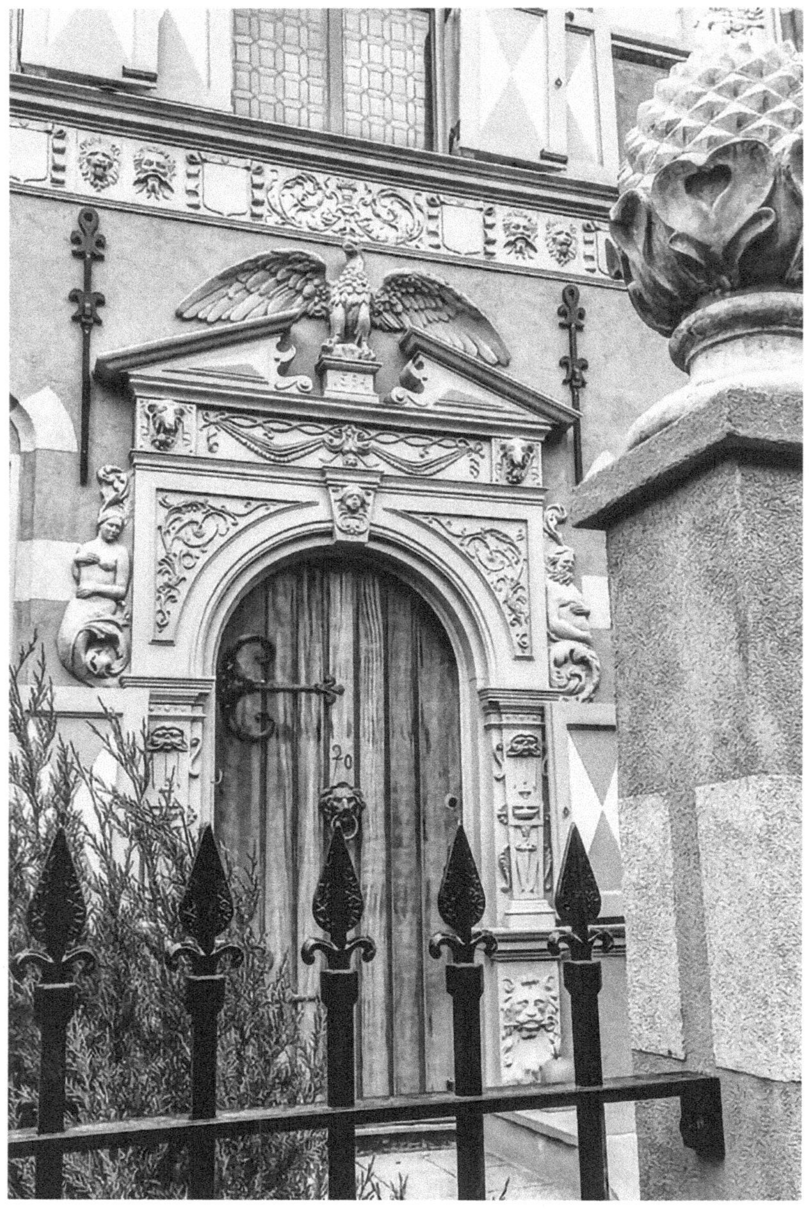

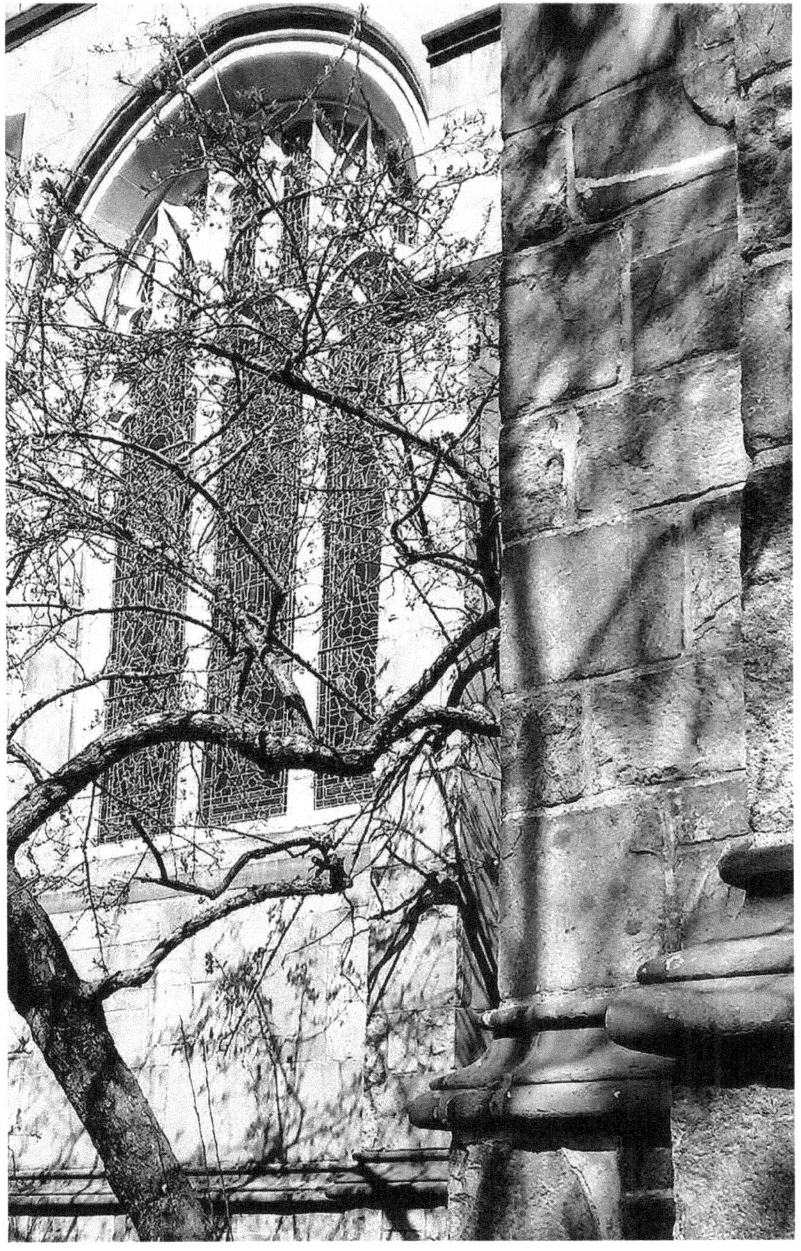

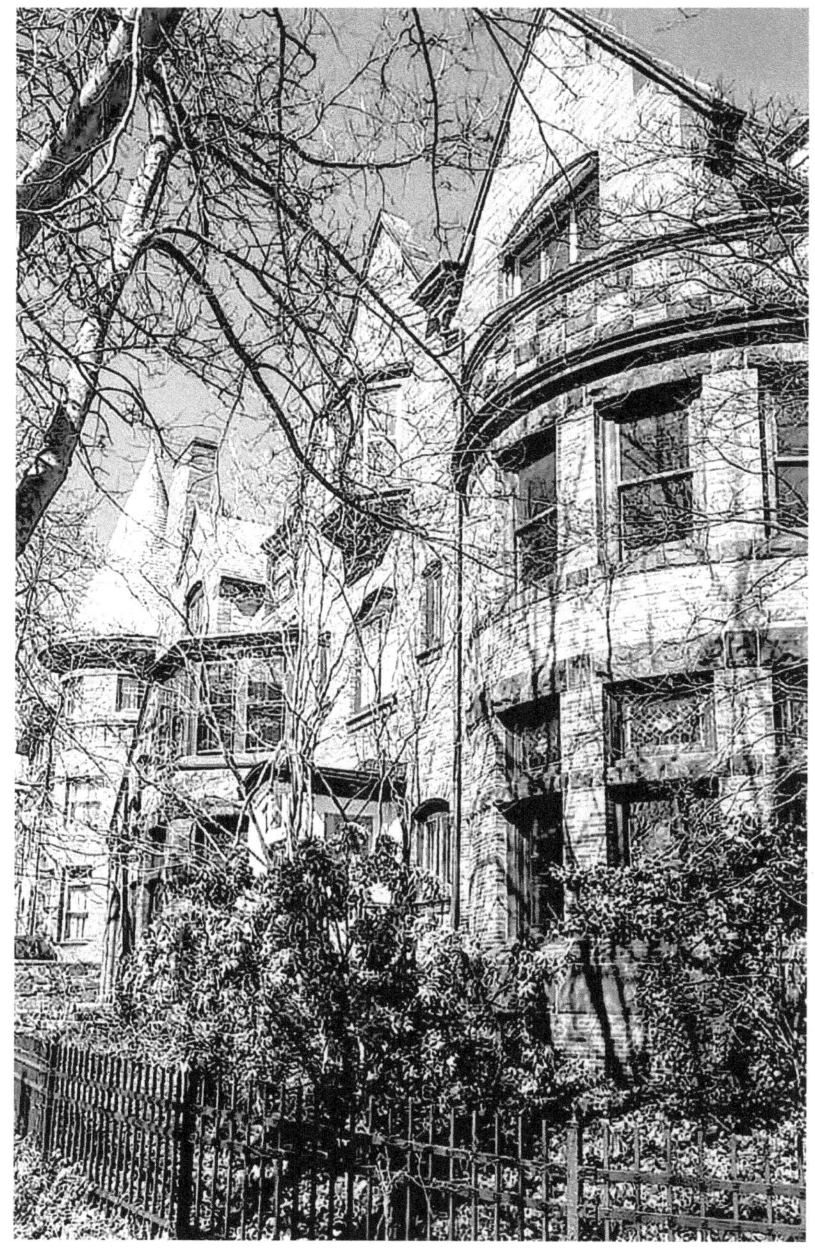

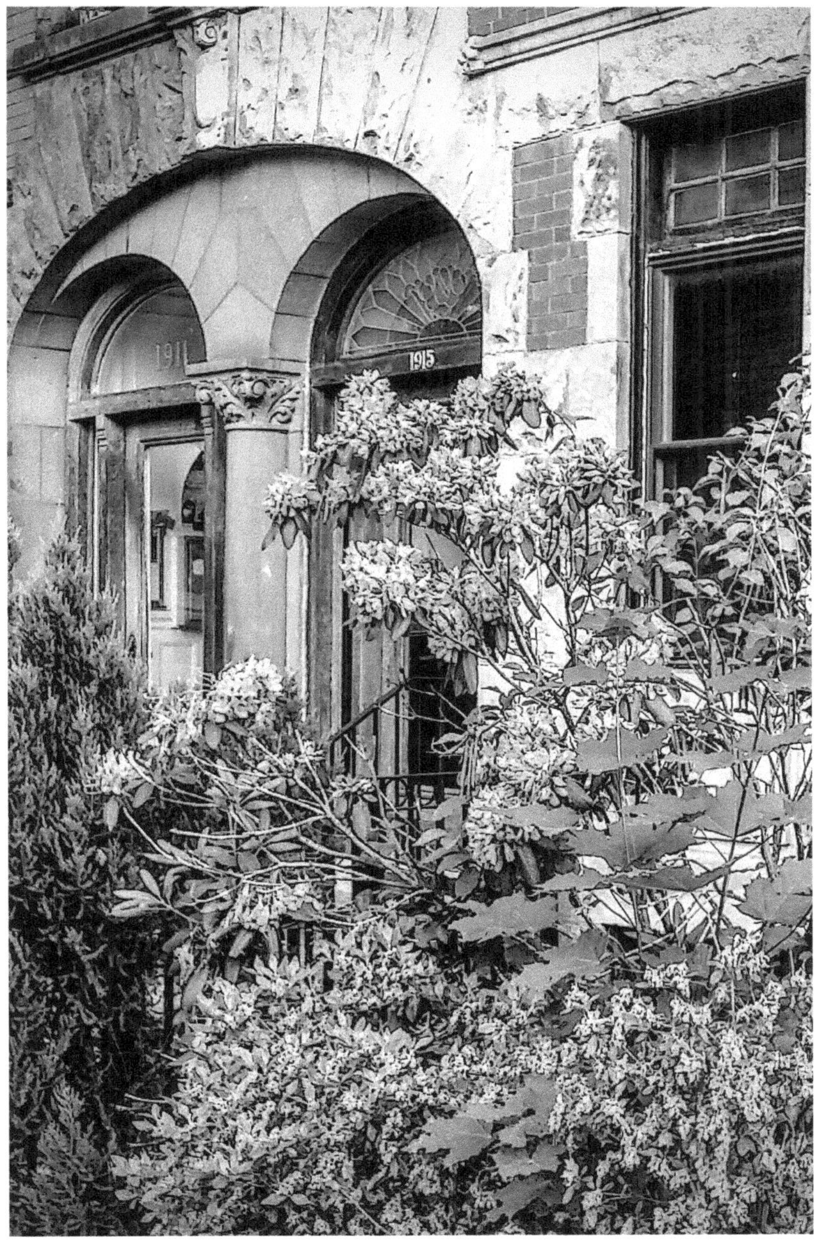

1911
1915

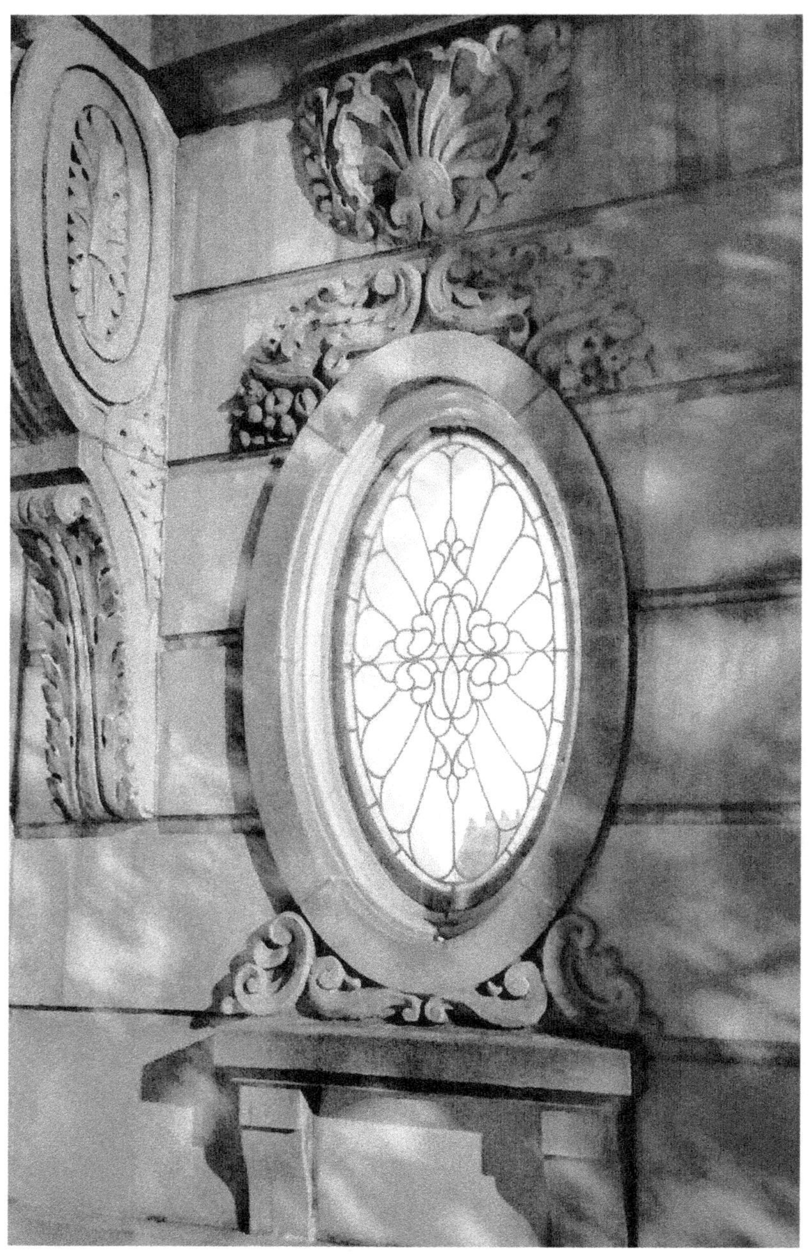

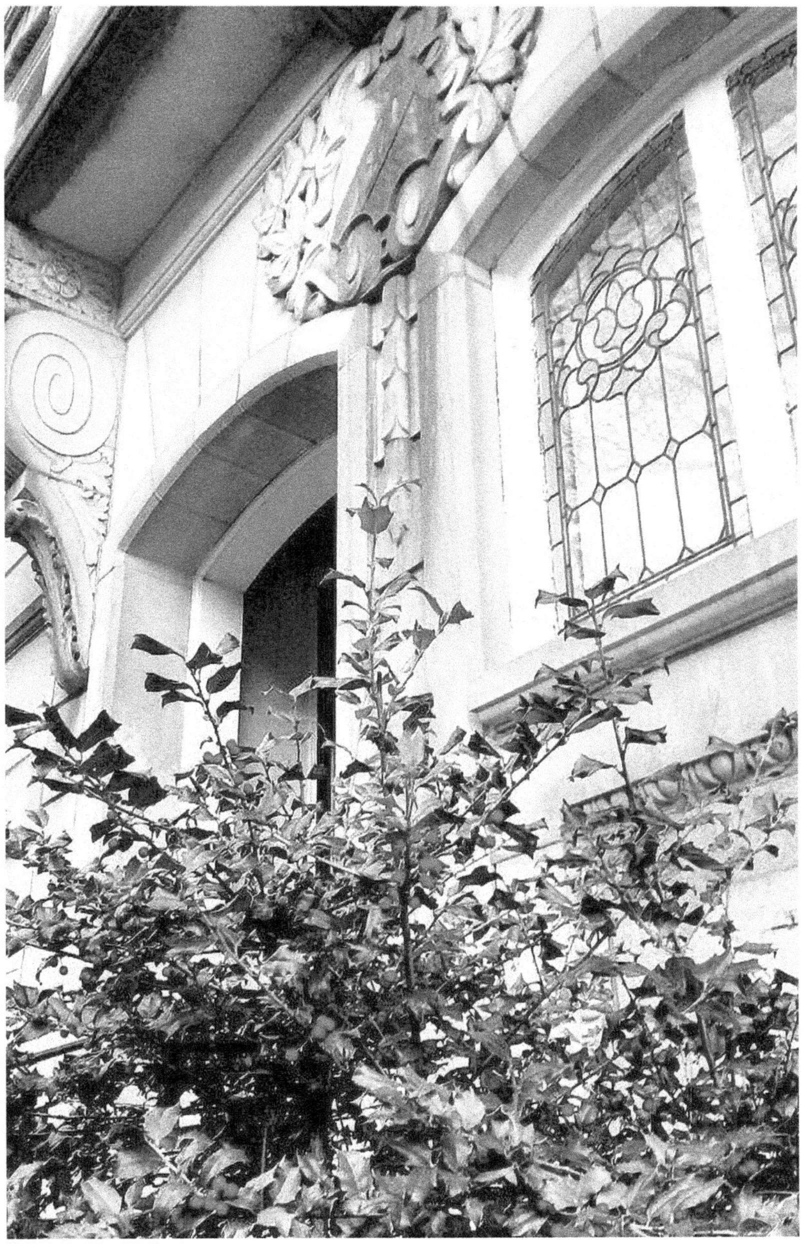

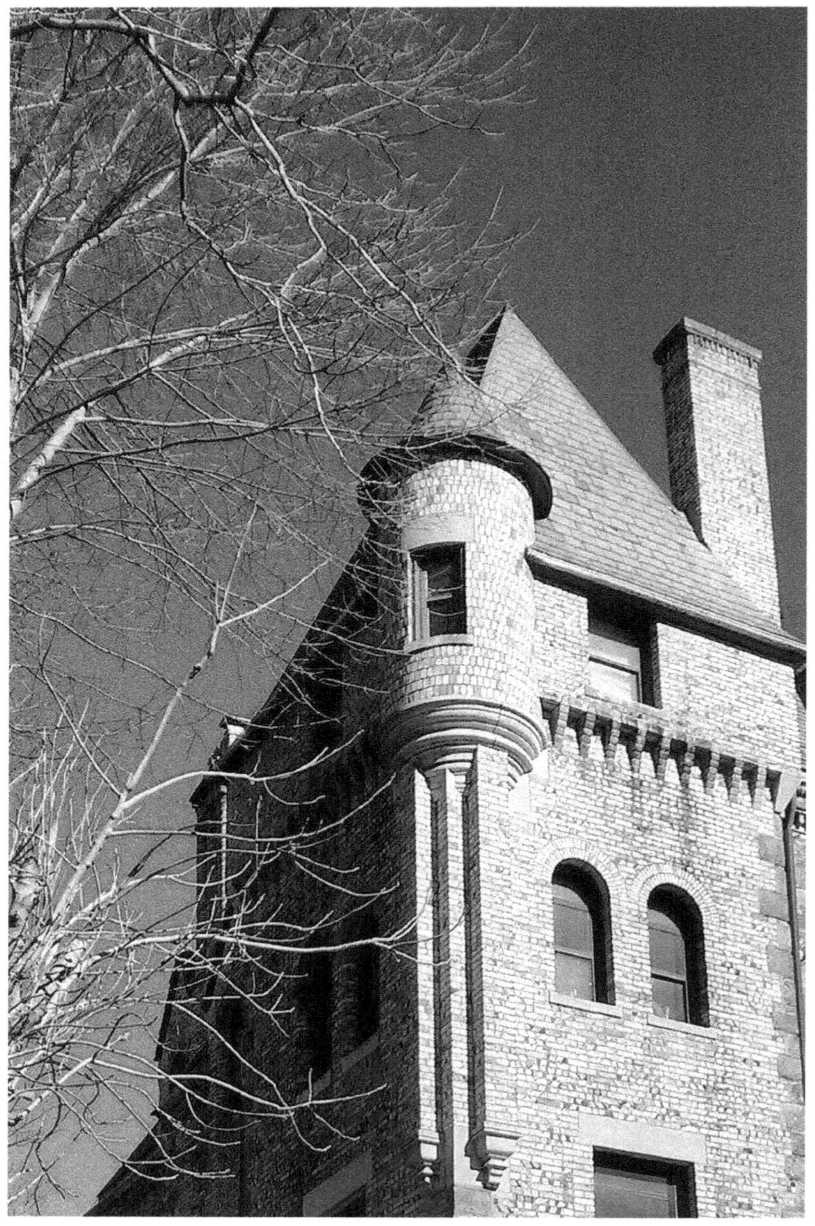

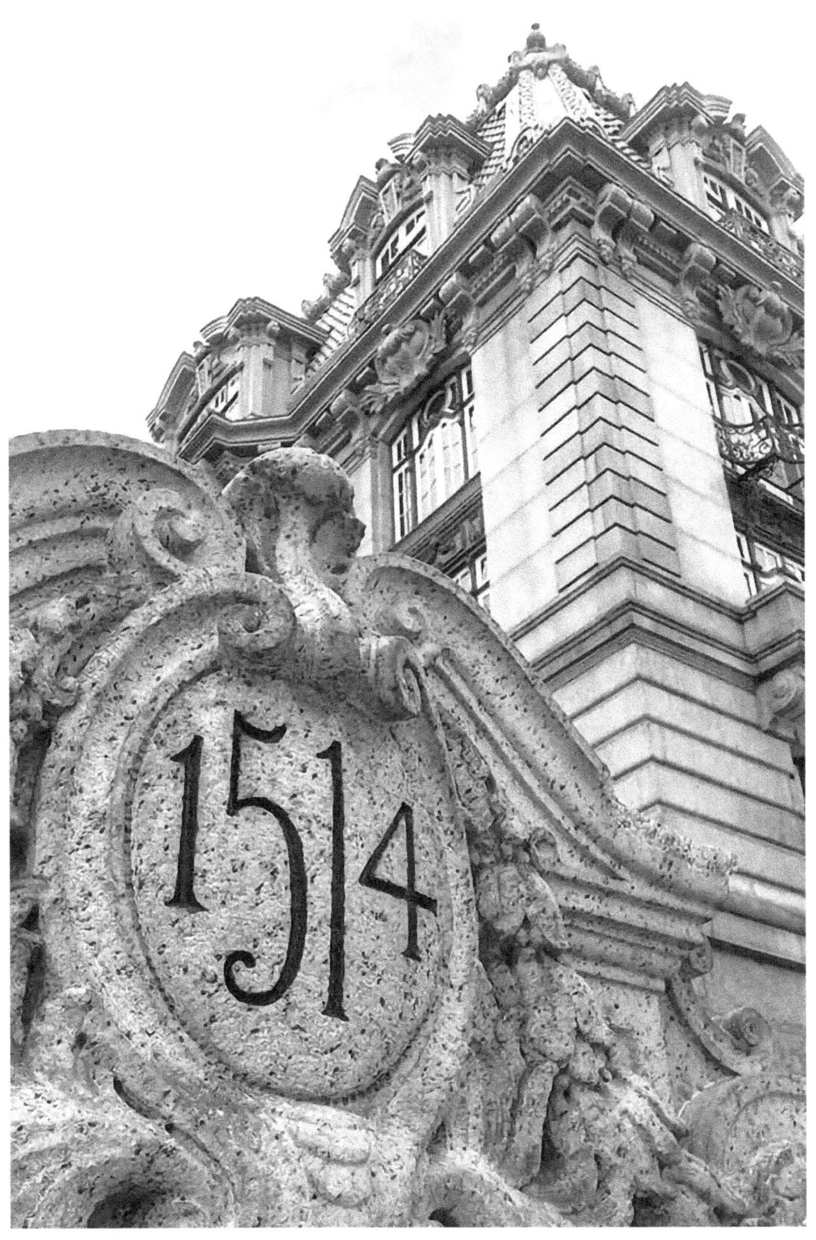

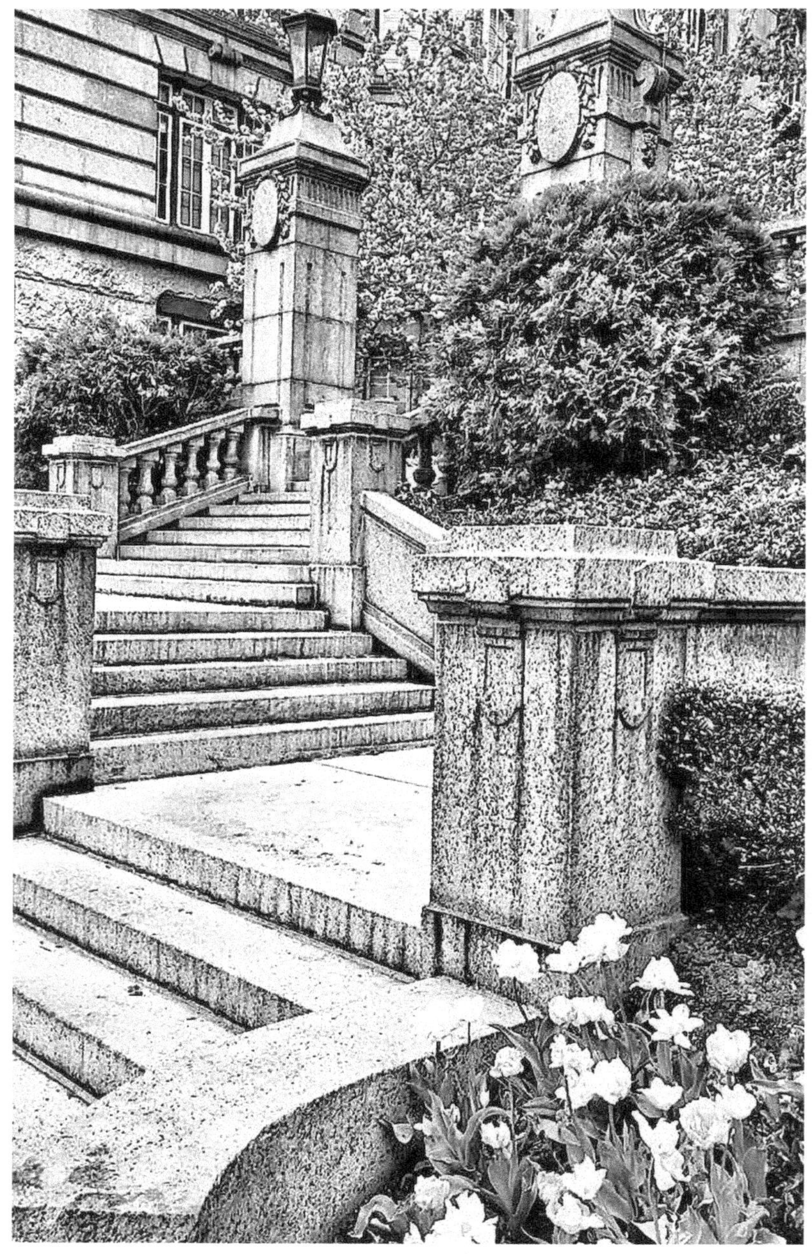

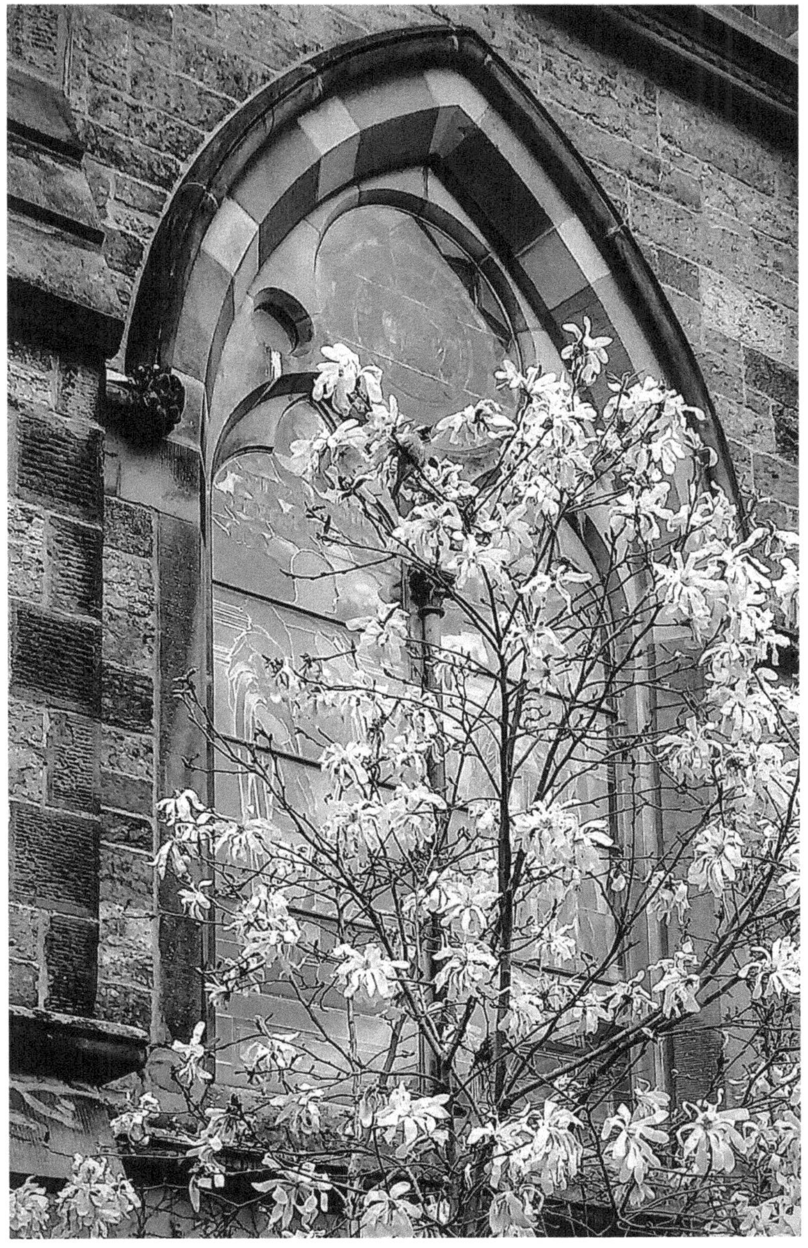

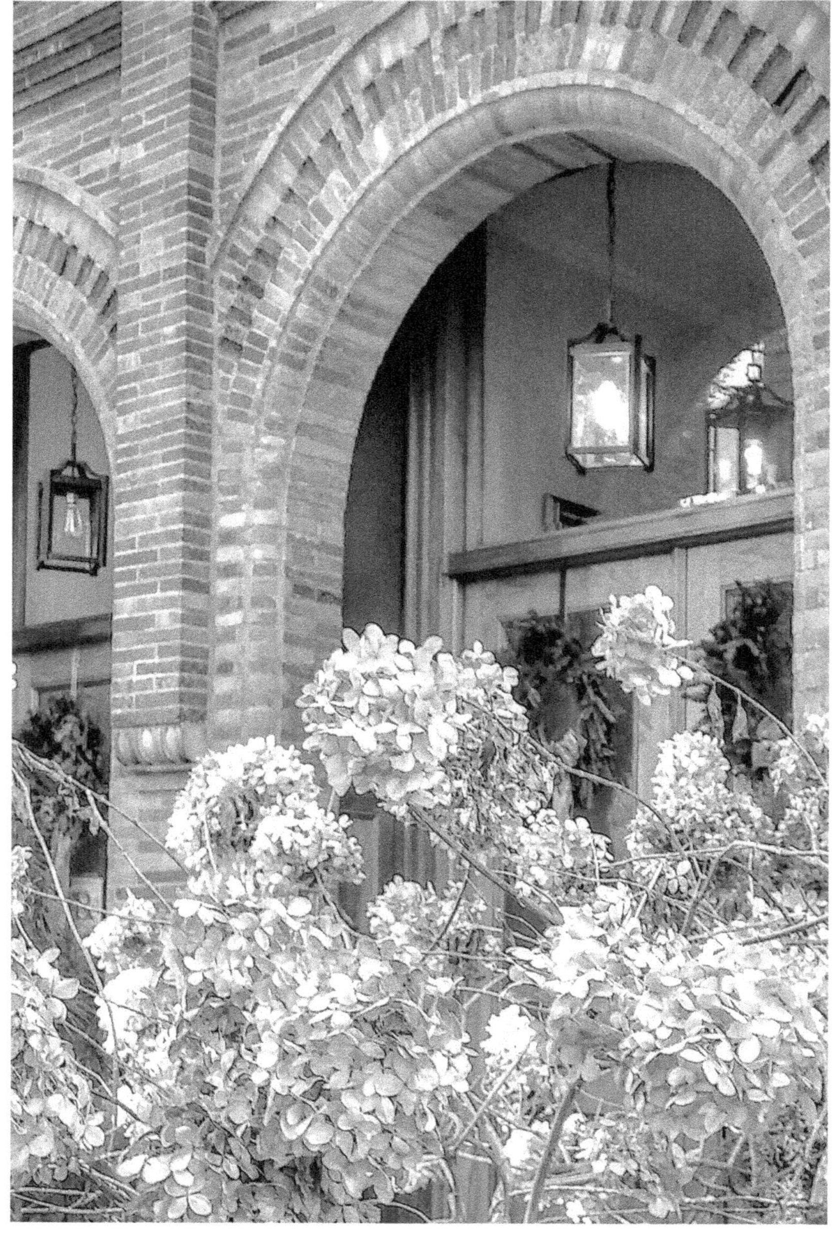

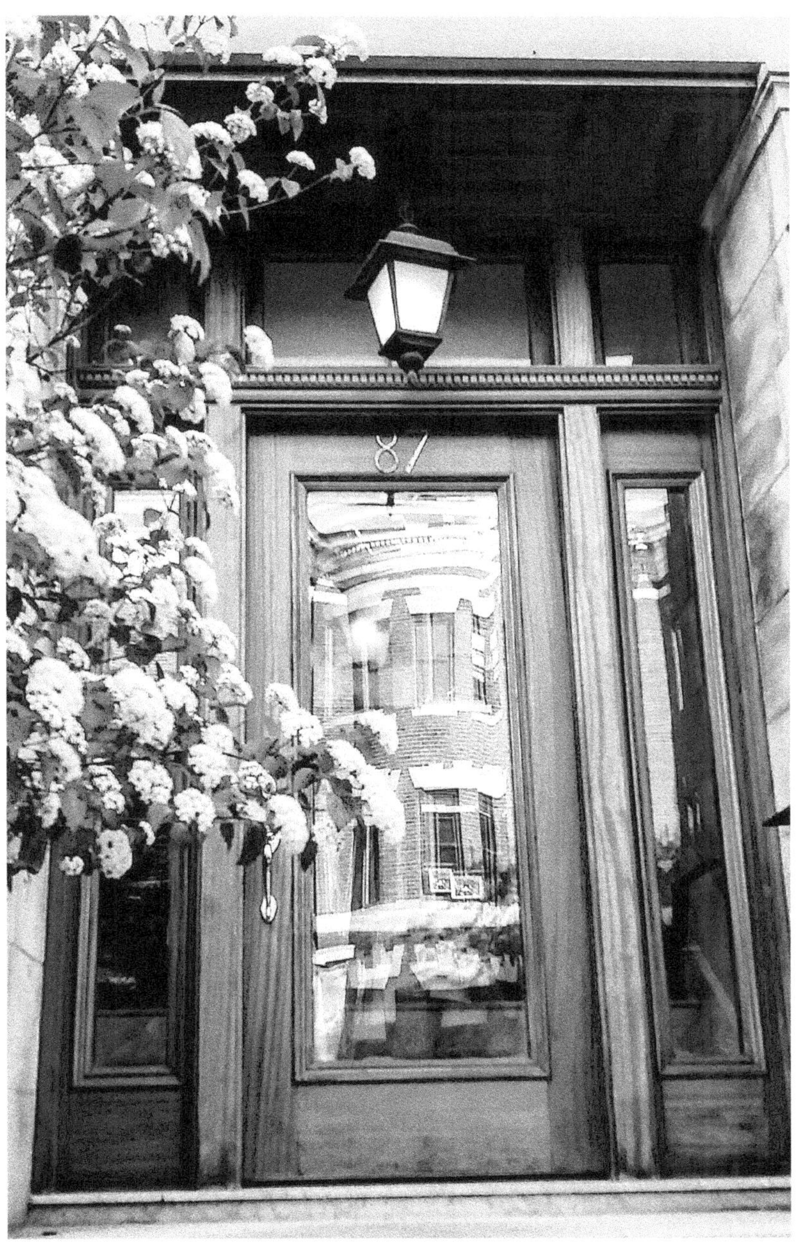

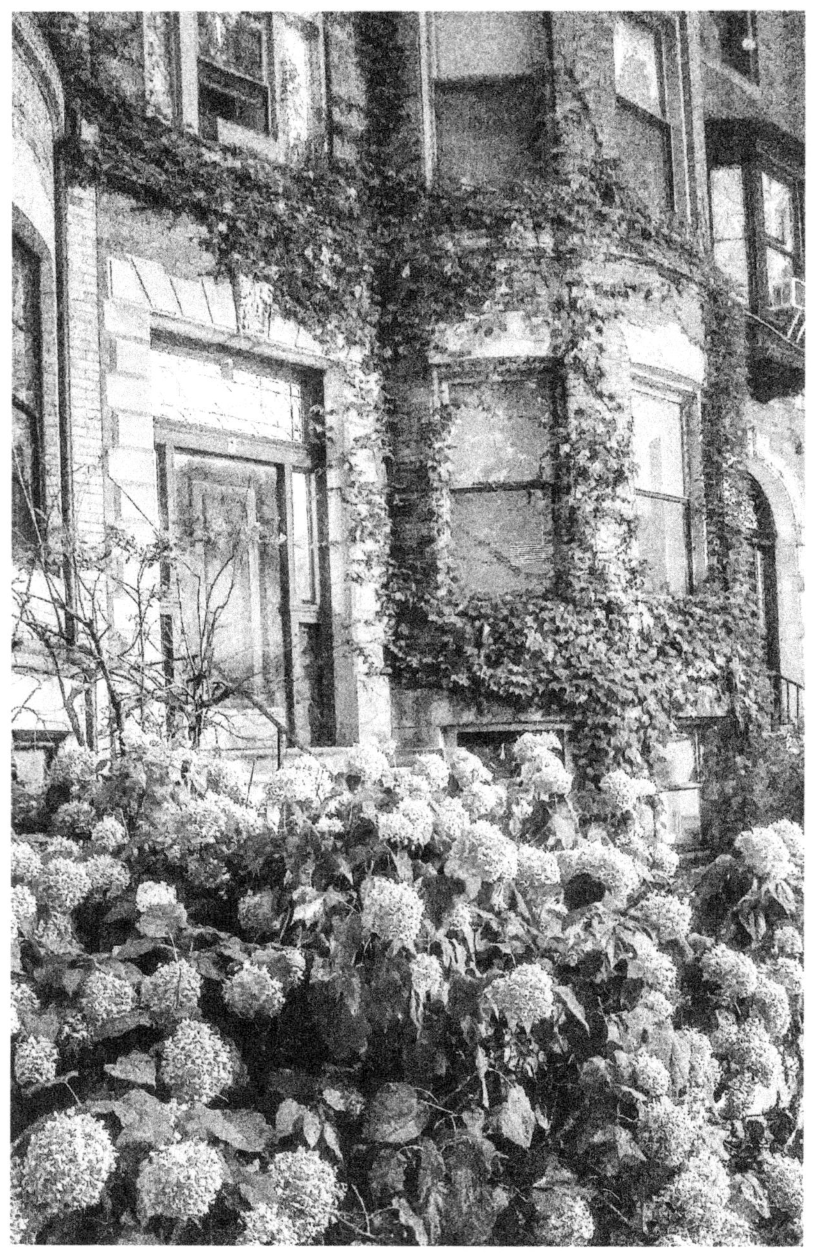

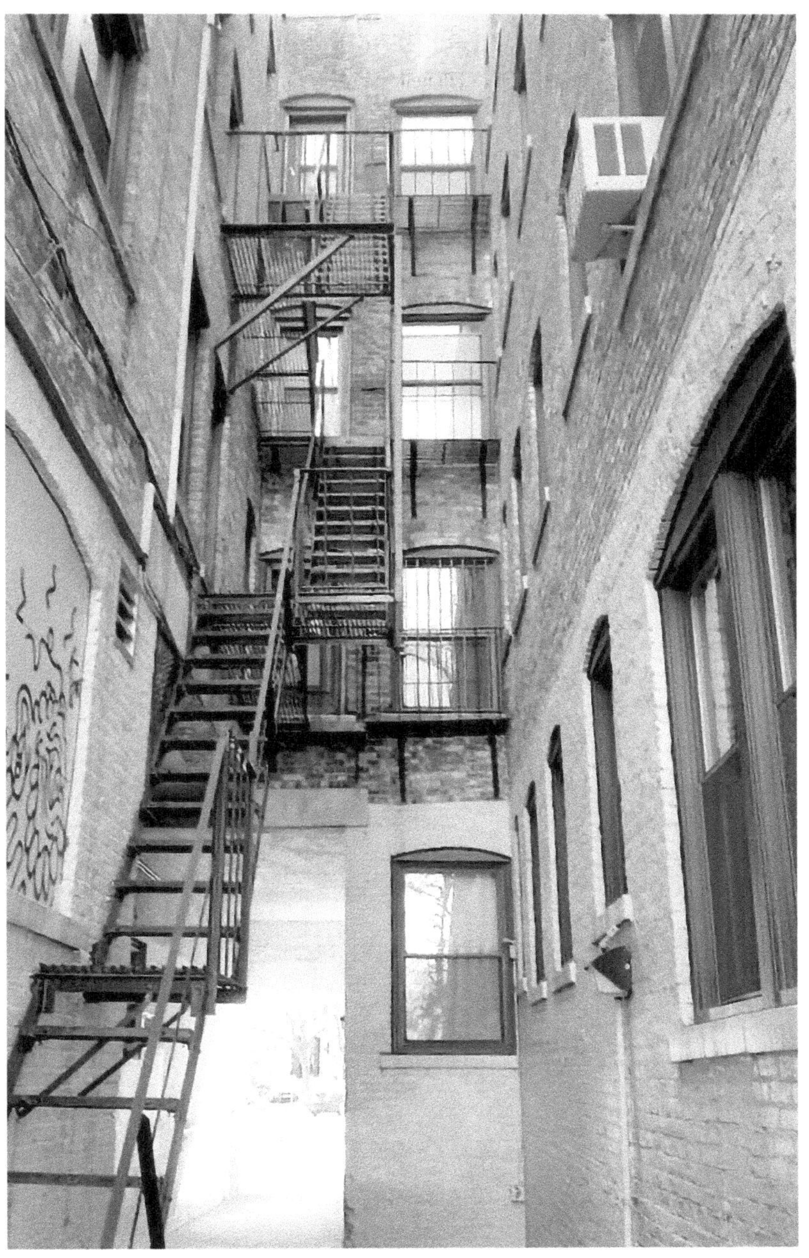

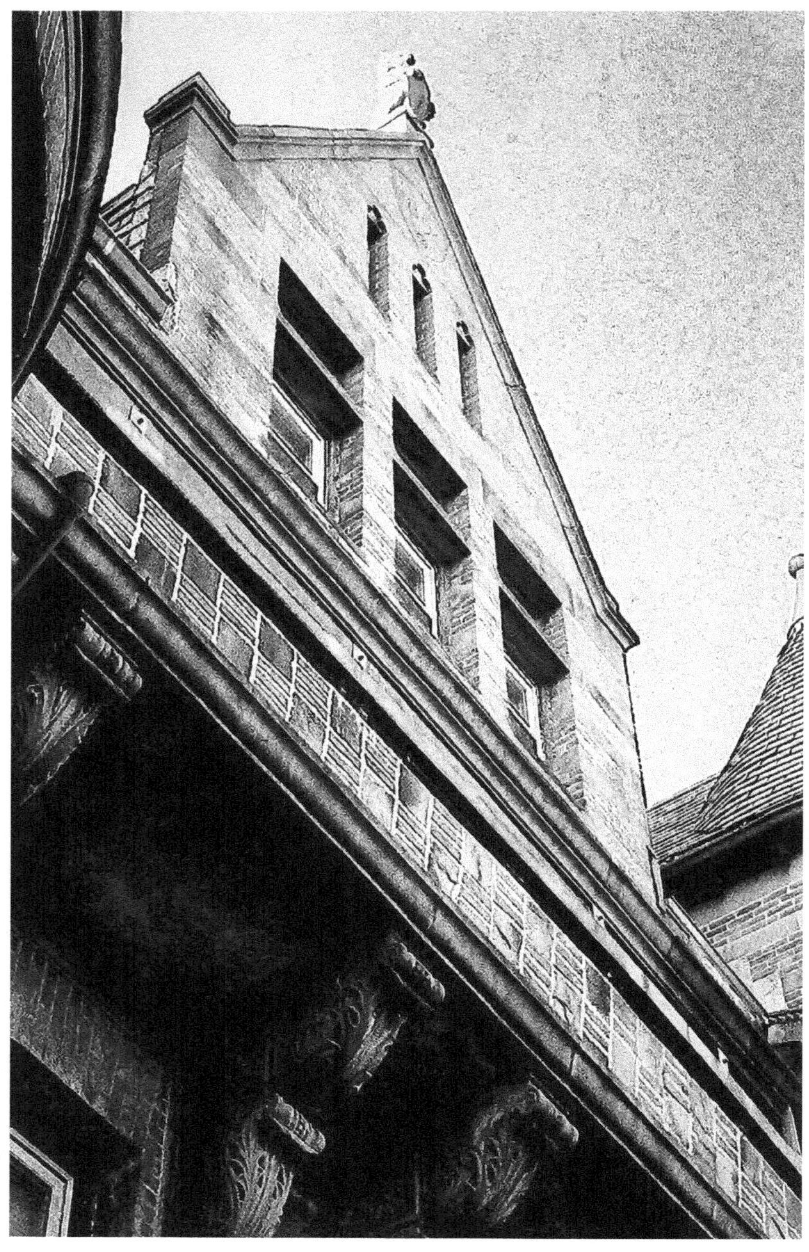

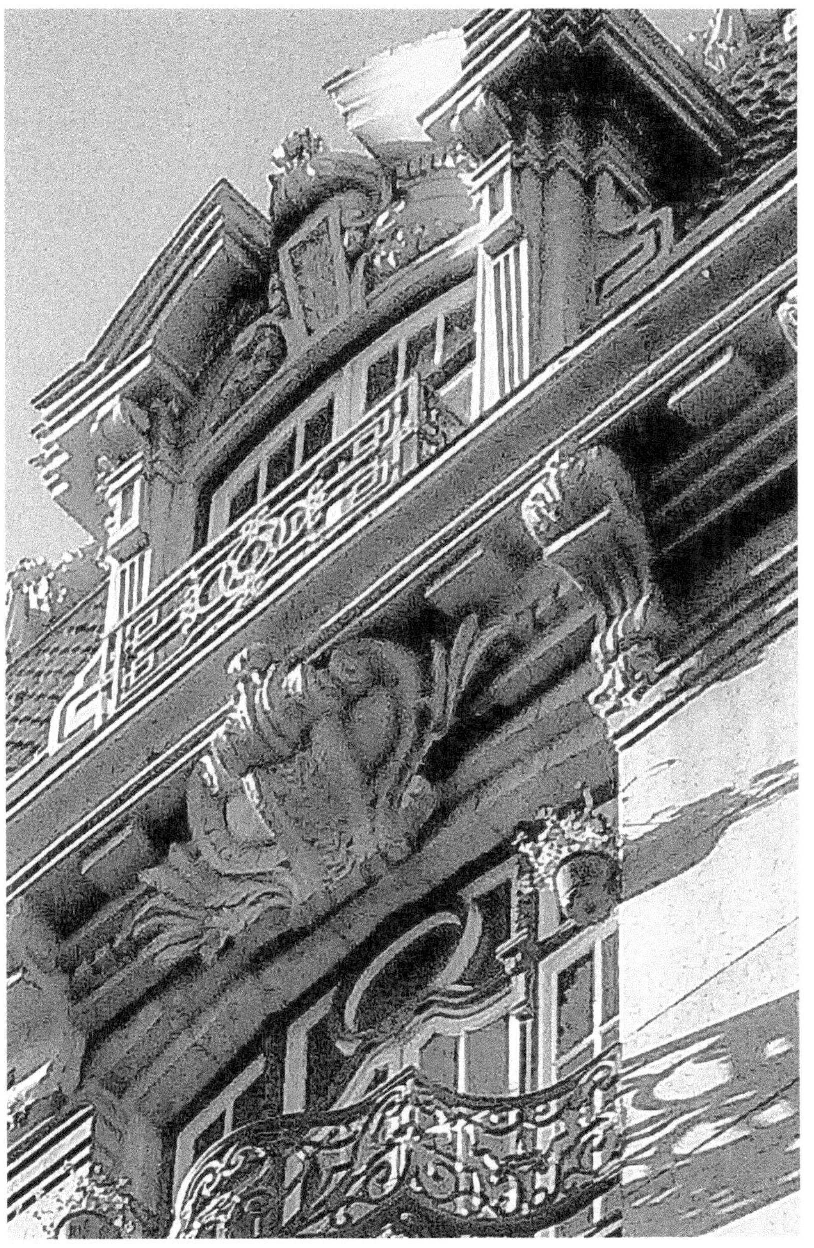

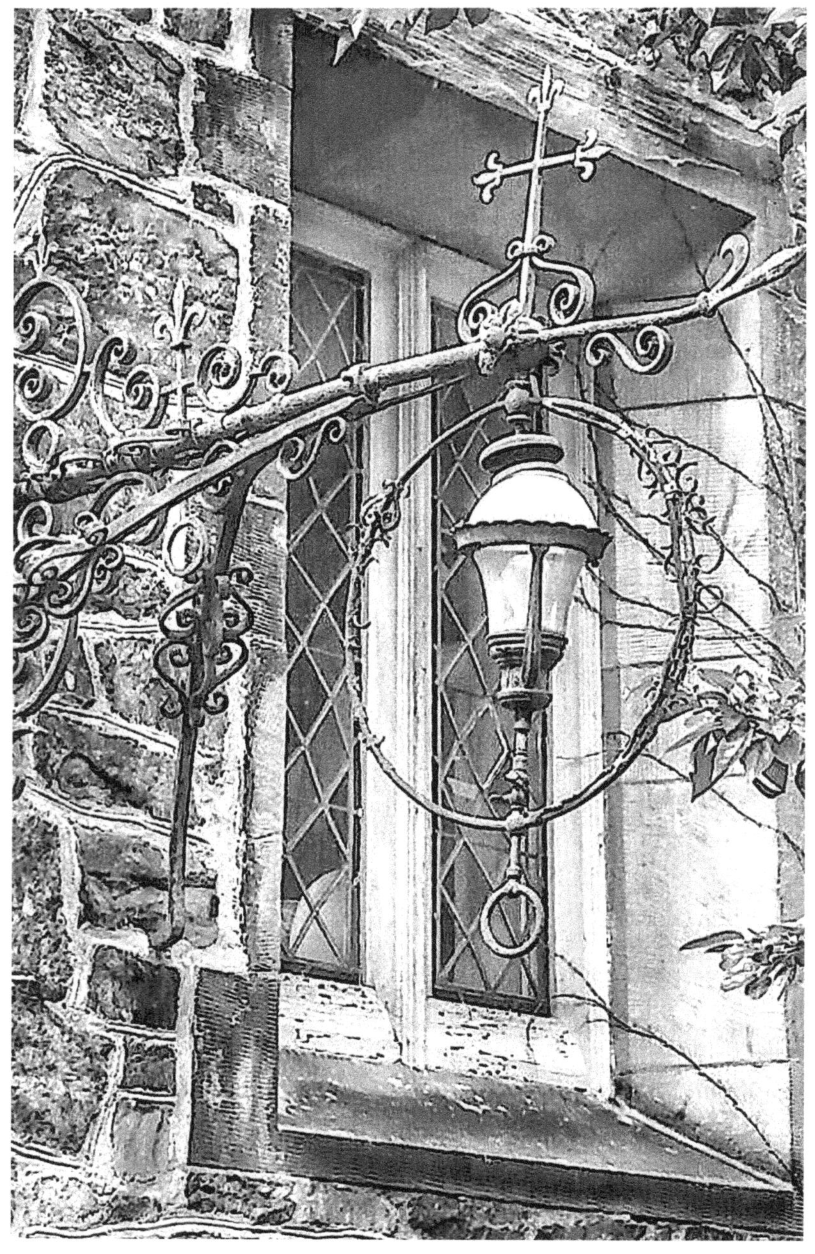

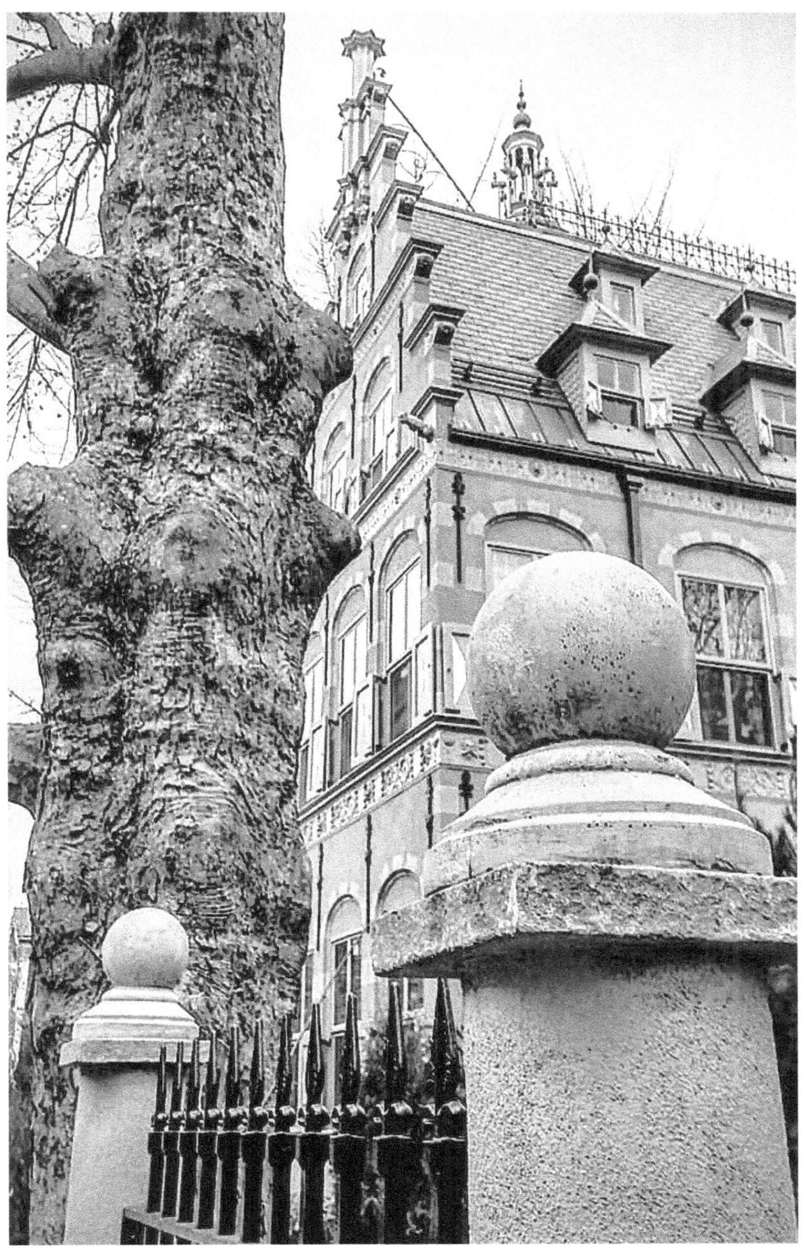

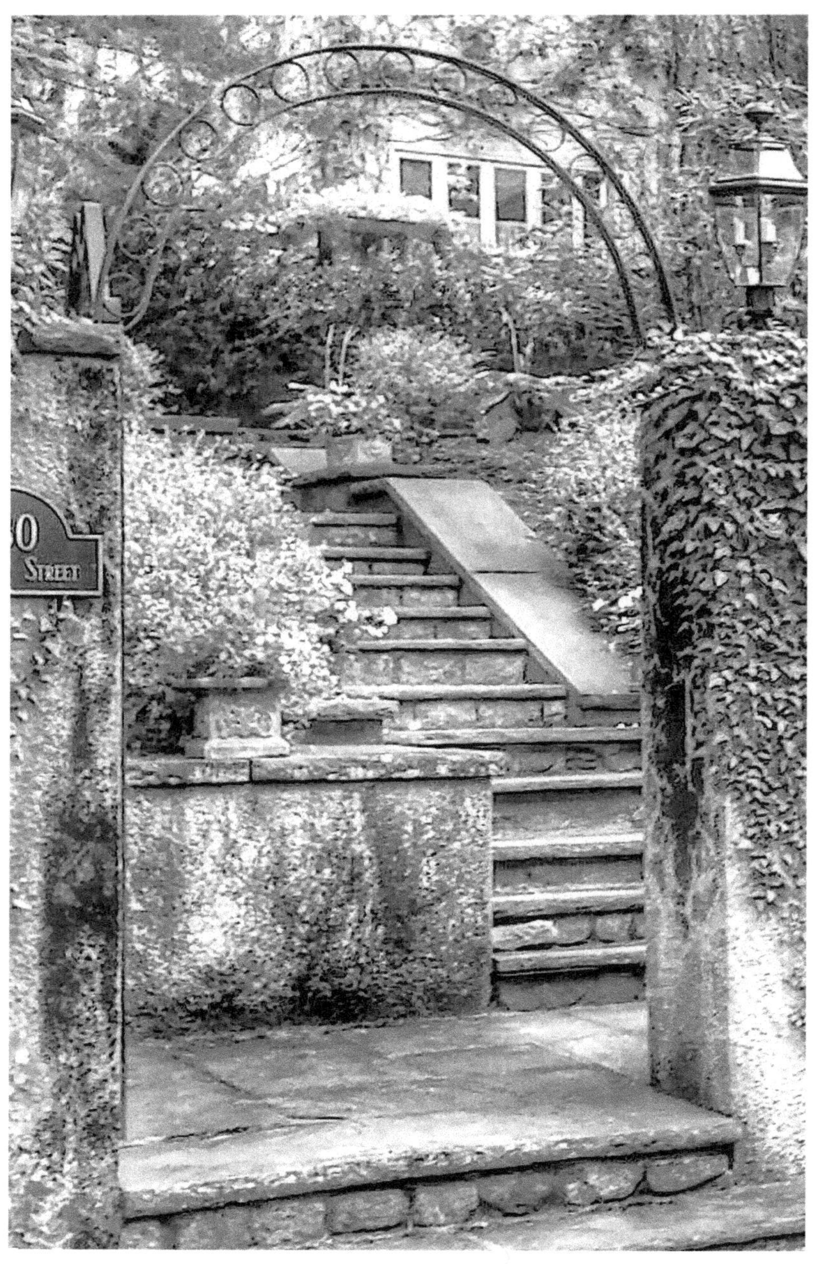

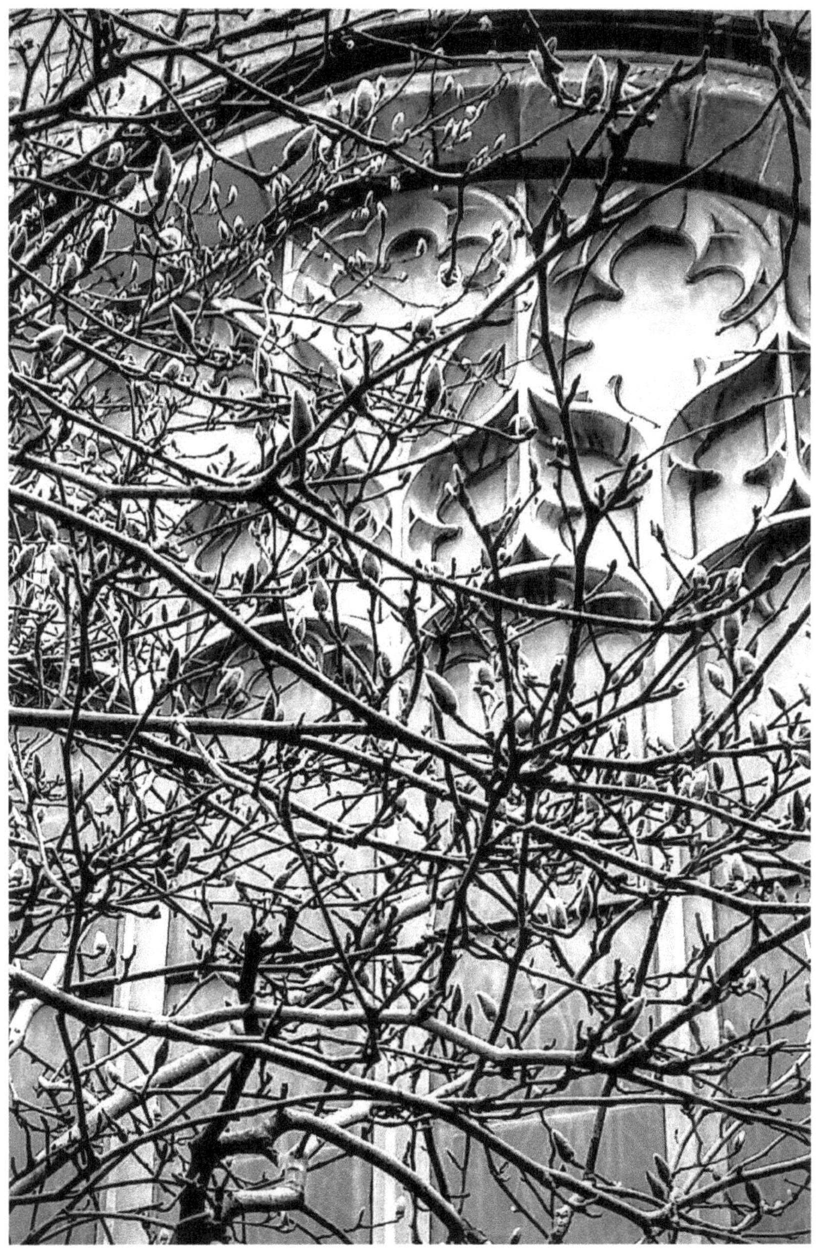

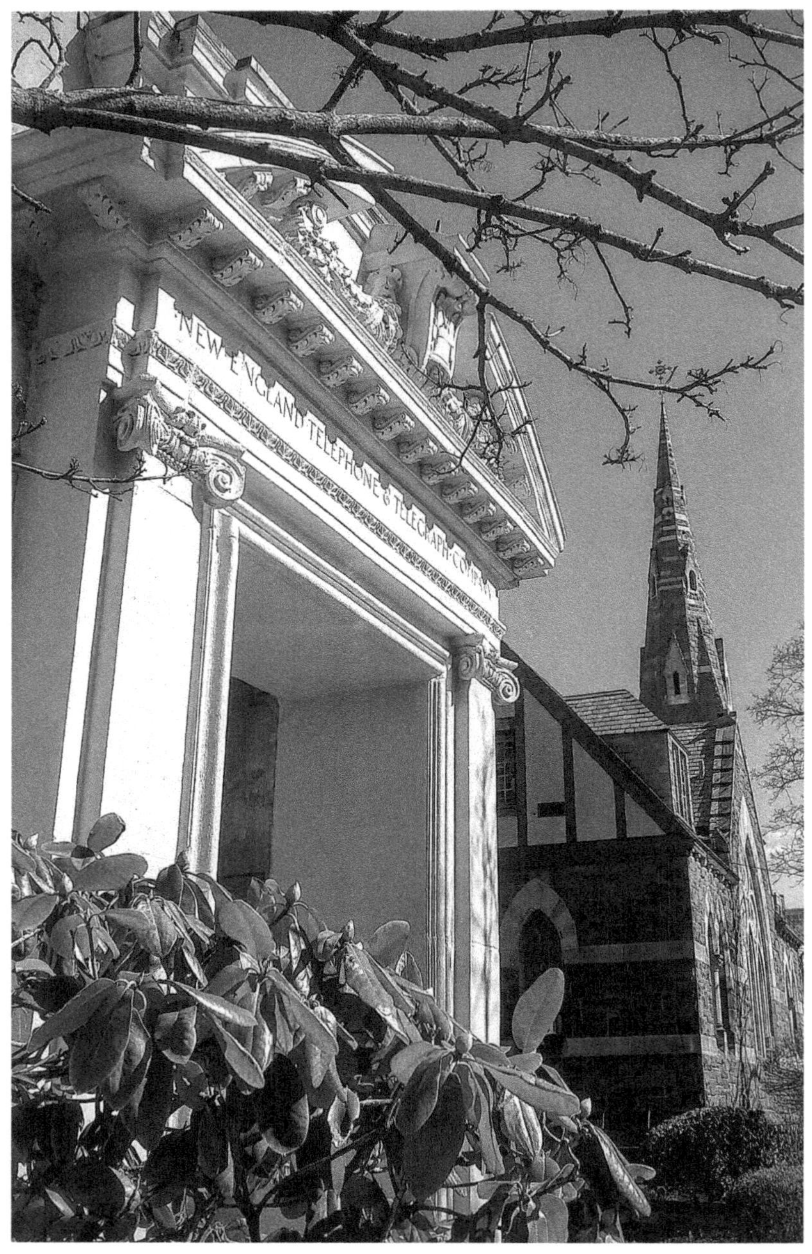

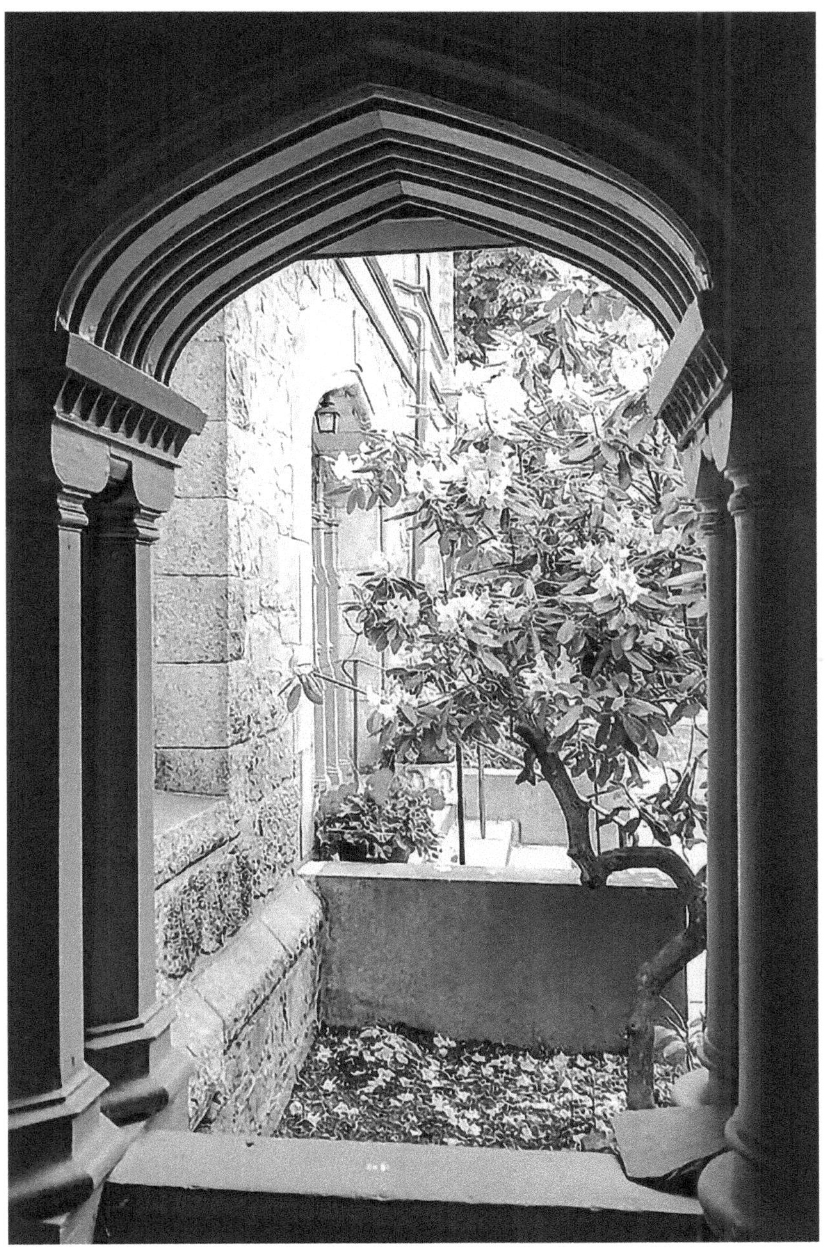

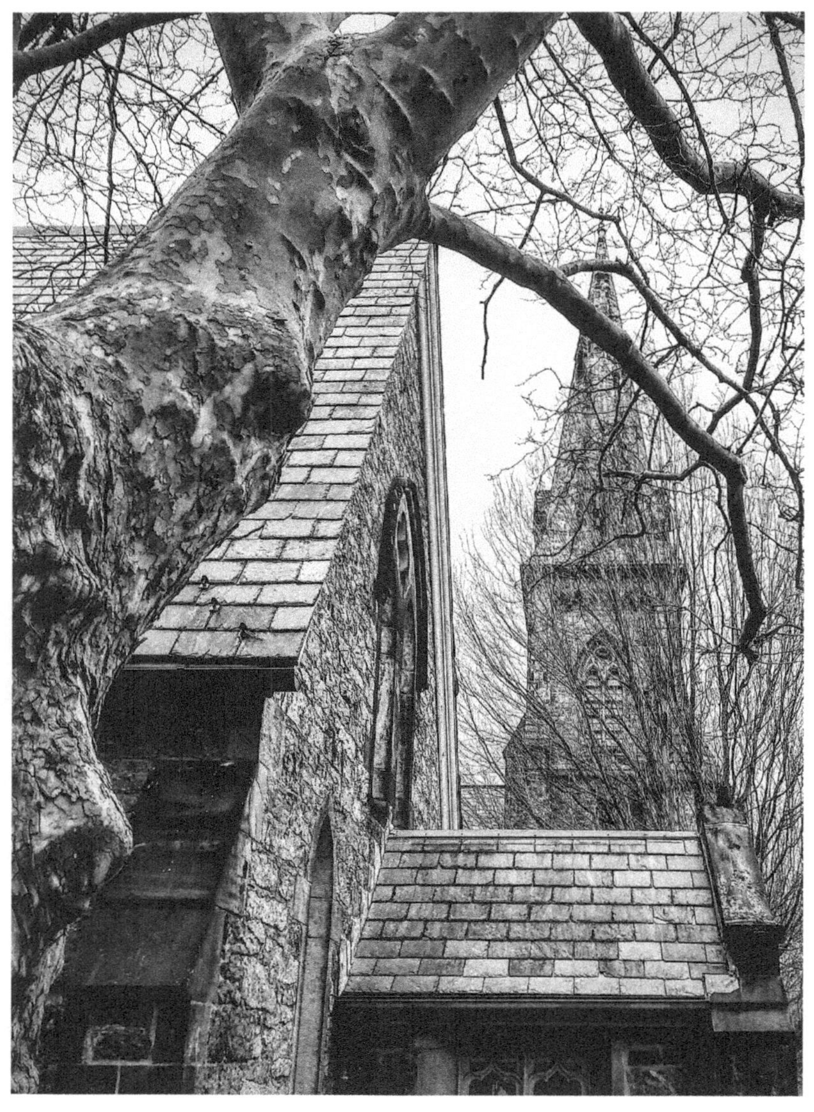

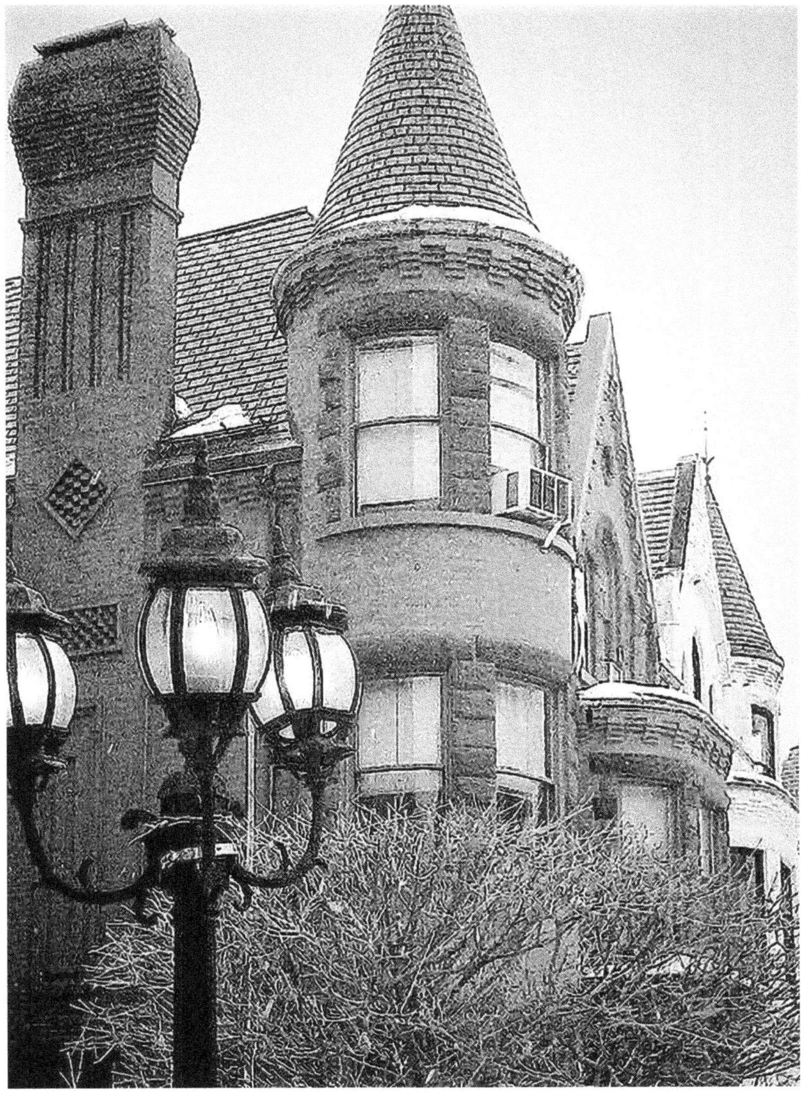

Wellesley

Life is beautiful. Life is sad.
That is all you need to know.

Vladimir Nabokov (1899 – 1977)
novelist and poet
Advice to a Wellesley College literary student

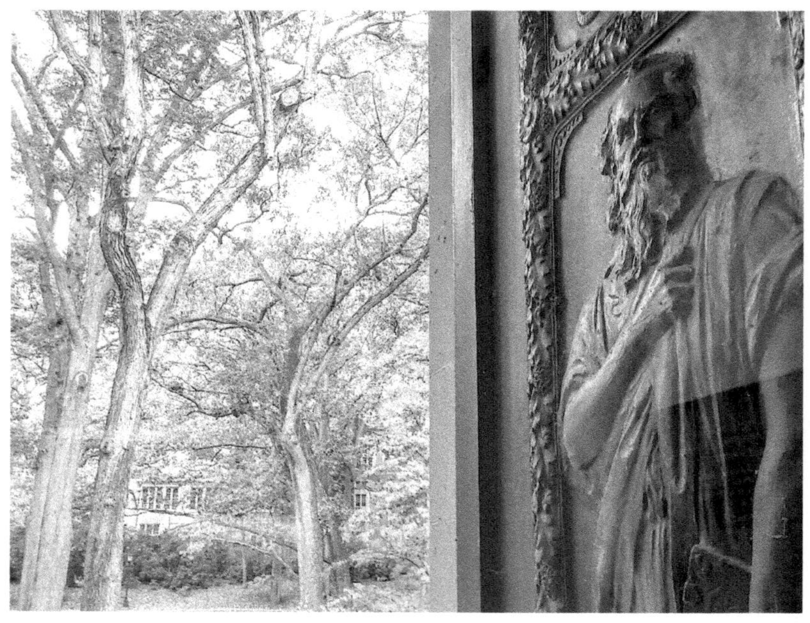

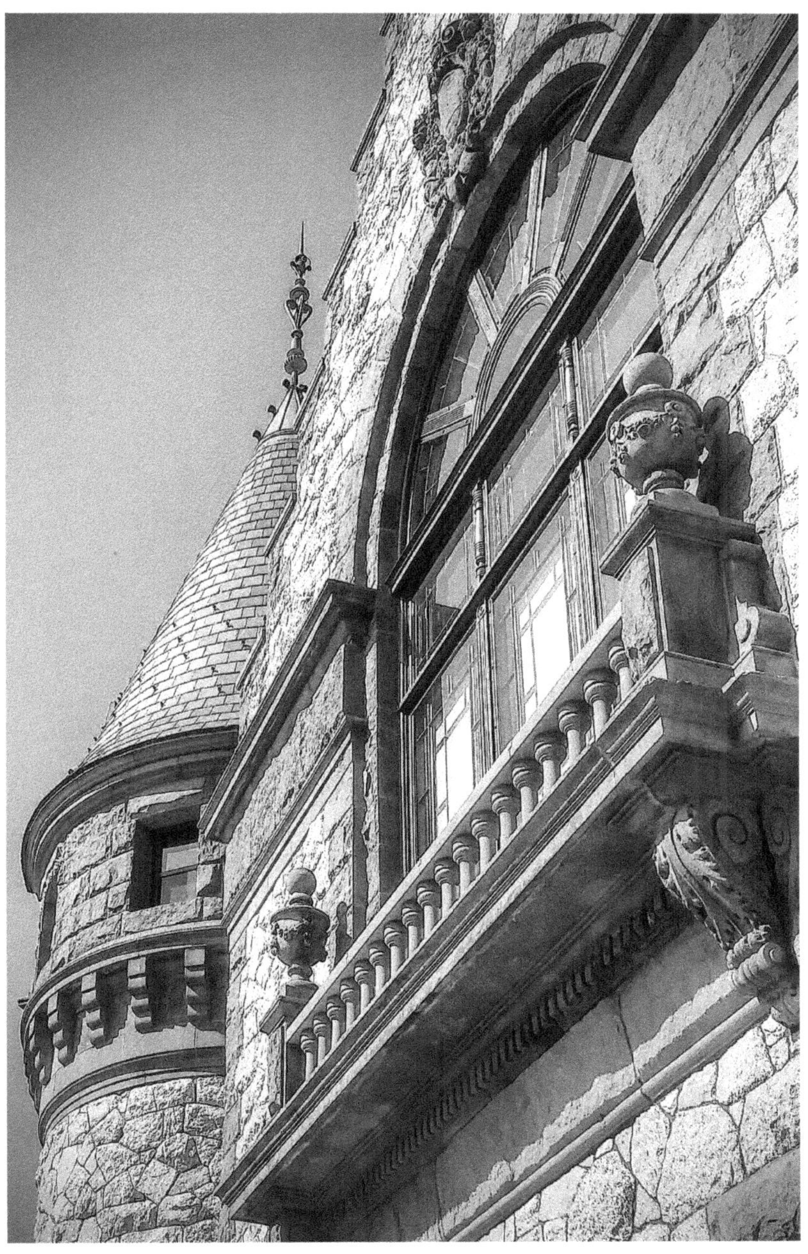

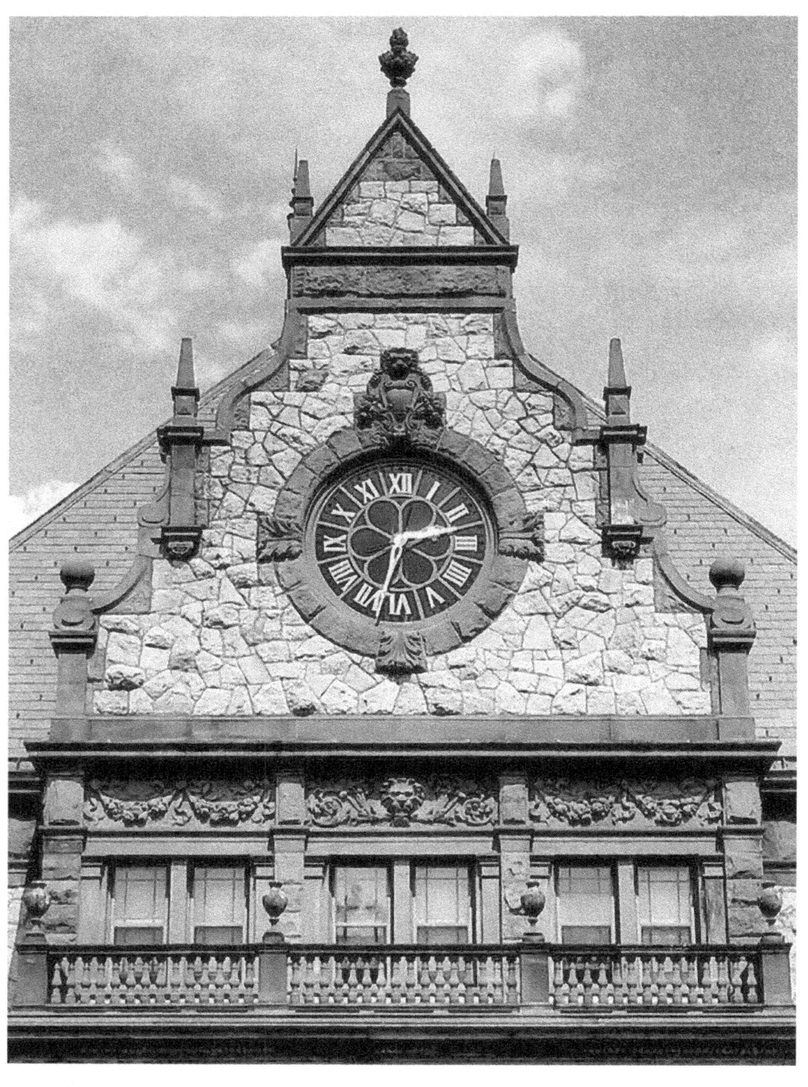

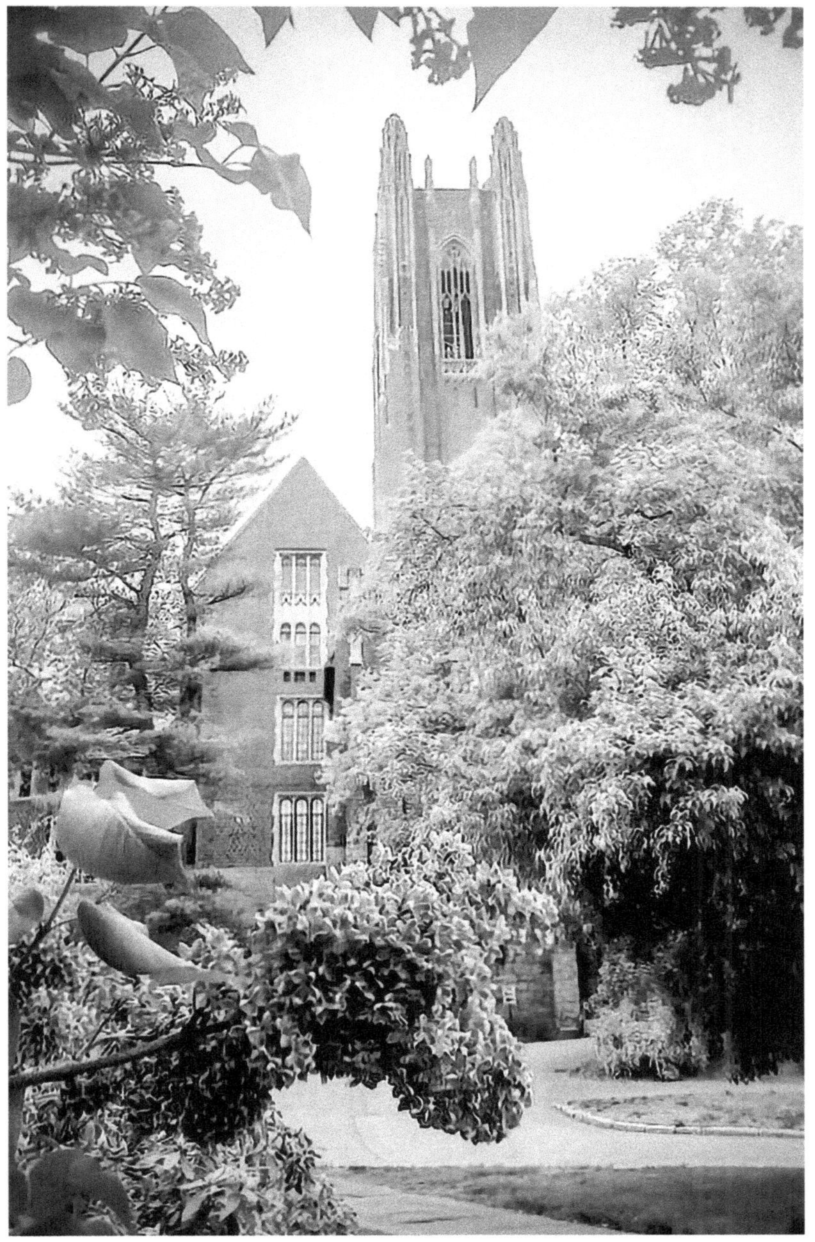

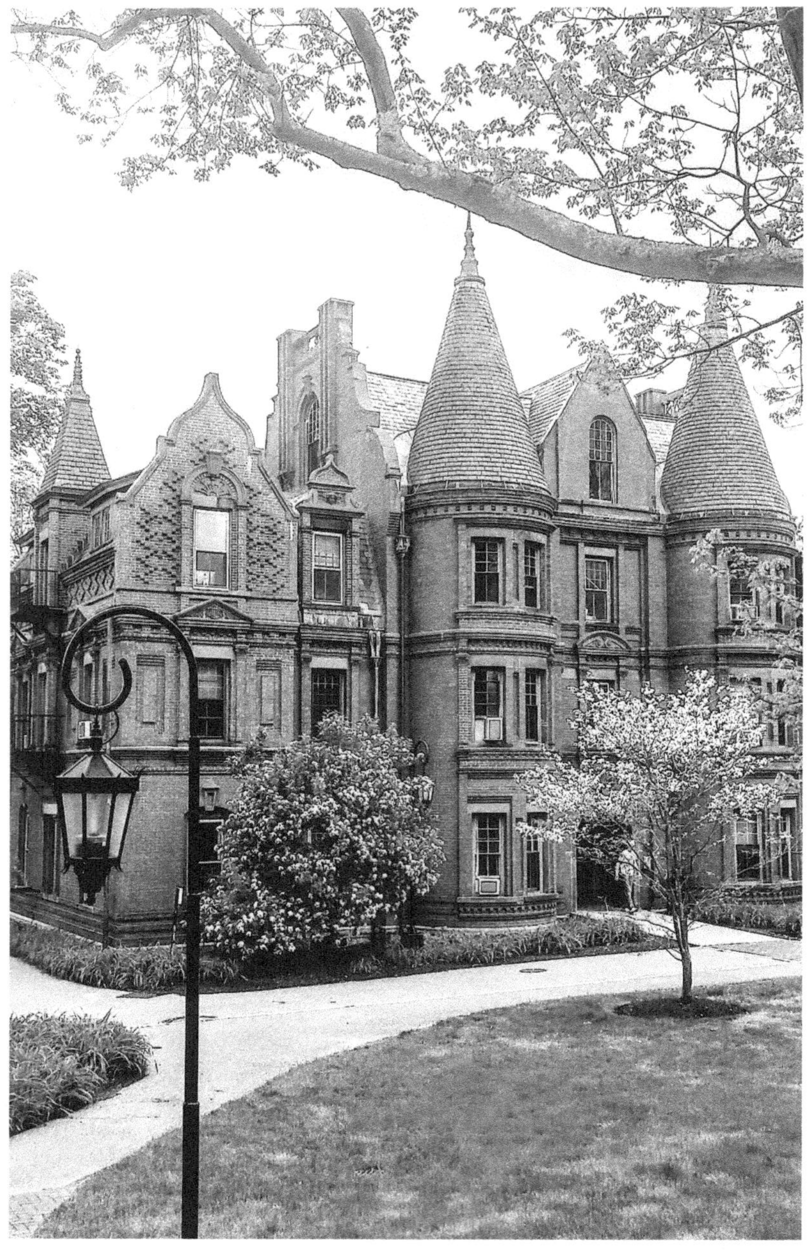

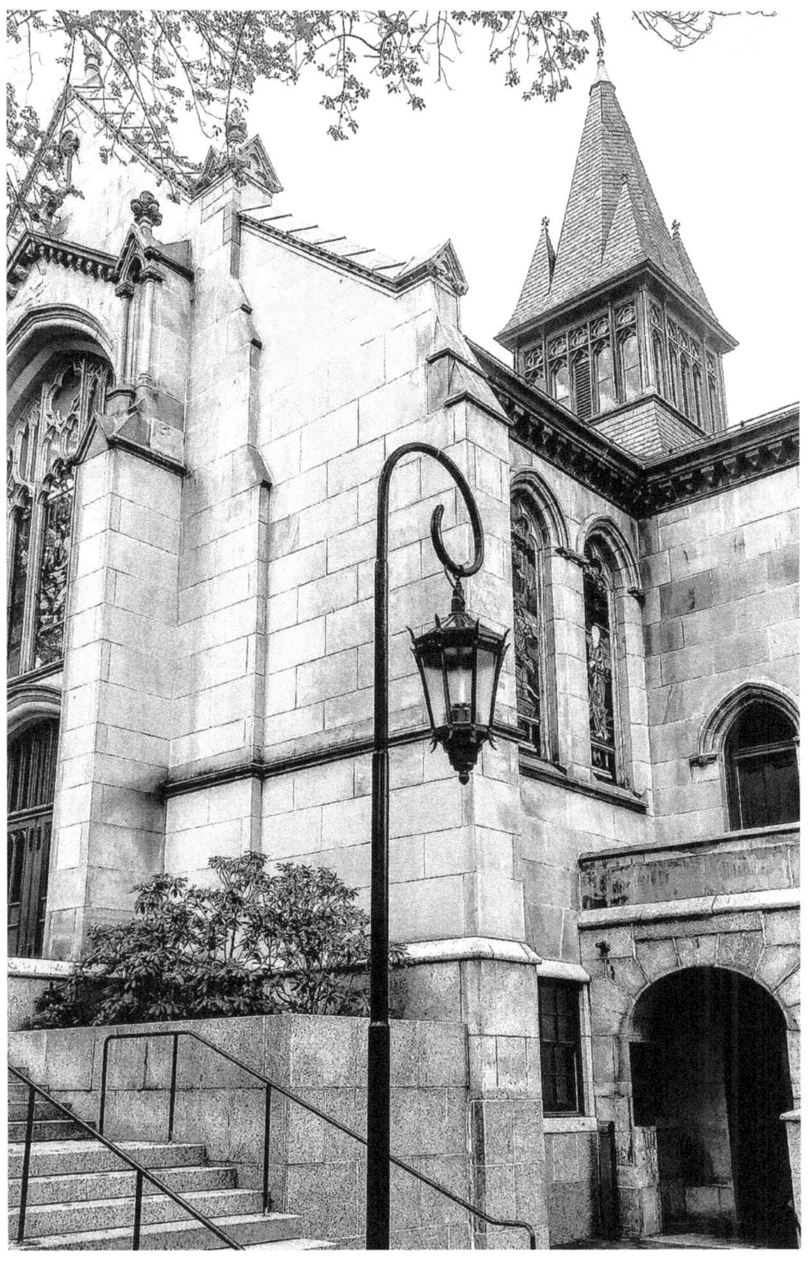

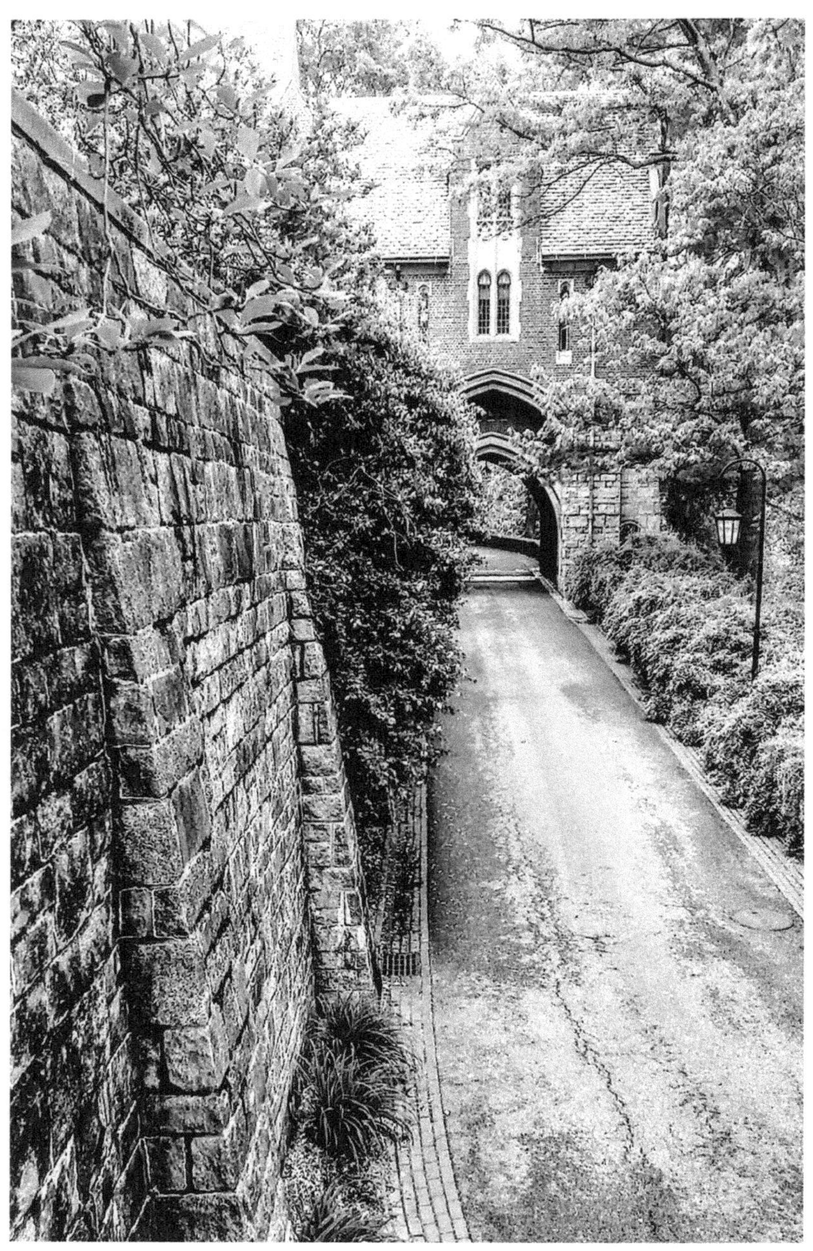

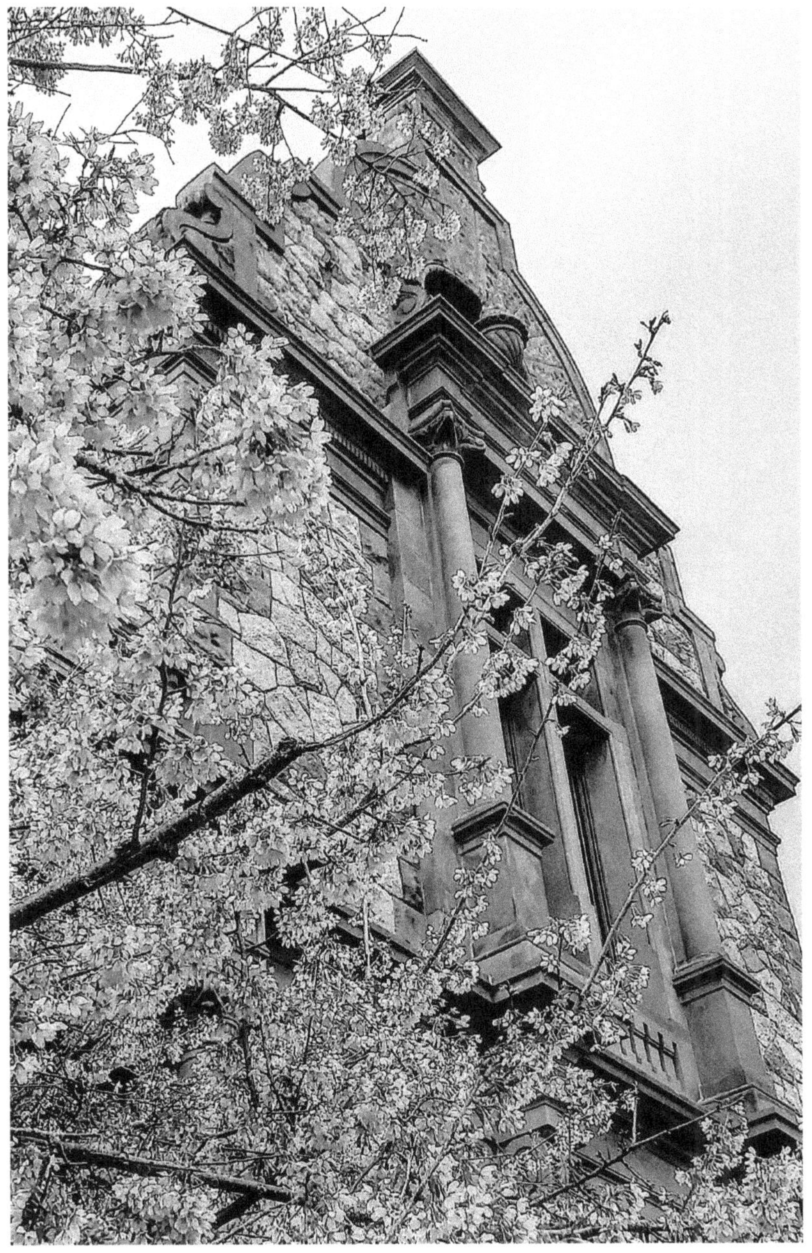

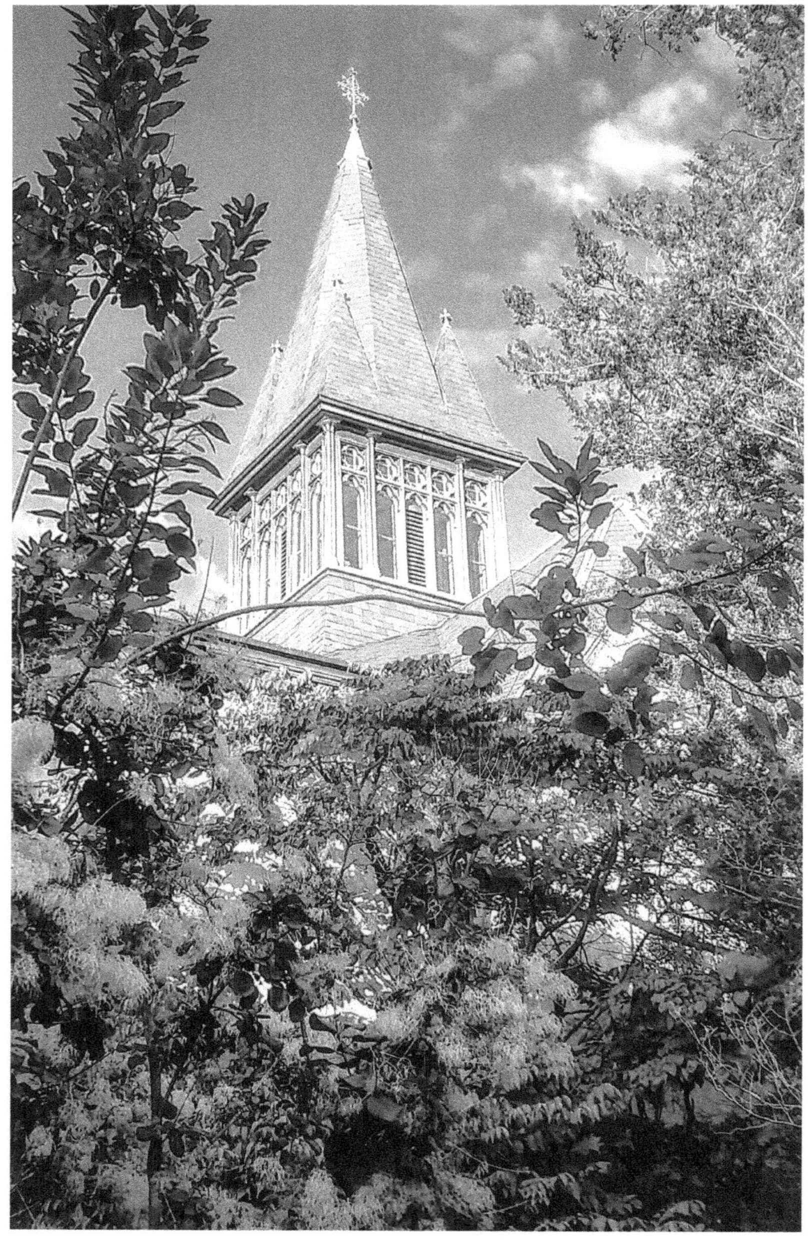

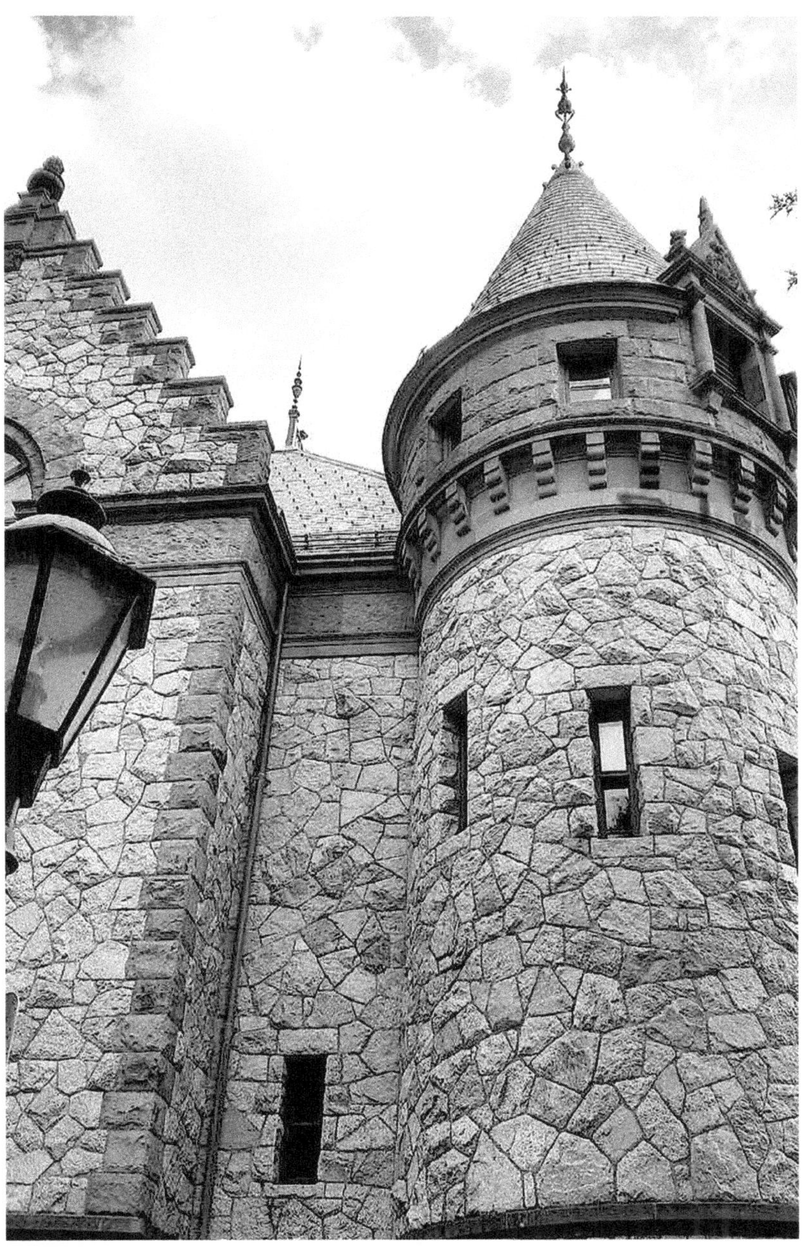

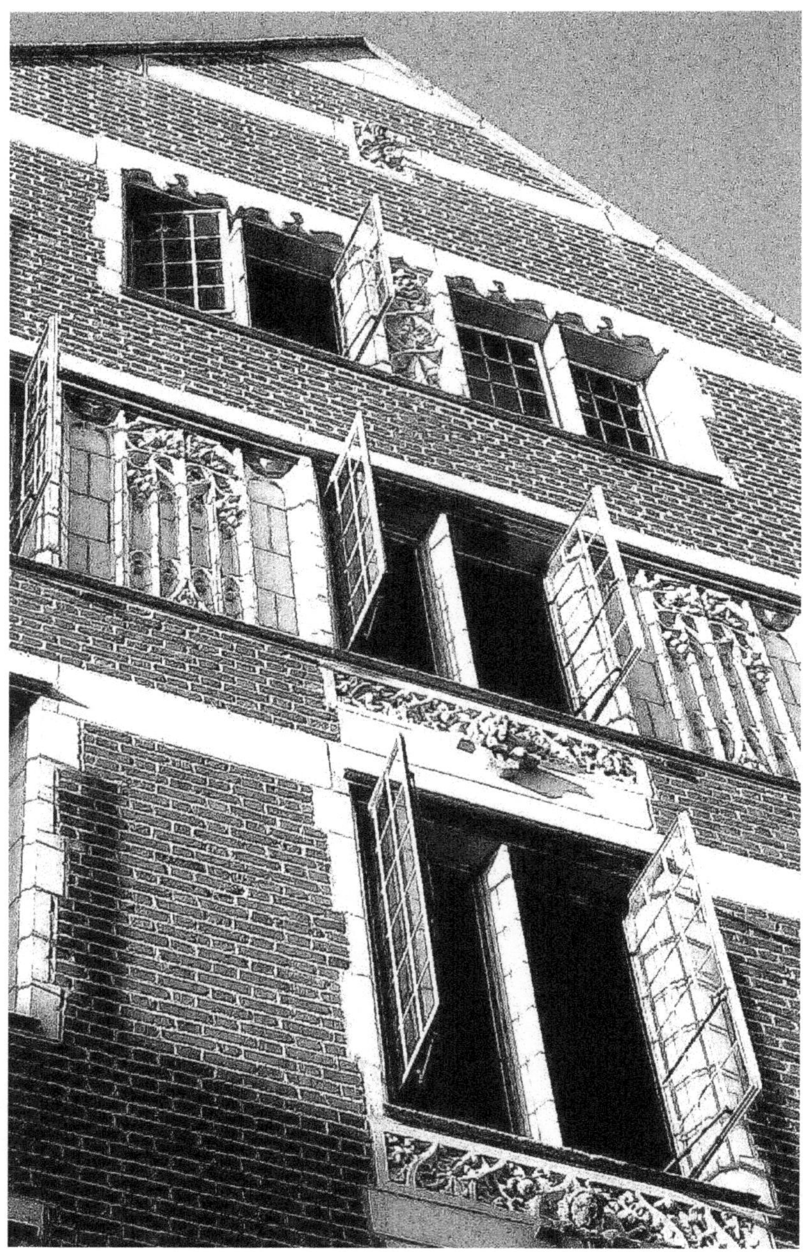

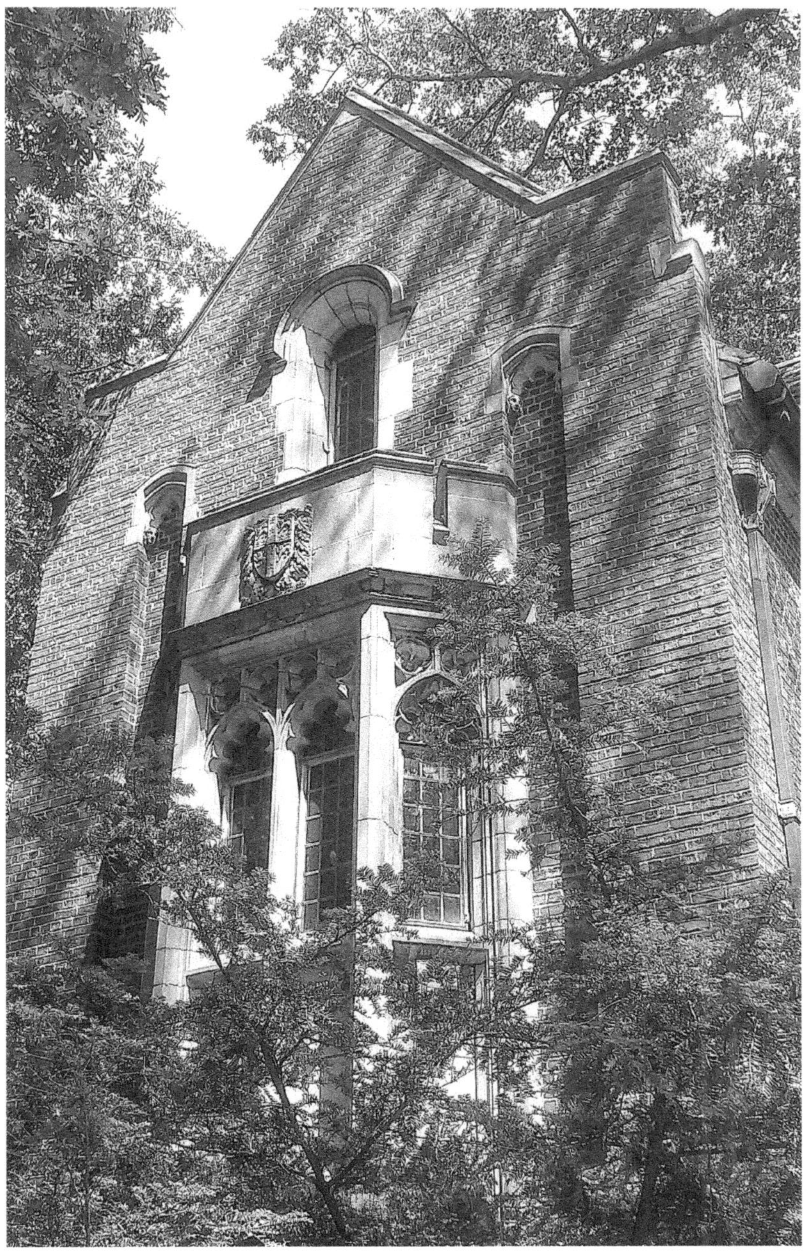

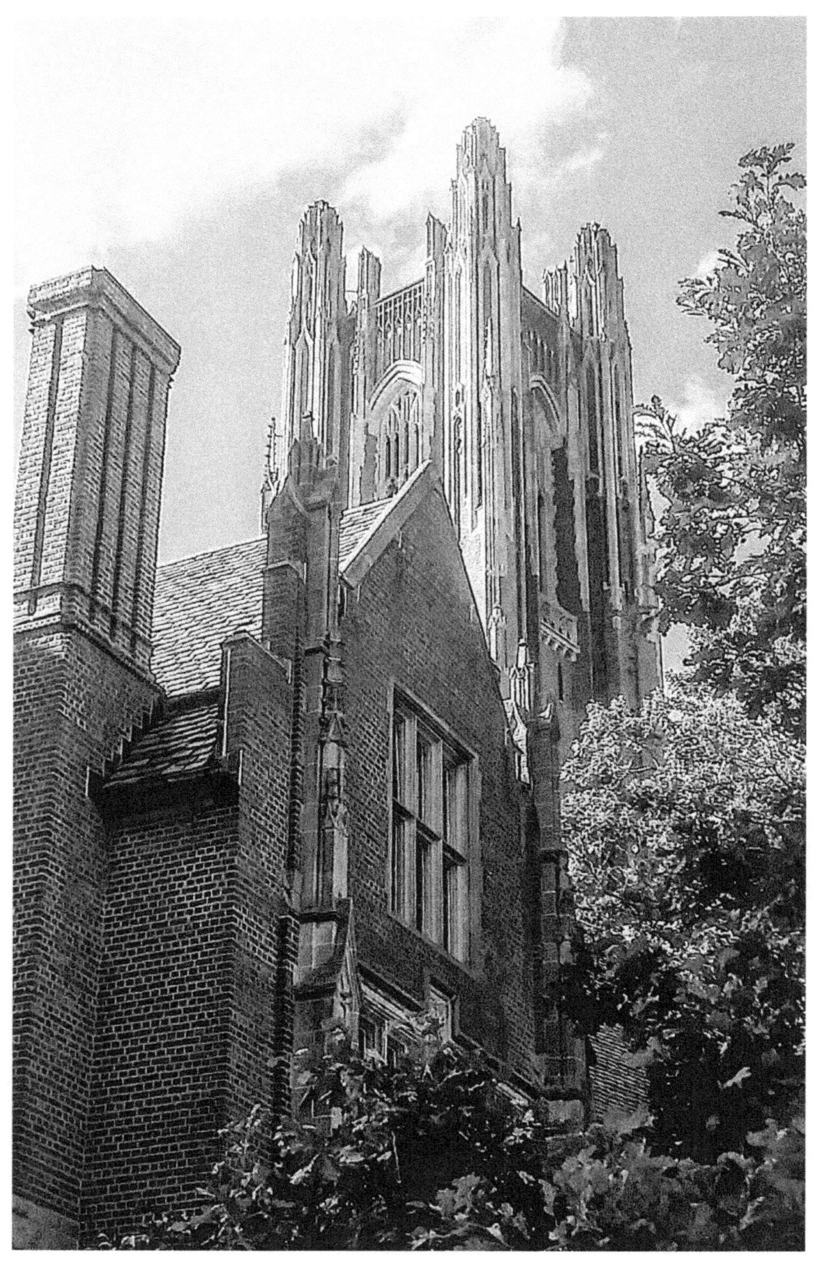

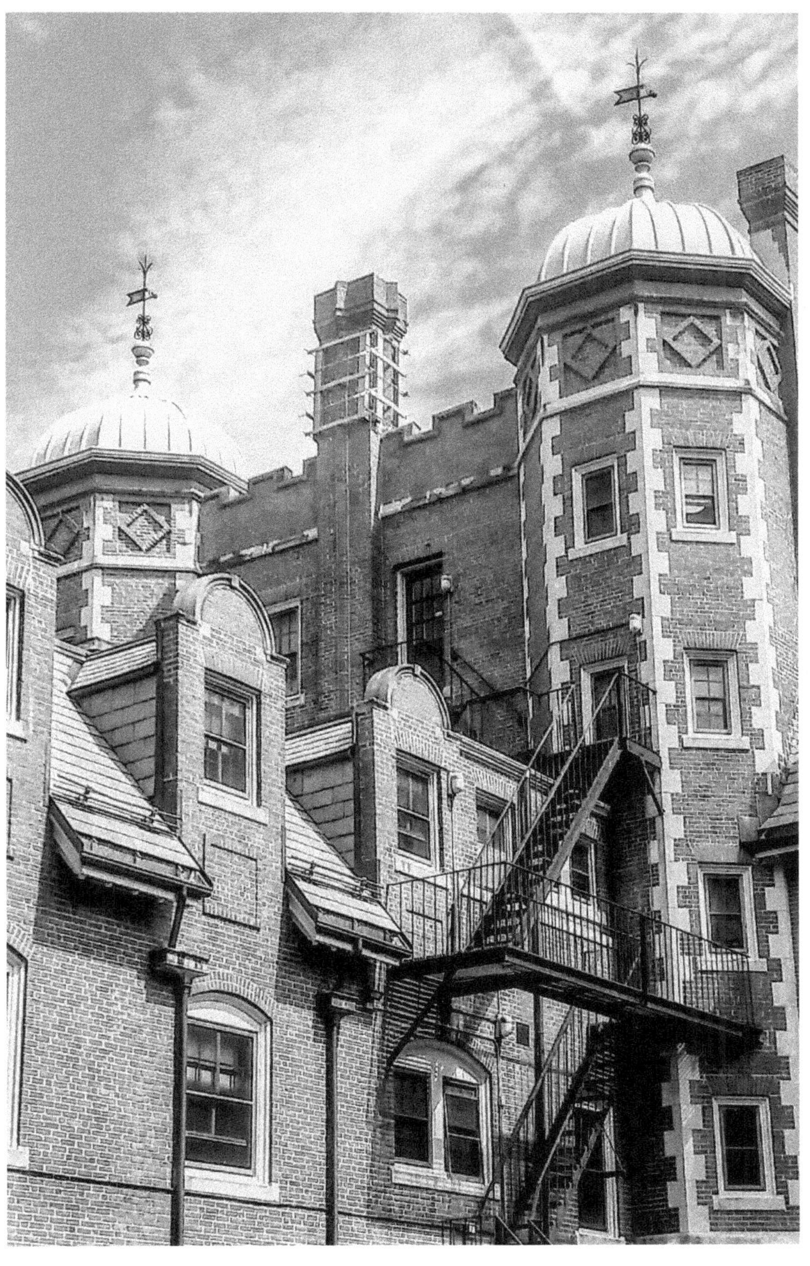

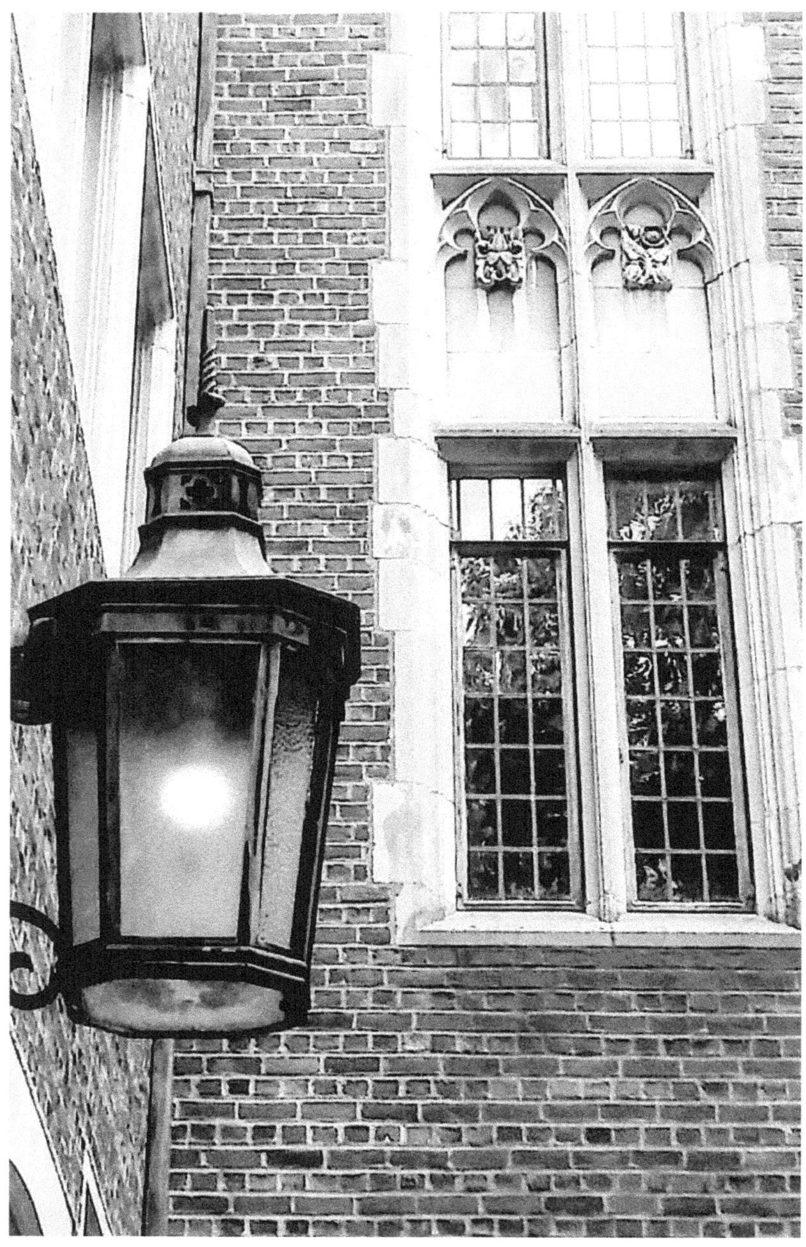

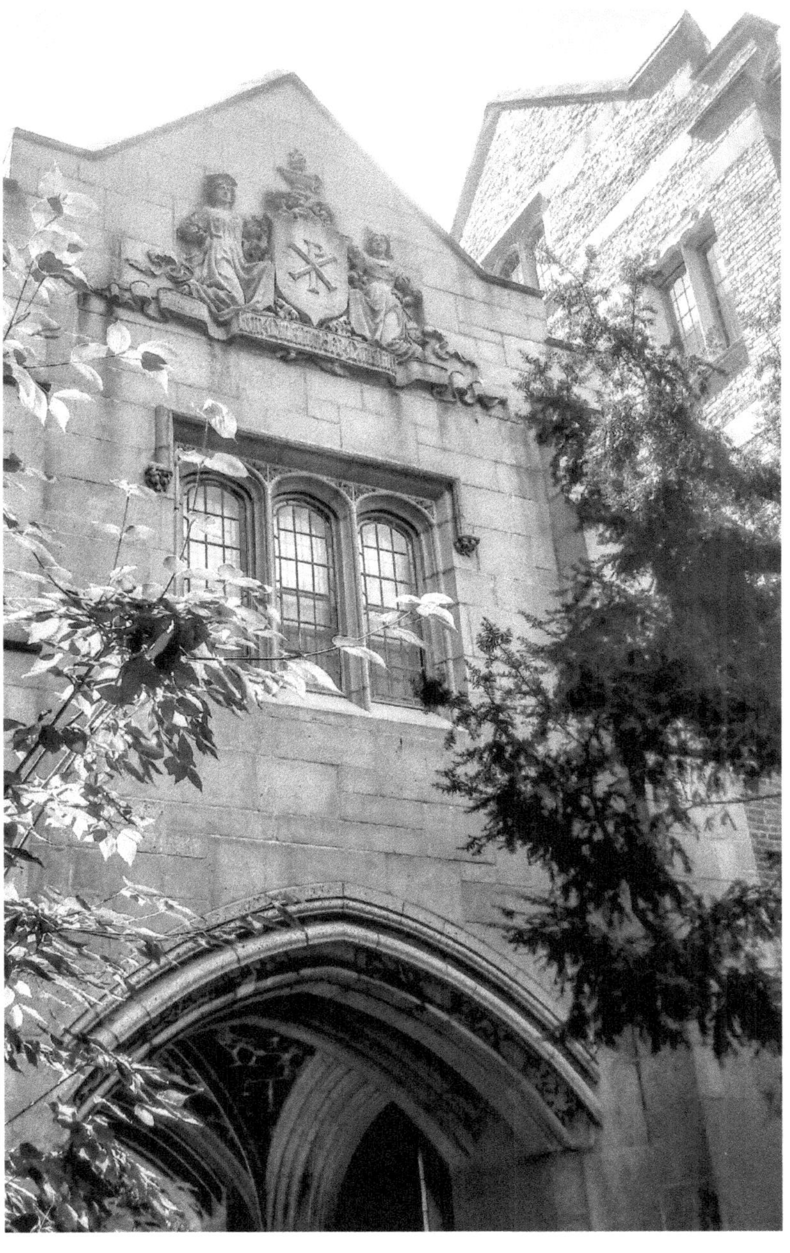

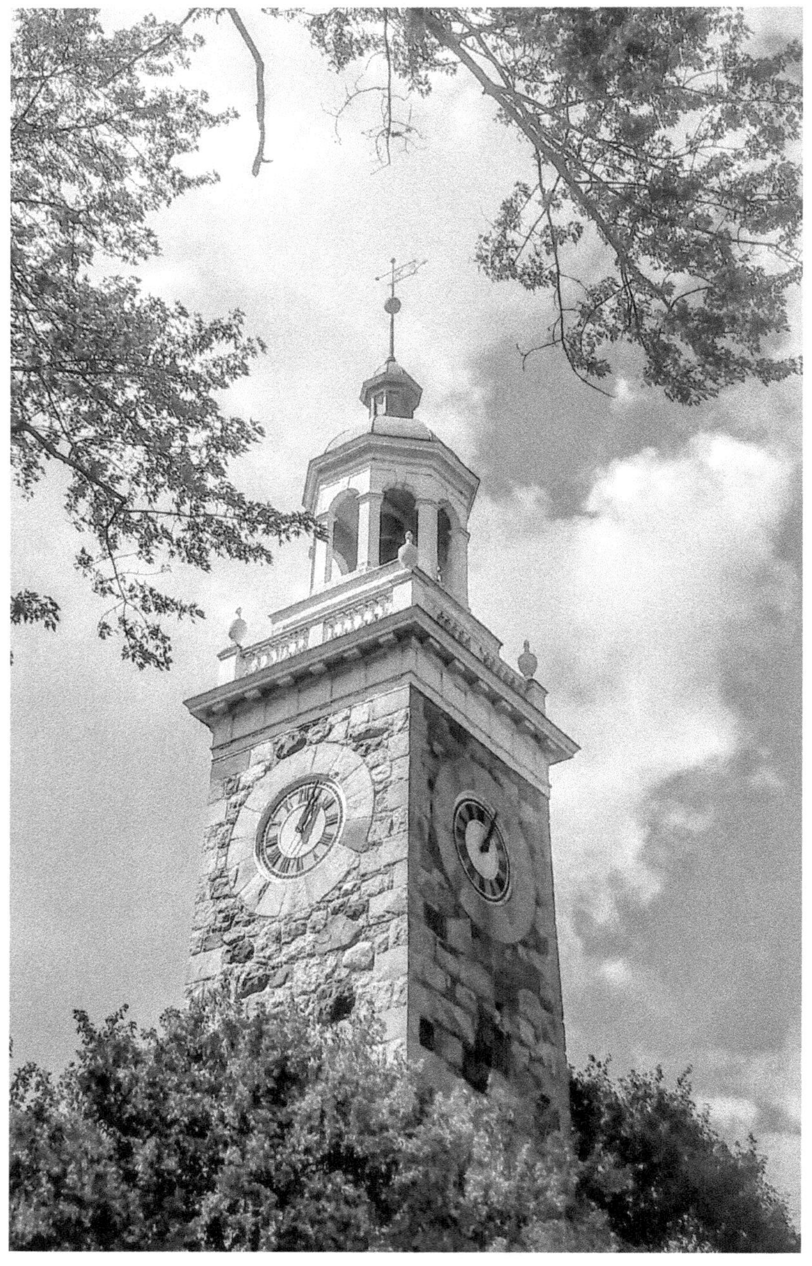

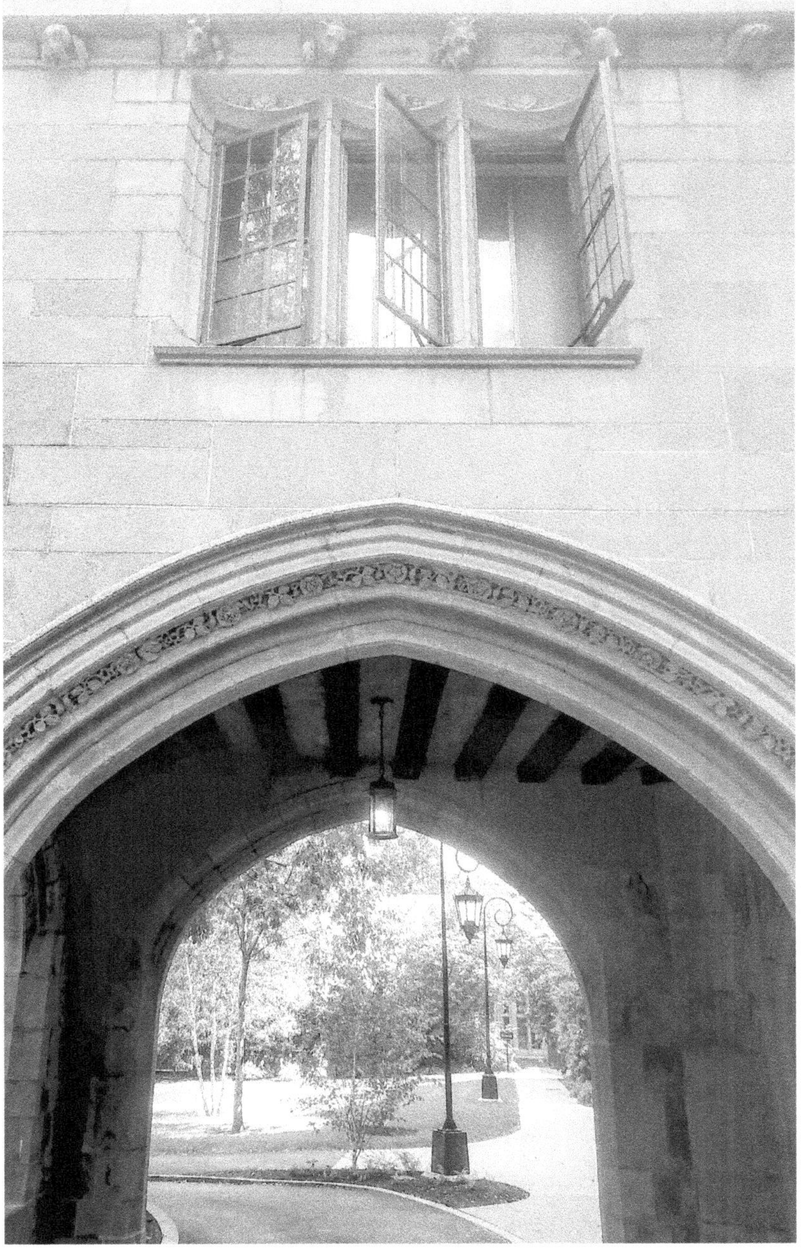

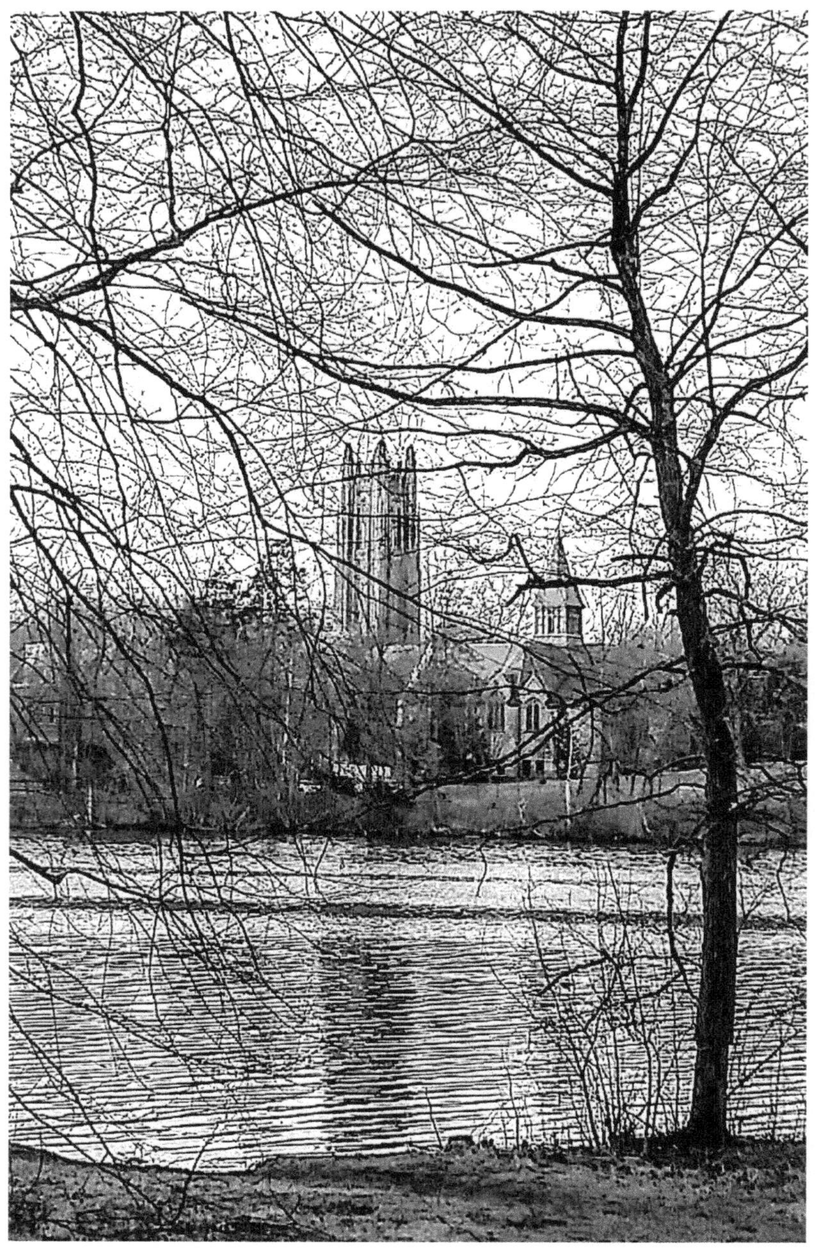

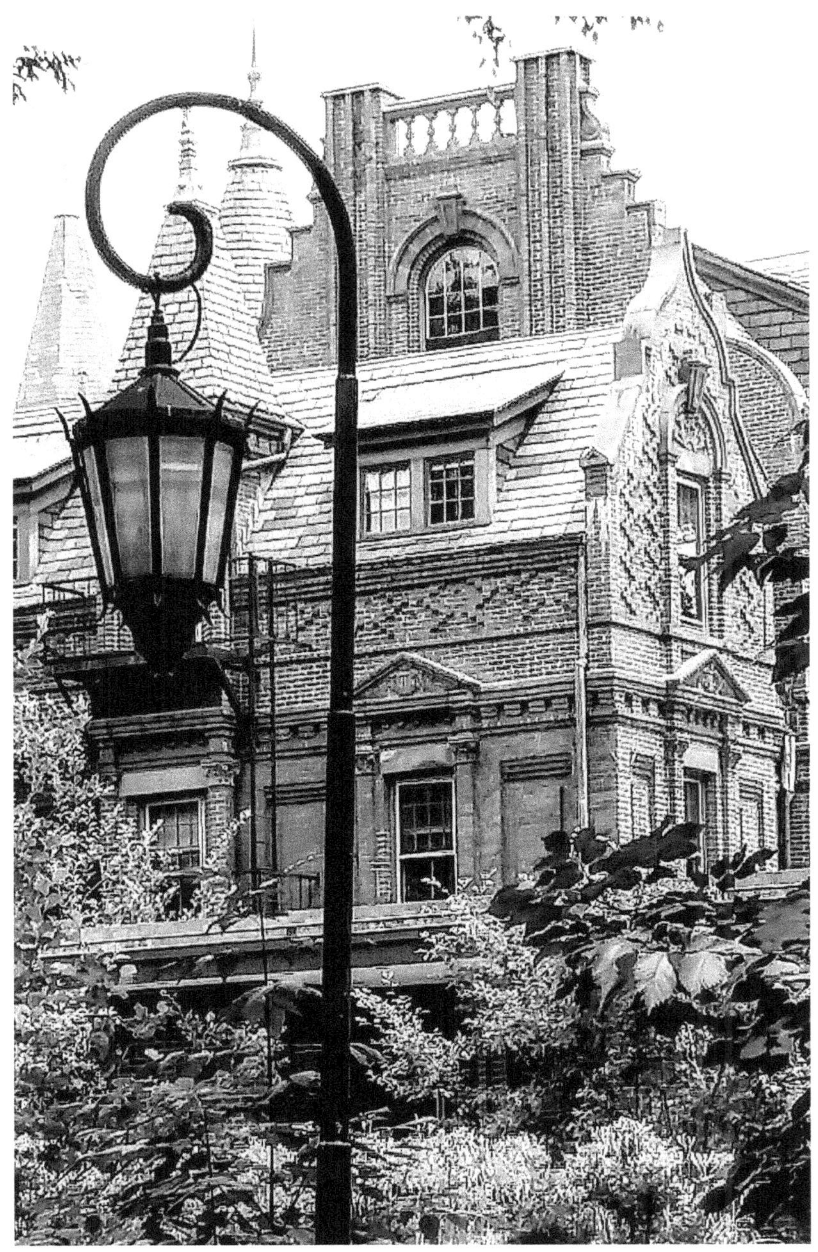

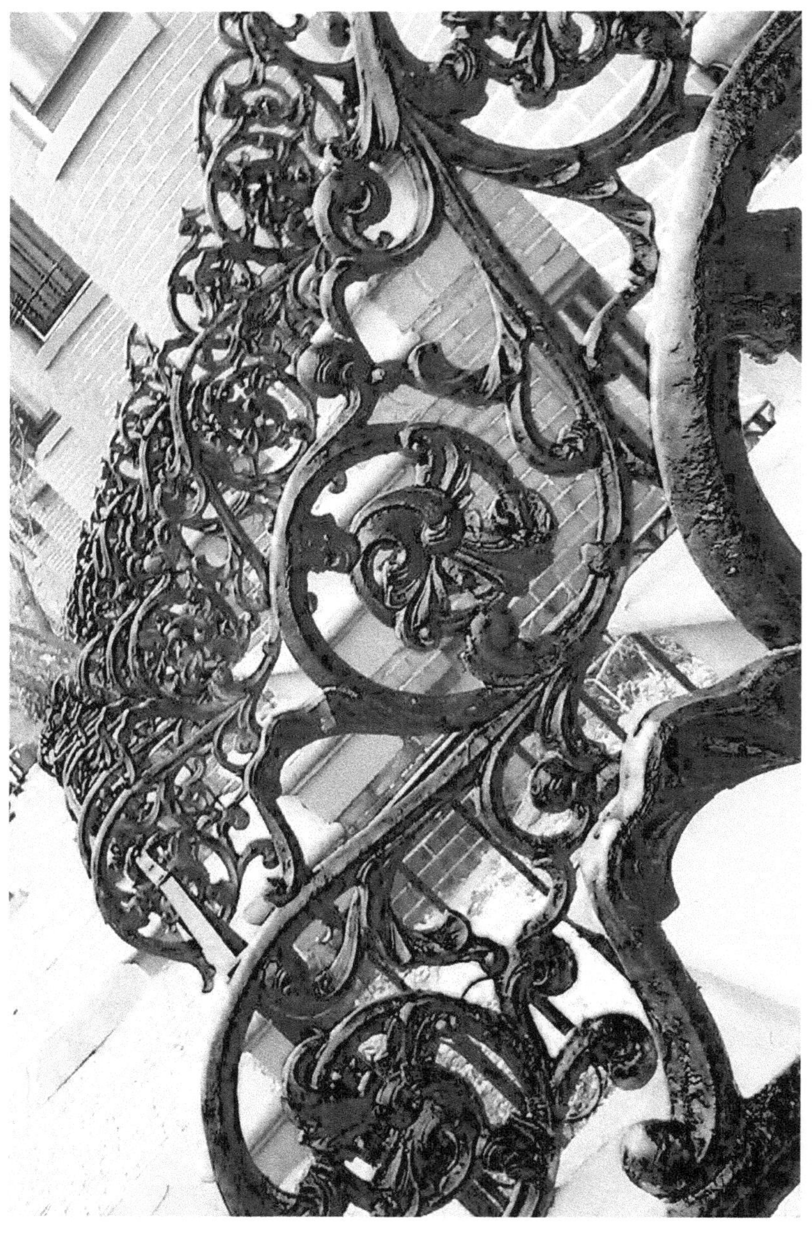

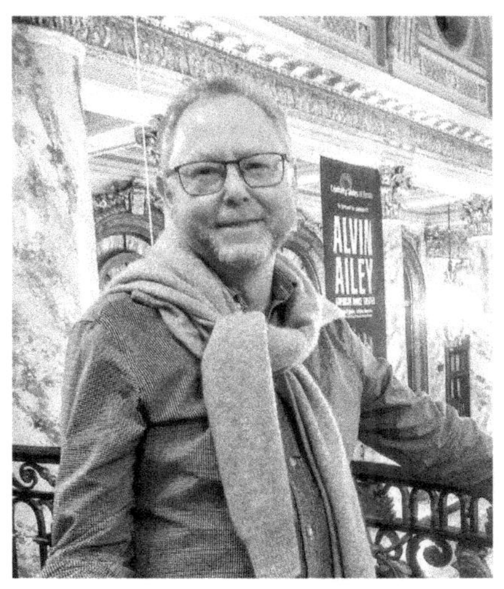

Dr. Leon Y. Spivak, originally from Saint Petersburg, Russia, is a graduate of New York University. A Bostonian since 1993, he is the author of numerous articles about Russian-American cultural ties from the 18th to 20th centuries. His documentary novelettes, including *Stories of the City of Boston*, *A Diplomat's Solitude*, and *When There Was No America*, are devoted to lesser-known moments in American history.

Leon Spivak

A DIPLOMAT'S SOLITUDE

Surprisingly little has been written about the main character of the book — William C. Bullitt. A few boring political studies and one biography just don't do justice to his amazing, event-filled life in Washington, Moscow, Paris and Vienna.

A journalist and a diplomat, a writer and a foreign affairs analyst — the whimsical twists and turns of our hero's biography found their way into novels by F. Scott Fitzgerald and Mikhail Bulgakov. A student of Freud and one of his exceedingly rare coauthors, Bullitt also managed to save his mentor from inevitable death after Hitler's annexation of Austria. He was the first U.S. Ambassador to Soviet Russia; indeed, the Nazis blamed Bullitt for being one of the culprits of World War II. During their occupation of France, he became the only "American Mayor of Paris."

After being a close friend and employee of President Franklin D. Roosevelt, he broke off ties with him in the 1940s, left his service in the capital, and signed up as a volunteer with de Gaulle's army. In this whirlwind of historical events, we can discern the diplomat's main character traits: his unique mindset, a rare ability to see far beyond the obvious, and an astuteness occasionally bordering on prophecy.

The book can be purchased on Amazon.com:
https://www.amazon.com/dp/1940220548

www.ingramcontent.com/pod-product-compliance
Lightning Source LLC
Chambersburg PA
CBHW041104090726
47602CB00018B/7